S. M. EISENSTEIN
Writings, 1922-34

S. M. EISENSTEIN

Selected Works

VOLUME I

Writings, 1922-34

Edited and translated by

RICHARD TAYLOR

BFI PUBLISHING
London

INDIANA UNIVERSITY PRESS
Bloomington and Indianapolis

S. M. Eisenstein
SELECTED WORKS
General Editor: Richard Taylor
Consultant Editor: Naum Kleiman

Volume I: Writings, 1922-34
Edited by Richard Taylor

First published in Great Britain in 1988 by the
British Film Institute
21 Stephen Street
London W1P 1PL
and published in the United States of America by
Indiana University Press
10th and Morton Streets
Bloomington, Indiana
Typeset by KC Graphics, Shrewsbury
Printed in Great Britain by
Anchor Brendon Ltd, Tiptree, Essex

British Library Cataloguing in Publication Data

Eizenshtein, Sergei
  Writings 1922-34.
  1. Moving-pictures
  I. Title   II. Taylor, Richard, *1946-*
  III. British Film Institute
  791.43   PN1994

  ISBN 0-85170-206-6

Library of Congress Cataloging-in-Publication Data

Eisenstein, Sergei, 1898-1948.
  Eisenstein, selected writings.

  Contents: v. 1. 1922-1934.
  1. Moving-pictures.   I. Taylor, Richard, 1946-
  II. Title.
  PN1998.A3E515   1987   791.43   86-45516   ISBN 0-253-35042-5 (v. 1)

  1 2 3 4 5   91 90 89 88 87

This volume
is dedicated to the memory of
Pera Attasheva, Bella Epstein and Sergei Yutkevich
the courageous and conscientious guardians
of Eisenstein's legacy

Acknowledgments

Any work on this scale owes a great deal to both people and institutions too numerous to mention. I hope therefore that those whose names have been omitted will understand and forgive.

My greatest debt is to Naum Kleiman, the Curator of the Eisenstein Museum in Moscow, who has agreed to be Consultant Editor for this edition. His knowledge of, and enthusiasm for, Eisenstein are such that no serious scholarly work would be possible without his generous assistance. I am grateful to Jay Leyda, who has done more than anyone else to bring Eisenstein to the attention of the English-speaking world, for his support and encouragement. I should also like to thank Alan Bodger for his generous advice and assistance with translation problems and problem translations. I owe the usual enormous debt to family and friends who have kept the train on the rails when the engine-driver was tempted to jump off, and in this case to five people in particular: Ian Christie in London, Jeffrey Richards in Lancaster and George Boyce, Neil Harding and Gareth Evans in South Wales. Last, but certainly not least, I should like to thank Mrs Pat Rees for typing a considerable part of the manuscript, and my wonderful secretary, Mrs Phyllis Hancock, for doing the rest and for remaining calm and serene during all-too-frequent crises.

I have received assistance from a number of institutions but I should like to express my particular gratitude to the following: VNIIKI (The All-Union Institute for the History of Cinema), the Lenin Library, the USSR Union of Cinematographers and TsGALI (the Central State Archive for Literature and the Arts) in Moscow; the British Library and the British Film Institute in London; the Library and the Centre for Russian and East European Studies at University College, Swansea; the Fellows of St Antony's College, Oxford, for a period as Senior Associate Member; the Museum of Modern Art Library, New York, and the Library of Congress, Washington D.C.

The work on this volume would not have been possible without these people and institutions; any faults in the volume are mine and mine alone.

R.T.

Contents

GENERAL EDITOR'S PREFACE ix

INTRODUCTION 1

TRANSLATOR'S NOTE 25

ABBREVIATIONS 27

1922

1. Sergei Yutkevich and Eisenstein: The Eighth Art.
   On Expressionism, America and, of course, Chaplin 29

1923

2. The Montage of Attractions 33

1924

3. The Montage of Film Attractions 39

1925

4. The Problem of the Materialist Approach to Form 59
5. The Method of Making a Workers' Film 65

1926

6. Constanța (Whither *The Battleship Potemkin*) 67
7. However Odd – Khokhlova! 71
8. Eisenstein on Eisenstein, the Director of *Potemkin* 74
9. Béla Forgets the Scissors 77
10. The Two Skulls of Alexander the Great 82
11. The German Cinema. A Traveller's Impressions 85

1927

12. Give Us a State Plan 89

1928

13. Literature and Cinema. Reply to a Questionnaire 95
14. What We Are Expecting from the Party Conference on Cinema 100
15. Our *October*. Beyond the Played and the Non-Played 101
16. For a Workers' Hit 107
17. Eisenstein, Vsevolod Pudovkin and Grigori Alexandrov:
    Statement on Sound 113
18. An Unexpected Juncture 115

19. Eisenstein and Grigori Alexandrov:
     The Twelfth Year   123
20. The GTK Teaching and Research Workshop. A Conversation
     with the Leader of the Workshop, S.M. Eisenstein   127

1929

21. Conversation with Eisenstein on Sound Cinema   131
22. The Form of the Script   134
23. *The Arsenal*   136
24. Beyond the Shot   138
25. Perspectives   151
26. The Dramaturgy of Film Form
     (The Dialectical Approach to Film Form)   161
27. The Fourth Dimension in Cinema   181

1930

28. The Principles of the New Russian Cinema   195
29. Rin-Tin-Tin Does His Tricks for Noted Russian Movie Man   203
30. The Dynamic Square   206

1932

31. Help Yourself!   219
32. In the Interests of Form   238

1933

33. Through the Revolution to Art:
     Through Art to the Revolution   243
34. Pantagruel Will Be Born   246
35. To Your Posts!   250
36. Georges Méliès's Mistake   258
37. An Attack by Class Allies   261
38. Cinema and the Classics   276

1934

39. For Elevated Ideological Content, for Film Culture!   277
40. On Fascism, German Cinema and Real Life.
     Open Letter to the German Minister of Propaganda,
     Dr Goebbels   280
41. 'Eh!' On the Purity of Film Language   285
42. At Last!   296

NOTES   301
INDEX   329

General Editor's Preface

Sergei Eisenstein is by general consent the most important single figure in the history of cinema. His contribution to the practice of film-making is universally acknowledged and his films, from *The Strike* to *Ivan the Terrible* are well known, if not always as widely shown as we might assume. But the bulk of Eisenstein's theoretical writings has remained largely inaccessible and, despite the invaluable efforts of Jay Leyda in particular, the English-speaking world has only a partial acquaintance with the ideas that underlay his films.

It is the primary purpose of this edition to make available the most important of Eisenstein's writings in a comprehensive and scholarly, but nevertheless accessible, form to the English-speaking reader for the first time. The nature of those writings posed considerable editorial problems concerning the organisation of the volumes in the series. Different editions in different languages have resorted to different solutions. The German edition is grouped around the films, the French and Italian editions are arranged thematically, while the Russian edition from which all other versions ultimately derive their inspiration is arranged in a manner that can only be described as esoteric. In this edition we have opted wherever possible for a chronological approach: the ultimate justification is quite simply that this is the order in which Eisenstein himself wrote and therefore the order which enables the reader most easily to trace the development of his ideas. Sometimes the sheer amount of material has rendered a chronological approach unsustainable, as in the second volume, *Towards a Theory of Montage*: there understanding is better served by grouping Eisenstein's sometimes fragmentary and often unfinished writings on montage from the 1930s and 1940s together in one large volume. But the first and third volumes in this edition follow his career from his first published article in November 1922 to the end of 1934 and then from the Party Conference on Cinema in January 1935 until his death in February 1948. The documents have been chosen not merely to record the development of his aesthetic ideas but also to illuminate the context in which that development occurred. Although each volume focuses on Eisenstein's writings on film, the thoughts he expressed on theatre and the other arts and on politics and current events have been included wherever relevant to illustrate that Eisenstein was not just an artist but a *Soviet* artist, with all that that entailed in the thirty turbulent years after the October Revolution.

It is the aim of this edition to make Eisenstein and his ideas more accessible to the English-speaking reader. If the organisation of the volumes or the quality of the translations or the annotation obstructs that purpose, then we shall not only have failed in our duty to the reader, we shall have failed in our responsibility towards Eisenstein.

RICHARD TAYLOR
Swansea, Wales, June 1987

Introduction

Eisenstein: On Socialism, Soviet Cinema and Reel Life

In 1911 the popular Russian writer Leonid Andreyev, enthusing about the potential of what he called 'the miraculous cinema', predicted:

> There will be no limits to the freedom of an author creating action, his imagination will have been enriched – and new cinema dramatists, as yet unknown talents and geniuses, will emerge. A cinema Shakespeare, after abandoning the inconvenience of words, will deepen and broaden action to such an extent, will find such new and unexpected combinations for it, that it will become as expressive as speech and at the same time it will convince with the incomparable conviction that is inherent only in the visible and the tangible.[1]

If there was one person who could properly lay claim to the title of 'cinema Shakespeare' it would have to be Eisenstein. His position in the development of cinema as an art form was in many ways similar to that of Shakespeare in the development of modern drama and it was certainly as seminal. But, unlike Shakespeare, Eisenstein was more than the leading practitioner of his art: he was also its principal theorist. He was therefore not only cinema's Shakespeare: he was also in some sense its Stanislavsky, its Brecht – or, perhaps most appropriately, its Meyerhold.[2]

Eisenstein has become a myth. He has been acclaimed as a genius, as the greatest film-maker of all time and as one of the great philosophers of art of our century. More has been written about him than about any other film director and he himself wrote more than any other film director both about his own work and about his medium. It is therefore a rather daunting task to introduce the first volume of Eisenstein's *Writings* in this edition. Until now the English-speaking reader has in a sense had to read Eisenstein backwards: his later writings were published first and his earlier work has appeared only partially and gradually in scattered tomes. The chronological order of the present volume enables us to trace the organic development of Eisenstein's thought more clearly. In the limited space available all that I can hope to do is to suggest some continuities in his argument and some avenues for further exploration. But I want above all to argue that there is a very considerable coherence and consistency in Eisenstein's thought even if ultimately his theory of art remained both partial and fragmentary.[3] I shall confine myself to the period covered by this first volume, that is the period until the end of 1934, and, since the basic details of Eisenstein's biography are well known, I shall refer to them only in so far as they help us to understand the development of his ideas.

Eisenstein's first involvement in the performing arts was, of course, theatrical rather than cinematic: he came to cinema through theatre and through an increasing frustration, shared with many others at that time, with theatre's limitations. But his artistic activity began as a child with drawings and sketches and he continued to produce these, sometimes in connection with his film and theatre work and sometimes not, throughout his adult life. It was his draughtsmanship that provided him with the additional income as a student that enabled him to pursue his interest in theatre[4] and ultimately to break away from the engineering career that his father had mapped out for him, via the Red Army into theatre itself. In this respect Eisenstein was typical of other Soviet artists of the time: the October Revolution not only broke down the old social, economic and political order, it also overthrew the traditional notions of art and of the arts. If one thing characterises the revolutionary Soviet artists of the 1920s it is the relative ease with which they moved from one art form to another, from literature to scriptwriting, from painting to set design – in Eisenstein's case from sketching through set design and stage direction to film-making – and this in turn helps to explain the ease with which they drew upon the techniques of those various art forms to enhance the effectiveness of their own activity in one particular form. It was Eisenstein's association with the Petrograd-based Factory of the Eccentric Actor (FEKS)[5] that convinced him of the utility of circus forms. While Grigori Kozintsev's contribution to the FEKS manifesto, 'Eccentrism', demanded 'art without a capital letter, a pedestal or a fig-leaf',[6] Leonid Trauberg's denounced 'serious people in galoshes'.

> The slogan of their time is: 'Revolution brings tasteful art out of the palaces and on to the streets!' It's a religious procession, take off your hats, just imagine it!
> Guilty, comrades! Not that one! To the ABC! From the streets into the palaces with the revolution! The streets bring revolution to art. Our street mud now is circus, cinema, music-hall, Pinkerton.[7]

These preoccupations are reflected in the first document in this collection. 'The Eighth Art', written in November 1922 by Eisenstein and Yutkevich (who had been one of the founder members of the FEKS) (pp. 29-32). In this, the first of Eisenstein's published articles, the techniques of the circus (Eccentrism), of the detective story (Pinkerton) and of Chaplin were held up as examples: indeed, it was Chaplin who was credited with having given cinema 'the eighth seat in the Council of the Muses', of having, in other words, 'moved from the streets into the palaces with the revolution'. The streets had indeed brought revolution to art.

The influence of Eccentrism was just as strong in 'The Montage of Attractions', Eisenstein's first major theoretical work, published in 1923 (pp. 33-38). Although his concern here was with the methods by which *theatre* could be made more effective, many of the arguments used were later to be applied to *cinema*, when theatre's limitations had proved all too apparent. Kozintsev had, on behalf of FEKS, proclaimed:

Life requires art that is
   *hyperbolically crude, dumbfounding, nerve-wracking, openly utili-
tarian, mechanically exact, momentary, rapid,*
otherwise no-one will hear, see or stop.[8]

Eisenstein argued that 'the moulding of the audience in a desired direction (or mood) is the task of every utilitarian theatre'. But, whereas Kozintsev proposed a hegemony of the new 'low' art forms to the exclusion of the traditional 'high' forms, encapsulated in the slogan, 'We prefer Charlie's arse to Eleonore Duse's hands,'[9] Eisenstein was prepared to utilise whatever was to prove most *effective*:

> all the parts that constitute the apparatus of theatre (Ostuzhev's 'chatter' no more than the colour of the prima donna's tights, a roll on the drums just as much as Romeo's soliloquy, the cricket on the hearth no less than a salvo under the seats of the auditorium) because, despite their differences, they all lead to one thing – which their presence legitimates – to their common quality of *attraction*.

The concept of attractions was central to Eisenstein's thought at this time and was to recur in different guises throughout his later career. The ends justified the means and for Eisenstein the ends were always *ultimately* ideological, even if they were frequently expressed in aesthetic terms:

> An attraction . . . is any aggressive moment in theatre, i.e. any element of it that subjects the audience to emotional or psychological influence, verified by experience and mathematically calculated to produce specific emotional shocks in the spectator in their proper order within the whole. These shocks provide the only opportunity of perceiving the ideological aspect of what is being shown, the final ideological conclusion.

The attraction was 'an independent and primary element in structuring the show': it derived its coherence from the perception of the 'final ideological conclusion' that it facilitated.

Eisenstein reiterated the purpose of the attraction in 'The Montage of Film Attractions', written in 1924 but not published in his lifetime (pp. 39-58):

> An attraction . . . is in our understanding any demonstrable fact (an action, an object, a phenomenon, a conscious combination, and so on) that is known and proven to exercise a definite effect on the attention and emotions of the audience and that, combined with others, possesses the characteristic of concentrating the audience's emotions in any direction dictated by the production's purpose.

3

Introduction

Without this overarching purpose the independent and primary elements would fall apart, as in the work of Vertov and the Cine-Eyes, which Eisenstein characterised at this stage as a mere 'montage of separate sequences'. Each montage element, each attraction, had to contribute towards the total effect of the work. These attractions worked on the audience's psyche through their associations and through chains of such associations: the effect of each attraction depended to a great extent on its montage context, on the relationship of each individual shot and its associations to the associations of the shots that surrounded it. Eisenstein chose the slaughter sequence from *The Strike* to illustrate his point.

In 'The Montage of Film Attractions' Eisenstein also broached the problem of the role of the script in film-making. Given his experiences in making *The Strike* and those he was to have with *The Battleship Potemkin*, it is perhaps hardly surprising to find him describing the script as 'a "prescription" that summarises the general projected emotional effect on the audience and the pressure that will inevitably be exerted on the audience's psyche' and arguing:

> More often than not, given our scriptwriters' utterly feeble approach to the construction of a script, this task falls entirely to the director. The transposition of the theme into a chain of attractions with a previously determined end effect is the definition we have given of a director's work. The presence or absence of a written script is by no means all that important.

The script was justified only if it performed a useful function in furthering the effectiveness of the film, in facilitating the communication of its ideological purpose.

This too was the actor's role and Eisenstein judged the concept of the *naturshchik* or model actor[10] accordingly. In so far as the model actor succeeded in exposing the underlying motivation of a character through the expressiveness of his external movements, his technique was justified. He discerned a productive conflict in the model actor between the desires of the actor and the inertia of his body: this notion of conflict contained the germ of the idea of the centrality of conflict to art that Eisenstein was to develop later. It also presaged the perception of montage as a means of resolving such conflict through the Marxist notion of the dialectic (even if it had come down to Eisenstein in a rather functional, perhaps even mechanistic, version through Engles and Lenin): thesis – antithesis – synthesis. The test for all the various elements employed in cinema was then, as it was to be later, its efficiency in communicating the purpose of the film:

> An idea expressed in its completeness is photogenic; that is, an object is photogenic when it corresponds most closely to the idea that it embodies. (A car is more photogenic than a cart because its whole

structure corresponds more closely to its purpose of transportation, and so on.)[11]

The montage of attractions in cinema was justified by its utility, just as it had previously been justified in theatre as long as it had been effective in that medium.

By the time that Eisenstein wrote 'The Problem of the Materialist Approach to Form' (pp. 59-64) he had already completed his first feature-length film, *The Strike*. He claimed that the film represented 'an ideological victory in the field of form' because of its

> discovery of the manufacturing logic and the exposition of the technique of the methods of struggle as of a 'living' current process that knows no inviolable rules other than its final aim and the methods that are varied and devised at a particular moment according to the conditions and the balance of forces at that particular phase of the struggle.

Here again the purpose was the overriding consideration. Before *The Strike*, he argued, cinema had absorbed 'the external characteristics of "neighbouring arts"' but the 'revolutionary quality' of *The Strike* lay in the fact that its 'renewing principle' was a 'directly utilitarian' one and, more specifically, an *industrial* one. Eisenstein denied a conflict of interest between form and content but argued instead that revolutionary form would derive from revolutionary ideology, just as the locomotive had derived from the discovery of steam as a motive power:

> It is not by 'revolutionising' the forms of the stage-coach that the locomotive is created but through a proper technical calculation of the practical emergence of a *new and previously non-existent kind of energy* – steam. It is not the 'research' for forms that correspond to the new content but the logical *realisation of all the phases of the technical production of a work of art consonant with* the 'new *kind* of energy' – the *ruling ideology* – that will produce the forms of revolutionary art.

The decisive factor 'for art in general and revolutionary art in particular' was the 'maximum intensification of the emotional seizure of the audience' and 'a formal approach that is *correctly* conducted in Marxist terms [and that] results in an ideologically valuable and socially useful product'. Eisenstein argued that formal effectiveness was impotent if it was not thematically effective and in this context he renewed his attack on the work of Vertov and the Cine-Eyes as 'primitive Impressionism'. He compared art, a 'tractor ploughing over the audience's psyche', with Vertov's position, the *'reductio ad absurdum* of the technical methods that are valid for newsreel', and noted the different effect of 'the abattoir that is *recorded* in *Cine-Eyes* and *gorily effective* in *The Strike*'.

He attributed the difference to the method by which in *The Strike* he had snatched 'fragments from our surroundings according to a conscious and pre-determined plan calculated to launch them at the audience in the appropriate combination, to subjugate it to the appropriate association with the obvious final ideological motivation.'

The Cine-Eyes, with their view of the essence of cinema as 'life caught un-awares', were accused of 'passionless representation', of 'the fixing of pheno-mena that goes no further than fixing the audience's attention' rather than 'ploughing the audience's psyche'. By implication Eisenstein was here engag-ing in the same kind of critique of the Cine-Eyes as those who were later to accuse them of empty Formalism.[12] Their work certainly had form, but it lacked ideological direction: 'It is not a "Cine-Eye" that we need but a "Cine-Fist".'

The Strike, or rather the vitriolic dispute over the authorship of the film,[13] also marked the end of Eisenstein's association with Proletkult, which had exerted a formative influence on him. With the severing of this link, he was in a sense cast adrift not only from the Proletkult collective but from other artistic groupings. He continued to play a leading part in LEF but that was an organisation broad enough to encompass both him and the Cine-Eyes. A sense of creeping isolation might help to explain why Eisenstein became more dogmatic in 'The Method of Making a Workers' Film' (pp. 65-66). He insisted that, 'There is *one* method for making *any* film: the montage of attrac-tions.' He re-defined the content of a film as 'the socially useful emotional and psychological effect that infects the audience and is composed of a chain of suitably directed stimulants'. The determination of the purpose of the film defined its class character and Eisenstein reiterated his earlier argument that without that purpose the individual attractions would not function as a total-ity but as essentially counter-revolutionary art for art's sake.

In January 1926 Eisenstein's second feature-length film, *The Battle-ship Potemkin*, was given its première. It was not popular with Soviet audi-ences reared on the same diet of popular Hollywood films as their counter-parts in the West. But when it reached the West it created a sensation amongst the intelligentsia and a *succès de scandale* in the press because of attempts to censor it or suppress it altogether.[14] Eisenstein became an international celebrity and the principal ambassador abroad of Soviet art. He made his first visit abroad as an adult by going to Berlin to promote the film and had his first taste of life in the West. His comparisons between film-making in the Soviet Union and in Germany were conveyed in his interview with the *Berliner Tageblatt* (pp. 74-76) and in 'The German Cinema. A Traveller's Impressions' (pp. 85-88). But it was *Potemkin* that dominated Soviet cinema in 1926 and *Potemkin* that gave him a reputation and raised expectations that he perhaps never subsequently fulfilled, nor could have fulfilled.

'Constanţa (Whither *The Battleship Potemkin*)' was Eisenstein's first attempt to explain the intentions and significance of what was to become his most famous film (pp. 67-70). He argued that *Potemkin* marked an advance on *The Strike* because '*The Strike* is a treatise; *Potemkin* is a hymn.' Citing the roaring lions as his example, he suggested that in his latest work, 'the object is not just an illustration acting as an object (an accordion, a toilet); the object is psychologised both by way of its positioning and in its very presentation.' This represented a further distancing from the Vertov school and, indeed, from what Eisenstein now called 'the Cine-Eye qualities of *The Strike*'. He explained the modification of his methods by arguing:

> There is one thing we have no right to do and that is to *make general-isations*. The current phase of audience reaction determines our methods of influence: what it reacts to. Without this *there can be no influential art and certainly no art with maximum influence.*

It was once more a matter of the end justifying the means: 'Art admits *all* methods except those that fail to achieve their end.' In 'The German Cinema' Eisenstein mocked the view of *Potemkin*, expressed to him in Germany, that there were 'simply not enough men and women in love with one another'. In 'Constanţa' he asserted that the end of art, at least of Soviet art, was not to lull the audience (a point reiterated in his interview with the *Berliner Tageblatt*) but to provoke and challenge it: 'art always exacerbates a current conflict rather than distracting audiences from it'. *Potemkin*, by 'psychologising' objects, marked a logical progression from the chains of associations that he had identified at an earlier stage in the development of his ideas:

> For those of us who take our stand on the basis of the montage of attractions, this change is neither an overturning of the foundations of cinema nor a change in course in understanding our cinema. For us it is the next consecutive stage of attraction – the next tactical man-oeuvre in the attack on the audience under the slogan of October.

Eisenstein thus felt that his arguments, despite their modification, retained an underlying coherence and consistency. It is not therefore surprising to find him developing his earlier statements on the model actor in 'However Odd – Khokhlova!' (pp. 71-73). Comparing the role of women in Soviet and Western cinema, Eisenstein presented the actress Alexandra Khokhlova, the archetypal example of the *naturshchik*, as a specifically Soviet phenomenon. His essential functionalism led him to believe that Soviet cinema should play to its strengths, Khokhlova being one of them: 'To keep Khokhlova, who is, I repeat, perhaps our only original actress . . . "veiled" is simply criminal.'

But the two most important writings from 1926 are undoubtedly 'Béla Forgets the Scissors' (pp. 77-81) and 'The Two Skulls of Alexander the Great' (pp. 82-84). The first was a response to an article by the Hungarian critic Béla Balázs in which he had argued that the role of the cameraman was central to the specificity of cinema. Eisenstein viewed this, from his own experience of German cinema, as a reflection of German conditions. He characterised what he termed Balázs's 'starism' as

> the individualism of bourgeois countries in general. They do not think beyond this in the West. Someone has to be the 'star'. *One* person. Yesterday it was the actor. This time let's say it's the cameraman. Tomorrow it will be the lighting technician.

By contrast with the Soviet Union, in the West 'the idea that a film is the result of *collective* efforts goes to the devil.' Balázs's individualism had led him to an erroneous belief in 'the shot itself as "star"'. Eisenstein, on the other hand, repeated his view that it was montage, which enabled the individual shot to be seen in the context of a particular sequence that gave it meaning through association – what he here called 'contextual confrontation' – that defined the specificity of cinema.

In 'The Two Skulls' Eisenstein re-examined the relationship between cinema and theatre, comparing them to the skulls of Alexander the Great at different ages. His arguments very much reflected the progress of his own career. While cinema had derived originally from theatre ('Cinema is the contemporary stage of theatre. The next, consecutive phase.'[15]), it was an offshoot that had outgrown its parent plant. As an effective medium theatre was finished and the past role of theatre would in future 'be fulfilled by by-passing theatre'. Using an analogy he had employed before, Eisenstein called for efforts to be concentrated on developing cinema at the expense of theatre:

> There's no point in perfecting the wooden plough. The tractor has been invented. Drawing attention to the success of tractorisation, i.e. to cinema, and organising life through clubs are the task of every serious theatre worker.

The analogy with the plough and the tractor was not fortuitous, for Eisenstein was already working on his next film, *The General Line*, which dealt with collectivisation in the Soviet countryside. Although this film is still not nearly as well known as his much more controversial anniversary film, *October*, Eisenstein considered it much more important. His view is summed up in his remark in 'Give Us a State Plan' (pp. 89-94): '*October* was an overtime job: our main job was and is *The General Line*, a film that we consider to be the next new stage in our film work.'

That article was largely an account of Eisenstein's working methods to date. He was principally concerned to reiterate his earlier statements on the need to calculate the content of a film for maximum effect in the same way that a loaded train is despatched to its destination. He called again for unified central control of film: 'The tractors whose movements are not organised by a single will do not plough the fields.' If the fields were not ploughed, nor would the audience's psyche be ploughed. Planning was the only answer: 'When that happens the freight trains will perhaps arrive at their destinations with a full and valuable load.' It was a call that was to be taken up by the Party Conference on Cinema that was held in March 1928. But by December 1927, when the article was published, neither of Eisenstein's freight trains had yet arrived at their destinations. *The General Line* had been interrupted by the making of *October*, but *October*, although completed, had still to be re-edited for general release. The attacks on Eisenstein's anniversary film were to mark the beginning of a downward slide from the apparently unassailable position in which *Potemkin* had placed him.

The year 1928 marked a turning-point in the history of Soviet cinema. The tenth anniversary of the October Revolution had focused attention on the continuing failure of the authorities to organise cinema as an effective ideological weapon, on their failure to effect the kind of centralised control that Eisenstein had called for. Cinema audiences were still being fed a diet of the kind of fiction films that Eisenstein and other intellectual film-makers despised, the kind of films that imitated the commercial films produced in the West. In the words of one film journal, Soviet cinema had been 'allowed . . . to drift on the Soviet sea "rudderless and without sails"'.[16] The Party Conference already mentioned constituted the official response to the crisis; Eisenstein made his thoughts clear in 'What Are We Expecting from the Party Conference on Cinema' (p. 100), the kind of statement of political identification that was itself already becoming expected of Soviet film-makers and that was to become *de rigueur* in the 1930s. His critique of the existing policies of Sovkino, the state cinema organisation, was elaborated in both 'For a Workers' Hit' (pp. 107-112) and 'The Twelfth Year' (pp. 123-126), which he jointly signed with Alexandrov. In this latter piece the authors reiterated the importance of a 'tendentious' cinema and argued the need for an improved training programme for young directors in order to overcome 'the unprincipled behaviour of our industry and its leadership' and ensure that 'we shall be able to meet the thirteenth October *with a fully armed Cinema October*.' Some of the elements of such a programme are to be seen in the interview entitled 'The GTK Teaching and Research Workshop' (pp. 127-129).

Eisenstein's principal concern was still as always the theory and practice of the film-making process. In a series of major articles in 1928 he re-examined the central tenets of cinema, moved towards the notion of 'intellectual cinema' and confronted for the first time the problems associated with the advent of sound. In 'Our *October*: Beyond the Played and the Non-Played' (pp. 101-106) he was defending his anniversary film against the thrust of the attacks made on it. Just as he had earlier argued that *Potemkin* should not be judged by the standards of *The Strike*, so he now argued that *October* should not be judged by the standards of his earlier work, but as a further stage on the path towards his next film. He compared *October* to the stage in life at which the male voice breaks:

The voice has a habit of 'breaking' at a transitional age.
At an age when you are growing. The transition to adulthood.
October appears at a similar turning-point for cinema.
October spans two epochs in cinema.

It represented the transition from the uttermost limits of the old forms to new forms that had 'by no means all yet been found'. *October* represented the transition from the old dichotomy between fiction and documentary film, between played and non-played, to a new and as yet unclearly defined stage 'beyond the played and the non-played' where 'cinema . . . stands on its *own two* feet with its own, admittedly as yet undesignated terminology'. We are back to the dialectic: thesis – antithesis – synthesis. In this dialectical process

A theoretical novelty – the 'non-played' film – has in due course re-placed plot by *fact*.
Illusion by *raw material*.

But the new synthesis was characterised not by fact or raw material, but by what Eisenstein rather provocatively called 'CONTEMPT FOR RAW MATERIAL'. Using an analogy only slightly less dismissive of the Cine-Eyes than his earlier remarks, he observed:

slaves of the machine are becoming masters of the machine.
Slaves of raw material are becoming exploiters of raw material.
If in the preceding period the material prevailed, the object re-placed 'soul and mood', then the next stage will replace the presen-tation of a phenomenon (material, object) by a *conclusion* based on the phenomenon and a *judgment* on the material, given concrete form in finished concepts.

We are back here to the 'tendentiousness' of cinema, to its 'ruling ideology' and its 'final ideological motivation'. Attractions still worked through their chains of associations, objects were still 'psychologised', but what Eisenstein had on a previous occasion called 'the next tactical manoeuvre in the attack on the audience under the slogan of October' meant now that 'Cinema is ready to begin operating through the abstract word that leads to a concrete *concept.*' This was 'intellectual cinema' in all but name: 'The sphere of the new film language will, as it happens, not be the sphere of the presentation of phen-omena, nor even that of social interpretation, but the opportunity for *abstract social evaluation.*' The paradigm of this 'abstract social evaluation' was to be Eisenstein's projected film version of Marx's *Capital*, but that film was never made.

Those who had felt unduly constrained by the limitations of cinema as a *silent* medium welcomed the advent of sound as a liberating force, but to the majority it was a cause of considerable trepidation. Some feared the loss of their jobs, others worried about the destruction of cinema as an art form. The significance of sound was examined by Eisenstein and his colleagues Alexandrov and Pudovkin in their 'Statement on Sound' (pp. 113-114). Their principal concern was that sound would be used merely as an addition to images, creating the illusion of naturalism, destroying the 'culture of montage' and thus the autonomy of cinema as an art form by re-establishing the hegemony of theatrical methods ('"dramas of high culture" and other photographed representations of a theatrical order'). To avoid this 'blind alley' the writers argued that film-makers should experiment first and foremost with '*the contrapuntal use* of sound *vis-à-vis* the visual fragment of montage' with a view to enhancing cinematic language by 'the creation of a new *orchestral counterpoint* of visual and sound images.' We have seen from Eisenstein's comments on *October*, especially in 'Our *October*. Beyond the Played and the Non-Played', that he regarded that film in particular and cinema in general as having reached the limits of its old cinematic language. Used properly, sound offered a way out of the impasse:

> Sound, treated as a new element of montage (as an independent entity combined with the visual image) cannot fail to provide new and enormously powerful means of expressing and resolving the most complex problems, which have been depressing us with their insurmountability using the imperfect methods of a cinema operating only in visual images.

The 'Statement on Sound' left matters there: it fell to Eisenstein himself to pursue the argument further and this he began to do in 'An Unexpected Juncture' (pp. 115-122).

This article reflected Eisenstein's long-standing interest in Japanese art and letters, an interest which was regenerated by the visit to Moscow of the Kabuki theatre in 1928, when one of the actors demonstrated his techniques to the students in Eisenstein's GTK workshop. Eisenstein's vision of Japanese culture was, of course, an incomplete and, in many ways, a misleading one. He was fascinated by the conventions of the Kabuki, by 'the peculiar quality that manifests itself clearly during the direct *perception* of the performance and that no *description* has managed to convey to us'. The manifestation of this 'peculiar quality' appeared to echo his own experiments with the chains of associations that were linked to the montage of attractions:

> Here we find an *unexpected juncture* between the Kabuki and those extreme experiments in theatre in which theatre has already ceased to exist and has become cinema. What is more, it has become cinema at the latest stage of its development: *sound* cinema.

But the principal lesson that the Kabuki had to teach was what Eisenstein characterised as the sense of 'monistic ensemble', which appealed to him

11

because of his continuing concern with the overall direction and purpose of a work of art. In the Kabuki, 'sound, movement, space and voice *do not accompany* (or even parallel) one another but are treated as *equivalent elements.*' The Kabuki operates through 'a single monistic sensation of theatrical "stimulation"', using all the elements of theatre that contribute towards the end of the production: 'Addressing himself to the sense organs, he bases his calculations on the final *sum* of stimulants to the brain, ignoring *which* path that stimulation takes.' Each element was a 'single unit of theatre' in the same way that Eisenstein had defined the attraction in 1923. But the Kabuki had found a method for 'the transference of the basic affective intention from one material to another, from one category of "stimulant" to another', so that 'we actually "hear movement" and "see sound".' This transference could be effected not merely because the Japanese treated sound and image as 'equivalent elements' but because they had discovered the 'common denominator' between them. This was an essential precondition for the realisation of the orchestral counterpoint that was to preserve montage and thus the autonomy of cinema:

> In our 'Statement' on sound cinema we wrote about the contrapuntal method of combining visual and sound images. To master this method you have to develop within yourself a new *sense*: *the ability to reduce visual and sound perceptions to a 'common denominator'.*
> The Kabuki has this ability down to a fine art.

As we shall see, he was to develop these ideas the following year.

In January 1929 Eisenstein returned to the problem of the role of the script in the process of film-making. In 1924 he had argued in 'The Montage of Film Attractions' that 'The presence or the absence of a written script is by no means all that important' and that the script, like the other elements that constituted a finished film, was justified only by its utility in effecting the director's aims. In his interview with the *Berliner Tageblatt* in June 1926 he had stated:

> My artistic principle was therefore, and still is: not intuitive creativity but the rational constructive composition of affective elements; the most important thing is that the affect must be calculated and analysed in advance.

Now, in 'The Form of the Script', (pp. 134-5) he argued that the script was 'a stage in the condition of the material', 'a shorthand record of an emotional outburst striving for realisation in an accumulation of visual images'. The script, written in literary language, was like 'a boot-tree, preserving the shape of the boot when there is no living foot inside it', 'a bottle that is necessary only so that the cork can explode and the character of the wine foam into the greedy gullets of the onlookers'. The script represented a blueprint for the director to translate into film language, 'a cipher communicated by one character to another', 'the cinematic equivalent of literary expression'. The script expressed 'the purpose of the experience that the audience must undergo': 'The script sets out the emotional requirements. The director provides its visual resolution.' The 'heart of the matter' lay in the 'tension or passion' that should be employed in order to exert the maximum desired effect on the audience:

> Let the scriptwriter and the director expound this in their different languages.
>
> The scriptwriter puts: 'Deathly silence.'
>
> The director uses: still close-ups; the dark and silent pitching of the battleship's bows; the unfurling of the St Andrew's ensign; perhaps a dolphin's leap; and the low flight of seagulls.
>
> The audience experiences the same emotional spasm in the throat, the same anxiety rising in his throat as that which seized the author of the memoirs at his writing desk and the director of the film at the cutting table or while shooting in the boiling sun.

The essence of the activity is the communication of that 'emotional spasm' to the audience: the end is the same, but the methods of the scriptwriter and the director are different.

In 'Beyond the Shot' (pp. 138-150) Eisenstein returned to the ideas that he had been exploring in 'An Unexpected Juncture'. He argued that Japanese script, with its use of ideograms – or, as he called them, hieroglyphs – had lessons for cinema:

> The point is that . . . the combination . . . of two hieroglyphs of the simplest series is regarded not as their sum total but as their product, i.e. as a value of another dimension, another degree: each taken separately corresponds to an object but their combination corresponds to a *concept*. The combination of two 'representable' objects achieves the representation of something that cannot be graphically represented.

Thesis, antithesis, synthesis. This was precisely the aim that Eisenstein had set out in 'Our *October*. Beyond the Played and the Non-Played': 'the next stage will replace the presentation of a phenomenon (material, object) by a *conclusion* based on the phenomenon and a *judgment* on the material, given concrete form in finished concepts.' There was no better way to achieve the aim of 'operating through the abstract word that leads to a concrete *concept*' than to employ the 'hieroglyphic' method of Japanese script, which was, in turn, effectively a montage of associations. This was 'the starting point for "intellectual cinema"'. In Eisenstein's analysis the hieroglyphic method of 'denotation through representation' involved 'splitting endlessly into two'. It was the interplay between the two elements (both of the method itself and of each splitting) that created 'something that cannot be graphically represented', something akin to 'abstract social evaluation'. This led Eisenstein to challenge the Kuleshovian notion of serial montage, with each shot as an 'element of montage' building up 'brick by brick' to the construction of a sequence. He regarded serial montage as 'merely one possible *particular* case', in the same way as he had considered the illustrative use of sound as just one, not very exciting, possibility:

> The shot is by no means a montage *element*.
> The shot is a montage cell. Beyond the dialectical jump in the *single* series: shot – montage.
> What then characterises montage and, consequently, its embryo, the shot?
> Collision. Conflict between two neighbouring fragments. Conflict. Collision.

Eisenstein compared montage with 'the series of explosions of the internal combustion engine', separate 'fragments' combining into a 'dynamic'. But, if 'montage is conflict', then the shot, as a 'montage cell', had also to be 'examined from the point of view of *conflict*', in this instance of 'conflict within the shot'. He delineated various types of such conflict:

> the conflict of graphic directions (lines)
> the conflict of shot levels (between one another)
> the conflict of volumes
> the conflict of masses (of volumes filled with varying intensities of light)
> the conflict of spaces, etc.

He also identified: 'the conflict between an object and its spatial nature and the conflict between an event and its temporal nature.' This particular aspect of conflict within the shot owed much to Shklovsky's notion of 'impeded form' and his belief in *ostranenie* or 'de-familisarisation'.[17]

The range of different conflicts both within the shot and between one shot and another could all too easily cause a film 'to break up into antagonistic pairs of fragments'. This could be avoided by the discovery of 'a single system of methods of cinematic expression that will cover all its elements', by the exposure of the 'single indicator' that lay at the basis of that mode of expression. Here Eisenstein was returning to the lesson that he had drawn in 'An Unexpected Juncture': the Kabuki theatre had discovered 'the ability to reduce visual and sound perceptions to a "common denominator"', thus enabling them to achieve 'the contrapuntal method of combining visual and sound images.' Now the discovery of conflict provided the necessary denominator for cinema. In the instance of conflict within the shot this could be expressed as 'the principle of optical counterpoint'. But conflict was not a new discovery for Eisenstein. In 1923 in 'The Montage of Attractions' he had implicitly recognised the significance of conflict in his assertion: 'These shocks [i.e. attractions] provide the only opportunity of perceiving the ideological aspect of what is being shown, the final ideological conclusion.'

Eisenstein's last concern in 'Beyond the Shot' was with the frame that actually surrounded the shot and here too he argued that the West could and should learn from the tenets of Japanese culture. Whereas in the West, or so he claimed, the film-maker began with the frame and then composed the shot within its confines, 'the Japanese do it the other way round': the image dictates the shape of the frame. The West 'staged' the scene, the Japanese 'captured' it, using the camera to organise the raw material, 'Cutting out a fragment of reality by means of the lens'. But, having reached this point in his argument about the frame, Eisenstein pushed it no further for the time being but turned instead back to the acting method of the Kabuki theatre. He called the method 'decomposed acting' because 'the whole process of the death agony was decomposed into solo performances by each "party" separately: the legs, the arms, the head.' It was quite simply 'decomposition into shot levels'. The analogy with cinematic montage was crystal clear. Eisenstein concluded that 'the most varied branches of Japanese culture are permeated by a purely cinematic element and by its basic nerve – montage'. It was therefore appropriate that cinema should learn from Japanese artistic practice.

In 'Perspectives' (pp. 151-160), also written in 1929, Eisenstein returned to problems of form and content, and to his attack on the supposed antithesis between them. Arguing that 'the role of the preacher has merged with the role of the artist. The *propagandist* has emerged', he confirmed content as 'the principle of the organisation of thinking'. Content dictated form, just as in Japanese art (according to 'Beyond the Shot') the image dictated the shape of the frame. Content and form were joined together by ideology, just as the montage of attractions had been given coherence by the 'final ideological conclusion':

> The *content* of a newspaper is the principle by which the *contents* of the paper are organised and processed, with the aim of processing the reader from a class-based standpoint.
> Herein lies the production-based inseparability of the sum total of content and form from *ideology*.

Similarly cognition and construction could not be separated because 'For us, to know is to take part':

> Cognition is construction.
> The cognition of life is inseparable from the construction of life, from its *recreation*.

15

Introduction

Cognition involved the deconstruction and reconstruction of life, as already outlined in 'Beyond the Shot', through conflict, through a constant dialectical process of thesis, antithesis and synthesis. Using the analogy of music, Eisenstein argued for 'a mnemonic of *collectively* experienced *perception*' that would by implication lead to '*collective action*'. Through the process of the dialectic art had to achieve a new synthesis:

> The new art must set a limit to the dualism of the spheres of 'emotion' and 'reason':
> It must restore to science its sensuality.
> To the intellectual process its fire and passion.
> It must plunge the abstract process of thought into the cauldron of practical activity.
> Restore the splendour and wealth of gut-felt *forms* to the emasculated speculative *formula*.
> Give the clarity of ideological *formulation* to *formal arbitrariness*.
> That is the appeal that we are making. Those are the demands we are directing at the coming period of art.
> Which art form will be able to meet the challenge?
> *Purely and solely the medium of cinema.*
> *Purely and solely intellectual cinema, the synthesis of emotional, documentary and absolute film.*
> Only *intellectual* cinema will be able to put an end to the conflict between the 'language of logic' and the 'language of images'. On the basis of the language of the cinema dialectic.
> An *intellectual* cinema of unprecedented form and social functionalism. A cinema of extreme cognition and extreme sensuality that has mastered the entire arsenal of affective optical, acoustical and biochemical stimulants.

This intellectual cinema had an ideological purpose: 'the task of irrevocably inculcating communist ideology into the millions'. It was, in Eisenstein's view, destined to play a central role in the coming age of communism. This was not an empty phrase, nor was it a phrase put into Eisenstein's mouth by the authorities: he was and remained, despite his later travails, a convinced Marxist, a devoted Party member and a loyal Soviet artist until his death. His Marxism was central to his artistic life: the dialectic informed the way he thought and it informed the way he wrote.

It is therefore not surprising that 'The Dramaturgy of Film Form' (pp. 161-180) should have been given the alternative title 'The Dialectical Approach to Film Form'. This piece can be seen largely as a schematisation of the ideas that Eisenstein had already expressed elsewhere. He repeated his view that, 'In the realm of art [the] dialectical principle of the dynamic is embodied in CONFLICT.' It was the collision between the 'logic of organic form' (nature) and the 'logic of rational form' (industry) that 'produces and determines the dynamic'. He reiterated the argument that 'both the whole and the minutest detail must be permeated by a *single principle*'. However the synthesis that montage represented 'is not an idea composed of successive shots stuck together but an idea that DERIVES from the collision between two shots that are independent of one another'. The notion of synthesis and of montage as 'blending' was therefore a 'vulgar description of what happens'. One new element was Eisenstein's analysis of the way in which 'each sequential element is arrayed, not *next* to the one it follows, but on *top* of it'. The retained impression of the first image (thesis) had a second image superimposed upon it (antithesis) and this produced a totality that was greater than the sum of the parts, 'a completely new higher dimension' (synthesis). He also analysed the nature of pictorial dynamism and, for the first time, the use of colour and concluded that the basis of dynamic effect lay with counterpoint or conflict. Film was essentially visual (or, in the case of sound film, audio-visual) counterpoint. There were three 'different *phases in the formation of a homogeneous expressive task*': formulation, conflict and explosion – thesis, antithesis, synthesis.

In further analysing the different kinds of conflict that might arise in film form Eisenstein borrowed from music the idea of the dominant as the principal sign of each shot, although he did not at this stage develop the analogy. He proposed what he, perhaps rather unwisely, called 'a tentative film syntax', a series of examples of the ways in which the film director could realise the 'emotional dynamisation' of the raw material. The concept of emotional dynamisation was itself a development of Eisenstein's earlier notions of 'ploughing the audience's psyche' ('The Problem of the Materialist Approach to Form') and of 'psychologising objects' ('Constanţa'). Despite his view, expressed in opposition to the Kuleshov/Pudovkin concept of serial montage, that the shot/montage relationship was not analogous to the word/sentence relationship, he was now arguing that film should use language, rather than theatre or painting, as its model:

> Why then should cinema in its forms follow theatre and painting rather than the methodology of language, which gives rise, through the combination of concrete descriptions and concrete objects, to quite new concepts and ideas?

Each montage fragment 'has in itself no reality at all'. It had associations and it was the accumulation of associations through the composition of the montage sequence as a whole that made it 'work emotionally'. The isolated word acquired meaning in the context of the sentence: the isolated shot acquired meaning in the context of the montage sequence. Intellectual cinema too depended upon the montage of associations and the final ideological conclusion. Citing the sequence of images of various gods from *October*, Eisenstein suggested that:

The conventional *descriptive* form of the film becomes a kind of reasoning (as a formal possibility).

Whereas in the conventional film the film directs and develops the *emotions*, here we have a hint of the possibility of likewise developing and directing the entire *thought process*.

Intellectual cinema, while 'still embryonic', would 'construct a really quite new form of filmic expression', which

will achieve direct forms for thoughts, systems and concepts without any transitions or paraphrases.

And which can therefore become a

SYNTHESIS OF ART AND SCIENCE.

Once again Eisenstein expressed his intention of experimenting with this synthesis in his projected film version of Marx's *Capital*.

In 'The Dramaturgy of Film Form' Eisenstein had for the first time suggested that a montage sequence might derive its expressive effect from the conflict between the dominant sign of each shot within the sequence, in the same way that in music the dominant related to the scale. He developed this idea in 'The Fourth Dimension in Cinema' (pp. 181-194). This level of intensity of the conflict could range: 'from a complete opposition between the dominants, i.e. a sharply contrasting construction, to a scarcely noticeable "modulation" from shot to shot.' What is more this dominant could be 'more or less specifically defined, but never absolutely'. Each montage sequence took its general meaning from an indicator or signpost shot 'that immediately "christens" the whole series with a particular "sign"': each combination of dominants had its own dominant. The rejection of the Kuleshov/Pudovkin analogy between shot/montage and word/phrase was now complete:

The shot never becomes a letter but always remains an ambiguous hieroglyph.

It can be read only in context, just like a hieroglyph, acquiring specific *meaning, sense* and even *pronunciation* (sometimes dramatically opposed to one another) only *in combination with* a separate reading or a small sign or reading indicator placed alongside it.

But the dominant was, after all, only the dominant; there were other signs contained within the shot as well. Eisenstein claimed that *The General Line* (which was the film he had been working on since the completion of *Potemkin* and the project that he regarded as artistically more important than *October*) had been edited 'by the method of "democratic" equal rights for all the stimulants, viewed together as a complex'. In other words, in this film he had applied the Kabuki method of calculating the sum of equivalent elements on order to determine the overall effect. He applied the argument that 'a whole complex of secondary stimulants always accompany the *central* stimulant' to both the acoustical and optical aspects of montage. These 'secondary resonances' (continuing the musical analogy) provided a whole complex of overtones and undertones to complement the dominant: 'This is the method on which the montage of *The General Line* is constructed. This montage is not constructed on the *individual dominant* but takes the sum of *stimuli* of all the stimulants as the dominant.' In a sense Eisenstein was now applying the methodology of the montage of attractions to the construction of the individual shot: thesis (tone/dominant), antithesis (overtone/undertone), synthesis (sum total/new dominant). Each shot was constructed on the basis of internal conflict, in the same way that each phrase of montage was constructed. But each shot, like each note in a musical phrase, was meaningless in isolation:

> Both emerge as a real constant only in the dynamics of the musical or cinematic *process*.
>
> Overtonal conflicts, which are foreseen but not 'recorded' in the score, emerge only through dialectical formation when the film passes through the projector or an orchestra performs a symphony.

This then was the significance of the 'fourth dimension' – time – in cinema.

Eisenstein offered the overtone as the long sought-after common denominator between sound and image in audio-visual montage counterpoint: 'Because, while a shot is a visual *perception* and a tone is a sound perception, *both visual and sound overtones are totally physiological sensations*'. It was the conflict between visual and sound overtones that, echoing the stipulation for 'orchestral counterpoint' in the 'Statement on Sound', 'will give rise to the composition of the Soviet sound film' and also provide the basic method for intellectual cinema:

> For the musical overtone (a beat) the term 'I hear' is no longer strictly appropriate.
>
> Nor 'I see' for the visual.
>
> For both we introduce a new uniform formula: '*I feel*'.

He then went on to analyse the four different 'methods of montage' that cinema could utilise: metric, rhythmic, tonal and overtonal. He made it clear that he regarded overtonal montage as 'an advance on the other stages': it therefore followed that *The General Line* marked for him an advance on his other films, just as *Potemkin* had earlier marked an advance on *The Strike*. 'Cinema,' he remarked, 'begins where the collision between different cinematic measures of movement and vibration begins.' This dialectic lay at the basis of what Lenin, in Eisenstein's paraphrase, had called 'an endless process of deepening the human cognition of objects, phenomena, processes, etc. from appearances to essence and from the less profound to the more profound essence.' As the next stage in this process Eisenstein proposed the notion of 'intellectual montage'. Whereas overtonal montage depended on the stimulation of physiological reactions:

> Intellectual montage is montage not of primitively physiological overtonal resonances but of the resonances of overtones of an intellectual order,
> i.e. the conflicting combination of accompanying intellectual effects with one another.

Once more the justification for the means was the end: he had ended 'The Dramaturgy of Film Form' with a call for intellectual cinema as 'a synthesis of art and science', but he concluded 'The Fourth Dimension in Cinema' with a call for a synthesis of art, science and ideology:

> Intellectual cinema will be the cinema that resolves the conflicting combination of physiological overtones and intellectual overtones, creating an unheard-of form of cinema which inculcates the Revolution into the general history of culture, creating a synthesis of science, art and militant class-consciousness.

We are back yet again to the 'final ideological conclusion' that underpinned the montage of attractions in 1923.

A week before the publication of 'The Fourth Dimension in Cinema' and two months before the première of *The General Line*, Eisenstein, Alexandrov and Tisse left the Soviet Union in order to study the latest developments in sound film in the West. Eisenstein's reception was warmest in that other outcast country of the Europe of the 1920s, Germany: at least there his films were shown and his ideas treated with respect. After attending the Congress of Independent Film Makers at La Sarraz, he was expelled from Switzerland. When he lectured at the Sorbonne ('The Principles of the New Russian Cinema' (pp. 192-202)) the Prefect of the Paris Police banned the proposed showing of what was by then called *The Old and the New* at short notice. When he came to Britain he was greeted with the news that *Potemkin* could not be shown publicly because it was regarded as too inflammatory. When he arrived in the United States he was treated as something of a curiosity. The contrast between the attitude implicit in 'Rin-Tin-Tin Does His Tricks for Noted Russian Movie Man' (pp. 203-205) and the interviews that had been published in German newspapers and French and British journals provided eloquent testimony to the different cultural traditions that prevailed on the two sides of the Atlantic and should have furnished a timely warning of the almost inevitable conflict that was to come between the collectivist approach of Eisenstein and the individualism of the USA. His time in North America was no more fruitful in terms of completed writings than it was in terms of finished films: his only major piece was the lecture delivered in

Hollywood ('The Dynamic Square' (pp. 206-218)), which echoed the point made in 'Beyond the Shot' about the relationship between shot and frame and probably went over the heads of the audience to whom it was addressed. Having arrived in 1930 as a curiosity, Eisenstein was to leave the United States in 1932 after the collapse of his Mexican project, denounced as 'a sadist and a monster', as a 'Jewish Bolshevik', as a wastrel and a pornographer:[18] he returned to the Soviet Union in May 1932 as a frustrated artist and a bitterly disillusioned man.

He also returned to a different Soviet Union from the one he had left in 1929. Both the country and the cinema were in the throes of the cultural revolution that accompanied the first Five-Year Plan. Soviet cinema had been centralised into Soyuzkino in 1930 under the firmer hand of Boris Shumyatsky whose first priority was to produce a 'cinema for the millions', one that would be both popular and ideologically effective. Eisenstein had left as the undisputed 'master' but he had been abroad at a crucial period of transformation. There had been rumours, repeatedly denied, that he had intended to defect and his absence at a critical time for Soviet cinema increased the resentment that resulted from the petty – and not so petty – jealousies of colleagues envious of his previous elevated and apparently unassailable position in the iconostasis of Soviet art. He came back to find that the reservations expressed about *October* and *The General Line* had now hardened into open allegations of Formalism.[19] He returned, not as the 'master' but as the man who had not made a film for three years and whose last two films had been 'unintelligible to the millions'.

Eisenstein had therefore to re-establish his credentials as a filmmaker, as a film theorist and, above all perhaps, as a loyal Soviet artist. In 'Help Yourself!', published in October 1932 (pp. 219-237), he argued that the purpose of cinema should be 'to grip and not to amuse' the audience, the difference lying in the particular 'ideological premiss' that should underpin Soviet films but that was missing from Hollywood: he cited his disagreements over *An American Tragedy* as symptomatic of this difference. In the same month he was put in charge of the Faculty of Direction at the State Film School, GIK, and he attacked the practice of encouraging each student to produce a short graduation film, a 'little episode'. The need was for a collective approach; instead of 'pissoirs' the students would work together to produce a 'cathedral': 'The art lies in the fact that every fragment of a film should be an organic part of an organically concerned whole.' That organic whole was, of course, still the 'final ideological conclusion'. It was in 'Help Yourself!' that Eisenstein for the first time introduced the idea of inner monologue as an essential element of sound film, comparing it to the literary technique of James Joyce. Inner monologue made possible the revelation of the thought processes that were central to intellectual montage and that in turn was to form the basis of intellectual cinema.

It was, however, this idea of inner monologue that unleashed a further attack on Eisenstein, to which he responded in Feburary 1933 in

'Pantagruel Will Be Born' (pp. 246-9). In his view, inner monologue provided a way out of the impasse in which sound cinema might find itself if it were unable to free itself from the theatricalism that he had warned of in the 'Statement on Sound'. Inner monologue would reconstruct dialogue along non-theatrical lines: 'In terms of both its quality and its stage of development it will stand in the same relationship to theatrical dramaturgy as does the thought process to ordinary walking.' Sound cinema would then presumably stand in relation to silent cinema as silent cinema had once stood to theatre: its next consecutive stage as a result of the dialectical process of development. In other writings of this period Eisenstein again returned to earlier themes: to the overriding importance of ideology in 'In the Interests of Form' (pp. 238-42), 'Through the Revolution to Art: Through Art to the Revolution' (pp. 243-5), 'For Elevated Ideological Content, for Film Culture!' (pp. 277-9) and 'On Fascism, German Cinema and Real Life' (pp. 280-4), to the relationship between script and film and the collective nature of film work in 'To Your Posts!' (pp. 250-7) to the dialectics of superimposition and juxtaposition in 'Georges Méliès's Mistake' (pp. 258-60).

Eisenstein was, however, still revising his ideas. In 'An Attack by Class Allies' (pp. 261-75) he recognised that Soviet cinema had reached a point where it was appropriate to abandon previous opposition to plot and script: 'At this particular stage we need plot. Just as at a different stage we managed without it.' But this did not mean that he had performed a *volte-face*. He had always recognised that plot had a certain role in the film-making process: now he was talking about 'new forms of plot-based cinema' which had overcome the weaknesses of Americanism and assimilated the achievements of the 'preceding stage of development'. It may seem surprising to find Eisenstein arguing in 1933 that the past should be assimilated, whereas in 1923 he had argued, in opposition to Lunacharsky among others, that the past should be rejected; but we should not fall into the trap of assuming that he had suddenly become an artistic conservative. One difference was that in 1933 Soviet cinema had a past to be assimilated, while ten years earlier cinema's past had been a bourgeois one.

Far from being conservative, Eisenstein launched an attack on Soviet films for their artistic conservatism, their theatricality in the use of both sound and actors, in 'Eh! On the Purity of Film Language' (pp. 285-95). He argued that the poor quality of the montage had led to disjointed and meaningless films. This was hardly progress:

> We must demand that the quality of montage, film syntax and film speech not only matches the quality of earlier works but exceeds and surpasses them. That is what the battle for the high quality of film culture requires of us.

He argued once more than Soviet cinema should learn from its own past, citing *Potemkin* as one example, and reiterated the importance at this stage of plot:

Now Soviet cinema is historically correct in joining battle for plot. There are still many obstacles along the path, many risks of a false understanding of the principles of plot. The most terrible of these is the underestimation of the opportunities that a temporary emancipation from the old traditions of plot has given us:

the opportunity to re-examine in principle and once more the bases and problems of film plot

and advances in a progressive cinematic movement not 'back to plot' but 'forward to plot'.

These ideas were to be developed in the writings that are included in the second and third volumes of this English-language selection of his *Writings*. At this juncture Eisenstein held up one film as a model and that film was *Chapayev*.[20] It was also held up as the official model film because of its 'intelligibility to the millions' but for Eisenstein its significance consisted in its synthesis of the achievements of the first (poetic) and second (prosaic) five-year periods[21] in the history of Soviet cinema. As a synthesis of this sort it also 'opens the fourth five-year period in our cinema': 'It is not a return to the old plot forms that were filmed in the first stage of our cinema. It is not "back to plot". But "forward to a new kind of plot".' Forward to that final ideological conclusion, that 'great synthesis, when all the achievements of the whole preceding era of Soviet cinema in their uncompromisingly high quality become at the same time the property of the many millions of the masses, infecting them with the new energy of heroism, struggle and creativity.'

This has of necessity been a highly reductive account of the development of Eisenstein's ideas in the period to the end of 1934. For reasons of space I have had to leave a great deal unsaid and a great deal of what I have said unargued and unjustified. I have kept close to the texts that are included in this volume, partly because that is, after all, the function of an introduction, but also partly because at the present stage of Eisenstein scholarship it seemed to me that my most important responsibility was to demonstrate the consistency and coherence of Eisenstein's thought as it developed – and that could obviously only be done chronologically. That consistency and coherence can only be understood within the framework of Eisenstein's attempts to apply the Marxist dialectic to the problems of cinematic form, for it is the notion of the totality, the synthesis dialectically achieved, that gives meaning to the constituent parts. Just as the shot is composed from the conflict between attractions (later refined to a dominant tone and overtones), just as the montage sequence is composed from the conflict between the shots, and the film from the conflict between the sequences, so cinema itself develops through thesis and antithesis to a synthesis, which in turn becomes a new catalytic thesis.

The proper comparison is not between Eisenstein and Shakespeare: it is between Eisenstein and Lenin. One applied the tenets of Marxism to the political conditions of Russia in the 20th century but his work remained unfinished: the other applied them to its cultural conditions – and his work also remained unfinished. But with this edition of Eisenstein's *Writings* in English we can follow his ideas chronologically as he himself developed them, we can see how his system of thought was developing towards its own synthesis and we can move closer to a proper understanding of his role in the cultural history of our century:

AT LAST!

R<small>ICHARD</small> T<small>AYLOR</small>
Swansea, June 1987

Translator's Note

Transliteration from the Cyrillic to the Latin alphabet presents many problems and no system will resolve them all. Perhaps the most important is the difficulty of reconciling the two principal requirements of transliteration: on the one hand the need to convey to the non-Russian-speaking reader a reasonable approximation of the original Russian pronunciation, and on the other the necessity of rendering for the specialist an accurate representation of the original Russian spelling. There is a further complication in that some Russian names have a non-Russian origin or an accepted English spelling that takes little heed of the two requirements just mentioned. I have therefore used two systems of transliteration in this edition. In the main text and in the index I have used the generally accepted spellings of proper names (such as Lunacharsky or Mayakovsky) or the spellings that reflect their linguistic origins (such as Meyerhold, Strauch and, indeed, Eisenstein), whereas in the endnotes (at least where these names are inflected) I have attempted to cater for the needs of the Russian-speaking specialist. There the names listed above will be found as: Lunacharskii, Mayakovskii, Meierkhol'd, Shtraukh and Eizenshtein. There are inevitably some inconsistencies in this practice but I hope that the system I have adopted will clarify rather than confuse the issue.

Eisenstein was unfortunately not always consistent in his use of key terms and the reader should bear this in mind. In this and subsequent volumes the translator and editor have offered a particular version of a particular term but some degree of ambiguity, if not downright confusion, must always remain. When talking about 'plot' Eisenstein, like other Russian writers of the time, distinguishes between *fabula* and *syuzhet*, which I have normally rendered as 'story' and 'plot' respectively. Naum Kleiman, Consultant Editor on this edition, has offered the following distinction:

fabula: a Formalist concept, the structure of events, what actually happened, the facts.
syuzhet: everything connected with the characters, all the associations, motivations, etc. Formalist critics also used the term to include technical aspects of film-making such as lighting, camera angle, shot composition and montage.

Other problematic words include the following, and the reader is strongly advised to bear the alternatives constantly in mind:

kadr: shot or frame
kusok: piece or fragment or sequence of montage
material: material or raw material
montazh: montage or editing, the arrangement of the shots, frames or sequences through cutting. In Eisenstein's view, as in the view of others, it was

montazh that distinguished the specificity of cinema as opposed to related art forms such as theatre, literature or painting.

To minimise the risk of confusion, the original Russian word is occasionally given in square brackets [...] in the text.

Lastly, Russian does not have either an indefinite or a definite article and it is a moot point whether one sometimes needs to be supplied in the English translation. I have preferred *The Strike* to *Strike* as a translation of the title of Eisenstein's film *Stachka*. Similarly I have used *The Mother* rather than *Mother* for Pudovkin's *Mat'*, *The Earth* rather than *Earth* for Dovzhenko's *Zemlya*, and so on. I have done this in the hope of clarifying the meaning of the original Russian title for the English-speaking reader.

Abbreviations

agitprop	contraction of 'agitation' and 'propaganda', used for both the Party Agitprop Department and the activity
AKhRR	*Assotsiyatsiya khudozhnikov revolyutsionnoi Rossii*: Association of Artists of Revolutionary Russia
ARK	*Assotsiyatsiya revolyutsionnoi kinematografii*: Association of Revolutionary Cinematography
ARRK	*Assotsiyatsiya rabotnikov revolyutsionnoi kinematografii*: Association of Workers of Revolutionary Cinematography
FEKS	*Fabrika ekstsentricheskogo aktëra*: Factory of the Eccentric Actor
GIK	*Gosudarstvennyi institut kinematografii*: State Cinema Institute 1930-4
GIKhL	*Gosudarstvennoe izdatel'stvo khudozhestvennoi literatury*: State Publishing House for Fiction
Glavpolitprosvet	contraction of *Glavnyi politiko-prosvetitel'nyi komitet Narkomprosa RSFSR*: Chief Political-Educational Committee of RSFSR Narkompros – the main censorship body 1920-30
Glavrepertkom	*Glavnyi komitet po kontrolyu za zrelishchami i repertuarom*: Chief Committee for the Control of Spectacles and the Repertoire – the principal organ of censorship for theatre and cinema
Goskino	contraction of *Tsentral'noe gosudarstvennoe fotokinopredpriyatie Narkomprosa*: Central State Photographic and Cinematographic Enterprise – the central state cinema organisation 1922-4
GTK	*Gosudarstvennyi tekhnikum kinematografii*: State Cinema Technical College 1925-30
GUKF	*Gosudarstvennoe upravlenie kinofotopromyshlennosti*: State Directorate for the Cinematographic and Photographic Industry, 1933-7
GVYRM	*Gosudarstvennye vysshie rezhissërskie masterskie*: State Higher Theatre Workshops
Komsomol	contraction of *Kommunisticheskii soyuz molodëzhi*: Communist Youth League
LEF	contraction of *Levyi front iskusstv*: Left Front of the Arts
LenARRK	the Leningrad branch of *ARRK*
Mezhrabpom	contraction of *Mezhdunarodnaya rabochaya pomoshch'*: International Workers' Aid
Mezhrabpom-Rus	joint-stock film-producing company that concentrated on producing films for the international market, 1924-8
Mezhrabpomfilm	film-producing company, 1928-36, based on *Mezhrabpom-Rus'*
MKhAT	*Moskovskii khudozhestvennyi akademicheskii teatr*: Moscow Art Theatre

Narkompros	contraction of *Narodnyi komissariat po prosveshcheniyu*: People's Commissariat for Enlightenment, headed by Lunacharsky 1917-29
NEP	*Novaya ekonomicheskaya politika*: New Economic Policy
ODSK	*Obshchestvo druzei sovetskogo kino*: Society of Friends of Soviet Cinema
OGPU	*Ob"edinënnoe gosudarstvennoe politicheskoe upravlenie*: Unified State Political Directorate, 1922-34 – secret police
Osoaviakhim	*Obshchestvo sodeistviya oborone i aviatsionno-khimicheskomu stroitel'stvu SSSR*: Society for Assisting the Defence of Aviation and the Chemical Development of the USSR
Proletkino	contraction of *Proletarskoe kino*: Proletarian Cinema organisation, 1923-5
Proletkult	contraction of *Proletarskaya kul'tura*: Proleterian Culture organisation, 1917-32
Rabkrin	contraction of *Raboche-krest'yanskaya inspektsiya*: Workers' and Peasants' Inspectorate
RAPP	*Rossiiskaya assotsiyatsiya proletarskikh pisatelei*: Russian Association of Proletarian Writers, 1925-32
Repertkom	see *Glavrepertkom*
RossARRK	*ARRK* for the RSFSR
RSFSR	Russian Soviet Federated Socialist Republic
Sovkino	contraction of *Sovetskoe kino*: Soviet Cinema – centralised state cinema organisation, 1924-30
Sovnarkom	contraction of *Sovet narodnykh komissarov*: Soviet of People's Commissars, the ruling ministerial body of the USSR at that time
Soyuzkino	contraction of *Soyuznoe kino*: Union Cinema – centralised state cinema organisation, 1930-3
TsGALI	*Tsentralnyi Gosudarstvennyi Arkhiv Literatury i Iskusstva*: Central State Archive of Literature and Art
Vesenkha	see *VSNKh* below
Vkhutemas	contraction of *Vysshie khudozhestvenno-tekhnicheskie masterskie*: Higher Artistic-Technical Workshops, 1921-6
VSNKh	*Vysshii sovet narodnogo khozyaistva*: Supreme Council for the National Economy, 1917-32

1. The Eighth Art. On Expressionism, America and, of course, Chaplin[1]

1922

Sergei Yutkevich and Eisenstein

A chapter from a story: 'At the end of the Great War an improbable thing happened. The Festive Parnassus of the seven classical muses who were officially in session was invaded by a long-legged man with a rapid, somewhat surprisingly erratic gait, shaking his curly head of hair and the bowler perched on top of it and invariably waving a cane which he did not hesitate to poke under the nose of one of the respected muses. He took a jump and flopped down into the chairman's seat. Then, making a very funny face and tugging at the black whiskers above his upper lip, he shouted (with difficulty, because he was obviously unaccustomed to speaking in such brilliant company) a strange phrase that amazed the inhabitants of Parnassus:

"DO YOU LIKE CHARLIE?"'

That is how, unnoticed by the inhabitants of the RSFSR, the transformation of the poor old 'bioscope' into a powerful art was accomplished and the genius of Charlie Chaplin took the eighth seat in the Council of the Muses.

That is already past history and, since we do not like archaeological excavations, we shall, now that we have brought this remarkable fact to the attention of citizens, pass on to the present day. In France, which is the country that is now richest in theoretical research in cinema, Claude Blanchard[2] has raised the question of 'synchronism' or sound in cinema. Analysing this problem, he writes:

> Many people have spoken recently about a new application of synchronised sound to cinema. It is an extremely interesting problem, though by no means a new one, as we can demonstrate. People who visited the darkened halls in 1905-6 will of course remember the primitive imitation sounds that invariably accompanied the showing of a film (the crashing of the waves, the roar of an engine, the sound of breaking crockery, etc. etc.).
>
> As for me I can vividly recall an unforgettable film in the Dufahel cinema in which a schoolboy appeared smoking a gigantic cigar and he suddenly disappeared from the screen. This was followed by sounds that left you in no doubt as to the sad state of his digestive tract. These imitation sounds were soon abandoned because of their technical imperfection. The engineer who had charge of the sound had at his disposition equipment that was unreliable and imperfect and as a result he was deprived of the opportunity of effecting a

complete coordination between his sound and what was happening on the screen, i.e. to produce synchronism.

'The illusion did not work!'

In France there have still not been any practical achievements in this field and the only thing that Claude Blanchard can point to is the case of the Swedish film *The Phantom Carriage*[3] that is accompanied by a successful combination of bells and percussion instruments. This made a powerful impression on Blanchard but the replacement of the engineer of 1905 by the band-leader of 1922 is not an achievement from the point of view of perfecting the technique of synchronism.

As far as the invention of highly complex technical apparatuses capable of combining sound, music and film is concerned, a series of extremely interesting experiments has recently been carried out by Charles de la Commune,[4] the inventor of new synchronous equipment. Claude Blanchard, who was present at the demonstration of his successes in this field, foresees in the expansion of what has been achieved the creation of a 'powerful dramatic or comic atmosphere (rejoice, Tairov![5]) but only, of course, within the limits of the necessary musical stylisation'.

It is embarrassing to read of this kind of attitude to sound on the part of his contemporary and fellow-countryman, A. Tanneret, a critic living in a country that has already had a 'jazz band' for two years. The question inevitably arises: does the final resolution of this problem in the proper direction lie with that same long-suffering RSFSR that has, in Meyerhold's[6] words, taken upon itself the role of mouthpiece for the new theatrical (and now also cinematic) theories?

We see that the word 'illusion', so frequently repeated in the respected critic's articles, has done a great deal of harm to the real work of French cinema.

The majority of recent films suffer from this affliction that we have now overcome. Even Louis Delluc,[7] the prominent theoretician of contemporary cinema and author of a fine monograph on Chaplin and a book on *Photogeny*, was unable to resist the corrupting influence of naturalism in his films *The Woman from Nowhere* and *Fever*. Finally, in America, where it would seem that the perfect models for the new Eccentric[8] cinema should originate, the temptations of 'illusion' have not yet been overcome.

In his article on American cinema the Frenchman Galtier Boissière[9] writes:

The Americans have taken scenery and *trompe l'oeil* to the height of perfection. The smallest studio in Los Angeles doesn't think twice before building a whole suburb of New York, a facsimile of the Avenue de l'Opéra, a Chinese quarter, the slums of Rio, mosques, Hindu temples, and so on. If you follow with consuming interest the thrilling round-up in the dubious back-alleys of the suburbs of San

Francisco you may not even suspect that all this is taking place among buildings made of papier mâché which have only the one façade. And when a samurai disembowels himself in a Japanese garden you would never guess that this quaint little garden with the miniature trees is only ten square metres large – precisely the size that the camera lens can take in.

It is, of course, difficult for us, as we have departed from the Meiningen approach,[10] to assess the degree to which the French and Americans have submitted to illustration but, if the constructions that Boissière writes about are built like Polenova's saccharine Jerusalem,[11] a toy Paris of Catherine de'Medici, a cardboard Babylon of Balthazar or a badly glued Golgotha (photographed simply from a scale model in the well-known film *Intolerance* in the production by the American director Griffith) then we do not congratulate those refined critics who laughed at *Father Sergius*,[12] the only Russian film to have reached America, and said it was 'impossible to sit through to the end'. Films of that kind, which also flourish in Europe (Marcel L'Herbier's *Don Juan and Faust*,[13] Louis Delluc's *The Woman from Nowhere*, Zoë Fuller's *Lily of Life*[14] and the majority of the Swedish films now running in Paris), ought to provoke laughter but not, of course, because people moved from 'daylight' in a garden to 'twilight' in a drawing-room or because the lighting in a cell does not change when a candle is carried from one corner to another – the reasons why the American cinema entrepreneurs who saw *Father Sergius* in Berlin did not buy it for New York.

As a counterbalance to this naturalistic tendency in Western cinema a new tendency, which we might christen 'stylised', has emerged in Germany. *The Cabinet of Dr Caligari*,[15] directed in six acts by Robert Wiene from a script by Carl Meyer and Hans Janowitz, is the first experiment in Expressionist montage carried out by the artists Rodstadt and Arpke.

On the subject of 'stylised' cinema we should also mention the 'animated film' defended by Hugues Boffe in his reports of the latest successes of the artists Matras and Boucher in bringing colours and the principles of shading into the techniques of animated film.

Lastly, the third and most powerful trend in cinema, which originates in America and offers new opportunities for genuine Eccentrism: the detective adventure comedy film has produced a whole series of wonderful actors, whom Léon Moussinac[16] has contrasted with the most remarkable actors of the French theatre. These are the fearless cowboy, Rio Jim, the 'chevalier sans peur et sans reproche' of the American prairies, Mary Pickford, the ideal Anglo-Saxon woman, the heroine of improbable adventure films, Douglas the sportsman and optimist, Hayakawa the Japanese man, Fatty Arbuckle[17] in his check trousers, the doltish but amusing Dudul and above all, of course, the incomparable *Charlie Chaplin!*

The craze everywhere is for Chaplin – Charlie! The newspapers enthuse, 'Charlie goes for a walk . . . Charlie on his bike . . . Charlie on skates . . . Charlie with Millerant . . .[18] Charlie in love . . . Charlie the drunkard'. That is the title of an article by the Frenchman Dreuse in which he poses the question of the difference between two views of the world in connection with Charlie.

Everyone is aware of the enormous influence that cinema now exerts on all the other arts. A number of French artists have reflected the images of contemporary cinema in their works: Fernand Léger, Picasso, Georges LeNain, Auberlot. Louis Latapie has produced a series of beautiful posters for the foyer of the cinema in Grenelle in which he portrays Chaplin in his films and Rio Jim.

Thus the 'happy infant' (as Ilya Ehrenburg[19] called it) grows bigger and prettier and the directors, artists, poets and technicians of the whole world who are interested in the victory of the new art must devote all their efforts to ensuring that their favourite infant does not fall into the obliging clutches of a 'heliotrope auntie'[20] and the sanctimonious watchdogs of morality.

2. **The Montage of Attractions**[1]   1923

(On the production of A.N. Ostrovsky's *Enough Simplicity for Every Wise Man* at the Moscow Proletkult Theatre[2])

I. Proletkult's[3] Theatrical Line

In a few words: Proletkult's theatrical programme consists not in 'using the treasures of the past' or in 'discovering new forms of theatre' but in abolishing the very institution of theatre as such and replacing it by a showplace for achievements in the field at the *level of the everyday skills of the masses*. The organisation of workshops and the elaboration of a scientific system to raise this level are the immediate tasks of the Scientific Department of Proletkult in the theatrical field.

The rest we are doing under the rubric 'interim', carrying out the subsidiary, but not the fundamental tasks of Proletkult. This 'interim' has two meanings under the general rubric of revolutionary content:

1. The *figurative-narrative theatre* (static, domestic – the right wing: *The Dawns of Proletkult*,[4] *Lena*[5] and a series of unfinished productions of a similar type. It is the line taken by the former Workers' Theatre of the Proletkult Central Committee).
2. The *agitational theatre of attractions* (dynamic and Eccentric – the left wing). It is the line devised in principle for the Touring Troupe of the Moscow Proletkult Theatre by Boris Arvatov[6] and myself.

This path has already been traced – in outline, but with sufficient precision – in *The Mexican*,[7] a production by the author of the present article and V.S. Smyshlyayev[8] (in the First Studio of the Moscow Art Theatre). Later, in our next collaboration (V. Pletnyov's *On the Abyss*[9]) we had a complete disagreement on principle that led to a split and subsequently to our working separately, as you can see by *Wise Man* and *The Taming of the Shrew*, not to mention Smyshlyayev's *Theory of Construction of the Stage Show*, which overlooked all the worthwhile achievements of *The Mexican*.

I feel that I must digress because any review of *Wise Man* that tries to establish a common link with other productions completely ignores *The Mexican* (January-March 1921), whereas *Wise Man* and the whole theory of attractions are a further elaboration and a logical development of my contribution to that production.
3. *Wise Man* was begun in the Touring Troupe (and finished when the two troupes combined) as the first work of agitation based on a new method of structuring a show.

II. The Montage of Attractions

This term is being used for the first time. It requires explanation.

Theatre's basic material derives from the audience: the moulding of the audience in a desired direction (or mood) is the task of every utilitarian theatre (agitation, advertising, health education, etc.). The instrument of this process consists of all the parts that constitute the apparatus of theatre (Ostuzhev's[10] 'chatter' no more than the colour of the prima donna's tights, a roll on the drums just as much as Romeo's soliloquy, the cricket on the hearth[11] no less than a salvo under the seats of the auditorium[12]) because, despite their differences, they all lead to one thing – which their presence legitimates – to their common quality of *attraction*.

An attraction (in our diagnosis of theatre) is any aggressive moment in theatre, i.e. any element of it that subjects the audience to emotional or psychological influence, verified by experience and mathematically calculated to produce specific emotional shocks in the spectator in their proper order within the whole. These shocks provide the only opportunity of perceiving the ideological aspect of what is being shown, the final ideological conclusion. (The path to knowledge encapsulated in the phrase, 'through the living play of the passions', is specific to theatre.)

Emotional and psychological, of course, in the sense of direct reality as employed, for instance, in the Grand Guignol, where eyes are gouged out or arms and legs amputated on stage, or the direct reality of an actor on stage involved through the telephone with a nightmarish event taking place dozens of miles away, or the situation of a drunkard who, sensing his approaching end, pleads for protection and whose pleas are taken as a sign of madness. In this sense and not in the sense of the unravelling of psychological problems where the attraction is the theme itself, existing and taking effect *outside* the particular action, but topical enough. (Most agit-theatres make the mistake of being satisfied with attractions solely of that sort in their productions.)

I regard the attraction as being in normal conditions an independent and primary element in structuring the show, a molecular (i.e. compound) unity of the *effectiveness* of theatre and of *theatre as a whole*. It is completely analogous to Grosz's[13] 'rough sketches', or the elements of Rodchenko's[14] photo-illustrations.

'Compound'? It is difficult to distinguish where the fascination of the hero's nobility ends (the psychological moment) and where the moment of his personal charm (i.e. his erotic effect) begins. The lyrical effect of a whole series of Chaplin scenes is inseparable from the attractional quality of the specific mechanics of his movements. Similarly, it is difficult to distinguish where religious pathos gives way to sadistic satisfaction in the torture scenes of the mystery plays, and so on.

The attraction has nothing in common with the stunt. The stunt or, more accurately, the trick (it is high time that this much abused term was returned to its rightful place) is a finished achievement of a particular kind of mastery (acrobatics, for the most part) and it is only one kind of attraction that is suitable for presentation (or, as they say in the circus, 'sale'). In so far as the trick is absolute and complete *within itself*, it means the direct opposite of the attraction, which is based exclusively on something relative, the reactions of the audience.

Our present approach radically alters our opportunities in the principles of creating an 'effective structure' (the show as a whole) instead of a static 'reflection' of a particular event dictated by the theme, and our opportunities for resolving it through an effect that is logically implicit in that event, and this gives rise to a new concept: a free montage with arbitrarily chosen independent (of both the PARTICULAR *composition and any thematic connection with the actors) effects (attractions) but with the precise aim of a specific final thematic effect – montage of attractions.*

The path that will liberate theatre completely from the yoke of the 'illusory depictions' and 'representations' that have hitherto been the decisive, unavoidable and only possible approach lies through a move to the montage of 'realistic artificialities', at the same time admitting to the weave of this montage whole 'illusory sequences', and a plot integral to the subject, not something self-contained or all-determining but something consciously and specifically determined for a particular purpose, and an attraction chosen purely for its powerful effect.

Since it is not a matter of 'revealing the playwright's purpose', 'correctly interpreting the author' or 'faithfully reflecting an epoch', etc., the attraction and a system of attractions provide the only basis for an effective show. In the hands of every skilled director the attraction has been used intuitively in one way or another, not, of course, on the level of montage or structure but at least in a 'harmonic composition' (from which a whole new vocabulary derives: an 'effective curtain', a 'rich exit', 'a good stunt', etc.) but essentially this has been done only within the framework of the logical plausibility of the subject (it has been 'justified' by the play) and in the main unconsciously and in pursuit of something entirely different (something that had been enumerated at the 'start' of the proceedings). What remains to us in reorganising the system we use to structure a show is merely to shift the focus of attention to the essential (what was earlier regarded as attendant decoration but is in fact the principal messenger of the abnormal intentions of a production and is not logically connected with the run-of-the-mill reverence of literary tradition), *to establish this particular approach as a production method* (which, since the autumn of 1922, has been the work of the Proletkult Workshops).

The school for the montageur[15] is cinema and, principally, music-hall and circus because (from the point of view of form) putting on a good show means constructing a strong music-hall/circus programme that derives from the situations found in the play that is taken as a basis.

As an example here is a list of the sections of numbers in the epilogue to *Wise Man*:

35

1. The hero's explanatory monologue. 2. A fragment from a detective film. (A classification of 1., the theft of the diary.) 3. An Eccentric[16] music-hall entrée (the bride and her three rejected suitors – all one person in the play – in the role of best men): a melancholy scene reminiscent of the song 'Your hands smell of incense' and 'May I be punished by the grave' (we intended that the bride would have a xylophone and this would be played on six rows of bells, the officers' buttons). 4.5.6. Three parallel two-phrased clowning entrées (the theme: payment for organising the wedding). 7. An entrée with a star (the aunt) and three officers (the theme: the restraint of the rejected suitors), punning (by reference to a horse) on a triple volte number on a saddled horse (on the impossibility of bringing it into the room, traditionally, in 'triple harness'). 8. Good agit-songs ('The priest had a dog' accompanied by a rubber priest like a dog. The theme: the start of the wedding ceremony). 9. A break in the action (a paper-boy's voice announcing that the hero is leaving). 10. The villain appears in a mask. A fragment from a comedy film. (A résumé of five acts of the play. The theme: the publication of the diary.) 11. The continuation of the (interrupted) action in another grouping (a simultaneous wedding with the three rejected suitors). 12. Anti-religious songs ('Allah-Verdi'[17] – a punning theme tune on the need to bring in a mullah because of the large number of suitors that one bride is marrying) from the choir and a new character used only in this scene, a soloist dressed as a mullah. 13. General dancing. Some play with a poster inscribed: 'Religion is the opium of the people.' 14. A farcical scene. (The bride and her three suitors are packed into a box and pots are smashed against the lid.) 15. The marital trio – a parody of life. (The song: 'Who here is young?') 16. A precipice. The hero's return. 17. The hero's winged flight beneath the big top (the theme: suicide in despair). 18. A break. The villain's return. The suicide is held up. 19. A sword fight (the theme: enmity). 20. An agit-entrée involving the hero and the villain on the theme of NEP.[18] 21. An act on a sloping wire (crossing from the arena to the balcony over the audience's heads. The theme: 'leaving for Russia'). 22. A clowning parody of this number (with the hero). Descent from the wire. 23. A clown descends the same wire from the balcony, holding on by his teeth. 24. The final entrée with two clowns throwing water over one another (as per tradition), finishing with the announcement: 'The End'. 25. A volley of shots beneath the seats of the auditorium as a finale. The connecting features of the numbers, if there is no direct transition, are used as linking elements: they are handled with different arrangements of equipment, musical interludes, dancing, pantomime, carpet-clowns.

Editor's Note

The final section of Eisenstein's 'The Montage of Attractions', where he characterises the Epilogue to *Enough Simplicity for Every Wise Man*, makes little sense to the reader who is not acquainted with the production or with the Ostrovsky play upon which it is very loosely based. The editors of the six-volume Eisenstein *Selected Works* in Russian have included a reconstruction of the Epilogue provided by the surviving members of the production led by Maxim Strauch. It is reproduced here:

1. On stage (in the arena) we see Glumov who, in an ['explanatory'] monologue, recounts how his diary has been stolen and he has been threatened with exposure. Glumov decides to marry Mashenka immediately and so he summons Manefa the clown on to the stage and asks him to play the part of the priest.

2. The lights go down. On the screen we see Glumov's diary[19] being stolen by a man in a black mask – Golutvin. A parody of the American detective film.

3. The lights go up. Mashenka appears, dressed as a racing driver in a bridal veil. She is followed by her three rejected suitors, officers (in Ostrovsky's play there is just one: Kurchayev), who are to be the best men at her wedding to Glumov. They act out a separation scene ('melancholy'). Mashenka sings the 'cruel' romance, 'May I be punished by the grave'. The officers, parodying Vertinsky,[20] perform 'Your hands smell of incense'. (It was Eisenstein's original intention that this scene should be regarded as an Eccentric music-hall number ('xylophone') with Mashenka playing on the bells sewn as buttons on to the officers' coats.

4.5.6. Exit Mashenka and the three officers. Enter Glumov. Three clowns – Gorodulin, Joffre, Mamilyukov – run out from the auditorium towards him. Each performs his own curious turn (juggling with balls, acrobatic jumps, etc.) and asks for his payment. Glumov refuses and leaves. (The 'two-phrased clowning entrées': for each exit there are two phrases of text, the clown's and Glumov's rejoinder.)

7. Mamayeva appears, dressed in extravagant luxury (a 'star'), carrying a ringmaster's whip. She is followed by the three officers. Mamayeva wants to disrupt Glumov's wedding. She comforts the rejected suitors and after their rejoinder about the horse ('My friendly mare is neighing') she cracks the whip and the officers scamper around the arena. Two imitate a horse while the third is the rider.

8. On stage the priest (Manefa) begins the wedding ceremony. Everyone present sings, 'There was a priest who had a dog'. Manefa performs a circus turn (the 'rubber priest'), imitating a dog.

9. Through a megaphone we hear the paper-boy shouting. Glumov, abandoning the wedding, escapes to find out whether his diary has appeared in print.

10. The man who stole the diary appears. He is a man in a black mask (Golutvin). The lights go out. On the screen we see Glumov's diary. The film tells of his behaviour in front of his great patrons and accordingly of his transmogrifications into various conventional figures (into a donkey in front of Mamaev, a tank-driver in front of Joffre, and so on).

11. The wedding ceremony resumes. Glumov has fled; his place is taken by the rejected suitors, the three officers ('Kurchayev').

12. As Mashenka is simultaneously marrying three suitors, four men in uniform carry a mullah on a board out from among the audience. He continues the wedding ceremony, performing songs parodying topical themes – 'Allah-Verdi'.

13. When he has finished singing, the mullah dances the *lezginka*[21] and everyone joins in. The mullah raises the board he had been sitting on. On the back there is an inscription: 'Religion is the opium of the people.' Exit the mullah, holding this board in his hands.

14. Mashenka and her three suitors are packed into boxes (from which, unseen by the audience, they disappear). The participants in the wedding ceremony smash clay pots against the box, parodying the ancient wedding rite of 'packing off the young couple'.

15. The three participants in the wedding ceremony (Mamilyukov, Mamayev, Gorodulin) sing the wedding song 'Who here is young, who here's not wed?'

16. The wedding song is interrupted by Glumov who runs in with a newspaper in his hand: 'Hurrah! There's nothing in the paper!' Everyone makes fun of him and leaves him alone.

17. After the publication of his diary and his failure to wed, Glumov is in despair. He decides to commit suicide and asks one of the men in uniform for a 'rope'. They lower a lead to him from the ceiling. He attaches 'angels' wings' to his back and they start to raise him towards the ceiling with a lighted candle in his hands. The choir sings 'At midnight the angel flew across the heavens' to the tune of 'My beauty's heart'. This scene is a parody of the Ascension.

18. Golutvin (the 'villain') appears on stage. Glumov, seeing his enemy, starts showering him with abuse, descends on to the stage and rushes after him.

19. Glumov and Golutvin fight with swords. Glumov wins. Golutvin falls and Glumov tears a large label off Golutvin's trousers. It bears the word 'NEP'.

20. Golutvin sings a song about NEP. Glumov accompanies him. Both dance. Golutvin invites Glumov to be his 'apprentice' and go to Russia.

21. Golutvin, balancing an umbrella, walks up the sloping wire over the audience's heads to the balcony: he is 'leaving for Russia'.

22. Glumov decides to follow his example, clambers up on to the wire but falls off (the circus 'descent') with the words 'It's slippery, slippery: I'd be better off in a back alley.' He follows Golutvin 'to Russia' but takes a less dangerous route – through the auditorium.

23. Enter a clown (with red hair) on stage. He cries and says over and over again, 'They've gone and left someone behind.' Another clown descends from the balcony on the wire, holding on by his teeth.

24.25. The two clowns start squabbling. One throws water over the other who falls over with surprise. One of them announces 'The End' and makes his bow to the audience. At this moment there is a pyrotechnical explosion beneath of the seats of the auditorium.

3. The Montage of Film Attractions[1]   1924

These thoughts do not aspire to be manifestos or declarations but they do represent an attempt to gain at least some understanding of the bases of our complex craft.

If we regard cinema as a factor for exercising emotional influence over the masses (and even the Cine-Eyes,[2] who want to remove cinema from the ranks of the arts at all costs, are convinced that it is) we must secure its place in this category and, in our search for ways of building cinema up, we must make widespread use of the experience and the latest achievements in the sphere of those arts that set themselves similar tasks. The first of these is, of course, theatre, which is linked to cinema by a common (identical) *basic* material – the *audience* – and by a common purpose – *influencing this audience in the desired direction* through a series of calculated pressures on its psyche. I consider it superfluous to expatiate solely on the intelligence of this ('agit') kind of approach to cinema and theatre since it is obvious and well-founded from the standpoint both of social necessity (the class struggle) and of the very nature of these arts that deliver, because of their formal characteristics, a series of blows to the consciousness and emotions of the audience. Finally, only an ultimate aspiration of this sort can serve to justify diversions that give the

E's production of *Enough Simplicity for Every Wise Man*

39

Boris Pasternak, Eisenstein, Olga Tretyakova, Lily Brik, Vladimir Mayakovsky

audience *real* satisfaction (both physical and moral) as a result of *fictive* collaboration with what is being shown (through motor imitation of the action by those perceiving it and through psychological 'empathy'). If it were not for this phenomenon which, incidentally, alone makes for the magnetism of theatre, circus and cinema, the thoroughgoing removal of accumulated forces would proceed at a more intense pace and sports clubs would have in their debt a significantly larger number of people whose physical nature had caught up with them.

Thus cinema, like theatre, makes sense only as 'one form of pressure'. There is a difference in their methods but they have one basic device in common: the montage of attractions, confirmed by my theatre work in Proletkult and now being applied by me to cinema. It is this path that liberates film from the plot-based script and for the first time takes account of film material, both thematically and formally, in the construction. In addition, it provides criticism with a method of objective expertise for evaluating theatre or film works, instead of the printed exposition of personal impressions and sympathies spiced with quotations from a run-of-the-mill political report that happens to be popular at a particular moment.

An attraction (NB for more details, see: *Lef*, 1923, No. 3,[3] and *Oktyabr mysli*, 1924, No. 1) is in our understanding any demonstrable fact (an action, an object, a phenomenon, a conscious combination, and so on) that is known and proven to exercise a definite effect on the attention and emotions of the audience and that, combined with others, possesses the characteristic of concentrating the audience's emotions in any direction dictated by the production's purpose. From this point of view a film cannot be a simple presentation or demonstration of events: rather it must be a tendentious selection of, and comparison between, events, free from narrowly plot-related plans and moulding the audience in accordance with its purpose. (Let us look at *Cine-Pravda*[4] in particular: *Cine-Pravda* does not follow this path – its construction takes no account of attractions – but 'grabs' you through the attraction of its themes and, purely superficially, through the formal mastery of its montage of separate sequences, which by their short footage conceal the 'neutral' epic 'statement of facts'.)

The widespread use of all means of influence does not make this a cinema of polished style but a cinema of action that is useful to our class, a class cinema due to its actual formal approach because attractional calculation is conceivable only when the audience is known and selected in advance for its homogeneity.

The application of the method of the montage of attractions (the comparison of facts) to cinema is even more acceptable than it is to theatre. I should call cinema 'the art of comparisons' because it shows not facts but conventional (photographic) representations (in contrast to 'real action' in theatre, at least when theatre is employing the techniques we approve of). For the exposition of even the simplest phenomena cinema needs comparison (by means of consecutive, separate presentation) between the elements which constitute it: montage (in the technical, cinematic sense of the word) is fundamental to cinema, deeply grounded in the conventions of cinema and the corresponding characteristics of perception.

Whereas in theatre an effect is achieved primarily through the physiological perception of an actually occurring fact (e.g. a murder),*[5] in cinema it is made up of the juxtaposition and accumulation, in the audience's psyche, of associations that the film's purpose requires, associations that are aroused by the separate elements of the stated (in practical terms, in 'montage fragments') fact, associations that produce, albeit tangentially, a similar (and often stronger) effect only when taken as a whole. Let us take that same murder as an example: a throat is gripped, eyes bulge, a knife is brandished, the victim closes his eyes, blood is spattered on a wall, the victim falls to the floor, a hand wipes off the knife – each fragment is chosen to 'provoke' associations.

An analogous process occurs in the montage of attractions: it is not in fact phenomena that are compared but chains of associations that are linked to a particular phenomenon in the mind of a particular audience.† (It is quite

---

* A direct animal audience action through a motor imitative act towards a live character like oneself, as distinct from a pale shadow on a screen. These methods of theatrical effect have been tested in my production of *Can You Hear Me Moscow?*

† In time (in sequence) clearly: here it plays not merely the role of an unfortunate technical condition but of a condition that is necessary for the thorough inculcation of the associations.

41

clear that for a worker and a former cavalry officer the chain of associations set off by seeing a meeting broken up and the corresponding emotional effect in contrast to the material which frames this incident, will be somewhat different.) I managed to test quite definitively the correctness of this position with one example where, because what I should call this law had not been observed, the comic effect of such a well-tried device as the alogism[6] fell flat. I have in mind the place in *The Extraordinary Adventures of Mr West in the Land of the Bolsheviks*[7] where an enormous lorry is pulling a tiny sledge carrying Mr West's briefcase. This construction can be found in different variants in any clown's act – from a tiny top hat to enormous boots. The appearance of such a combination in the ring is enough. But, when the whole combination was shown on the screen in one shot all at once (even though it occurred as the lorry was leaving the gates so that there was a short pause – as long as the rope joining the lorry to the sledge), the effect was very weak. Whereas a real lorry is immediately perceived in all its immensity and compared to a real briefcase in all its insignificance and [for comic effect] it is enough to see them side by side, cinema requires that a 'representation' of the lorry be provided first for long enough to inculcate the appropriate associations – and then we are shown the incongruous light load. As a parallel to this I recall the construction of an analogous moment in a Chaplin film where much footage is spent on the endlessly complicated opening of the locks on a huge safe* and it is only later (and apparently from a different angle) that we are shown the brooms, rags and buckets that are hidden inside it. The Americans use this technique brilliantly for characterisation – I remember the way Griffith 'introduced' the 'Musketeer', the gang-leader in *Intolerance*:[8] he showed us a wall of his room completely covered with naked women and then showed the man himself. How much more powerful and more cinematic this is, we submit, than the introduction of the workhouse supervisor in *Oliver Twist* in a scene where he pushes two cripples around: i.e. he is shown through his deeds (a purely theatrical method of sketching character through action) and not through provoking the necessary associations.

From what I have said it is clear that the centre of gravity of cinema effects, in contrast to those of theatre, lies not in directly *physiological* effects, although a purely *physical* infectiousness can sometimes be attained (in a chase, with the montage of two sequences with movements running against the shot). It seems that there has been absolutely no study or evaluation of the purely physiological effect of montage irregularity and rhythm and, if it has been evaluated, this has only been for its role in narrative illustration (the tempo of the plot corresponding with the material being narrated). 'We ask you not to confuse' the montage of attractions and its method of comparison with the usual montage parallelism used in the exposition of a theme such as the narrative principle in *Cine-Pravda* where the audience has first to guess what is going on and then become 'intellectually' involved with the theme.

---

* And a large number of bank premises are shown first.

The montage of attractions is closer to the simple contrasting comparisons (though these are somewhat compromised by *The Palace and the Fortress*[9] where the device is naively revealed) that often produce a definitely powerful emotional effect (chained legs in the ravelin and a ballerina's feet). But we must point out that in *The Palace and the Fortress* [from which this example comes] any dependence on comparison in the construction of the shots for this sequence was completely ignored: their construction does not assist association but disrupts it and it enters our consciousness through literary rather than visual means. For example, Nechayev, seen from the waist up and with his back to the camera, hammers on a barred door and the prison warder, seen in long shot somewhere in a corner by a window, holds a canary in a cage. The chained legs are shown horizontally whereas the ballerina's points are shot about four times larger and vertically, etc.

The method of the montage of attractions is the comparison of subjects for thematic effect. I shall refer to the original version of the montage resolution in the finale of my film *The Strike*: the mass shooting where I employed the associational comparison with a slaughterhouse. I did this, on the one hand, to avoid overacting among the extras from the labour exchange 'in the business of dying' but mainly to excise from such a serious scene the falseness that the screen will not tolerate but that is unavoidable in even the most brilliant death scene and, on the other hand, to extract the maximum effect of bloody horror. The shooting is shown only in 'establishing' long and medium shots of 1,800 workers falling over a precipice, the crowd fleeing, gunfire, etc., and all the close-ups are provided by a demonstration of the real horrors of the slaughterhouse where cattle are slaughtered and skinned. One version of the montage was composed roughly as follows:

1. The head of a bull. The butcher's knife takes aim and moves upwards beyond the frame.
2. Close-up. The hand holding the knife strikes downwards below the frame.
3. Long shot: 1,500 people roll down a slope. (Profile shot.)
4. Fifty people get up off the ground, their arms outstretched.
5. The face of a soldier taking aim.
6. Medium shot. Gunfire.
7. The bull's body (the head is outside the frame) jerks and rolls over.
8. Close-up. The bull's legs convulse. A hoof beats in a pool of blood.
9. Close-up. The bolts of the rifles.
10. The bull's head is tied with rope to a bench.
11. A thousand people rush past.
12. A line of soldiers emerges from behind a clump of bushes.
13. Close-up. The bull's head as it dies beneath unseen blows (the eyes glaze over).
14. Gunfire, in longer shot, seen from behind the soldiers' backs.
15. Medium shot. The bull's legs are bound together 'according to Jewish

43

custom' (the method of slaughtering cattle lying down).

16. Closer shot. People falling over a precipice.

17. The bull's throat is cut. Blood gushes out.

18. Medium close-up. People rise into the frame with their arms outstretched.

19. The butcher advances towards the (panning) camera holding the blood-stained rope.

20. The crowd rushes to a fence, breaks it down but is met by an ambush (two or three shots).

21. Arms fall into the frame.

22. The head of the bull is severed from the trunk.

23. Gunfire.

24. The crowd rolls down the precipice into the water.

25. Gunfire.

26. Close-up. Teeth are knocked out by the shooting.

27. The soldiers' feet move away.

28. Blood flows into the water, colouring it.

29. Close-up. Blood gushes from the bull's throat.

30. Hands pour blood from a basin into a bucket.

31. Dissolve from a platform with buckets of blood on it . . . in motion towards a processing plant.

32. The dead bull's tongue is pulled through the slit throat (one of the devices used in a slaughterhouse, probably so that the teeth will not do any damage during the convulsions).

33. The soldiers' feet move away. (Longer shot.)

34. The head is skinned.

35. One thousand eight hundred dead bodies at the foot of the precipice.

36. Two dead skinned bulls' heads.

37. A human hand in a pool of blood.

38. Close-up. Filling the whole screen. The dead bull's eye.

Final title.

The downfall of the majority of our Russian films derives from the fact that the people who make them do not know how to construct attractional schemas consciously but only rarely and in fumbling fashion hit on successful combinations. The American detective film and, to an even greater extent, the American comedy film (the method in its pure form) provide inexhaustible material for the study of these methods (admittedly on a purely formal level, ignoring content). Griffith's films, if we had seen them and not just known them from descriptions, would teach us a lot about this kind of montage, albeit with a social purpose that is hostile to us. It is not, however, necessary to transplant America, although in all fields the study of methods does at first proceed through imitation. It is necessary to train ourselves in the skill of selecting attractions from our own raw material.

Thus we are gradually coming to the most critical problem of the day: the script. The first thing to remember is that there is, or rather should

be, no cinema other than agit-cinema. The method of agitation through spectacle consists in the creation of a new chain of conditioned reflexes by associ-
ating selected phenomena with the unconditioned reflexes they produce
(through the appropriate methods). (If you want to arouse sympathy for the
hero, you surround him with kittens which unfailingly enjoy universal sympathy: not one of our films has yet failed to show White officers juxtaposed to
disgusting drinking bouts, etc.). Bearing this basic situation in mind we
should handle the question of played films with great care: they wield such
enormous influence that we cannot ignore them. I think that the campaign
against the very notion of such films has been caused by the really low level of
scripts as well as the technique of the performers. I shall return to the latter in
greater detail later. As far as the former is concerned, our approach allows us
to conceive of arranging something other than 'little stories' and 'little ro-
mances' with a 'little intrigue', kinds of film which on the whole (and not
without reason) frighten people away. An example of this sort of arrangement
may be provided by the project that I put forward for the treatment of historical-revolutionary material and that was accepted after long debates with the
supporters of 'Rightist' real-life films who dream of filming the life of some
underground conspirator or notorious *agent provocateur,* or an imaginary
story based on real-life materials. (Incidentally, these materials are completely ignored by the 'wistful' men of cinema and left at the disposal of right-
wing directors who abuse them: viz. *Andrei Kozhukhov, Stepan Khalturin*[10]
and *The Palace and the Fortress!*)

The most important consideration in my approach to this theme was
to give an account of and depict the *technique of the underground* and to provide
an *outline of its production methods* in individual characteristic examples. How
they sewed boots – how they prepared for the October Revolution. Our audience, trained to take an interest in production, is not the least interested in,
and *should not be* interested in, the emotions of an actor made up as Beideman
or in the tears of his bride. It is interested in the prison regime at the Peter
and Paul Fortress and this is to be presented not through the personal sufferings of the hero but through the direct exposition of its methods.

It is not the life of Malinovsky the *agent provocateur* that interests us
but the varieties and types (what are the characteristics of a particular type)
and what makes an *agent provocateur,* not the presence of someone in a de-
portation prison but the prison itself, the conditions there, the mores in their
numerous variants. In a word, the presentation of every element of underground work as *phenomena that are represented in the greatest possible number of
varieties and examples.* The conditions in which proofs were corrected, the
underground printing press, etc., in the form of sequences characterising particular moments and not joined into a seamless plot centred on an underground printing press but edited with a view to the thorough exposure, for
example, of the underground printing press as one of the facts of underground work. The emphasis is on the most interesting montage tasks. Without 'staging' this is quite unthinkable but in a quite different context! There is

an example of the montage (e.g. in the episode of the 'flight') of pure adventure material preserving all its attractional quality in the orientation towards historical familiarisation. The theme of a strike was chosen first of all for the transition to constructions of this kind: in terms of its saturation with the mass it is most suited to the intermediate form between a film whose purpose is a purely emotional revolutionary effect conditioned by the plot and the new way of understanding its construction. For a number of reasons, dictated mainly by the material itself, it has to adhere more closely in its form to the first of these.

As far as the question of the necessity or otherwise of a script or of free montage of arbitrarily filmed material is concerned, we have to remember that a script, whether plot-based or not, is (as I wrote with reference to theatre: see *Lef*[11]), in our view, a prescription (or a list) of montage sequences and combinations by means of which the author intends to subject the audience to a definite series of shocks, a 'prescription' that summarises the general projected emotional effect on the audience and the pressure that will inevitably be exerted on the audience's psyche. More often than not, given our scriptwriters' utterly feeble approach to the construction of a script, this task falls in its entirety to the director. The transposition of the theme into a chain of attractions with a previously determined end effect is the definition we have given of a director's work. The presence or absence of a written script is by no means all that important. I think that, when it is a matter of operating on the audience through material that is not closely plot-based, a general scheme of reference that leads to the desired results is enough, together with a free selection of montage material based on it (the absence of such a scheme would not lead to the organisation of the material but to hopeless Impressionism around a possibly attractional theme). But, if it is carried out by means of a complex plot construction, then obviously a detailed script is necessary. Both kinds of film have the same citizenship rights because in the final analysis we are going above all to see in *Nathan the Wise*[12] the amazing work of the cavalry, its jumping past the camera, exactly as we see it in Vertov's work at the Red Stadium.

Incidentally I shall touch here on one purely directorial moment in our work. When, in the process of constructing, shooting and moulding the montage elements, we are selecting the filmed fragments, we must fully recall the characteristics of cinema's effect that we stated initially and that establish the montage approach as the essential, meaningful and sole possible language of cinema, completely analogous to the role of the word in spoken material. In the selection and presentation of this material the decisive factor should be the immediacy and economy of the resources expended in the cause of associative effect.

The first practical indication that derives from this is the selection of an angle of vision for every element, conditioned exclusively by the accuracy and force of impact of the necessary presentation of this element. If the montage elements are strung together consecutively this will lead to a constant movement of the angle of vision in relation to the material being demonstrated (in itself one of the most absorbing purely cinematic possibilities).

Strictly speaking, the montage elision of one fragment into another is inadmissible: each element can most profitably be shown from just one angle and part of the film fact that proceeds from, let us say, an inserted close-up, already requires a new angle that is different from the fragment that preceded the close-up. Thus, where a tightly expounded fact is concerned, the work of the film director, as distinct from the theatre director, requires, in addition to a mastery of production (planning and acting), a repertoire of montage-calculated angles for the camera to 'capture' these elements. I almost managed to achieve this kind of montage in the fight scene in *The Strike* where the repetition of sequences was almost completely avoided.

These considerations play a decisive role in the selection of camera angles and the arrangement of the lights. No plot 'justification' for the selection of the angle of vision or the light sources is necessary. (Apart, that is, from a case where the task involves a particularly persistent emphasis on reality. For instance, *contre-jour* lighting is by no means 'justified' in American interior shots.)

On a par with the method of staging a scene and taking it with a camera there exists what I should call the Futurist method of exposition, based on the pure montage of associations and on the separate depiction of a fact: for example, the impression of that fight may be represented through the montage of the separate elements that are not joined by any logical sequence in the staging of the scene. The accumulation of the details of conflicting objects, blows, fighting methods, facial expressions and so on produces just as great an impression as the detailed investigation by the camera of all the phases in a logically unfolding process of struggle: I contrast both kinds of montage, done separately, in the scene of the shooting. (I do not, for example, use the chain: the gun is cocked – the shot fired – the bullet strikes – the victim falls, but: the fall – the shot – the cocking – the raising of the wounded, etc.)

If we move on to the persistently posed question of the 'demonstration of real life' as such, we must point out that this particular instance of demonstration is covered by our general position on the montage of attractions: but the assertion that the essence of cinema lies only in the demonstration of real life must be called into question. It is, I think, a matter of transposing the characteristics of a '1922/3 attraction' (which was, as is always the case, a response to social aspirations – in this instance, the orientation towards 'construction' as the raw material for these aspirations and towards a 'presentation' that advertised this construction, e.g. an important event like the Agricultural Exhibition) to the entire nature of cinema as a whole. The canonisation of this material and of this approach as the only acceptable ones deprive cinema of its flexibility in relation to its broadly social tasks and, by deflecting the centre of gravity of public attention to other spheres (which is already noticeable), it leaves only a single aesthetic 'love for real life' (to what absurd lengths the game of love for 'machines' has been taken, despite the example of a very highly respected Soviet whodunit in which the cartridge-producing and dual-printing presses of the 'short film' begin to work for a mechanical conglomeration when the military chemical factory is set in motion!). Or we shall have to effect a 'revolution in the principles of cinema' when it will be a matter of a simple shift of attractions.

This is by no means a matter of trailing under the cover of 'agit tasks' elements that are formally unacceptable to, and uncharacteristic of, cinema in the same way as an incalculable amount of pulp literature, hack-work and unscrupulous behaviour in theatre is justified as agitational. I maintain my conviction that the future undoubtedly lies with the plot-less actor-less form of exposition but this future will dawn only with the advent of the conditions of social organisation that provide the opportunity for the general development and the comprehensive mastering of their nature and the application of all their energy in action, and the human race will not lack satisfaction through fictive energetic deeds, provided for it by all types of spectacle, distinguished only by the methods by which they are summoned forth. That time is still a long way off but, I repeat, we must not ignore the enormous effectiveness of the work of the model actor [*naturshchik*][13] on the audience. I submit that the campaign against the model actor is caused by the negative effect of the lack of system and principle in the organisation of his work.

This 'play' is either a semi-narcotic experience with no account of time or space (and really only a little off the 'place where the camera is standing'), or a stereometric spread in three-dimensional space of the body and the extremities of the model actor in different directions, remotely recalling some forms of human action (and perceived by the audience thus: 'Aha, apparently he's getting angry') or consecutive local contractions of facial muscles quite independent of one another and their system as a whole, which are considered as mime. Both lead to a superb division of space in the shot and the surface of the screen that follow strict rhythmic schemas, with no single 'daubing' or unfixed place. But . . . a rhythmic schema is arbitrary, it is established according to the whim or 'feeling' of the director and not according to periods dictated by the mechanical conditions of the course of a particular motor process; the disposition of the extremities (which is precisely not 'movement') is produced outside any mutual mechanical interaction such as the unified motor system of a single organism.

The audience in this kind of presentation is deprived of the emotional effect of perception which is replaced by guesswork as to what is happening. Because emotional perception is achieved through the motor reproduction of the movements of the actor by the perceiver, this kind of reproduction can only be caused by movement that adheres to the methods that it normally adheres to in nature. Because of the confirmation of the correctness of this method of influence and perception I agree in this matter (this problem has been examined and elaborated in detail in my brochure on expressive movement published by Proletkult[14]) even with Lipps* who cites as proof of

---

* Lipps, *Das Wissen vom fremden 'Ich'* [The Consciousness of the Alien Ego].

the correctness of his investigations into the cognition of the *alter ego* the statement that (citing Bekhterev) 'the emotional understanding of the *alter ego* through the imitation of the other leads only to a tendency to experience one's own emotion of the same kind but not to a conviction that the *alter ego* exists.'

Leaving aside the last statement, which hardly concerns us, we have a very valuable confirmation of the correctness of our approach to construction, to an 'effective construction' (in the particular instance of film), according to which it is not the facts being demonstrated that are important but the combinations of the emotional reactions of the audience, It is then possible to envisage in both theory and practice a construction, with no linking plot logic, which provokes a chain of the necessary unconditioned reflexes that are, at the editor's will, associated with (compared with) predetermined phenomena and by this means to create the chain of new conditioned reflexes that these phenomena constitute. This signifies a realisation of the orientation towards thematic effect, i.e. a fulfilment of the agitational purpose.*

The circle of effective arts is closed by the open essence of the agitational spectacle and a 'union' with the primary sources is established: I think that the celebrated dances in animal skins of the primitive savages 'whence theatre derived' are a very reasonable institution of the ancient sorcerers directed much less towards the realisation of figurative tendencies ('for what purpose?') than towards the very precise training of the hunting and fighting instincts of the primitive audience. The refinement of imitative skill is by no means a matter of satisfying those same figurative tendencies but of counting on the maximum emotional effect on the audience. This fundamental orientation towards the role of the audience was later forfeited in a purely formal refinement of methods and it is only now being revived to meet the concrete requirements of the day. This pure method of training the reflexes through performance effect deserves the careful consideration of people organising educational films and theatres that quite unconsciously cram children with an entirely unjustified repertoire.

We shall move on to analyse a particular, but very important, affective factor: the work of the model actor. Without repeating in brief the observations I have already made as to what that work is and what it should be, we shall set out our system of work, endeavouring somehow to organise this branch of our labour (reforging someone else's psyche is no less difficult and considerable a task than forging iron and the term 'playing' is by no means appropriate).

---

* We must still bear in mind that in a spectacle of dramatic effect the audience is from the very first placed in a non-neutral attitude situation and sympathises with one party, identifying itself with that party's actions, while opposing itself to the other party, reacting from the very first through a *feeling of direct opposition* to its actions. The hero's anger provokes your own personal anger against his enemies; the villain's anger makes you jeer. The law of effect remains essentially the same.

The Basic Premiss

1. The value lies not in the figurativeness of the actions of the model actor but in the degree of his motor and associatively infectious capabilities vis-à-vis the audience (i.e. the whole process of the actor's movement is organised with the aim of facilitating the imitative capacities of the audience).

2. Hence the first direction concerns the *selection* of versions presented to the audience: a reliance on invention, i.e. on the *combination* of the movement, required by the purpose, from the versions that are most characteristic of real circumstances (and consequently automatically imitated by the audience) and simplest in form. The development and complication of motivations in the matter of 'delays' (as literature treats them). NB Cinema makes very frequent use, apart from delays, of montage methods and this method too. I can cite an example of a moment that is constructed cinematically in this way from my theatre production of *Can You Hear Me, Moscow?*,[15] when the *agent provocateur* is handed an empty envelope that purports to contain evidence of his provocations. (There will be no reference in this section to the film I am working on in so far as the film as a whole is not orientated in its construction towards this group of actions whereas the work of the model actor is a matter of investigating the methods of 'free work'.) Here the de-texturisation [*rasfakturennost'*] of the elements taken from the simplest versions of the movement of handing the envelope over and attempting to take it so excites the emotion of the audience with its delay that the 'break' (the transition to the murder) makes the same impression as a bomb exploding. (In a film treatment you would add a montage section following the same rhythmic module.)

3. The refinement of this version of movement: i.e. the ascertainment of the purely mechanical schema of its normal course in real life.

4. Breakdown of movement into its pseudo-primitive primary component elements for the audience – a system of shocks, rises, falls, spins, pirouettes, etc. – for the director to convey to the performer the precise arrangement of the motor version and to train these inherently neutral expressive (not in terms of plot but in terms of production) motor units.

5. Assembly (montage) and co-ordination into a temporal schema of these neutral elements of the movements in a combination that produces action.

6. Obfuscation of the schema in the realisation of the difference in execution that exists between the play of a virtuoso with his own individual reordering of rhythm [*pereritmovka*] and the play of a pupil metrically tapping out the musical notation. (NB The completion of the minor details in fixing the version also enters into this obfuscation.)

The realisation of the movement does not proceed in a superficially imitative and figurative manner vis-à-vis a real action (murder, drunkenness, chopping wood, etc.) but results in an organic representation that emerges through the appropriate mechanical schema and a real achievement of the motor process of the phenomena being depicted.

50

The norms of organicism (the laws of organic process and mechanical interaction) for motor processes have been established partly by French and German theoreticians of movement (investigating kinetics in order to establish motor primitives) and partly by me (kinetics in its application to complex expressive movements – and the dynamics of both: see below) in my laboratory work at the Proletkult Theatre.

Briefly, they lead to the following: the basic raw material – and the actor's real work lies in overcoming its resistance – is the actor's body: its resistances to motor intentions comprise its weight and its ability to conserve motor inertia.

The methods for overcoming these resistances dictated by their very nature are based on the following premises.

The basic premiss was stated by G. B. Duchenne in *Physiology of Motion* as early as 1885:[16] 'l'action musculaire isolée n'est pas dans la nature',[17] i.e. a particular muscular action with no connection with the muscular system as a whole is not characteristic of nature and is found only in the pathological phenomena of cramps, hysterics and convulsions.

Furthermore, the consequences of Rudolph Bode's* premiss, the results of long years of practical research are:

1. The principle of 'totality' [*tselokupnost'*][†] according to which the body as a whole participates in the execution of every movement.
2. The principle of a 'centre of gravity'. Because of the inorganic nature of the process of directing effort to individual muscles, only the centre of gravity of the entire system can serve as the sole permissible point of application. (Hence it follows that the movements of the extremities are not independent but the mere mechanical result of the movement of the body as a whole.)
3. The principle of emancipation, i.e. given general work selection, the periodic positioning – by means of the appropriate muscular relaxation [*Entspannung*] – of an extremity, of the extremities or of the body as a whole, becomes the positioning of the purely mechanical actions of the forces of gravity and inertia.

These premisses were expounded without being applied to any special kind of movement and, principally, to the norms of physical education. None the less, even the first attempts to normalise the working movements of a worker at a lathe (at that time this was mainly with a view to protecting him against occupational physical distortions of the body and the spine) led to the application of those same principles, as is clear from the motor schemas and descriptions appended to the work of Hueppe who (in 1899) first raised the question of the physical organisation of labour.

---

* R. Bode, *Ausdrucksgymnastik* [The Gymnastics of Expression] (Munich, 1921).

† *Totalität* in Sergei Tretyakov's Russian translation.

In the application of these principles to the movement being demonstrated the emphasis is on the utmost expressiveness as the bearer of the influence: I have studied this further. By expressive movement I understand movement that discloses the realisation of a particular realisable motor intention in the process of being realised, i.e. the appropriate arrangement of the body and the extremities at any particular moment for the motor execution of the appropriate element necessary for the purpose of the movement. Expressive movements fall into three[18] groups:

1. A set of rational directions in the direct execution of common motor intentions (all aspects of an appropriately constructed movement – of a boxer, a hammerman, etc. – and also reflex movements that have at some time been automated into conscious purposes – the leap of a tiger, etc.).
2. A set of instances with varying purpose with two or more motivations for their realisation when several purposes that resolve particular motivations build up in the body and, lastly:
3. The most interesting case in terms of its motor formation is the case of a psychologically expressive movement that represents a motor exposure of the *conflict* of motivations: an instinctively emotional desire that retards the conscious volitional principle.

It is realised in the motor *conflict* between the desires of the body as a whole (which respond to the tendency of instinct and represent material for the exposure of reflex movement) and the retarding role of the consciously preserved inertia* of the extremities (corresponding to the role of the conscious volitional retardation that is realised through the extremities).

This mechanical schema, first elaborated by me, for expressive movement finds confirmation in a series of observations by Klages[†] and the premisses put forward by Nothnagel.[19] We value the former's statements that only the affect can serve as the cause of organic motor manifestation and not the volitional impulse whose fate it usually is to act merely as a brake on and a betrayer of intentions. The latter has stated that the actual means of communicating cerebral stimulation through the facial muscles (he is writing about mime) are achieved by quite different methods depending on whether the movement is determined by the surface of the face or as a result of affective stimulation. The latter methods involve a specific part of the brain (the so-called *Sehhügel*[20]), the former do not. As confirmation Nothnagel cites some very interesting cases of paralysis. Given the appropriate affects, the paralysed part of the face of certain patients was able to cry and laugh whereas the patient was incapable of the smallest movement of the lips or eyes consciously (freely) in the absence of affective prerequisites. Or the inverse in-

---

* A state of tranquillity or of the preservation of the preceding movement of the object.
† Klages, *Ausdrucksbewegung und Gestaltungskraft* [Expressive Movement and Formative Power] (Leipzig, 1923).

stance when, in cases of very powerful emotional shock, a paralysed face preserved a stony immobility whereas the patient was able at will to produce any muscular contractions in his face (knit his brows, move his mouth, and so on).*

It would be a great error to perceive our statement as advocating in the model actor's work the affective condition that was long ago condemned in theatre and is absolutely unthinkable in cinema, given the peculiarities of its production. It is here a matter of assessing the mechanical interactions that constantly occur within us but that flow from us in cases where a similar process has to be consciously realised in front of an audience or a camera.[†] We must also bear in mind that both series of movements that are coming into conflict are equally consciously constructed and the effect of the affective movement is achieved by the artificial mechanical setting in motion of the body as a whole and must in no way result from the emotional state of the performer. The biodynamic method of translating artificially induced movement to the conditions of the organic flow of the process of movement through a dynamic and powerful deployment of the so-called 'denying' movement (understood even by schools of movement which included it in their system merely in its spatial sense[‡]) is an attitude expressed by theoreticians of theatre as long ago as the 17th century[§] and due to inertia. I shall here only remind you of the particular kind of certain neutrally affective 'working conditions' that also facilitates this translation. A detailed exposition of these questions, which are less important to cinema than to theatre, would lead us into too much technical detail.

We should do better to concentrate on selecting a particular example of this kind of expressive movement. A particularly clear example is the 'baring of teeth': in our view this is *not* a parting of the lips *but* a pushing on the part of the head which, as the 'leading' part of the body, is striving to break through the inert restraints of the surface of the face. The motor process is

---

* I am quoting from: Krukenberg, *Vom Gesichtsausdruck des Menschen* [Human Facial Expression] (Stuttgart, 1923).
† The majority of movements are reflex and automatic and it was Darwin who pointed out the difficulties involved in reproducing these kinds of movements. One example is the difficulty involved in reproducing a 'premeditated' swallow. It is interesting to note the immediate departure from the laws of movement that occurs when they are consciously reproduced: whereas if the hands of an actor (which, according to the general laws, are part of his body as a whole) are in real life always engaged in motor movement, on stage 'they do not know what to do' because this law is being broken.
‡ 'Denial' in this sense in a small preparatory movement in the reverse direction to the movement being executed which serves to increase the amplitude of the movement and underline more strongly the beginning of the movement not as a starting-point but as an extreme point of denial that is no longer static but is a turning-point in the direction of the movement.
§ See: Vsevolod N. Vsevolodskii-Gerngross, *Istoriya teatral'nogo obrazovaniya v Rossii* [The History of Theatrical Training in Russia], vol. 2 (St Petersburg, 1913).

quite analogous to a particular psychological situation: in the final analysis the baring of the teeth is a gesture towards an opponent, constrained by consciousness for one reason or another. Thus, according to the stated premises, 'psychological expression' also leads to unique dual gymnastics in reproducing the conflict between the motor tendencies of the body as a whole and the extremities. In the process of this 'struggle' distortions arise on the surface of the face and in the centrifugal spatial trajectories of the extremities and of the interrelationships of the joints just as there will also be countless shades of expression subjected to strict calculation and conscious construction given an adequate command of this system of dual motor process. (It is very interesting that even the apparently 'intellectual' parts of the body are involved in the realisation of the delaying role of the intellect, i.e. those parts that have been emancipated with the cultivation of the individual from 'unskilled' labour in the motor servicing of the body – moving and feeding it – the hands, that we have stopped walking on, and the face, that has ceased to be a snout gulping down food – a kind of 'class struggle' in its own way!)

The material that I analysed and selected in these principles of movement is for the time being a base schema which will begin to come to life only when real forces are set in motion, and a rhythmic scale which is appropriate to the particular expressive manifestation cannot be established until that moment. (It is unnecessary to say anything about the need for a rhythmic formula in general: it is quite obvious that the same sequence of movements, with the addition of different combinations of duration, will produce quite different expressive effects.) The principal distinction of this approach will be the establishment of temporal values, selected in a far from arbitrary way, for any elements in whatever combination, and they will represent the result of the processes of distribution of power loads for shocks, and the intensity of muscular responses; the forces of centrifugal inertia on the extremities; the neutralisation of the inertias of preceding elements of the movements, the conditions that arise in connection with the general position of the body in space, etc., in the process of realising the expressive objective.

Thus, a precise organic rhythmic schema is taking shape that corresponds to the intensity of the course of the process and itself changes in changing conditions and in the common character of the precise resolution of the objective: it is individual to each performer and corresponds to his physical characteristics (the weight and size of his extremities, his muscular state, etc.). In this context we note that in the rhythmic construction of the process of movement its degree of arbitrariness is extremely limited. In rhythmic movement we are a long way from being able to behave as we please: the actual biomechanical structure of the working organ inevitably conducts our movement towards a regular function that breaks down into the sum of simply and strictly motivated harmonic components. The role of random innervation in this process amounts to a spasmodic disturbing intervention in the organically progressing motor process and the possibility of automating this process (which represents the ultimate aim in the realisation of its conviction and is achieved by training in rehearsal) is in these circumstances excluded.*

On the other hand, to fit temporal segments artificially to a desired expressive schema is much less economical and presents enormous difficulties. I might even go as far as to say that it is impossible because of the fact that I verified this in my production of *Gas Masks*.[21] When a man suffocates in the hatch where a pipe is being mended the intervals between beats increase and their force abates. From the sound throughout the auditorium you could detect unmistakably each time the combination of the performer's beats occurred at a break in the movement and the artificial selection of the intervals between, and the intensity of, the beats and when they were part of an uninterrupted process, achieving the necessary effect by overcoming in the longer term the inertia of preceding movements through introducing successively weaker new shocks in the repeated blows. A visually similar phenomenon would strike us even more powerfully.

An example of the ideal form of the verbal-rhythmic effect of movement (constructed on the basis of matching a sound schema as we match the schema of an expressive objective) is provided by the performer in a jazz band: his command of movement consists in an amazing use of the process of neutralising the inertia of a large-scale movement into a series of pantomime and percussive movements, and in their combination with small-scale new elements of movement. If this process is replaced by a process of newly emerging innervations of certain limbs (if the jazz-player is not a good dancer), without regard for the rhythmic oscillations of the body as a whole, his exaggerated movements, ceasing to fit into an organic schema, would have the effect of pathological grimaces (precisely because of the inorganic character of their origin).

Even this one example should be enough to confirm the rule of the preservation of inertia, the rule that determines how convincing a motor process is by preserving the motor inertia of what becomes a single action. As an example of this use of inertia I shall cite the clowns in 'Fatty' Arbuckle's[22] film group. They employ this method in such a way that they unfailingly lend to each complex of complicated movement, liquidated in the conditions of one scene or another, a completely unfounded ending of pure movement. Given their skill this is always a brilliant little 'trick'. In mechanical terms it is this device that releases the accumulating reserve of inertia that permeates a whole complex of movement.

I shall not get involved in the details of their methodology. I shall merely point out that the basic requirement of a model actor for this kind of work is the *healthy organic rhythm* of his *normal physical functions*, without which it is impossible for him either to master this system or to perceive it via a rhythmically precise screen, despite the fact that in theatre success (i.e.

---

* See the collection of essays by the Central Labour Institute in their application to work movement.

emotional infectiousness) can be greater in the light of the nervous imbalance that accompanies, or rather conditions, this characteristic. (This has been tested on two of my actors: it was curiously impossible to find two or three 'unsoiled' in a row, whatever the tempo of their filmed movement, because the nervous foundation of their rhythm was so uneven.)

The question of fixation, which is so decisive for the screen, emerges here as the natural result since, whatever the outcome of the conflict depicted, that [conflict] passes through a moment of equalisation, i.e. a state of rest. If the disproportion of forces is too great there can be neither fixation nor expressive movement for it becomes either simply an act or a simple state of rest, depending on which tendency is dominant.

Thus we can realise a montage (assembly) of movements that are purely organic in themselves. I should call them the elements of the working movement of the model actors themselves and the arrangement assembled in this way involves the audience to the maximum degree in imitation and, through the emotional effect of this, in the corresponding ideological treatment. In addition as a whole it produces (although it is possible to construct them without this) the *visual* effect of the emotion apparently experienced. We see that the methods of processing the audience are no different in the mechanics of their realisation from other forms of work movement and they produce the same *real, primarily physical* work on their material – the audience.

In this approach to the work of the model actor there is no longer any question of the 'shame' of acting (an association with the concept of acting that has taken root because of the really shameful methods of experiential schools of acting). There will be no difference in the perception via the screen of a cobbler sewing boots or a terrorist throwing a bomb (staged) because, proceeding from the identical material bases of their work, both of them first and foremost process the audience through their actions: one plays (not directly of course but through appropriate presentation by the director) on pride in work well done (more precisely on illusory co-construction) while the other plays on the feeling of class hatred (more precisely, the illusory realisation of it). In both cases this constitutes the basis of the emotional effect.

I think moreover that this kind of movement, apart from its direct effectiveness which I have verified in theatre in both its tragic and its comic aspects, will be the most photogenic in so far as one can define 'photogenic' by paraphrasing Schopenhauer's good old definition of the 'beautiful'. An idea expressed in its completeness is photogenic; that is, an object is photogenic when it corresponds most closely to the idea that it embodies.* (A car

---

* This definition fully conforms to Delluc's observation that photogenic faces are those which first and foremost possess 'character', which, for a face, is the same as what we are saying about movement. [Note in E's MS.]

The 'character' of a face is the most frequent imitation, i.e. of the motivations (Klages). [Note in Belenson version.][23]

is more photogenic than a cart because its whole structure corresponds more closely to its purpose of transportation, and so on.)

That the objects and costumes of previous periods are not photogenic* can, I think, be explained by the way that they were made: for example, costumes were not produced by a search for normal clothing or by the forms of special clothing suitable for various kinds of production, i.e. for forms that corresponded most closely to the purpose they embodied, the 'idea', but were determined by purely fortuitous motivation like, let us say, the fashion for red and yellow combinations, the so-called 'cardinal sur la paille', named in honour of Cardinal de Rohan who was imprisoned in the Bastille in connection with the affair of the 'Queen's necklace'. Or lace headdresses 'à la Fontanges', connected with the saucy episode between Louis XIV and Mlle de Fontanges who lost her lace pantaloons and saved the situation by hurriedly adding them to her already elaborate hair-do. The approach that makes for photogenic costume, i.e. the search for functional forms in costume, is characteristic only of recent times (noted apparently for the first time by the Japanese General Staff) so that only contemporary costumes are photogenic. Working clothes[24] furnish the richest raw material: e.g. a diving suit.

In this particular instance movements are revealed that most logically and organically correspond to the phases of the flow of a certain action. Apart from theoretical probability, a practical indication that it is precisely this kind of movement that is most photogenic is provided by the photogenic quality of animals, whose movements are structured in strict accordance with these laws and do not infringe them by the intervention of the rational principle in their automatic nature (Bode). Labour processes, which also flow in accordance with these stated laws, have similarly been shown to be photogenic.

There remains to add to the system we have elaborated only one more circumstance that formally is more critical for cinema than for theatre. For cinema the 'organisation of the surface' (of the screen) presents an even more serious problem, indissolubly linked to the organisation of the space encompassed by the frame and – and this is specific to cinema – by the fluctuation of this surface and the constant contrast between the surfaces thus organised in movement (the montage succession of shots). I think that, as far as establishing the necessary (in the sense of a correctly constructed superstructure to movement) consequent (deriving from this characteristic of cinema) spatial correctives is concerned, there is little to add to Kuleshov's 'axial system' that seemed to illuminate this problem so thoroughly. Its one fundamental error lies in the fact that those who elaborated it regard it as the basic approach to movement in general, which leads to its alienation from the mechanical and dynamic foundations of movement. In Kuleshov's view we do not have a smooth process of movement but an alternation of unconnected 'positions' (poses). The motor results of this lead to grimace instead of mime,

---

* As noted, for instance, by Delluc in the journal *Veshch'*, no. 3.

and movement over and above the energetic purpose of material work, and the model actors, by their appearance as mechanical dolls, undermine our trust in the extraordinarily valuable methods of spatial organisation of the material on the screen. In this instance only one thing can serve as the criterion for a production: it is the director's personal taste for overturning the rhythmic schemas of quiet scenes and [creating] chaos in the motor organisation of fights and other energetically saturated places, requiring that organisation be subjugated to the schemas of force and mechanics. It is only once this has been done that they can be subjected to some kind of external moulding. Inevitably this kind of approach must, and does, lead to stylisation.

The attractional approach to the construction of all elements, from the film as a whole to the slightest movement of the performer, is not an affirmation of personal taste or of the search for a polished style for Soviet cinema, but an assertion of the method of approach to the montage of effects that are useful to our class and of the precise recognition of the utilitarian goals of cinema in the Soviet Republic.

4. The Problem of the Materialist Approach to Form[1]

The unanimous and enthusiastic reception that the press has given *The Strike*, and the actual character of that reception, allow us to perceive *The Strike* as a revolutionary victory not merely for the work itself but also as an *ideological victory in the field of form*. This is particularly significant now at a time when people are ready to trample with such fanaticism on any work in the field of form, branding it as 'Formalism' and preferring . . . complete formlessness. But in *The Strike* we have the first instance of revolutionary art where the form has turned out to be more revolutionary than the content.

The revolutionary novelty of *The Strike* by no means derives from the fact that its content – the revolutionary movement – was, historically, a mass rather than an individual phenomenon (hence the absence of plot and hero, etc., that characterise *The Strike* as the 'first proletarian film'), but rather from the fact that it has promoted a *properly devised formal method of approaching* the exposure of the abundance of historical-revolutionary material in general.

The historical-revolutionary material – the '*manufactured*' past of contemporary revolutionary reality – was for the first time treated from a correct *point of view*: its characteristic movements were investigated as stages in a single process from the point of view of its 'manufacturing' essence.[2] The discovery of the manufacturing logic and the exposition of the technique of the methods of struggle as of a 'living' current process that knows no inviolable rules other than its final aim and the methods that are varied and devised at a particular moment according to the conditions and the balance of forces at that particular phase of the struggle, having depicted it in all its everyday intensity: that is the formal requirement I put to Proletkult in determining the content of the seven parts of the cycle *Towards the Dictatorship*.[3]

It is quite obvious that the specific quality of the actual *character* (the massness[4]) of this movement does not yet play any part in the construction of the logical principle that has been expounded and it is not its *massness* that defines it. The form of the plot [*syuzhet*], the treatment of the content (in this case the first use of the method of script montage: i.e. its construction not on the basis of some kind of generally accepted dramaturgical laws but in the exposition of the content by methods that define the construction of the montage as such in general terms, e.g. in the organisation of newsreel footage),*

---

* It is, however, interesting to note that, because of this feature of the actual technique of exposition of *The Strike* and the other parts of *Towards the Dictatorship*, there was, properly speaking, no script but there was a jump – subject: cue sheet – which was quite logical in terms of the montage essence of the matter.

even the very correctness of the arrangement of the visual angle towards the material were in this particular instance *consequences of the basic formal realisation of the material under consideration*, of the basic form-renewing 'trick' of direction in the construction of a film that defined it in the first instance.

On the level of the affirmation of a new form of film phenomenon as the consequence of a new kind of social command (stated baldly: the 'underground') the direction of *The Strike* followed the path that has always characterised the revolutionary affirmation of the new in the field of art, the path of the *dialectical* application, to a number of materials, of methods of treatment that were not normally used for them but that came from another field, either adjoining or opposite. Thus, the 'revolutionising' of the aesthetics of theatrical forms that have been transformed before our very eyes during the last twenty-five years has taken place under the guise of the absorption of the external characteristics of 'neighbouring' arts (the successive dictatorships of: literature, painting, music, exotic theatres in an era of conventional theatre, circus, the external tricks of cinema, etc.[5]). This involved the fertilisation of one series of exotic phenomena by another (apart, perhaps, from the role of the circus and of sport in the renewal of acting skills). The revolutionary quality of *The Strike* was exemplified by the fact that it took its renewing principle not from the ranks of 'artistic phenomena' but from those that are *directly utilitarian*: specifically, the principle of the construction of the exposition of manufacturing processes in the film, a choice that is significant because it goes beyond the limits of the aesthetic sphere (which is, in itself, quite logical for my works which are, always and in every case, orientated towards the principles not of aesthetics but of the 'mincer'), all the more so because what was in *material* terms correctly ascertained was precisely that *sphere* whose principles might alone *define the ideology of the forms of revolutionary art just as they have defined revolutionary ideology in general*: *heavy industry*, factory production and the forms of the manufacturing process.

When talking about the form of *The Strike* it is only very naive people who refer to the 'contradictions between the ideological requirements and the director's formal digressions'. It is time some people realised that form is *determined* much more profoundly than by any superficial 'trick', however successful.

Here we can and must talk not about a 'revolutionising' of the forms, in this particular instance of cinema, because this expression is in manufacturing terms devoid of common sense, but of an instance of revolutionary film form in general because it is in no way the result of a charlatan's 'researches', and certainly not of 'the synthesis of a good mastery of form and our content' (as Pletnyov writes in *Novyi zritel*[6]). *Revolutionary form is the product of correctly ascertained technical methods for the concretisation of a new attitude and approach to objects and phenomena* – of a new class ideology – of the true renewal not just of the *social significance but also of the material-technical essence of cinema*, disclosed in what we call 'our content'. It is not by 'revolutionising' the forms of the stage-coach that the locomotive is created but through a proper technical calculation of the practical emergence of a *new and previously non-existent kind of energy* – steam. It is not the 'research' for forms that correspond to the new content but the logical *realisation of all the phases of the technical production of a work of art consonant with* the 'new *kind* of energy' – the ruling *ideology* – that will produce the forms of revolutionary art that to the very last moment still *want like a spiritualist* to 'leave us guessing'.

So the principle of approach that I put forward and the point of view that I affirmed on cinema's use of historical-revolutionary material turned out to be correct, in terms of materialism, and was recognised as such in *Pravda* by, as one might expect, a *Communist*, who went as far as to call my (formal!) approach 'Bolshevik', and not by the *professional film critics* (who cannot see beyond the end of their noses, that is beyond my 'Eccentrism'[7]). It has been recognised even in spite of the weakness in its programme and plot: the absence of material that adequately describes the technique of the Bolshevik underground and of the economic preconditions for the strike which is, of course, an enormous flaw in the *ideological plot* part of the content, although in this particular instance it is merely regarded as a 'non-comprehensive exposition of the manufacturing process' (that is, the process of struggle). It determined a certain superfluous refinement in forms that were in themselves simple and severe.

Massness is the director's *second conscious* trick. As we can see from the above, it is by no means a logical necessity: in fact, of the seven parts of *Towards the Dictatorship*, which are impersonal throughout, only two have a mass character. It is no accident that *The Strike* (one of them, the *fifth* in the series) was selected to be made *first*. The *mass* material was put forward as the material *most capable* of establishing *in relief* the ideological principle being expounded of an approach to form in the new postulation of a particular resolution, and as *a supplement to the dialectical opposition* of this principle to the *individual plot material of bourgeois cinema*. It is also consciously established in formal terms through the construction of a logical antithesis to the bourgeois West, which we are in no way *emulating* but which we are in every way *opposing*.

The mass approach produces in addition the maximum intensification of the emotional seizure [*zakhvat*] of the audience which, for art in general and revolutionary art in particular, is decisive.

Such a cynical analysis of the basic construction of *The Strike*, while perhaps debunking the fine phrases about the 'elemental and collective' character of its 'creation', involves at the same time a more serious and businesslike base and confirms that a formal approach that is *correctly* conducted in Marxist terms results in an ideologically valuable and socially useful product.

All this gives us grounds to apply to *The Strike* the appellation that we are accustomed to using to mark revolutionary turning-points in art: 'October'.

An October that even has its own February because what are the

61

works of Vertov[8] if not the 'overthrow of the autocracy' of fiction cinema and . . . nothing more? In this context I am speaking merely of my only fore-runner: *Cine-Pravda*.[9] But *Cine-Eye*,[10] released when the shooting and part of the editing of *The Strike* were already completed, could not have exerted any influence, and by its very essence *there was no way in which it could exert any influence* because *Eye* is the *reductio ad absurdum* of the technical methods that are valid for newsreel, of Vertov's claims that they are *adequate* for the creation of a new cinema. In fact *it is merely an act of denial* filmed by the 'running of one camera', of one particular aspect of cinema.

Without denying a certain part of the genetic link with *Cine-Pravda* (the machine-guns fired just as much in February as they did in October: the difference lay in the target!), because, like *The Strike*, it derived from manu-facturing newsreels, I consider it all the more necessary to point to the *sharp distinction in principle*, that is the *difference in method*. *The Strike* does not 'de-velop the methods' of *Cine-Eye* (Khersonsky[11]) and it is not 'an experiment in grafting certain methods of construction in *Cine-Pravda* on to fiction cinema' (Vertov). Whereas, in terms of the *external form* of the construction you can point to a certain *similarity*, in precisely the most essential part, the *formal method of construction, 'The Strike' is the direct antithesis of 'Cine-Eye'*.

My starting-point is that *'The Strike' has no pretensions to being an escape from art and in that lies its strength*.

In our conception a *work of art* (at least in the two spheres in which I work: theatre and cinema) is first and foremost a *tractor ploughing over the audience's psyche in a particular class context*.

The work that the Cine-Eyes produce has neither this characteristic nor this premiss and, I think, because of a certain degree of 'mischief' on the part of these producers that is inappropriate to our epoch, their work con-stitutes a *denial* of art instead of a *recognition of its materialist* essence or, if not, then at least its *utilitarian application*.

This flippancy puts the Cine-Eyes in a quite absurd position because no analysis can fail to establish the fact that their works belong very much to art *and, what is more, to one of its least valuable expressions in ideological terms, to primitive Impressionism*.

With a set of montage fragments of real life (of what the Impressionists called *real tones*), *whose effect has not been calculated, Vertov weaves the causes of a pointillist painting*.

This is of course the most 'felicitous' form of *easel* painting, just as 'revolutionary' in its subjects as AKhRR, which takes pride in its affinity with the Wanderers.[12] Hence the success of the *Cine-Pravdas* that are always top-ical, i.e. *thematically effective*, rather than of *Cine-Eye* which is thematically less satisfactory and which in its non-primitively agitational moments (its major part) *miscarries because its formal effectiveness is impotent*.

Vertov takes from his surroundings the things that impress *him* rather than the things with which, by impressing the *audience*, he will plough its psyche.

The practical distinction between our approaches emerges most sharply in the limited amount of material that *The Strike* and *Cine-Eye* have in common. Vertov considers this to be virtual plagiarism (there's not much material in *The Strike* that would make you rush to *Cine-Eye*!); in particular, the abattoir that is *recorded* in *Cine-Eye* and *gorily effective* in *The Strike*. (This extremely powerful effect – 'pulling no punches' – is responsible for 50 per cent of the opposition to the film.)

Like the well-known Impressionist, *Cine-Eye*, sketchbook in hand (!), rushes after objects as they are *without rebelliously interrupting the inevitability of the statics of the causal connection between them, without overcoming this connection through a powerful social-organisational motive but yielding to its 'cosmic' pressure.* Vertov uses the fixing of its external dynamics to mask the statics of a manifest pantheism (a position that in politics is characteristic of opportunism and Menshevism) in the dynamics of the methods of alogism,[13] in this context a purely aesthetic concept: winter-summer in *Cine-Pravda* no. 19,[14] or simply through the short footage of the montage fragments, and he dutifully reproduces it in sequences of quite impassive consistency.*

[All this is] instead of (as in *The Strike*) snatching fragments from our surroundings *according to a conscious and predetermined plan calculated to launch them at the audience in the appropriate combination, to subjugate it to the appropriate association with* the obvious *final ideological motivation.*

You should by no means conclude from this that I am not prepared to eliminate the remnants of the theatrical element that is organically inconsistent with cinema from my future works, perhaps through that *apology for a predetermined plan – the 'production' –* because the important element – *the direction (the organisation of the audience through organised material)* is, in this particular instance of cinema, possible, and not just through the *material* organisation of the effective phenomena that are filmed but *optically*, through the actual shooting. Whereas in *theatre* the director, in his *treatment*, recarves the *potential dynamics* (statics) of the dramatist, the actor and the rest into a

---

* With reference to Vertov's static quality, it is in the final analysis interesting to note one instance from one of the most abstractly *mathematically* successful places in the montage: the raising of the flag over the pioneer camp (I don't remember which *Cine-Pravda* it is in). This is a striking example of resolution, not in favour of *the emotional dynamism* of the actual fact of the flag being raised, but in favour of *the statics of the examination* of this process. Apart from *this* directly sensed characterisation, there is in this context a characteristic deployment in the actual technique of montage of (for the most part, short sequences of) *static* (and, what is more, *contemplative*) *close-ups* that are, of course, because of their tri- and quatercellular quality, ill fitted to dynamism within the shot. But here, in this particular instance (and it should be noted that, generally speaking, this method is very widespread in Vertov's 'style') we have, as it were, brought into focus (the 'symbol') the relationships between Vertov and the external world that he is examining. We are face to face with precisely that montage 'elaboration' into a dynamic of static fragments.

We should also bear in mind that in this case, and in that of exposed montage material, the montage combination bears the *ultimate* responsibility.

socially effective construction, here in *cinema*, *by selective treatment*, he recarves *reality* and real phenomena through montage *in the same direction*. This is still *direction* and it has nothing in common with the *passionless representation* of the Cine-Eyes, with the fixing of phenomena that goes no further than *fixing the audience's attention*.*

The *Cine-Eye* is not just a symbol of *vision*: it is also a symbol of *contemplation*. But we need *not contemplation but action*.

It is not a 'Cine-Eye' that we need but a 'Cine-Fist'.

Soviet cinema must cut through to the skull! It is not 'through the combined vision of millions of eyes that we shall fight the bourgeois world' (Vertov): we'd rapidly give them a million black eyes!

We must cut with our cine-fist through to skulls, cut through to final victory and now, under the threat of an influx of 'real life' and philistinism into the Revolution we must cut through as never before!

Make way for the cine-fist!

---

* Justice requires me to note that Vertov is making attempts at a different, an *effective*, organisation of material, particularly in the second reel of the *Lenin Cine-Pravda* (January 1925). It is true that here it still shows itself for the moment in the form of a groping towards ways of 'tickling' the emotions, in the creation of 'moods' with no consideration of the use that they might be put to. But when Vertov progresses beyond this first stage of mastering effect and learns to provoke the states of mind he requires in his audience and, through montage, supplies the audience with a predetermined emotional charge, then . . . there will be scarcely any disagreement between us – but then Vertov will have ceased to be a Cine-Eye and will have become a *director* and perhaps even an 'artist'.

Then we could raise the question of the use by someone of certain (but by whom and which?) methods because it is only then that we shall be able to speak *seriously* of certain Vertov methods which in the meantime lead only to the intuitive method he has expounded of the practice of his constructions (which, in all probability, Vertov himself acknowledges only faintly). We must not call *practical skills a method*. In theoretical terms the doctrine of 'social vision' is nothing more than an unconnected montage of high-flown phrases and commonplaces that in montage terms yield easily to the simple montage 'sleight of hand' that he is attempting with conspicuous lack of success to substantiate and extol.

5. **The Method of Making a Workers' Film**[15]

There is *one* method for making *any* film: the montage of attractions. For what this is, and why, see the book *Cinema Today*.[16] In this book – albeit rather confused and unreadable – my approach to the construction of films is expounded.

Class character [*klassovost'*[17]] emerges:

1) *in the determination of the purpose of the film*: in the socially useful emotional and psychological effect that excites the audience and is composed of a chain of suitably directed stimulants. I call *this socially useful effect the content of the film*.

Thus, for instance, you can define the content of the production, *Can You Hear Me, Moscow?*.[18] The maximum tension of the aggressive reflexes of social protest in *The Strike* is an accumulation of reflexes which make no allowance for relaxation (satisfaction), i.e. a concentration of the reflexes of struggle (a raising of the potential class tone).

2) *in the selection of the stimulants themselves*. In two directions. In the correct evaluation of their inevitably class-based effectiveness: i.e. a particular stimulant is capable of provoking a particular reaction (effect) only from an audience of a particular class character. To achieve a more specific effect the audience must be even more unified particularly if this is done by profession: any producer of 'living newspaper' performances in the clubs knows, for instance, the difference between an audience of, let us say, metal workers and one of textile workers who will react quite differently and in different places to one and the same work.

Class-based 'inevitability' in matters of effectiveness is easily illustrated by the hilarious failure of one attraction that has had a very powerful influence on film-makers in the context of the worker audience. I have in mind the slaughter [sequence in *The Strike*]. Its exaggeratedly bloody associative effect on a certain stratum of the public is well enough known. The Crimean censors even cut it along with the latrine scene. (One of the Americans who saw *The Strike* pointed out that such harsh effects are unacceptable when he said that this scene would have to be cut out for showing abroad.) But on a worker audience the slaughter *did not have* a 'bloody' effect for the simple reason that the worker associates a bull's blood above all with the processing plants near a slaughter-house! While on a peasant, used to slaughtering his own cattle, there will be no effect at all.

The second aspect of selecting stimulants is the *class-related acceptability* of a particular stimulant.

Negative examples are: the variety of sexual attractions that lie at the basis of the majority of market-oriented bourgeois films – leading one away from the concrete reality of a method like, for example, the Expressionism of a *Caligari*[19] – the sweet petty-bourgeois poison in the films of Mary Pickford[20] that exploit and train by systematically stimulating the remaining petty-bourgeois inclinations even among our healthy and progressive audiences.

Bourgeois cinema is just as aware as we are of these kinds of class-based 'taboos'. Hence, in the book *The Art of the Motion Picture* (New York, 1911)[21] in the analysis of thematic attractions in a list of themes unsuitable for use first place is given to '*the relationship between labour and capital*', closely followed by 'sexual perversions', 'excessive cruelty', 'physical deformity'. . . .

The study of stimulants and their montage for a particular purpose should provide comprehensive material on the question of *form*. Content, as I understand it, is *the summary of the series of shocks* (to which you wish to subject the audience in a particular sequence). (Or, put crudely: a certain percentage of the material fixes the attention, another percentage provokes anger, and so on.) But this material must be organised in accordance with a principle that leads to the desired effect.

Form is the *realisation of these dimensions* in a particular raw material by creating and assembling precisely those stimulants that are capable of provoking the necessary percentages, i.e. the concretising and the factual aspects of the work.

We must, moreover, remember particularly the 'attractions of the moment', i.e. the reactions that erupt temporarily in connection with particular currents or events in public life.

In contrast to them there is a series of 'eternally' attractional phenomena and methods.

Some of these are useful from the class standpoint: for example, an epic of class struggle inevitably has an effect on a healthy and integrated audience.

And on a level with these are the 'neutrally' effective attractions like, for instance, alogisms, death-defying stunts, double meanings, etc.

Their independent use leads to *l'art pour l'art* whose counter-revolutionary essence is obvious enough.

As with the attractional moments, which we must not use to gamble on the events of the day, we must never forget that the ideologically acceptable use of a neutral or accidental attraction may serve only as a method of provoking those unconditioned reflexes that we need, not for their own sakes but to train the conditioned reflexes that are useful to our class and which we wish to combine with the defined objectives of our social principle.

6. Constanţa
(Whither 'The Battleship Potemkin')[1]

'But where does the *Potemkin* go?' That is a question that very many viewers ask. They met, they waved, they passed, but where did they go?

This is not, of course, just the average man in the street's curiosity or a worker's thirst for knowledge gaining the upper hand over his consciousness of the great public significance of the fact that the admiral's squadron did not open fire.

In the light of this revolutionary consciousness, the maximum conceivable in the circumstances, making the *Potemkin* (the moral victor over the guns of tsarism) into the occasion for an anecdote, albeit a sublime and tragic one, about a 'wandering ship' is, however, to demean the significance of this event.

We stop the event at this point where it had become an 'asset' of the Revolution. But the agony goes on.

The bewilderment of the audience does of course testify to something else: how far the squadron's refusal to open fire is seen in the present state of consciousness as something natural and proper rather than as something 'striking'.

Hence the inconceivability of this event today seems very 'average' to the audience, who have in short 'waved', and their interest is transferred from the great significance of the event to its anecdotal aspect, 'what comes next?'

Perhaps we should prefer it if the audience did not know. Perhaps it is a matter for our conscience. But that is immaterial here.

What is material is the fact that the critics unfortunately do not act in the way my audiences do.

God Himself commanded them to examine the question, 'Where does the *Potemkin lead*?' That is, to draw conclusions from it on matters of film policy.

Instead they write me compliments or they dig out who I 'stole' it from and they do it so intensely that I begin to think of myself as a 'thief of Bagdad'.[2]

The term 'thieving' is just as appropriate here as it is to the confiscation of Church valuables. But we shall return later to the 'Church's right' to the valuables confiscated.

Now we shall try to plot the course taken by the *Potemkin* and determine its further voyage

The time has come to establish the NEP tactic in art – and remember that, despite the NEP of the nepmen, NEP is still Ilyich's [Lenin's] most inspired tactical manoeuvre.

What characterises NEP in formal terms? It is the achievement of a particular effect by methods that are the logical opposite to the trend being followed: moving towards socialism by trading, and so on.

It is just the same in policy for the arts.

If people ask me what I myself value in *Potemkin* I tell them it is the fact that it is the first step in the 'NEP' phase of the struggle.

Because in *Potemkin* the complete review of attractions (albeit of *The Strike*) and the positive effect (the pathos) – the stern appeal to activity – are achieved by three 'negative' methods, all of them the methods of passive art: doubt, tears, sentiment, lyricism, psychologism, maternal feelings, etc. These elements are removed from the harmony of their traditional composition with the resultant 'withdrawal symptoms', with a suspension of reality and other pacifying effects (Chekhov, *The Station Master*[3]). These elements of 'right' art are dismembered and reassembled 'business fashion'. In a new setting. This is the bourgeoisie forced to work on a *subbotnik*![4]

It is not my fault that I am not a lyric poet. But our contemporaries are even less to blame if, after the battle, they need a dose of sentimentalism. I consider that it is only through sentimentalism that they *can be given the necessary*, correct, left, *active 'once over'*.

Do you really think that the classic 'mists' (a masterpiece of Tisse's photography) are my 'nightingale's song'?! (It's as if, in making propaganda for co-operation, you were to set yourself the ideal of turning the future USSR into an All-Union Muir & Merrilees.[5]) Not at all, I admire them as a sharply honed razor that will cut the viewer 100 per cent in the place that needs it at a particular moment. The mists in *Potemkin* are the 'cows' in *The Strike* . . . amended for the year that has passed!

In reflexology[6] the term 'stimulant' encompasses at the same time both the blow of a stick on the pate and the softness of pale blue light.

As far as *methods* of influence are concerned *Potemkin* is not a continuation of *The Strike* but a contrast to it. The full force of psychologism is here contrasted with the plotlessness, the protocolism, the abstract naturalism and, if you will, the Cine-Eye qualities [*kinoglazistost'*] of *The Strike*. In a new role, certainly, and by new methods. The object is not just an illustration acting as an object (an accordion, a toilet); the object is psychologised both by way of its positioning and in its very presentation: the rotation of the gun is an action but not by virtue of its presentation. The 'roaring lions' are the clearest instance of the new psychologism, the apogee of the psycho-effect elicited from the *object*. The skiffs and the battleship act not through *formal* juxtaposition but through a profoundly psychological contrast – the defenceless clinging to the strong. How many times have I heard how 'touching' destroyer no. 267 appeared, so 'tiny' beside the battleship. But in the encounter with the squadron the machines were almost like the heart of Harry Lloyd,[7] jumping out of his waistcoat because it was so agitated!

Let us compare the 'water hosing' sequence in *The Strike* with the 'Odessa Steps'. The difference is colossal with due regard for the technicism of public sentiment – ascertaining what was the basic emotion of the mass that was just making heroic progress with *construction* – the hosing sequence is elaborated as illustration, logically, as a technical analysis of the combination of bodies and rushing water. On the whole, that is how *The Strike* (or more accurately 'an illustration of the strike') was constructed. The 'Odessa Steps' sequence appeared at the time of an emerging flood of emotionalism. It is no accident that this flood of emotionalism overflows when women Party members leave their Party work and return to their families. A part of the worker's personality is *demobilised* for his personal life, his 'experience'. The resolution of this problem is quite different: a factual line (means and effect: there, water and bodies – here, shots and people falling) demoted to at least a secondary role, and a combination of boot and body, a combination of a 'psychological' rather than a 'production' effect, not to mention the 'episodisation' of the theme of fear that is indiscriminately resolved in *The Strike*, for instance, by a montage of the shot and the carriage.

The continuity from *The Strike* to *Potemkin* lies in the development of a pathos emerging dialectically in *The Strike* that is based on the principle of abstraction and logical technicism.

The Strike is a treatise; *Potemkin* is a hymn.

With *Potemkin* we reach a new era, that of the new psychologism.

What will it be like? . . .

But first, a series of resolutions we must make about it:

1. There is one thing we have no right to do and that is to *make generalisations*. The current phase of audience reaction determines our methods of influence: what it reacts to. Without this *there can be no influential art and certainly no art with maximum influence.*

2. However much the real state of affairs may be unsympathetic to the preceding period and however much it may contradict it we are obliged to produce a slogan that derives from it. We have no right to alter our policy in the name of scholastic doctrines (and that is what even the *most topical* of *yesterday's* slogans is). Art admits *all* methods except those that fail to achieve their end. It was Voltaire who said, 'Au théâtre il faut mieux frapper fort que frapper juste!' [In the theatre it is better to strike hard than true.]

3. What else do we not have a right to? In the 'slippery' methods that are standing in wait for us we must remember this with particular force. We have no right to only one thing that these dangerous attractions of tomorrow used to serve as – a means of 'lulling' the audience – and we must direct all our resources towards ensuring that art always exacerbates a current conflict rather than distracting audiences from it. The bourgeoisie is a great expert in smoothing over the critical questions of the present day which are so brilliantly resolved by the philosophy of 'happy endings'.

Hence the governing philosophy for the coming psychologism – no rigid development of psychological problems in the 'general sense' but on the level of a newspaper satire – is that you will pay some attention to the most painful current question that needs to be resolved, the question that, even though you cannot resolve it in the particular context, compels you not to 'gloss over' it but to *pose* it in concrete form.

We are, alas, on the threshold of a similar theatrical phenomenon in literature, Tretyakov's brilliant *I Want a Child*.[8] We shall see if the theatre staging it proves to be at the same peak of topicality!

It is in this that we find our guarantee against non-topicality and figurative (or, even worse, 'historical', i.e. narrative) psychologism.

4. Lastly – we must not drop the level of the qualifications of mastery and *formal* forward progress in our methods of handling the means of influence.

This concludes the concrete details on the theme 'Whither the *Potemkin*'.*

A more precise specification would be dogmatic charlatanism and playing with words. The question can be resolved only by selecting a new object from the raw material, selecting it properly from the point of view of the right theoretical presupposition and . . . the right intuition in the treatment of it – an intuition that, while not yielding to dissection or close analysis, can none the less be considered a powerful but for the time being an unknown form of energy.

For those of us who take our stand on the basis of the montage of attractions, this change is neither an overturning of the foundations of cinema nor a change of course in understanding our cinema. For us it is the next consecutive change of attraction – the next tactical manoeuvre in the attack on the audience under the slogan of October.

---

* This is enough to define the raw material for the treatment.

7. However Odd – Khokhlova![9]

The eighth of March rang out.

The pages of *Pravda* shimmered with: a woman captain, a woman mechanic, a woman master.

The film factory committees held fervent meetings for 'Women's Day'.[10]

Women's victories on all fronts were being celebrated.

Meanwhile darkly, as always, and only on the film front we heard: he can't add a master actress to the galaxy of master seamstresses.

They won't let an actress begin as a mistress.

Because on what we might call the cultural front – in cinema – a woman actress used to be a mere 'female'.

As far as the women's question is concerned our cinema is like pre-revolutionary Bombay and its nine hundred naked women in cages.

Let there be 'Komsomol girls', 'peasant women', 'women chieftains' but 'practice' requires that: a Komsomol girl must be chubby, a peasant woman must be fat, a woman chieftain must usually be a really 'meaty piece'.

Otherwise the public won't come.

Our cinema officials cling tenaciously to the traditions of the capitalist concept of women on the screen. When they say actor, they are recalling and demanding the mastery of Lon Chaney, Stroheim or Barthelmess.[11] The concept of a woman master, of an artist with equal rights, is not recognised here.

We are sufficiently grown-up to judge Valentino, Novarro[12] and others as 'mere good lookers'. As far as the culture of the actor is concerned, we require a high level of industrial technique.

The artistic councils of the studios look at a woman through the eyes of a primeval cattle-breeder.

The power to 'tie and untie the bonds' is a terrible economic power against which there is no appeal – and it's in their primeval hands.

Their deciding veto falls like a shattering blow and . . . for a second year Khokhlova sits idle without work. For a second year Kuleshov is not directing a film.

This is a luxury of positively tsarist proportions, given the miserable state of our reserves of real masters, directors and model actors.

Khokhlova has, of course, a talent for acting for today that is perhaps the only one of its kind that is worthy of serious mention.

She represents a stake in mastery. And one that is distinctively *original*.

She is neither a 'Soviet Veidt' nor a 'Soviet Pickford'. America and Europe have no knowledge of this kind of thing. They do not have it.

71

Priscilla Dean tries in some of her films (e.g. *The Virgin of Stamboul*[13]) to pass the severe test of 'male' technique but she rapidly and hopelessly slides into the ample beds of the Glorias, Barbaras and Leatrices.[14]

America is possessed by the ideal of the petty-bourgeois 'Bathing Girl'.[15]

The very 'existence' (presence) of Khokhlova frustrates that ideal. The firm grip of her bare-teethed grin tears to shreds the hackneyed formula of the 'woman of the screen', the 'woman of the alcove'.

Hence traditions are turned upside-down. But our Americanised executives see this as a pogrom.

Khokhlova can create a whole genre.

Khokhlova is precisely the raw material we can 'use' to make our own pictures. She has that 'uncommon' (extraordinary) quality that a clever boss would pay large sums for and out of which he would make a great deal more.

A limited company called 'Khokhlova-Film' has been set up abroad. But here she is consigned to the dusty stage props.

As always the inadequacy of straightforward honest ability to take responsibility is concealed by high-flown phrases: 'Khokhlova is decadent. Khokhlova is bourgeois . . . .'

That's what I want to dispute!

Even if in their search for genre Khokhlova and Kuleshov have not yet found the right solution, branding them as 'generally bourgeois' and depriving them of the opportunity to find their proper usefulness is sheer stupidity and bad management.

To define the genre for a great talent, especially one as varied as Khokhlova, is not such a simple matter. It is only now with *Sally of the Sawdust* that Carol Dempster[16] has found her rightful place and this after working for so many years with the patriarch himself, Griffith, and thinking that her vocation was for playing touching little girls in ringlets. (Read the ecstasies over *Sally* in the American press which wrote about her long years of melodramatic exercises with more than mere restraint.).

In this country we do not know how to tell when the material itself is at fault and when it is the *particular case* of the treatment. Here things are either criminally contrived (*The Bear's Wedding*[17]) or 'absolutely' incompatible. Some idiots are prepared to find a dialectic in the art of Ekaterina Geltser (*Art for the Workers*).[18]

What is more, they forget that 'everything is relative', that nothing is absolutely harmful or absolutely useful and that on the whole there can only be something that is used or for the moment not yet used intelligently.

Khokhlova has to be provided with a sharply Soviet repertoire and a proper interpretation to match her essential qualities.

Firmly rejecting demonic women, adventuresses and the rest, I would plait her hair, dress her in a *sarafan*[19] and release a cycle of grotesque comedies on a 'town and country' theme with the screen's first woman film

Eccentric *Khokhlova* (*Dunka in GUM*, *Dunka on the Bus*[20] or other titles of that sort).

Then perhaps I'd tag Okhlopkov[21] on to her and make a pair of real 'film masks', alive like the plaster figures of a man and a woman that you see on any chest of drawers or window-sill.

To keep Khokhlova, who is, I repeat, perhaps our only original actress, 'veiled' is simply criminal.

8. Eisenstein on Eisenstein, the Director of 'Potemkin'[22]

I am twenty-eight years old. I studied for three years until 1918; I wanted originally to be an engineer and architect. During the Civil War I was a sapper in the Red Army. At about this time I began to devote my free time to the problems of theatre and art: I had a lively interest in theatre history and theatre problems. In 1921 I joined the Proletkult organisation as a set-painter. It was the Proletkult Theatre's task to find a new art form that corresponded to the ideology and the actual state relations of the new Russia. The Theatre consisted of young workers who wanted to create a serious art and who brought with them a really new spirit and a new view of the world and of art. At that time these workers conformed completely to my artistic views and requirements, although I really belong to another class and came to the same point of view only through a purely theoretical analysis. In the years that followed I had to struggle hard. In 1922 I became sole director of the First Moscow Workers' Theatre and I got involved in the most violent differences of opinion with the leaders of Proletkult.[23] The Proletkult people shared Lunacharsky's view: they favoured the utilisation of the old traditions and were not afraid of compromise when it came to the question of relevance of the pre-Revolutionary arts. I was one of the most uncompromising champions of LEF, the left front, which wanted a new art that corresponded to the new social relationships. All the younger generation and all the innovators were on our side then, including the Futurists Meyerhold and Mayakovsky:[24] ranged in bitter opposition against us were Stanislavsky the traditionalist and Tairov the opportunist.[25]

I was all the more amused when the German press identified my 'simple people' as actors in the Moscow Art Theatre, my deadly enemy.[26]

In 1922 and 1923 I produced three dramas for the Workers' Theatre: the principle behind their production was the mathematical calculation of their effect and at the time I called them 'attractions'. In the first play, *Enough Simplicity for Every Wise Man*,[27] I tried like a Cubist to dissect a classical play into its individual effective 'attractions' – the setting for the action was a circus. In the second play, *Can You Hear Me, Moscow?*,[28] I worked more with technical resources and attempted to calculate mathematically the illusive potential of the art of drama. It was the first success for the new theatrical effects. The third play was called *Gas Masks*[29] and it was played in a gas works during working hours. The machines were working and the 'actors' were working: it was the first success for absolute reality, for objective art.

The path from this concept of the theatrical to film was now no more than simple consequence: only the most inexorable objectivity can be the sphere of film. My first film appeared in 1924; it was made in collaboration with the people from Proletkult and was called *The Strike*. It had no plot in the conventional sense: it depicted the progress of a strike, a 'montage of attractions'. My artistic principle was therefore, and still is: not intuitive creativity but the rational constructive composition of effective elements; the most important thing is that the effect must be calculated and analysed in advance. Whether the individual elements of the effect are devoid of plot in the conventional sense or whether they are linked together by a 'plot carcass', as in my *Potemkin*, I see no essential distinction. I myself am neither sentimental nor bloodthirsty nor especially lyrical, as has been suggested to me in Germany. But I am very well acquainted with all these elements and I know that one has only to stimulate them skilfully enough to provoke the necessary effect and arouse the greatest excitement. That is, I believe, a purely mathematical affair and it has nothing whatsoever to do with the 'manifestation of creative genius'. You need not a jot more wit for this than you need to design a utilitarian steel works.

As for my attitude to film in general, I must admit that by 'film' I understand tendentiousness and nothing else. Without a clear idea of the why and wherefore of a film one cannot, in my view, start work. Without knowing which latent moods and passions one has to speculate on (excuse this expression: it is 'not nice' but it is professional and it hits the nail on the head) one cannot create. We whip up the passions of the audience and we must therefore provide them with a safety-valve, a lightning-conductor, and this lightning-conductor is tendentiousness. I think that the avoidance of tendentiousness, the dissipation of energies, is the greatest crime of our age. What is more, tendentiousness in itself seems to me to provide a great artistic opportunity: it has by no means always to be as political, as consciously political as in *Potemkin*. But if it is completely absent, if people think of film as a plaything to pass the time, as a means of lulling and putting to sleep, then this lack of tendentiousness seems to me merely to reinforce the tendentious view that people are leading a glorious and contented existence. Just as if cinema's 'congregation', like the church's, should be brought up to be good, quiet and undemanding citizens. Isn't this the sum total of the philosophy of the American 'happy ending'?[30]

I have been criticised because *Potemkin* (and the German version has toned down the political purpose considerably) is too full of pathos. But are we not human beings, do we not have passions, do we not have aims and purposes? The [film's] success in Berlin, in post-war Europe, in the twilight of a still tottering and insecure status quo, had to mean an appeal to an existence worthy of mankind: is not this pathos justified? People must learn to hold their heads high and feel their humanity, they must be human, become human: the intention of this film is no more and no less.

The Battleship Potemkin was made for the twentieth anniversary of the 1905 Revolution. It had to be ready in December 1925 and that gave us three months. I believe that people in Germany too will regard this as a record. I had two and a half weeks for the editing and there were 15,000 metres altogether.

Even if all roads lead to Rome and genuine works of art do in the final analysis stand on the same spiritual level, I must nevertheless insist that this work has nothing to do with Stanislavsky and the [Moscow] Art Theatre. But it has just as little to do with Proletkult: it is a long time since I worked at that theatre. I have, as it were, organically transferred to cinema whereas the Proletkult people are still wedded to theatre. But in my view an artist must choose between film and theatre: you cannot 'do' both together if you want to achieve something important.

In *The Battleship Potemkin* there are no actors. There are only real people in the film and it was the director's job to find the right people. It was physical appearances rather than proven artistic abilities that were decisive. The opportunity to work in this way is of course only available in Russia where each and everything is a matter for the state. The slogan 'All for one and one for all' was not confined to the screen. If we shoot a film about the sea, the whole navy is at our disposal; if we shoot a battle film, the Red Army joins in the shooting and, if the subject is an economic one, then the commissariats assist. Because we are not making films for me or for you or for any one person but for us all.

I anticipate enormous successes from co-operation in the film field between Germany and Russia. The combination of German technical resources and Russia's feverish creative drive is bound to produce something out of the ordinary. But it is more than questionable whether I myself might move to Germany. I should not like to leave the land that has given me both my strength and my subject matter. And I think people will understand me better if I refer to the story of Antaeos[31] rather than explaining the relationships between artistic creativity and the socio-economic base in Marxist terms. In addition it would be quite impossible for me to work, given the orientation of the German film industry towards cliché and commerce. There have of course been films in Germany that one had to respect but now people are wearing themselves out – I exclude *Faust* and *Metropolis*[32] – in absurd trivialities half-way between pornography and sentimentality. People in Germany have no guts. We Russians break our necks or we win the day and more often than not we win the day.

[I shall stay at home. I am now shooting a film about the development of agriculture in the countryside, the intense struggle for a new agriculture.[33]]

9. Béla Forgets the Scissors[34]

Balázs's article will surprise some people. Without its concluding stipulation: 'The cameraman is the alpha and omega of film.'[35]

We have such respect for foreigners that we might consider this a 'blessing'. The idiots on the Moscow evening paper who accorded recognition to the exercises by young Frenchmen that Ehrenburg brought from Paris have declared the article to be a 'revelation'.[36] These are sheer *enfantillages* – 'children's playthings' – based on the photographic possibilities of the photographic apparatus. I am not exaggerating when I say that: if we have these 'children's playthings' today, tomorrow they will be used to refurbish the formal methods of a whole branch of art (for instance, the 'absolute': the plotless film of Picabia, Léger or Chomette).[37]

We are taking our conviction that light can come only from the West to the point of absurdity.

Professor Meller journeyed to London, to the egg market. To seek out standard eggs.

He found unusual ones.

A search began.

Which farms, which ranches, which plantations? Where did this unusual breed of hens come from? Through a chain of Dutch egg wholesalers, agents, contractors and intermediaries they were traced to . . . the Novokhopyorsk district.[38] This 'Sirin', 'Alkonost', 'Firebird' turned out to be a peasant's hen.[39]

A peasant's hen from the Novokhopyorsk district. And a London market. . . .

But the hen is not a bird and Balázs is a great authority. Such a great authority that at a stroke his book is translated, published and paid for by *two* publishers. Why not, if it's all right to make *two* films from the same material? One set at sea, one in the mountains, and so on.

To understand Béla Balázs's position you have to bear two things in mind: the first and the second. The first is the basis (not the economic one): *where* and *for whom* his report was written. *Filmtechnik* is the organ of the German cameramen's club.[40]* Give the cameraman his due or, more exactly, give him the position of respect that he deserves – that is its fighting slogan.

But that is already an integral feature of the economic basis.

The cameraman achieves. He is obliged to achieve 'self-determination'. To us this kind of programme sounds somewhat savage.

What? In the cultured West?

---

* I refer those who are interested to nos 1 and 2, which contain a lengthy report by the most respected German cameraman Karl Freund (*Variété*, *Metropolis*) about the aims and purposes of the club.

Yes. In the cultured West. The steel jaws of competition in the Western metropolis are not accustomed to thinking of the 'service staff' as individuals. The director is just acceptable. But in fact the hero is of course the commercial director. And the cameraman? Round about where the camera handle ends, that's where this . . . mechanic apparently begins.

In the advertisements for *Potemkin* even the heroic Prometheus[41] wanted at first to leave Eduard Tisse[42] out altogether. So strong is the tradition. That is not surprising because in the UFA-Haus – the multi-storey headquarters of Universum-Film-Aktiengesellschaft[43] – they don't even know men like Karl Freund or Rittau[44] by sight. That's how it is. They told us themselves. Whereas even we know them by sight. They are like the Novokhopyorsk eggs . . . only from the Cöthenerstrasse, where UFA shares its enormous building with the 'Vaterland', the largest café in Berlin. And not for nothing. It is not coincidental that this corner is swarming with swastika-wearers (German Fascists) distributing news-sheets and leaflets. UFA will follow suit.[45]

The *Tägliche Rundschau* of 12 May 1926 writes:

> The declaration by the board of the leading German film organisation UFA of its truly national and commonsense interests is undoubtedly *a slap in the face* for the Committee of Censors: 'In view of the character of the political inclinations of the film we decline to include *The Battleship Potemkin* in the distribution plan for UFA theatres.'[46]

On the same subject *Film-Kurier* writes that, 'The wrath of a businessman who has missed the brilliant commercial success of the season is understandable.' But in other ways UFA remains true to itself. And not only UFA but Phoebus and the others, whatever they are called.

The cameramen are setting up a union to defend the character of their *activity*.

That is the first thing. It explains the emphatic nature of Balázs's positions.

The second thing concerns that same economic basis. Balázs is unaware of collectivism not just in film but also in its production, in work. There is nowhere that he can have seen it. He is due in the USSR in July. Then he'll realise. In Germany man is to man as wolf is to wolf and the link between the director and the cameraman is the banknote. Unity through non-material interest is unknown there.

Balázs's 'starism'[47] is the individualism of bourgeois countries in general. They do not think beyond this in the West. Someone has to be the 'star'. *One* person. Yesterday it was the actor. This time let's say it's the cameraman. Tomorrow it will be the lighting technician.

The idea that a film is the result of *collective* efforts goes to the devil. What about the man who is nearly dying from the heat of the burning sun, who has to be sponged down, the man Kivilevich whom nobody has ever heard of, who is bent down under the weight of a lighting mirror and dares not move in case a shaft of light should run across little Abraham while he's being trampled on the Odessa Steps?

Or what about the heroism of the five striped assistants?! The 'iron five',[48] taking all the abuse, shouting in all the dialects spoken by the crowd of 3,000 extras who were unwilling to rush around 'yet again' in the boiling sun. Leading this human current behind them. Regardless of its mood. By their own example. And what about the Odessa crowd itself?!

What of Kulganek, Stepanchikova, Katyusha, Zhenya, who stayed up *three nights in succession* to edit the negative for the demonstration copy that was shown on 28 December in the Bolshoi. Do you realise *what* it means to edit a negative of 15,000 metres down to 1,600?!

Who remembers them? . . . Even in our own country. Cheap over-time workers who were viewed with suspicion by the work inspectorate. Their collective enthusiasm a mere debit in the 'administrative plan'.

Balázs cannot yet conceive of the idea of the cameraman as a free member of a *union of equally creative individuals*, not the cameraman as a 'star' but the camera operator as a co-operator. There the camera crew is a transient pact between self-seeking individuals, here it is a 'creative collective'.

In his approach Balázs makes the same mistake in his theoretical principles as he makes in his section on creative organisation. Because he dissociates himself from a rigid view of the *externality* of the shot, from 'living pictures', but bases his view on the *figurative quality of the shot as the decisive factor*, he falls into rigidity himself in his definition of methods of influence.

It cannot be the decisive factor. Even though it responds to such an undeniable sign as the specific result of specific (i.e. peculiar to it alone) characteristics of the instruments of production, i.e. it corresponds to the possibilities that are the exclusive prerogative of cinema. But Balázs's individualism encourages him to dwell on this.

The shot itself as 'star'.

His stipulation about the staccato effect between 'beautiful shots' is extremely woolly even in the case of 'symbolic shots' because for Balázs the compositional harmony would be preserved in the film as a whole. He does not mention the conditions for a 'genetic' (constructive) amalgamation of the shots.

A long time ago, before *The Strike* was released, we wrote in Belenson's ill-fated book *Cinema Today*[49] opposing the individualism of the West: '*a)* down with individual figures (heroes isolated from the mass), *b)* down with the individual chain of events (the plot intrigue) – let us have neither personal stories nor those of people "personally" isolated from the mass. . . .' It remains to add one more 'down with' – the personification of cinema in the *individualised shot*. We must look for the essence of cinema not in the shots but in the relationships between the shots just as in history we look not at individuals but at the relationships between individuals, classes, etc.

In addition to the lens Balázs has forgotten another *defining* 'instrument of production': the scissors.

The expressive effect of cinema is the result of juxtapositions.

It is *this* that is specific to cinema. The shot merely *interprets* the object in a setting to use it in juxtaposition to other *sequences*. That is characteristic. Balázs always says 'picture', 'shot', but not once does he say '*sequence*'! The shot is merely an extension of selection. That is, the selection of one object rather than another, of an object from one particular angle, in one particular cut (or *Ausschnitt*, as the Germans say) and not another. The conditions of cinema create an 'image' [*obraz*] from the juxtaposition of these 'cuts' [*obrez*].

Because the symbolism (in the decent sense of the word!) of cinema must not be based on either the *filmed symbolism of the gesticulation* of the filmed person, even if there is more than one (as in theatre) or the autonomous pictorial symbolism of the emerging shot or picture (as in painting).

However strange it may seem, we must not look for the symbolism of cinema – for its own peculiar symbolism – in the pictorial or spatial arts (painting and theatre).

Our understanding of cinema is now entering its 'second literary period'. The phase of approximation to the symbolism of *language*. Speech. Speech that conveys a symbolic sense (i.e. not literal), a 'figurative quality', to a completely concrete material meaning through something that is uncharacteristic of the literal, through *contextual confrontation*, i.e. also through *montage*. In some cases – where the juxtaposition is unexpected or unusual – it acts as a 'poetic image'. 'Bullets began to whine and wail, their lament growing unbearably. Bullets struck the earth and fumbled in it, quivering with impatience' (Babel).[50]

In cases other than those of traditional juxtaposition the meaning acquires its own autonomous sense, distinct from the literal, but no longer featuring as an element of its figurative quality (no literary Darwinism!). The notion of 'swine' has its own independent legitimacy and nobody thinks of the figurative fascination of the results of 'swinish' behaviour. Why? Clearly there is little demand. But figurative expression, generally speaking, forever represents a 'mutation' that emerges only in context. When someone says, 'I feel crushed', you still do not know whether 'grief' or a 'tram' is responsible. It becomes obvious from the context.

But Balázs gets bogged down in skiffs and his own definitions which are far removed from ours: the effect of hauling down the sails (simultaneously) appears to have been *created* by the symbolism of the collective gesture (*Gebärde*) and not by the lens.[51] The way the image is cut [*obrez*], of course, is here exactly as decisive – no more, no less – in the final analysis as the Sebastopol fishermen's union *in toto* once they are resolved and able to 'symbolise' this scene!

Nevertheless we must welcome Balázs for his good intention of constructing a cinema aesthetic on the basis of the possibilities that are unique to cinema, i.e. on pure raw material.

In this respect he has, of course, rather fallen behind the USSR. But we must not expect a man to discuss the 'montage shot' when this concept is generally unknown in Germany.

There are 'literary' shots and 'pictorial' shots, i.e. those that tell us what is happening (an acted sequence), and those that constitute a *performed* intertitle (the scriptwriter's responsibility) or a series of easel paintings (the cameraman's responsibility).

Germany is unaware of the *director's shot that does not exist independently but is a compositional shot, a shot that, through composition, creates the only effect specific to cinema thought.*

People still speak of 'American montage'.[52] I am afraid that the time has come to add this 'Americanism' to the others so ruthlessly debunked by Comrade Osinsky.[53]

America has not understood montage as a new element, a new opportunity. America is honestly narrative; it *does not 'parade' the figurative character of its montage but shows honestly what is happening.*

The rapid montage that stuns us is not a construction but *a forced portrayal, as frequent as possible, of the pursuer and the pursued.* The spacing out of the dialogue in close-ups is necessary to show one after another the facial expressions of the 'public's favourites'. Without regard for the perspectives of montage possibilities.

In Berlin I saw the last two reels of Griffith's 1914 film *The Birth of a Nation*: there is a chase (as always) and *nothing* formally different from more recent similar scenes. But in twelve years we might have 'noticed' that, apart from its *narrative* possibilities, such – 'if you'll pardon the expression – montage' could offer the prospect of something more, something effective. In *The Ten Commandments*,[54] where there was no special need to portray the Jews separately, the 'Flight from Egypt' and the 'Golden Calf' are shown without recourse to montage but, technically speaking, by long shots alone. Hence the little nuances of the composition of the masses, that is the action of the mass, go to the devil.

In conclusion, a word about Béla Balázs's style. His terminology is unpleasant. Different from ours. 'Art', 'creativity', 'eternity', 'greatness' and so on.

Although some prominent Marxists write in the same dialect and this counts as dialectics.

It looks as if this style has become acceptable.

10. The Two Skulls of Alexander the Great[55]

In every decent private collection you will always find two skulls of Alexander the Great: one when he was fifteen years old and the other when he was forty-five.

Cinema stands in contrast to theatre like two completely different elements. Correct. Like different ways of thinking. Also correct. Like influences that operate through quite different methods. Correct again. Such contrasts are not without their uses. We still have so little practical acquaintance with methods of influencing people that these contrasts are by no means superfluous.

But suddenly someone comes up to us and says: 'Now you're a Catholic, a Stundist,[56] or an Anabaptist or some such (a cinematographer). You're probably made to go to a mosque or a pagoda (stage a theatre production). Make another change.'

Comrades, we can talk, make distinctions and comparisons between Buster Keaton's locomotive and a long-distance express. At any rate in circumstances where considerations of time and space are not applicable. This may even be very instructive. But, if you wanted to go somewhere, you would take an express and not *Our Hospitality*.[57]

If you move away from this kind of abstract Formalist point of view and begin to view theatre and cinema in a general perspective, seeing the dynamics of the development of a revolutionary spectacle as a single gradual process, you will realise the obvious absurdity of this outlook. The two skulls of Alexander the Great at different ages confront one another, laughing scornfully and baring their teeth.

In the general run of events it is, of course, cinema that has outgrown the fifteen-year-old head of theatre by forty-five years.

In other words cinema is the contemporary stage of theatre. The next, consecutive phase.

Theatre as an independent unit in revolutionary construction, revolutionary theatre as a problem, has virtually ceased to exist. The universal fraternisation is not surprising. It is nothing to quarrel with.

Four productions have rapidly taken theatre to its limits: beyond these limits theatre has ceased to be theatre and has had to become an apparatus of real social utility.

Four productions. The last in theatre.

The Magnanimous Cuckold[58] posed the question of the organisation of displayed movement. With particular reference to the actor. It led to the organisation of human movement in everyday life and to the establishment of pedagogical institutes of everyday management.

Enough Simplicity for Every Wise Man[59] laid bare the mechanism and the essence of theatrical effect in its 'montage of attractions'. The next stage is the replacement of the intuitively artistic composition of effects by the scientific organisation of socially useful stimulants. Psychotherapy through entertainment methods.

Earth Rampant[60] was an experiment in the organisation of mass manifestations. The theatrical collective as a particular instance of the mass. The 'staging' of public holidays, court hearings, conferences, etc. in advance.

Gas Masks[61] with its general aims and its tendency towards the material was the last possible attempt within the confines of theatre to overcome its sense of illusion. The montage of effects was composed of real, materially existing constants and objects: the factory as an element in the show and not as a mere 'receptacle' for it, the production processes and situations as part of the action, etc. – in fact that was already almost cinema, which builds its effects on precisely that kind of theatrical 'material' through montage juxtaposition.

None of the first three witnessed their next stage. Theatre surrendered on these points. Only my *Gas Masks* led completely logically to *The Strike* as its next stage structured entirely around the fact that it was contained within it as a 'stunt'. A real stunt is innovatory. It represents a small fragment of a *future stage* borrowed for a present-day production.

The whole 'point' of the matter lies in this dialectically occurring detail that places the whole order of things in doubt or negates it. The order which this detail will at the next stage overturn.

In other instances theatre, by remaining within its own confines, has discounted itself as an organism with developing form. There can be no more 'stunts', comrades, within the 'grand style'. It cannot be moved any further!

Theatre is like a telescope. The greatest possible magnification. But, as the magnification increases, the intensity of the light decreases. There is apparently a formula devised by Nikolai[62] that defines once and for all the limit of possible magnification. On the basis of these two factors. The same formula also governs theatre. The limitations of its gradual movement and development are well known. People try to avoid them rather than cross them. They prefer to run round desperately in circles on the revolving stage of *The Warrant!*[63]

Not forwards, but backwards. So biomechanics becomes 'biomechanical ballet' and is indistinguishable from all Goleizovsky's other dances in *Give Us Europe!*.[64] The search for working clothes becomes the green and gold wigs of *The Forest*,[65] and so it goes on.

At best these will create a storm in a teacup. A shock like a 'damp squib'. Then theatre will return to its good old position. It will once more become a church, a school, a library. Whatever you will. But by no means an apparatus for independent aggressive opportunities, a blow aimed at life, etc.

A megaphone. An intermediary. And that's a good thing. In the final analysis, its general role in social organisation is important. It is not important that from now on this role, although it will be fulfilled in theatre, will be fulfilled by bypassing theatre.

83

Roar, China!, The Storm, The Meringue. . . .[66] What's theatrical about them? They are brilliant journalism. A response to urgent enquiries.

For the moment it doesn't matter a bit that *Roar, China!* is a first-rate play, *The Meringue* an insignificant one, and that *The Storm* is not a play at all – no staging, no acting, but a bit of genuine civil war. Perhaps for this reason almost the most remarkable thing we've seen on the boards for the last few years.

In whatever formal sense you like the actual object is now taking over. Form in theatre has ceased to slumber. And not by chance.

There's no point in perfecting the wooden plough. The tractor has been invented. Drawing attention to the success of tractorisation, i.e. to cinema, and organising life through clubs are the task of every serious theatre worker.

11. The German Cinema.
A Traveller's Impressions[67]

While I was in Germany with Eduard Tisse, the cameraman, I visited the big film centres.

The largest covered studio in the world is situated at Staaken, a few kilometres' journey from Berlin. This vast studio is housed in a former Zeppelin hangar. The large-scale scenes in *The Nibelungs*, *Metropolis*[68] and other big pictures were filmed here. They shoot mass scenes with 3,000 people in this studio. The studio has five power-stations of its own, producing 12,000 amps of direct current and an unlimited amount of alternating current. It is interesting to note that the staff servicing this vast undertaking consists of 225-250 people in all.

Then we visited the smaller but better equipped studio at Tempelhof.

The next largest German film-producing centre is Neubabelsberg. The studios are small and they are used only for filming trifles. But the sets that are being erected for filming at Neubabelsberg are really enormous. The most successful sets are being retained for future films. The Gothic cathedral from *The Chronicles of the Grey House*[69] has been preserved there as has the ancient castle into whose moat they threw live frogs during the filming 'for atmosphere'. This moat with its live frogs is still complete and untouched. Neubabelsberg is notable for an exceptionally well-built Berlin street. It was used in the film *The Last Laugh* with Emil Jannings in the principal role.[70] The same street has already been used six or seven times for various films and in *The Fire*[71] it is burnt to the ground. All these sets are made on a stock basis. They take planks that are 3 or 4 metres long, make them into a cross shape and, using large concrete foundations, they erect colossal buildings. They have a whole series of pre-built walls, towers, etc. to which they can attach various sets as required. You can see how solidly these structures are built from the fact that for *Metropolis* the entire square that was built for the film was specially covered in asphalt, which we cannot always manage even in real cities. Apart from the fact that all new sets become part of the stock held, their individual and best-made details are preserved in full. Thus, for instance, there is an enormous quantity of windows and doors built in various styles. All these things are made with typically German precision. For example, I saw the carved altars made for *Faust*:[72] they are an exact copy of the ones in Nuremberg. All these difficult, painstaking and expensive works are made with documentary precision.

Two mechanical elephants have been made for *Faust*. They walk and move like live ones. These elephants are better made than the dragon in *The Nibelungs*. A monster horse has also been made for *Faust*: people will fly on it in the Walpurgis Night scene. The studio has a permanent menagerie. Apart from the commonly used animals, it also contains rare species of animals and birds, like, for instance, white peacocks.

In Neubabelsberg they are currently making a film about cats. The director who is making the film made his name with his first film *Cock-a-Doodle-Doo*, which depicted the loves and adventures of hens. Now, however, he is making a cat film in which the mother cat saves her kittens from a fire, etc. For this film UFA is keeping fifteen different breeds of cat in special cages.

Of the sets that have been preserved I must single out the model of a provincial German town that was built for the film *Waltz Dream*[73] based on the operetta by Oscar Strauss and that will be in great demand for future productions.

As far as the actual 'principle' behind these sets is concerned, it has to be said that we must not be too carried away by dreams of creating a similar cine-city. I suggest that the impoverishment of German cinema on the artistic level derives in part from the fact that what might be called its cinematic 'being' is entirely determined by 'consciousness'. There the sets are devised in the mind 'once and for all' within pre-determined limits and these sets cannot produce an independent charge from the material to add to the director's intentions. This is especially true when only the lower part of the set is built and the upper part is filmed simultaneously through trick photography. This kind of limited number of simply pre-determined points of view removes the opportunity for new discoveries on the spot and does of course mean that directorial invention is impoverished.

In German production conditions the opportunities that the USSR gives us are quite unthinkable. The resources we had for *Potemkin* 'slayed' the Germans: the fact, for instance, that we were given command of the streets, that we were allowed to cordon off the Odessa Steps for six days and film there. These conditions are quite unthinkable in Germany. If we had had to film a city street in Germany we should have had to pay more money in bribes alone than the cost of the whole picture.

The Battleship Potemkin made an enormous impression on the Germans but they said that in the film there were quite simply not enough men and women in love with one another and uniting at the end. That would give them what they need. It is curious that, after seeing *The Strike* in Odessa, the actor Saltykov once sighed and said, 'If only it were me against that background!'

In Germany a director is very rarely able to display the breadth of his initiative and skill. This usually happens if he can exploit the competition between two firms. For example, the transfer of the major part of the shares in UFA to the Deutsche Bank was marked by the fact that the Deutsche Bank embarked on a production like *Metropolis* to show how much richer it was, and how much greater its potential, than the bank it was competing with. That was the origin of this grandiose film. The tendentiousness of *Met-*

ropolis is quite obvious: it is a pure *agitka*[74] and you can see the Deutsche Bank behind it.

In Germany I got to know the scriptwriter for *Metropolis* and *The Nibelungs*, the wife of the director Fritz Lang, Thea von Harbou.[75]

When I asked what the idea behind the film was, because there are rumours in Germany that *Metropolis* is a revolutionary film and that it will be a great success in Russia but will scarcely be shown at all in America, Thea von Harbou said, 'It is, of course, difficult to say in two words, but the message of the picture is that there must be some kind of compromise between the men who work with their hands and the creative brain of the factory owner.'

It is personalised in this way: a girl worker in a white coat like Ophelia falls in love with the son of the man who owns the factories. The plot develops to the point where the workers revolt, destroy the machines, tear down the city of Metropolis and face certain death because they are incapable of creating anything. Then they turn to their former 'leader' (for this, read: boss) and there is a reconciliation between them: against this background the lovers are united. I leave the reader to judge how 'revolutionary' this is.

The director of *Metropolis* is Fritz Lang. Who is this Lang? The man who took *Metropolis* six million marks which not unnaturally left an impression. Facially he resembles Kuleshov if the latter had been well fed over a period of time. This similarity extends to the sphere of taste. The style and spirit of *Metropolis* are extremely close to what Kuleshov was endeavouring to do, and in part did, in *The Death Ray*.[76] Quite simply the special 'denuded' style that is characteristic of Kuleshov is also noticeable in Lang. If you gave. Kuleshov six million marks he would do just as well.

As far as the organisation of artistic work among film workers themselves is concerned, it has to be said that the kind of collective approach that we have, that is developing and that must exist, cannot be discerned at all there. People there are held together exclusively by financial interest. Give any cameraman an extra hundred marks and he will go and join the next firm without hesitation. There the cohesion of ideas is replaced by the drill and discipline of the establishment. The conditions in which workers have to work are quite dreadful. This is how they treat the workers in one firm, for instance: their only right is to know in the evening whether they will be taken on the following morning.

If shooting is postponed all the workers are laid off for the day with the right to come back the following morning and ask whether they are needed.

As for the work of the director, despite the great precision and thoroughness, both outwardly and in terms of the sets, the situation as far as the internal technical organisation of the director's work is concerned is, for the most part, as dismal as it is here. The director does not give the actor any substantial instructions.

The actor lamely copies the director without knowing what the director wants. The director shouts and forces the actor to redo it a dozen times without giving him any instructions. By chance it all works out the twelfth time, more or less. They begin shooting. During the shooting things do not, of course, go well. The actor does not know what he has to do whereas the most elementary instructions would have been quite enough.

It transpires that sometimes they film a 'passage' as many as twelve times and the thirteenth time they rehearse it to no avail. (What a passage!)

We watched the filming of *Faust* in Tempelhof. Jannings is playing the part of Mephistopheles in the film.

German film production has been cut back by 70 per cent and is gradually falling into American hands.

Firms that used to make large-scale productions are now going over to making small-scale films which they exchange for films imported from America.

I think that *Metropolis* and *Faust*, if the economic situation in Germany does not change, will probably be the last large-scale national films. The rest will be trifles.

We had one other task: to force *Potemkin* through the censorship. Some of the details are interesting. The German censors cut out the scene where the officer is thrown into the water but it was all right for the doctor to be thrown into the water because he was, after all, the 'original cause' of the mutiny by the Black Sea Fleet. He committed the sin of lying and vice must be punished. So they allowed us to throw just the doctor into the sea. A close-up of a Cossack was also cut. The motive behind this was that the brutality of the Tsar's Cossacks was so well known in Germany that showing them once more than was necessary would only harden the public.

As is well known the War Ministry has forbidden members of the armed forces to see the film.

In total the censors cut 29 metres out of *Potemkin*.[77]

12. Give Us a State Plan[1]

I

There is no doubt that cinema, regardless of whether you view it as an art or an industry, suffers from many shortcomings. The most important, to my mind, is the fact that until now work in cinema has not been organised in accordance with the principle of the planned economy.

A State Plan for cinema is conspicuous by its absence. The production of films is significantly less well organised even than the production of home-distilled spirits [*samogon*]: in the case of the latter there is a localised division of the relevant market between individual producers.

This makes itself felt particularly in work on anniversary films.

Having some experience in that field we are inclined to the view that the absence of a planning system is one of our gravest misfortunes and the cause of all the unpleasant aspects of our work.

A work conceived on a monumental and thematically exhaustive plane must be compared to the composition of a goods train loaded with a mass of uniform material. It is only then that the possibility arises of evaluating the theme fully: the material completely covers the sector that is being explored.

The length of a train like this is a completely relative measurement but it is obviously greater than the length of any film that is being contemplated.

Anniversary themes (e.g. *The Year 1905, October*) are conceived only in series: the chronological and social weight of the material dictates that it be grouped compositionally into independent artistic units. It must, however, be noted that emotional correspondences that are repeated in each grouping are perfectly possible. But more of this in detail later.

Hence, when the anniversary train, loaded to the limit with valuable material, sets off on its path towards montage lists and the camera lens, it becomes quite obvious that only Gosplan[2] should control the points for this journey.

The train either does not follow the single track of a single film or it follows it at snail's pace. A whole series of wagons has to be despatched on to branch lines, whole groups – the units of uniform material – have to travel side by side but cannot travel in the general sequence.

This makes one think enviously of Thomas Ince,[3] a director-producer who divided even plot films according to their raw material, which he distributed to several different directors to work on at the same time.

His films were released on time.

Planning undoubtedly manifests itself in this unwelcome kind of standardisation.

But Ince's methods are useful if deployed in another way. Especially for anniversary films.

When Soviet cinema joined the ranks of those celebrating the anniversary of 1905, it was extremely badly handled: nobody knew where to begin. The themes of the proposed films overlapped.

Exactly the same thing happened for the anniversary of October. The scripts for *October* and *The End of St Petersburg* had to be forcibly divided on to different tracks when shooting was already under way: there was an obvious recurrent overlap in the material, particularly on the ethnographical and compositional level.

The revolution in Moscow was removed from the script of *October* because of lack of time but Barnet hurriedly filmed the same subject before the actual tenth anniversary.[4]

Had a State Plan existed, the production of anniversary films would have been organised in a fundamentally different way: the material of this single immense subject would have been conveyed in wagons on parallel tracks from the station of departure.

The subject would immediately have been secured in different sectors.

The State Plan must be the basis of film work.

Had that been the case we – personally – should not have needed in the course of each work to leave behind us a virgin land of unploughed, as yet unnecessary, material.

In that case we should not have had to reject many interesting things merely because their real-life dimensions were significantly greater and did not correspond to their artistic dimensions.

In that case there is no doubt that the need for forced and cruel selection would have disappeared.

The subject we were set would not have been transformed into a dream that could not be realised for crudely realistic and everyday reasons.

Creative work on broadening our horizons and on reducing the train's load would not have been stranded up a siding, restricted by the pages of a calendar that are being torn off or are still untorn, up a siding, a blind alley of unplanned time.

The past convinces us of this with tragic insistence.

II

If we take a retrospective look at our past anniversary works (even *The Strike* may be counted as having an anniversary purpose), we see how the raging of creative tension, expressed in the full load of a single train, incurs an inevitable penalty as the iron strength of this principle acts, invariable in its ever tightening movement in relation to any kind of material.

Our works – *The Strike*, *The Battleship Potemkin* and *October* – finally and inevitably served as the measure of those sectors of the circle of what was originally envisaged, sectors which willy-nilly emerged as 'representatives' of the ideas of a general mass of material loaded at the first station. These films passed through all the usual stages, and everyday and artistic conditions stimulated work on narrowing them down: the result of this narrowing down was useful in those instances where the most important thing, the ideological 'change' and the specification of the excised material, was preserved.

Perhaps the most noteworthy thing was the fact that the principle of diverting a wagon, a principle that had played a subconscious role in our work on *The Strike*, was recognised with some embarrassment as a necessary evil in *Potemkin* and had already emerged as an unavoidable stage in our work on *October*.

The film *The Strike* furnishes the most conclusive evidence of the steady uncoupling of wagons from a moving train. In the process of reworking the film the seven reels of our original conception grew through a full load of 'atmospheric' material into seven parts of a series.

In so far as the themes of our first work in cinema could be defined as 'the technique of struggle for the Revolution' ('From the underground to the dictatorship' it was called in short), we sooner or later came to the conclusion that the material could only be organised on – at least – seven levels closely bound to one another by the tempo and the sense of the transitions from one stratum to another.

The outline of our work on *The Strike* was mapped out as follows:

1. *Geneva – Russia*. (The technique of secret police work, the Black Cabinet,[5] police spies, revolutionary contraband, agitational literature.)
2. *The Underground*. (The technique of underground organisational work, underground printing presses.)
3. *The First of May*. (The technique of organising illegal May Day meetings.)
4. *1905*. (Demonstration of its characteristic features as the conclusion of the first stage of the Russian Revolution.)
5. *The Strike*. (The technique and method of revolutionary responses by the proletariat to the reaction.)
6. *Prisons, Revolts, Escapes*. (The technique of organising escapes, prison revolts, etc.)
7. *October*. (The technique of seizing power and establishing the dictatorship of the proletariat.)

A vast corpus of material, in terms both of everyday life and of ideas, from the whole underground history of the last quarter of a century of the Russian Revolution, was packed conveniently into the schemas of these distinctive educational films. As far as the organisation of things was concerned, we had already mapped out a long-range plan for the future. *1905* and *October* had already entered the orbit of our attention as subjects suitable for treatment.

But even the most primitive map immediately demonstrated to us that what we had devised was unrealisable at the present time: to realise it, seven locomotives would have to be coupled to the seven trains of the general theme and set in motion along seven parallel tracks.

Even Goskino put only one locomotive at our disposal. It took the *Strike* train.

To *The Strike* fell the responsibility of being the plenipotentiary representative of all our initial cinematic methods.

But the remaining material, six immobile projects for trains, lies in enforced oblivion in the depot of our creativity, waiting for the time when that same Gosplan will switch the points.

III

The theme of *1905* was outlined as an epic of events that had in fact been thoroughly researched.

As a demonstration of the stern annals of the revolutionary struggle.

For this reason the plan for the organisation of the film immediately required a complete reworking of the material.

Of the events covered by the script it was necessary to show:

1. The Russo-Japanese War. 2. The month of January and the ensuing wave of strikes. (A 'roll-call'.) 3. Peasant disturbances. 4. The General Strike and its liquidation. 5. The violence of the forces of reaction, the Jewish pogroms, the Armenian massacre. 6. Krasnaya Presnya.[6]

1905 was written by Agadzhanova-Shutko.[7] The Party commissioned her to 'script' an epoch and this immediately defines the full seriousness of her task. And, while we helped Agadzhanova to formulate what she had conceived in cinematic terms, she furnished the fundamental basis, creating the trampoline for the whole production.

She combined a whole mass of material into a single idea based on facts, she established the atmospheric and emotional value and character of *1905*.

Working with an author so close to the events of the period it was difficult to divest ourselves of a certain range, undoubtedly too much for a single film, in our inclusion of the raw material of the period. But, in the final analysis, *1905* was not supposed to be a *single* film. To make up for it, this work introduced a specific feeling for the period, which is the most valuable quality in any script, but especially in a historical one.

In this instance the charge turned out to be so fundamental that, even with the surrender of material due to the forced compression from a ten-reel epic into *Potemkin* (which itself developed from a half-reel episode into a film in its own right), this fermentation continued to react, determining even the new introductory, detailed or episodic material – unforeseen by the script – in the field of purely directorial work.

It was, by the will of the fates and because of the poor organisation of cinema, to *Potemkin* that the task fell of 'representing' the whole of 1905. Of course it by no means exhausts *1905* and *Potemkin* remains a fragment of a great epoch.

IV

The initial sketches for *October* were as usual broad in scope. The raw material that was absolutely essential and socially significant was gathered in a relatively short time. Literary and real-life sources gave us the opportunity to operate using the most varied objects. The first versions of the film encompassed, in chronological order, the stages of the Revolution from the overthrow of the monarchy to the end of the Civil War and the transition to peace-time construction.

The material included: the February Revolution, the organisation of the Provisional Government, the patriotic demonstrations in June, the 18 June offensive and the rout of the Russian Army, Lenin's arrival, the July days, the preparations for October, the organisation of the Military Revolutionary Committee, the October upheaval in Petrograd, the storming of the Winter Palace, Moscow in October, the funeral of the victims of the Revolution, the support for the Revolution from the Peasant Assembly, the Junker uprisings, the organisation of the White Guards on the Don, the Don government, the march on Moscow, the Civil War, starvation and devastation, the 'iron torrent', the stratification of the peasantry, the partisan war, the intervention, the Congresses of the Soviets, the execution of Nicholas II, the assassination of Mirbach, the formation of the Red Army, the merger of the partisans with the Red Army, the symbolic struggle of the Red Army with the Hydra of counter-revolution, synthesising in montage sequence the victory of the Revolution on the whole front ending with Perekop.[8]

When this vast train, loaded with a solid mass of material, was firmly settled on the rails, the formidable principle of forced selection came into play, consigning the cargo at its own discretion either to the screen or into oblivion.

October was an overtime job: our main job was and is *The General Line*, a film that we consider to be the next new stage in our film work. We had temporarily to put a full stop after this line and make *October*.

Time, inexorable like the board of Sovkino, has guillotined works that, because of their specific gravity, would inevitably have developed into separate films (like, for instance, *The Iron Torrent*).[9] In order to avoid this peculiar 'budding' of our routine work we rejected sectors of material that were historically and compositionally necessary. The surrender of material was carried out with unusual cruelty and with the routine sighs about the State Plan.

The damage done to the material did unprecedented violence to the nature of the film. Time compressed and nullified things that could never have been called superfluous.

The script for *October* was compressed not according to principle, but according to area: the front, as envisaged, went; Moscow in October went; the Civil War, the partisans went, as did a great deal of integral material that was harmless in terms of its composition but whose existence required something like Thomas Ince's system.

Although others filmed in parallel on the same theme we still suggest that the anniversary theme is as yet far from exhausted. The tractors whose movements are not organised by a single will do not plough the fields.

Film work, especially for anniversaries, is waiting to be included in the planning system. When that happens the freight trains will perhaps arrive at their destinations with a full and valuable load.

13. Literature and Cinema. Reply to a Questionnaire[1]

1928

THE EDITORS: In our questionnaire to film workers we put these questions: 1) Knowledge of literature. Literature and cinema. 2) Is there a common style of development in literature and cinema? 3) What is required of contemporary literature, etc.?

EISENSTEIN: This is not a question about specialised knowledge (of literature).

I confess that I am very ill acquainted with literature.

I have no time to acquaint myself.

Zola[2] did more than anyone else for cinema.

I don't know to what extent he counts as contemporary literature.

If he does, he's probably classified as a fellow traveller.

There's no doubt that the trend in Soviet cinema that my works represent is close to his.

A lot of people have read him.

I reread him.

Before each new project I reread the appropriate volume of his works.

Before *The Strike*: *Germinal*.

Before *The General Line*: *Earth*.

Before *October*: *The Débâcle* for the attack on 18 June 1917 and *The Happiness of Women* for the rape . . . of the Winter Palace.

As far as I can see, I infect my film colleagues with his works. The FEKS are basing *The Storm of the Heavens*[3] on *The Belly of Paris*.

I criticised Pudovkin because he did not reread *Money* before filming the stock exchange for *The End of St Petersburg*.

It would have turned out even better if he had.

I particularly recommend him to the younger generation.

Serafimovich will do a great deal for cinema when *The Iron Torrent* is filmed:[4] in my view it is a most remarkable work. (In this case, it seems, there's no doubt that it's contemporary.)

I have worked myself up to making it on two occasions, thinking of including it in the first part of *Red Cavalry* (1924)[5] and in the post-October section of *October*.

However, on the third occasion I think I will make it.

While Zola is in the methodological sense the greatest school for a film-maker (his pages read like complete cue sheets) only two of the few contemporary writers that I am acquainted with are *in this sense* of any use to me: Babel and Fedorchenko.[6] The former will always be an irreplaceable secondary 'reader' for the new *cinema figurativeness*. A concept that has only just come into cinema. I mentioned it in passing in *Kinogazeta*[7] and I shall soon write about it in greater detail. In the meantime I ask you to take it on trust.

Fedorchenko is interesting to us in the structural sense.

Our new cinema works are 'written' in a manner close to hers.

In a logically unmotivated associative transition from one theme to another.

For instance Kornilov's 'In the name of God and Fatherland' and the triad: linking the cyclists to the Second Congress, the bomb in the Winter Palace and the Cossacks' surrender to the artillery, or the structure of the 'Damn your mother' sequence, in *October*.

There are more cumbersome instances in *The Strike*.

A People at War may help the many people who want to work in the same way.

In this respect it would be true to say that Fedorchenko is a more accessible and less expensive 'edition' of James Joyce.

Ulysses is of course the most interesting phenomenon for cinema in the *West*.

I don't know about the literary aspect but I think the same applies there.

At any rate, however odd it may seem, I am familiar with Joyce's writings.

I don't have to read him at night in a hurry, like I did Dreiser the night before my official meeting with him.

Fedorchenko and Joyce are very close to contemporary cinema. Certainly more than half way to what lay ahead.

They use the same 'de-anecdotalisation' and the direct emergence of the theme through powerfully effective raw material.

This may be completely tangential to the plot that only figures in the work because the author is conscientious.

The same 'physiologism' of detail.

In close-up.

In a purely intellectual effect, an abstract conclusion from their physiological methods.

Cinema again.

There is, of course, significantly more in Joyce.

To meet the demands of the denunciatory, polemical and other multiple tasks that *Ulysses* or *The Portrait of the Artist as a Young Man* set themselves.

Fedorchenko is more like a fixing agent but her construction is the same.

The remainder of literature seems to me, from the point of view of its utility for cinema, to be merely – although this may be more than enough – an inexhaustible fund, a storehouse of materials.

Our literature consists mainly of factual materials.

That makes them all the more valuable.

For me they constitute a large store of everyday, social, etc. 'cuttings'.

Shishkov's[8] Kirzhak partisans, for example, are remarkable, not to mention *Chapayev* and other things that have gained 'general recognition'.

Certainly newspapers, memoirs or specialised research push them in this direction more often than not.

Kondurushkin's *Private Capital and Soviet Justice,*[9] for instance, is read with more fascination, greater economy and greater profit than any novel.

It even has its own peculiar 'refinement'.

What is wrong with this extract from the minutes?

A *list* of the Usha brothers and sisters, the Leningrad speculators who were tried in 1924 for systematically offering bribes in the affair of the North Western Railway. (They escaped from the court.)

Usha, Grigori: tradesman.

Usha, Lyubov: student at the 1st Leningrad State Institute.

Usha, Khaya: student at the Medical Institute.

Usha, Alexander: tradesman.

Usha, Wulf: student at the Polytechnic.

Usha, Meyer: student tradesman.

Usha, Zoya: student.

They had a lavishly furnished four-roomed flat, two servants and a *dacha*.

It's almost like the Rougon-Macquarts.

Other books too are quite exceptional, especially semi-statistics, when they are written with somewhat greater pathos than the writings of the Procurator of the Republic.

In first place here of course are O. Davydov's *The Macloteans* and Burov's *The Countryside in Crisis.*[10]

However, I do not know to what extent this is considered to be literature with a capital 'L'.

In any event, in terms of their social 'disembowelling' of contemporary problems and in terms of their accumulation of pure raw material, these are the most valuable examples (of contemporary literature).

Whereas *Cement*[11] is not even suitable building material for cinema.

I think it would be best suited to a metal sculpture (with 'bronze' for the whites of the eyes and the hair).

As for our 'mutual relations' I can say that we have now completed the process of purging cinema respectively of:

1) Literature (primitive and operating only through plot: pure adventurism, *Rocambole, 813, The Nibelungs* or psychological adventurism, for instance *A Woman of Paris*);[12]
2) theatre (the acted genre);
3) painting (the German 'school');[13]

4) the People's Commissariat of Posts and Telegraphs (the work of the Cine-Eyes).

In beginning to discover its own particular paths cinema is now displaying once more a curious conjunction with literature but, as distinct from the first period, with literature's formal side (see above).

In this regard we may mention the fact that there is without doubt a sense of a common style of development, although 'style' is a dubious designation when the terminology of genetics or experimental biology would be more appropriate.

In our current tendency to search for forms that are really characteristic of it cinema finds its best *support* in what is happening in the field of the renewal of literary forms.

This helps us to understand better the series of problems that arise quite independently from cinema's raw material by using the experience and the analogy of a 'neighbouring' sphere.

Here literature works 'hand in glove' with the jazz-band.

In response to the question as to what cinema needs from literature we can in any case say one thing with certainty.

Comrade man of letters, don't write scripts!

Force the production organisations to buy your commodities as novels.

Sell the rights to the novel.

You must force film directors to find the *cinema equivalents* of these works. (When required.)

In this way we can conceive of both the renewal and the fertilisation of both the formal aspect of and the opportunities for cinema, and not just of the thematic or plot aspect which, in the final analysis, is successfully implemented in other forms of literature (see above).

A 'numbered' script will bring as much animation to cinema as the numbers on the heels of the corpses in the morgue.

'Writing a script is like calling out the midwife on your wedding night.' These are Babel's priceless words from the time when we were doing a script 'from' *Benya Krik*.[14]

For the 'management'. Why should I bother to build on a full-blooded novella rather than a rickety 'shooting schedule' devoid of settings or tendencies of rhythm or tempo or physiological appreciation of why it is worth paying money to authors?

This is of course a theme in its own right which should have been raised for broad discussion a long time ago.

As far as the link between cinema and literature as such is concerned, we must admit that it is liable to be a platonic one.

Cinema is sufficiently independent to fulfil the details of its directives and the social command entrusted to it directly from its own raw material, ignoring literature for 75 per cent of the time.

It has already outgrown its period as the second derivative – taking literature as the first – of everyday prerequisites and the conditions for their reorganisation.

The programme remains as it was before: 'Peace to the cottages, war to the palaces.'[15]

In admitting any interrelationship in the present period of the formation of both Soviet literature and cinema we must at the same time keep cinema, which works *directly* as *agitprop*, in perspective.

In conclusion a couple of words about the critics.

Here, in my view, things don't look good at all.

At least as far as cinema is concerned.

The majority of them are by no means dedicated to the matters they write about.

It is simply a pity for cinema when you see the microscopic detail that literary criticism works in.

The critics make their judgments on cinema purely from their own 'individual perception' or . . . by clinging to the current 'vogue' expression that has been dropped in a political report on a quite different question.

Of course even individual perception is not so bad. It does naturally depend in the first place on the individual.

Or rather on the perception.

The fact is that all is not well in this matter of perception.

The perception of the professional critic has, if you will pardon the expression, been prostituted in comparison with the real 'untainted' healthy perception of the audience.

However, the critic is 'untainted' by any specialist knowledge of cinema.

That is why he flounders like someone in an ice-hole.

He has fallen behind some people and not joined up with others.

Personally I have a great deal of respect for Blyum.[16]

In any 'sleight of hand' he always knows the right moment to shout out (in his bass voice), 'But what good is this to an audience of workers and peasants?'

That's what happened in our discussion recently of *A Woman of Paris*.

Our appraisers, especially those who are more qualified, too often forget this formula.

You will agree that it is difficult to imagine an objective positive appraisal of a film that is absolutely right but has the misfortune not to be to a particular author's 'liking'.

Our professional critics who are at heart supporters of the Mezhrabpom salon frequently quote Lenin with ostentatious enthusiasm in defence of educational films.[17]

This is followed by an audible and mournful sigh asking why Ilyich thought it was precisely these educational films that were so useful. . . .

14. What We Are Expecting from the Party Conference on Cinema[18]

The dictatorship of the proletariat, at last, and in the cinema sector: socialist construction.

   With a view to the 'moral' replacement of vodka (in all kinds of bottles, including even Mezhrabpom-Rus).

– The merger of film-producing organisations and the transfer to the merged enterprise of all cinemas.

   With a view to its 'material' replacement.

– And, in any case, a rod of iron now for all those who bring disgrace on cinema.

15. Our 'October'. Beyond the Played and the Non-Played[19]

October is ready.

Ready and not ready.

A year of quite back-breaking toil.

A year in which coping with thirty to forty hours' shooting was regarded as the easy part of our job and most of our energy was expended on a fight with the slow, sluggish and malevolent machinery of the Leningrad studio.

Towards the end this year 'flattened' us.

We had no teeth left to bite out another ten days from the inexorable deadlines.

Ten days in which to erase the last specks of material that had not been fully integrated, to tighten the screws in the framework of the film, to eradicate the repetitions, remove some superfluous 'shock troops', some identical shots that appear twice, some scenes with similar rhythms – in other words, to remove everything that neither invention nor ingenuity required.

All we needed was a clear head and a little time.

We did not manage, as it were, to redeem our new-born infant.

So the film is tainted with a certain hint of negligence which in places hinders perception and everywhere provides 'dilettanti' with ammunition for their derision.

But, even if this secondary stage of work had been completed, would *October* have displayed that same taut clarity of purpose that distinguished *Potemkin*?

Potemkin.

It would be a very great mistake to judge *October* by the criteria generated by the appearance of *Potemkin*.

Just as *Potemkin* should not be judged by the rules of *Broken Blossoms*.[20] Only an extremely superficial analysis of *October* as a work would confine itself to evaluating it from the compositional point of view: even that would become a judgment on the work itself.

A cultural analysis in this particular case must address itself above all to questions of methodology.

Because the methodology of the work has taken precedence over the construction of the work.

The methodology of the work at the expense of the work as a whole has destroyed the work.

In this lies the 'tragic fault' of the direction of *October*.

In this lies its surprise for those who expected it to be, and wanted to see in it, its elder brother, *Potemkin*.

But this 'fault' is the fault of a man whose 'voice breaks' at a certain age.

October speaks with two voices.

Falsetto and bass.

'First you hear the flute and then the piano.'

The voice has a habit of 'breaking' at a transitional age.

At an age when you are growing. The transition to adulthood.

October appears at a similar turning-point for cinema.

October spans two epochs in cinema.

The poles are: AKhRR and *zaum*.[21]

AKhRR as the forward limit of certain forms of consumerism. Of memorial tablets. Commemorative oleographs.

Zaum as that stage in the process of correctly resolving a problem when the correct forms for using the results of this resolution have by no means all yet been found.

Is *October* now unique in this respect? Or is the internal contradiction merely particularly noticeable in it?

Here we should note that development 'within the work' *at the expense of the construction* might be defined as a general characteristic of films released in the current year.

And in every instance this is a sign of internal growth.

Development to the next stage along the path of its own individual development, within the limits of its own genre.

This is accompanied by an unavoidable dialectical 'break' within the work as such, unlike the integrity of the works of the previous period.

In actual fact the complete played 'chamber' quality[22] of *The Mother* and *The End of St Petersburg*[23] is suddenly overturned in the middle of the film by a whole swarm of mass-scale and impersonally expressed methods for the social characterisation of phenomena. The disproportion in the work is unavoidable and obvious.

Measured shots, beating the intervals between the pathos-filled intertitles in *A Sixth Part of the World*[24] like the balls of an abacus, have migrated from the Cine-Eye style to an immediate proximity to the notation marks of 'absolute' films.

The Eleventh Year[25] moves in a series of fragments from a *poem of facts* to a *symphony of facts*.

At last, the routine *Bag* has suddenly given birth to . . . a mountain.

The Diplomatic Bag . . . to *Zvenigora*.[26]

'An enormous distance!'[27]

To a polygamy of approaches, styles and genres turning upside-down the very concept of genre.

The future researcher will of course know how to link a particular phenomenon – the move towards inward-looking, more profound study of the methods of a work at the expense of the composition as a whole – with the general trend towards cultural revolution, the trend towards more profound study of the problems of culture in general.

For the present I wanted here to point out the feature of the 'period' that even *October* succumbed to. In the next issue we shall dwell in detail on those elements of forward movement that have fallen to its lot.

II

When there are two contestants it is usually the third who is right.

In the ring now:

played and non-played.

That means that justice lies with the third.

With the extra-played.

With cinema that places itself *beyond* the played and the non-played.

With cinema that stands on its *own two* feet with its own, admittedly as yet undesignated, terminology.

The trend in cinema that places itself beyond this opposition emerges quite legitimately and opportunely.

At a time when the slogans of the previous stage have achieved 100 per cent success. At a time when they are generally recognised. At a time when these slogans are reduced – through the stages of obviousness, vulgarisation and truism – to the level of the absurd.

At a time like this there is usually a dialectical overturning of a similar stage by one that is clearly opposed to it.

A theoretical novelty – the 'non-played' film – has in due course replaced plot by *fact*.

Illusion by *raw material*.

Aesthetic fetishisation was replaced by a fetish for raw material.

But a fetish for material is not quite materialism.

In the first instance it is still after all *fetishism*.

When the question of the hegemony of 'raw material' merged into general usage, a hysterical scream, the 'cult' of raw material, it meant the end of raw material.

A new page has to unfold under the precisely inverse slogan:

CONTEMPT FOR RAW MATERIAL.*

This sounds terribly unfamiliar.

But:

slaves of the machine are becoming masters of the machine.

Slaves of raw material are becoming exploiters of raw material.

---

* Wherever 'raw material' is mentioned, it must be understood in the formal cinematic sense and not as something historical or factual.

If in the preceding period the material prevailed, the object replaced 'soul and mood', then the next stage will replace the presentation of a phenomenon (material, object) by a *conclusion* based on the phenomenon and a *judgment* on the material, given concrete form in finished concepts.

Cinema is ready to begin operating through the abstract word that leads to a concrete *concept*.

The new stage will come *under the aegis of a concept – under the aegis of a slogan*.

The period of the 'free market' in cinema is coming to an end.

The played 'I am jealous' (*Variété*),[28] the transitional 'We shall fight' (*Potemkin*) and the non-played 'I see' (*A Sixth Part of the World* and *The Eleventh Year*) remain a page of the calendar that has already been torn off.

What is more, material as material is refusing to work further.

Material is beginning to be viable only in conditions of 'exoticism'.

In *The Eleventh Year* it is already painful to watch the machines.

The shooting, montage and use of a working machine are becoming traditional for us, just as Runich and Khudoleyev[29] are.

But there was a time when the spinning of the wheels of a machine was enough 'in itself'.

Now the slogans surrounding the machine have become more complex – the *interrelationships* surrounding the machine have been made more complex.

While the wheels turn in the same simple way as they did before.

But 'in themselves', *as raw material*, they cannot give more than they have to give – as they say about the most beautiful girl.

The period of the fuss about material was the period of the recognition of the montage fragment as a word and sometimes as a letter.

In some reels *October* is trying to take the next step, trying to seek out *speech* that in its construction will wholly correspond to a similar vocabulary.

The sphere of the new film language will, as it happens, not be the sphere of the presentation of phenomena, nor even that of social interpretation, but the opportunity for *abstract social evaluation*.

On a primitive level this is the line of harps and balalaikas. The discrediting of deities. 'What we fought for' over the piles of mass-produced Crosses of St George. The Kornilov restoration.[30] The debunking of the Winter Palace: its 'moral' defeat in the assault on it, etc.

At first this method seemed to be connected to working elements of – and for the moment it works in the depiction of – the 'enemy'.

The rest adhered to the more or less pathetic tradition of previous works.

But, if the duality of the object weakens perhaps its power to shock as a whole, one corresponding dialectical rupture is compensated by another.

By the fact that it testifies to its viability. By the fact that it has perspective. That it contains both a promise and a guarantee of the film of the future.

We must not forget that the balanced integrity of *Potemkin* paid the price for its maximum effect in the utter exhaustion of its stylistic method.

There can be no further progress along *Potemkin*'s path. There can only be variations in the same methods, possibly on other subjects.

We must also remember that the integrity of *Potemkin* occurred at the expense of *The Strike* which preceded it and which also displayed elements of duality and the dialectic.

I have in passing heard the view expressed that the style of *Potemkin* was missing from *October* and that *October* continues the style of *The Strike*.

This is an absolutely illiterate point of view.

It is not the *style* that *October* continues but, apart from its role as a work in its own right, it still plays the role of *The Strike* in relation to the next work, which for the moment is what it has to do.

A work in which we have perhaps already managed to approximate to genuine pure cinema, cinema beyond the played and the non-played, but equally distant from 'absolute' film.

Now that we have discovered what constitutes a word, a form, a fragment of speech in cinema language, we can begin to pose the question of what we can *express cinematically* and how.

It will be the realm of stating a concept that is free of plot and of the primitive level of 'love as I love', 'tiredness – a tired man'.

It will be the art of the direct cinematic communication of a slogan. Of communication that is just as unobstructed and immediate as the communication of an idea through a qualified word.

The epoch of the direct materialisation of a slogan takes over from the epoch of a slogan about material.

The position of the slogan as the backbone of our films, at least some of them and not just 'loyal' ones, can in no way serve as an objection to what I have stated here.

The time has come to learn to make films directly from a slogan.

To replace the formula 'deriving from raw material' by the formula 'deriving from a slogan'.

After *October* we can turn our hand to attempting the appropriate resolution of the problem. Our next work will try to resolve this problem.

It will not be *The General Line*. On that same formal level *The General Line* is the contemporary of *October*. To it will fall the role of popularising the partial *zaum* of *October* by making these methods generally more accessible.

The attempt to resolve the vast and very difficult problem that *October* proclaims can only be made by our next (planned) capital work.

Because it is only along these line that the resolution of the problems that it sets itself can be imagined.

This 'capital' work will be made from a 'libretto' by Karl Marx and it will be called:

CAPITAL.

105

Since we recognise the immensity of this theme as a whole we shall shortly proceed to delimit in the first instance which of its aspects can be cinefied.

This work will be carried out in collaboration with the historian A. Efimov,[31] our consultant in the preparation of the script for *October*.

16. For a Workers' Hit[32]

We can begin as we begin a film.

Prominently, across the whole screen, foam. Mountains of foam. More mountains of foam. Nothing but whipped foam.

Out of the foam there gradually emerges a head. A heavily soaped head.

That is how the idea of someone having their hair washed,[33] or even their head examined, is shown on the screen.

You must begin with such an examination in the case of Sovkino.

The allegorical head belongs to it.

Anyone who feels like it 'purges' Sovkino. It's such a thoroughgoing attack that even Sovkino is beginning to realise dimly that it serves it right – and why. Little by little it is beginning to correct its course. To paint it red. And the signposts, if they are not actually changing, are apparently shifting a little.

No doubt Sovkino will take – and on a certain plane is already taking – a down-wind course. It is trying to take at least a few paces to ensure that it is 'in step with the demands of the broad masses'.

The masses want a film of everyday life, the masses demand a workers' film.

The demands of the masses must be satisfied – why cause unpleasantness and two or three unnecessary and tactless debates?

No doubt Sovkino will make a 'token gesture' towards 'films from working-class life'.

They are starting to prepare the scripts hurriedly. A necessary requirement is to turn production activity upside-down. And the 'conflicts' that originate in production. And the raw material. And so on, and so on, and so on.

We do not have to indulge in hypothetical baptismal processes in order to imagine the plan for the films in the immediate future.

The 'everyday workers' film' will be allocated a significant percentage in the studios' production plans. They will start work on everyday life. Everyday films will crush the audience like herring in nets.

'Rich everyday life' will start to climb out of every little hole and crack.

But . . . supposing this natural (at least in its healthy part) current were to be treacherously diverted into other channels.

If the matter is carried to extremes, either in quite a minor careless way, or else with provocative deliberation, the audience's assessment of films of everyday life will match that of the notorious 'oriental films'.

Nothing is easier than discrediting a particular genre through *inattention* or an insufficiently *serious* attitude.

107

Let us recall how all kinds of films like *Red Partisans*[34] and *The Red Web*[35] have spoiled the Civil War theme through their hack superficiality.

Add to this a little prejudice, a little evil intent. . . .

And . . . on the shelves of the warehouses of the distribution departments pathetic rows of 'films for workers and middle peasants' will build up.

They are just that: middle, middling, mediocre. In quality. In the money spent on them. In the attention paid to them.

A real recipe for setting your teeth on edge.

Films like *Bulat Batyr*[36] will go on being hits. Films like *Princess Tarakanova* will go on exhausting the funds.

Instead of throwing all their efforts and resources into raising the production of 'workers' films' to the required level and thus ensuring their profitability, instead of this they will continue as before viewing workers' films as wholesale goods:

'on everyday themes, fifty-three items, for a total sum of . . .'

For the same sum they will have found it difficult to make, let us say, seventeen other 'commercial historical', 'commercial costume' and 'commercial plot' films. . . .

But the most militant theme – the theme of everyday workers' life – will be doomed to take shelter as a 'poor relation' and in grey and cheap neglect it will gradually grow sickly, wean the audience from itself, force it to recall tearfully the 'golden age' of cinema.

The cinema of films like *The Poet and the Tsar, House of Ice, The Lame Gentleman* and others.[37]

Of course nobody says that it will be like that.

That is why the Party Conference has been called.

But there is no harm in warning.

How much more gratifying it will be if the warning is not necessary.

Now for the standardised middlebrow film.

For America it is precisely the material base of the cinema industry.

The American hit is (with a few exceptions) really a matter of advertising. It is swallowed up by production expenses or expenditure on creating and maintaining personal reputations.

A neat little film stuffs the American pocket which has been carded with the cliché of the 'middlebrow'.

The material base of our cinema too (in the production supply plan) will be secure when the regular uninterrupted release of middlebrow films is assured. But our middlebrow film is something quite different. If only because its starting-point is a recognition that we have by no means yet mastered the Ford style of film production.

Sometimes we sinfully half manage a 'hit'.

But that is after all *easier*.

It is easier to write an essay with broad appeal than it is to compress everything into two or three slogans.

And conditions for a development of this kind in our country are extremely difficult. The qualifications of a middlebrow film here cannot rest on the moulds of the market stamp.

Because of the small number of films released in this country generally, each release attracts too much attention, too much individual notice.

In this country it is impossible to exploit mass middlebrow production along the lines of a fashion that has become a hit.

In the West this is one of the principal functions of a hit. A host of minor films completely 'wear out' the costumes, the props, the inventories of the major films that have set the fashion.

Currently countless costume films are being released following the success of *Monsieur Beaucaire*.[38]

Next there will be a new flowering of 'cowboy films' if they can unearth a horse that will run fast enough.

Even our *Potemkin* contrived to inaugurate a fashion in Germany for 'steamship' pictures.

In this country, I repeat, the field of 'fashion' has no place.

In this country *every picture is accountable*. Both in the financial sense, and in the ideological sector that it resolves. It is also accountable to the section of our reality that it deals with.

It is accountable because it has no chance of 'vanishing without trace', of slipping unnoticed into the general mass.

Any mistake it makes is dangerous to the cinema's interests in the area it touches.

Cinema will not be able to engage this theme again in the near future. Remember how those middlebrow films weaned us off the Civil War – the Civil War that had entered cinema so triumphantly with the hit *The Little Red Devils*.[39]

And how quickly in our circumstances we exhaust and spoil our raw material!

We must not condemn the themes we cherish to cheap productions.

We must not condemn the basic themes of the day to the risk of being discredited because we have not devoted sufficient care and resources to them.

Let us produce hits on themes from working-class life!

A hit because it has a fighting theme.

A hit because a hit is, in our present production circumstances, the only form that gives us the opportunity, in terms of raw material, time and production conditions, to deal *seriously* with a theme and raw material.

But this raises the question that is always at the centre of attention in discussions of this kind.

The question is: can a theme from working-class life meet the other 'requirements' of a hit? This is a question not just of profitability but also of great profit.

A question of 'commerce' in inverted commas.

A question that is, alas, *decisive* in the fight between 'our' film and 'local westernised production' (*The Three Millions Trial*,[40] etc.).

The most curious thing is that the point of view that is biased in its aims in favour of 'commercial non-profitability' in this matter appears in this context to result from ideological error in dealing with the actual raw material of working-class life.

Here ideology determines commerce.

The idea has become established in this country that you can only make 'minor pictures' from working-class life. Narrowly domestic pictures. Of microscopic individual dimensions.

Completely ignoring the social milieu, the grandiose social movements producing the shocks which also determine the eruption and re-arrangement of narrow everyday movements: on the shop floor, in the family, and elsewhere.

We are already delighted that production detail is driving the 'plot' forward. The link with everyday life has been forged. Hurrah!

People neglect the presentation of the monumental turn-around in social processes that is echoed in the particular case.

Falling into ideological error, we treat the phenomenon in an unco-ordinated way, in isolation and out of context. In so doing, we are robbing ourselves of really monumental, heroic raw material that cannot be found elsewhere!

We do not know how to select a theme 'with a capital T'. How to elevate a particular case into a social epic.

I repeat, in this country the Formalist critics are awfully pleased because the trite 'eternal triangle' is motivated by the fact of production. They consider this both 'necessary and sufficient', to use the formulation of a mathematics textbook.

This fact is necessary to create a 'collision'.

But it is by no means sufficient to create a large-scale class work. Classness does not begin with the moment when the raw material is altered or with a two-line maxim at the end.

The melodrama of a particular case becomes a tragedy of great pathos when it begins to be assessed according to the scales established by the epoch as a whole.

I refer to two concrete examples of two good films that had a right to be considered large scale but did not wish to use that scale.

It is, perhaps, true that they were not given the chance to use it. Because of the general prejudice against workers' film.

I am talking about *Potholes* and *Lace*.[41]

In neither case did the film pursue a course that exhausted its theme.

The catastrophic moment for the fate of the family in *Potholes* – the glass factory's transition from making vases, jugs and other petty-bourgeois rubbish to the production of window glass – is 'played' in the film only in terms of the concomitant reduction in the work-force.

The raw material for a work of high calibre in this context is certainly not to be found in a reduction in the work-force.

The raw material here lies in the *transition* to the production of window glass.

In the factory's transition from *private* apartments to a system of *state* construction.

And, next, family life. The 'cut glasses'. Personal life that does not keep pace with the advancing step of the proletarian government.

Using this method the particular case of a 'family history' may be elevated into significantly greater generalisation, greater scope and greater breadth.

On the other hand, the moment of unpremeditated agitation for the elements of petty-bourgeois custom – the factory's original product – would be avoided.

The nice, almost irresistible features of petty-bourgeois taste, these little objects are given the 'martyr's halo' of dead 'bread-winners'. The cessation of their production leads in general to a reduction in the work-force. Redundancy. Unemployment.

Window glass emerges as the enemy.

The stomach begins to agitate on behalf of the petty-bourgeois 'cut glass that has fallen from the table'.

Beyond the window glass the construction is invisible.

The film could be elevated into a tragedy of everyday life that could not keep pace with time. With economic progress.

Lace is another good film.

It deals with the very topical theme of the fight against hooliganism. All this is centred on the problem of a wall newspaper.

That the factory in this film is a lace factory is a result of two factors: 1) these events actually took place in a lace factory; 2) an interest in the machines themselves as raw material.

I am suggesting that it would have been possible to have broadened this theme by viewing the events that occurred in a more general context.

When you think of lace production in this country in 1928 you raise the troublesome question of harmful forms of production.

We know about professional physical illnesses and injuries.

Could there be forms of production that are harmful psychologically?

How does the character of production influence the psychology of the person working on it?

When I was employed in the Proletkult workers' theatre I personally observed a quite definite psychological distinction that depended on the kind of production the lads had been engaged in.

A metal worker is not the same as a catering worker.

I made my observations in theatre working conditions. There it was curious to see how that bane of theatre, 'bohemianisation', inevitably affected the various lads.

The ones who found it easiest to submit to bohemianisation, the ones who found the transition to 'artiness' least difficult, were the ones who had worked in perfume or tobacco factories, or similar plants.

The most unstable elements, the least reliable comrades-in-arms in the cruel battle against bohemianism in the context of workers' theatre turned out to be the comrades connected with production in fields where in our conditions there must be some question mark over their commitment.

Perfumes, lace, all sorts of 'goodies'.

I do not by any means wish to say that there is no place in the context of socialist construction for *compote* or fruit drops . . . .

Similarly, I do not think that under socialism people drink tea without sugar.

But to toss out the idea that the strength of class allegiance depends on the class utility of production is to raise a theme that is in itself extremely interesting.

By bravely breaching the front of working-class themes (*Potholes, Lace*) we must strengthen our positions, showing and distributing films on these themes.

There are already precedents for that kind of understanding of narrow domestic themes.

It is true that this precedent is for the moment unique and deals with its theme in a historical cross-section of the recent past.

Showing how the uneducated village lad, the unwilling strikebreaker, the lone rebel and the 'cannon-fodder', is forged into the Bolshevik who storms the Winter Palace during the October Revolution.

I am talking about *The End of St Petersburg*.

There it is after all not the 'pace of history' that is the focus of attention but the regeneration, the fall and rise, of one particle, the overcoming of the psychology of this lone lad by the implacability of the unfolding social process.

In order to show the psychological progress inside the brain of this village lad the vast machinery of war, the stock exchange, capitalist competition and revolution is set in motion.

Pudovkin's enormous achievement lies in the fact that, in taking the individual psychological theme of the growth of class consciousness in the village lad, he knew how to elevate it by involving in the film all the social factors of a similar regeneration and thus turning – by switching to a monumental scale – a particular episode into a vast epic. A hit 'in every way'.

We are acquainted with the epic of the collective.

It is Pudovkin who has created the first epic from an individual psychological theme of the past.

The time has come for an epic on the everyday life of today.

The way is open for 'film hits' of workers' life!

17. Statement on Sound[42]

Eisenstein, Vsevolod Pudovkin and Grigori Alexandrov

Our cherished dreams of a sound cinema are being realised. The Americans, having developed the technique of sound cinema, have embarked on the first stage towards its rapid practical implementation. Germany is working intensively in the same direction. The whole world now speaks of the 'silent' that has found its voice.

We who work in the USSR recognise that, given our technical capabilities, the practical implementation of sound cinema is not feasible in the near future. At the same time we consider it opportune to make a statement on a number of prerequisite theoretical principles, particularly as, according to reports reaching us, attempts are being made to use this new improvement in cinema for the wrong purposes. In addition, an incorrect understanding of the potential of the new technical invention might not only hinder the development and improvement of cinema as an art form but might also threaten to destroy all its formal achievements to date.

Contemporary cinema, operating through visual images, has a powerful effect on the individual and rightfully occupies one of the leading positions in the ranks of the arts.

It is well known that the principal (and sole) method which has led cinema to a position of such great influence is *montage*. The confirmation of montage as the principal means of influence has become the indisputable axiom upon which world cinema culture rests.

The success of Soviet pictures on world screens is to a significant extent the result of a number of those concepts of montage which they first revealed and asserted.

And so for the further development of cinema the significant features appear to be those that strengthen and broaden the montage methods of influencing the audience. If we examine every new discovery from this standpoint it is easy to distinguish the insignificance of colour and stereoscopic cinema in comparison with the great significance of *sound*.

Sound is a double-edged invention and its most probable application will be along the line of least resistance, i.e. in the field of the *satisfaction of simple curiosity*.

In the first place there will be commercial exploitation of the most saleable goods, i.e. of *talking pictures* – those in which the sound is recorded in a natural manner, synchronising exactly with the movement on the screen and creating a certain 'illusion' of people talking, objects making a noise, etc.

The first period of sensations will not harm the development of the new art; the danger comes with the second period, accompanied by the loss of innocence and purity of the initial concept of cinema's new textural possibilities can only intensify its unimaginative use for 'dramas of high culture' and other photographed presentations of a theatrical order.

Sound used in this way will destroy the culture of montage, because every mere *addition* of sound to montage fragments increases their inertia as such and their independent significance; this is undoubtedly detrimental to montage which operates above all not with fragments but through the *juxtaposition* of fragments.

Only the contrapuntal use of sound vis-à-vis the visual fragment of montage will open up new possibilities for the development and perfection of montage.

The first experiments in sound must aim at a sharp discord with the visual images. Only such a 'hammer and tongs' approach will produce the necessary sensation that will result consequently in the creation of a new *orchestral counterpoint* of visual and sound images.

The new technical discovery is not a passing moment in the history of cinema but an organic escape for cinema's cultural avant-garde from a whole series of blind alleys which have appeared inescapable.

We must regard as *the first blind alley* the intertitle and all the vain attempts to integrate it into montage composition as a unit of montage (fragmentation of an intertitle, magnification or contraction of the lettering, etc.).

The second blind alley comprises *explanatory* sequences (e.g. long shots) which complicate the composition of the montage and slow down the rhythm.

Every day the problems of theme and plot grow more complex; attempts to solve them by methods of purely 'visual' montage either lead to insoluble problems or involve the director in fantastic montage constructions, provoking a fear of abstruseness and reactionary decadence.

Sound, treated as a new element of montage (as an independent variable combined with the visual image), cannot fail to provide new and enormously powerful means of expressing and resolving the most complex problems, which have been depressing us with their insurmountability using the imperfect methods of a cinema operating only in visual images.

The *contrapuntal method* of structuring a sound film not only does not weaken *the international nature of cinema* but gives to its meaning unparalleled strength and cultural heights.

With this method of construction the sound film will not be imprisoned within national markets, as has happened with the theatrical play and will happen with the 'filmed' play, but will provide an even greater opportunity than before of speeding the idea contained in a film throughout the whole globe, preserving its world-wide viability.

18. An Unexpected Juncture[43]

> The famous comic actor from the Maly Theatre, Givochini, once had to stand in at very short notice for the popular Moscow bass, Lavrov, in the opera *The Amorous Bayadère*. But . . . Givochini had no singing voice. 'How will you manage to sing, Vasili Ignatevich?' His sympathisers shook their heads sadly. But Givochini himself was not downcast. 'The notes I can't reach with my voice I'll point to with my hands,' he replied merrily.
>
> (Tales about Givochini)

Milk a billy-goat? Agricultural practice is unaware of the operation. It is said that a billy-goat provides neither wool nor milk. It has another firmly established reputation and other honourable functions.

But, alas . . . our critical avant-garde does not see things in that light. The Kabuki[44] theatre, that most remarkable phenomenon of theatre culture, is visiting us.

Everyone showers praise on its really magnificent craftsmanship. But there has been absolutely no examination of what constitutes its remarkable quality. The museum elements are essential to an understanding of this remarkable phenomenon but they are by no means enough. Only things that promote cultural progress, that feed and stimulate the intellectual problems of the day are remarkable. But the Kabuki is dismissed with faint praise: 'How musical!' 'What handling of objects!' 'What plasticity!' And people come to the conclusion that there is nothing to be learned, that (as one senior critic spitefully remarked) there is nothing much here that is new: Meyerhold long ago 'fleeced' the Japanese!

That is not all. Our 'venerable' critics, making general remarks in their published writings about the positive aspects of the Kabuki, are in fact offended by their own better feelings. For pity's sake! The Kabuki provides 'neither wool nor milk'. The Kabuki is conventional![45] The Kabuki does not move Europeans like us! Its craftsmanship is the cold perfection of form! And lastly the plays they perform are feudal! . . . What a nightmare!?

But to expect *Lyubov Yarovaya* from the Japanese is as naive as it would be for us to tour with *A Life for the Tsar*[46] . . . . What is more, even our revolutionary theatre has only 'chanced' upon *The Collapse* and *Armoured Train* ten years after the Revolution.[47] I suggest that, as far as the Kabuki is concerned, we can look 'over the repertoire' and expect from it no more than we expect from the Bolshoi Theatre.[48] After all, Osoaviakhim, studying the experience of the West, is not embarrassed by the fact that gas-masks are a 'product' of imperialism! The borrowing of the technical elements of foreign, even to us alien, experience is as justified in cultural matters as it is in *the practice of the country's defence provided that it is in the interests of the working class.*

It is above all its conventionalism that prevents us from making thoroughgoing use of everything that could be borrowed from the Kabuki.

But the conventionalism that we know 'from books' proves in fact to be a conventionalism that has a very curious relativity. The conventionalism of the Kabuki is far removed from the stylised and premeditated mannerism that constituted, for example, the 'conventional' in our own theatre and that was artificially transplanted with no regard for the technical prerequisites. In the Kabuki this conventionalism is profoundly logical. The same applies, indeed, to every oriental theatre: let us take, for instance, Chinese theatre.

Among the characters in Chinese theatre there is one called the 'spirit of the oyster'! Just look at the actor performing this role: his face is made up in concentric circles with distorted centres radiating out to the right and left so that they all meet at the nose, graphically reproducing the halves of an oyster shell – and it will all seem quite 'legitimate' to you! It is no more and no less of a convention than a general's epaulettes. Their narrowly utilitarian origin, once serving to protect the shoulder from possible sword blows, has given way to the stars of rank so that the epaulettes are in principle indistinguishable from the blue frog imprinted on the forehead of the actor who 'functions' as the 'spirit' of that frog!

Another kind of convention derives directly from real life. In the first scene of *The Forty-Seven Samurai*[49] Syozyo plays a married woman and appears without eyebrows and with blackened teeth . . . . This convention is no more unreal than the custom of a Jewish woman who shaves her head so that her ears are exposed or a girl who joins the Komsomol and wears a red scarf as a kind of 'uniform'.

As distinct from European 'practice', in which marriage serves as a 'guarantee' against the unpleasant aspects of free love, in Japan a married woman destroyed her attractions 'once the need for them had passed'! She shaved her eyebrows, blackened her teeth and sometimes even pulled them out! . . .*

But let us move on to the most important issue – to the conventionalism that is explained by the specifically Japanese perception of the world, to the peculiar quality that manifests itself clearly during the direct *perception* of the performance and that no *description* has managed to convey to us.

Here we find an *unexpected juncture* between the Kabuki and those extreme experiments in theatre in which it has already ceased to be theatre and has become cinema. What is more, it has become cinema at the latest stage of its development: *sound* cinema.†

---

* These traditions are not, of course, observed among the Japanese who have been Europeanised, but they are still part of the code.

† It is my firm conviction that cinema is the *contemporary stage* of theatre. Theatre in its old form is dead and, if it exists, it is only through inertia.

The clearest distinction between the Kabuki and our own theatres is, if I may use the expression, a *monism of ensemble*.

We are familiar with the emotional ensemble of the Moscow Art Theatre, the ensemble of united collective experience,[50] and with the ensemble 'parallelism' of opera (the orchestra, the chorus, the soloist). The theatre that is denoted by that nasty word 'synthetic' has added to this parallelism with 'active sets' and now that ancient 'animal' ensemble is wreaking its revenge with hooters 'sounding' from various parts of the stage in imitation of a fragment of the everyday life of the audience 'witnessing' the performance.

The Japanese have shown us a different and extremely interesting form of ensemble, the *monistic ensemble*. Sound, movement, space and voice *do not accompany* (or even parallel) one another but are treated as *equivalent elements*.

The first association that occurs to us in our perception of the Kabuki is *football*, that most collective ensemble sport. Voice, rattle, mime, the narrator's cries, the folding sets seem like innumerable backs, half-backs, goal-keepers, forwards passing the dramatic ball to one another and scoring a goal against the astonished audience.

It is impossible to speak of 'accompaniments' in the Kabuki, just as we would not say that, when we walk or run, the left leg 'accompanies' the right or that they both 'accompany' the diaphragm!

Here a single monistic sensation of theatrical 'stimulation' takes place. The Japanese regards each theatrical element not as an incommensurable unit of the various categories of affect (on the various sensual organs) but as a single unit of *theatre*.

> Ostuzhev's 'chatter' no more than the colour of the prima donna's tights, a roll on the drums just as much as Romeo's soliloquy, the cricket on the hearth no less than a salvo under the seats of the auditorium.[51]

That is what we wrote in 1923 in the June issue of *Lef*, putting an equals sign between elements in various categories when we established theoretically the basic *unit of theatre* which we termed an 'attraction'.

The Japanese, in what is of course his instinctive practice, makes 100 per cent use of his theatre in precisely the way that we had in mind then. Addressing himself to the sensual organs, he bases his calculations on the final *sum* of stimulants to the brain, ignoring *which* path that stimulation takes.*

---

* Not even the *food eaten* in this theatre is accidental! I did not manage to discover whether ritual food is eaten in the theatre. Do they eat whatever happens to be available or is there a specific menu? If the latter, then we must include the sense of taste in the ensemble.

117

Instead of *accompaniment* the Kabuki reveals the method of *transference*: the transference of the basic affective intention from one material to another, from one category of 'stimulant' to another.

Watching the Kabuki, you involuntarily recall the novel by an American writer about a man whose auditory and optical nerves were transposed so that he perceived light vibrations as sounds and air tremors as colours: that is, he began to *hear light and see sounds*. The same thing happens in the Kabuki! We actually 'hear movement' and 'see sound'.

Here is an example: Yuranosuke leaves the besieged castle and moves from the back of the stage to the very front. Suddenly the backdrop with its life-size gate (close-up) is folded away. A second backdrop is visible: a tiny gate (long shot). This means that he has moved even further away. Yuranosuke continues his journey. A curtain of brown, green and black is drawn across the backdrop indicating that the castle is now hidden from Yuranosuke's sight. Further steps. Yuranosuke moves out on to the 'flowery way'. This further distancing is emphasised by the *samisen*,* i.e. by sound!!!

The first distancing is steps, i.e. a *spatial* distancing by the actor.

The second distancing is a *flat painting*: a change of backdrops.

The third distancing is an *intellectually* conditioned sign: the 'magic' of the curtain 'effacing' our vision.

The fourth distancing is *sound*!

There was a time when we used to hold up a blue speckled board and say that it was the visual representation of the word 'Marusya', while an orange one with little green crosses represented 'Katerina' and a pink one with mauve snakes was 'Sonya'.[52] This eccentricity, this *search for an equivalent*, has been brilliantly realised in the Kabuki theatre.

Here is an example of pure cinematographic method from the last section of *Tsyusingura*.

After a shortish battle 'for a few metres' we have an 'interval': an empty stage, a landscape. Then the battle starts again. Just as we cut into a film a fragment of landscape to create a mood in a scene, here an empty snow-covered nocturnal landscape (an empty stage) is cut in.

But after a few metres two of the 'forty-seven good men and true' notice a shack where the villain is hiding (the audience knows this). Just as in cinema, there has to be some damper at a moment of such heightened drama.

In *Potemkin*, when the command to 'Fire!' on the sailors covered by the tarpaulin is about to be given, there are metre-length shots of the parts of the battleship that are 'indifferent': the bows, the muzzles of the guns, the life-belt, and so on. The action is slowed down and the tension is 'screwed' tighter.

---

* *Samisen*: a Japanese musical instrument similar to a mandolin.

The moment when the hut is discovered must be stressed. In a *first-class* work this stress must be produced from the *same* rhythmic material, from a return to the night, the emptiness, the snow-covered landscape . . . .

But there are people on the stage! None the less the Japanese work is first class! And . . . it is a *flute* that enters triumphantly! And you *see* those same snow-covered fields, that same 'resonant' emptiness and night that you '*heard*' a short while before when you were *looking* at an empty stage . . . .

Occasionally (and then it seems as though your nerves are about to *break* with the tension) the Japanese double up their effects. With the *perfect* equivalent of visual and sound mirages at their disposal, they suddenly produce *both*, 'squaring' them and aiming a brilliantly calculated blow of the billiard cue at the audience's cerebral hemisphere. I do not know how else to describe the unique combination of the *hand movement* of Itsikawa Ensio as he slits his throat in the act of hara-kiri with the *sobbing sound* off-stage that *graphically* corresponds to the movement of the knife.

There it is: 'The notes I can't reach with my voice I'll point to with my hands.' But here the voice does reach and the hands do point! . . . And we stand numbed by such perfection . . . of montage.

We are all familiar with those three trick questions: what shape is a spiral staircase? what does 'compactly' mean? what is a 'surging sea'? There are no intellectually analysed answers to these questions. Perhaps Baudouin de Courtenay[53] knows some but we respond with gestures. We demonstrate the complex concept 'compactly' by clenching our fist, and so on.

Even better: this kind of explanation is *completely satisfactory. We also show a touch of the Kabuki*!!! But not enough!

In our *Statement*[54] on sound cinema we wrote about the contrapuntal method of combining visual and sound images. To master this method you have to develop within yourself a new *sense: the ability to reduce visual and sound perceptions to a 'common denominator'*.

The Kabuki has this ability down to a fine art. We too, crossing the successive Rubicons that flow between theatre and cinema and cinema and sound cinema, must also develop it! We must learn this necessary new sense from the Japanese. Just as painting owes an irredeemable debt to the Japanese for Impressionism and contemporary left sculpture is indebted to the child of Negro sculpture, so sound cinema will be no less indebted to those same *Japanese*!

And not just to the Japanese theatre because the features I have described do, in my view, penetrate deeply into the whole Japanese perception of the world. At least those incomplete fragments of Japanese culture that have been accessible to me.

In this same Kabuki we see examples of the identical perception of naturalistic three-dimensional form and flat painting. People may say this is 'alien'! But a 'pot must boil' in its own way so that a metal dragon-fish, suspended on a thread, can 'swim against the current' up a waterfall composed of a series of vertical lines. Or, folding back the screen-wall of a strictly Cubist 'house of the vale of fans', a hanging backdrop is disclosed with a 'perspective' gallery running right down the middle. Our set design is unfamiliar with this kind of spacious set, with such primitive painted perspective. And, even more, with such *simultaneity*. Here, it seems all-pervading.

Costume. In the Dance of the Snake Odato Goro enters bound with a rope that is also given expression through the transposition of a flat rope design on his robe into a three-dimensional rope-belt.

Written language. The Japanese has at his command an apparently incalculable number of hieroglyphs. The hieroglyphs consist of the conventionalised features of objects, comprising the concepts expressed in them, i.e. *the picture of a concept*, the image of an idea. Alongside these there exists a series of Europeanised alphabets: Kata-hana, hiragana, etc. And the Japanese writes using all these alphabets at once! He thinks nothing of mixing hieroglyphic *pictures* with the *letters* of several quite separate alphabets.

Poetry. The Japanese *tanka* is an almost untranslatable form of lyrical epigram with a strict metre: five, seven, five syllables in the first strophe (*kami-no-ku*) and seven, seven syllables in the second (*shimo-no-ku*). It must be the most unusual poetry in terms of both its form and its content. When it is written you cannot tell whether it is an ornament or an inscription! It is valued as *calligraphy* no less than as *poetry*.

As for the content . . . . It is not for nothing that Julius Kurth writes of the Japanese lyric: 'Japanese poems should be *seen* (i.e. visually *presented* – S.E.) *rather than heard.**

THE APPROACH OF WINTER

They leave for the East,
A bridge of magpies in flight,
A stream across the sky . . .
The nights edged with hoar-frost
Will be more tedious still.

The magpies stretched out in flight appear to Yakamosi (who died in 785!) like a bridge cast into the ether.

THE WILD GOOSE

Wild grey goose! Wild grey goose!
Swishing in the blue
Like a house in a willow grove.

---

* Julius Kurth, 'Japanische Lyrik aus 14 Jahrhunderten', *Die Fruchtschale, Eine Sammlung, Band 17* ['Fourteen Centuries of Japanese Lyric Verse', *The Fruit Bowl. A Collection. Vol. 17*] (2nd edn, Munich, 1909), p. iv.

In flight the goose's feathers are spread out and look like trees planted round a house.

CROW IN THE SPRING MIST

The crow was perched there
Partially concealed
In the kimono of mist,
Just like a silken songstress
In the folds of her sashes.

The anonymous author (1800) wishes to convey that the crow is not quite visible in the morning mist (just as the over-large birds embroidered on the sash are not quite visible when the belt is tied).

The strict limit on the number of syllables, the calligraphic charm of the script and the comparisons, striking in their improbability, and also in their wonderful proximity (the crow half-hidden in the mist and the embroidered bird half-hidden by the folds of the sash), are witnesses to a most interesting *'fusion'* of images that appeal to the most varied senses. This unique archaic 'pantheism' is undoubtedly based on a *non-differentiation of perceptions, the well-known absence of a sense of 'perspective'*. It could not be otherwise. The history of Japan is too rich in historical experience and the burden of feudalism, although it has been outgrown politically, still runs like a red thread through Japan's *cultural* traditions. The differentiation that emerges in society during its transition to capitalism and that brings in its wake, as a consequence of economic differentiation, a differentiated perception of the world, has not yet emerged in many areas of Japan's cultural life. And the Japanese goes on thinking in a 'feudal', or undifferentiated way.

It is just the same as in children's art. People cured of blindness experience the same thing when the world of objects both far and near does not seem to exist in space but to crowd in closely on them.

Apart from the Kabuki the Japanese have also shown us the film *Karakuli-musme*. But here the non-differentiation that is brought to such brilliantly unexpected heights in the Kabuki is realised *negatively*.

Karakuli-musme is a melodramatic farce. Beginning in the style of Monty Banks,[55] it ends in incredible gloom, and in between it is criminally torn in both directions.

The attempt to co-ordinate these two elements is, generally speaking, a most difficult task.

Even a master like Chaplin, whose *The Kid* was unsurpassable in this respect, was unable to 'balance' these elements in *The Gold Rush*.[56] The material 'slid' from one level to another. But in *Karakuli-musme* there is a complete 'collapse'. . . .

121

1928

As always the echo, the juncture, is found only at the polar extremes. The archaic non-differentiated sense of the Kabuki's 'stimulants' on the one hand and, on the other, the acme of the development of *montage thinking*.

Montage thinking, the peak of the differentiatedly sensed and expounded 'organic' world, is realised anew in a mathematically faultless instrument, the machine.

We recall Kleist's words that are so close to the Kabuki theatre that derives 'from puppets': 'The perfection of the actor lies either in the body that has no consciousness at all or has the maximum consciousness, that is, in the puppet or the "demi-god".'*

The extremes meet. . . .

There is no point in grumbling about the soullessness of the Kabuki or, even worse, in finding in Sadanji's acting a *'confirmation* of Stanislavsky's theory'! Or in looking for something that Meyerhold 'has not yet stolen'!

Broadly speaking, the goat has given us milk!

The Kabuki can only celebrate its juncture with the sound film!

---

* H. von Kleist, *Werke in einem Band* (Salzburg/Stuttgart), p. 1002.

19. **The Twelfth Year**[57]

Eisenstein and Grigori Alexandrov

Many people are wandering confused in the icy draught of the unprincipled behaviour of our industry and its leadership. But . . .

> To chatter about the dialectic and about Marxism, without knowing how to combine the necessary (if it is necessary at the time) submission to the majority with revolutionary work in any circumstances, is to mock the workers and deride socialism.[58]

'In any circumstances'. This means that revolutionary work dare not slacken even in the conditions of that cursed status quo in cinema which has managed to survive the criticism and the decisions of the Party Conference 'wholly and completely'.

The 'dismal exhaustion in the "underground"'* suddenly arises in quite a different guise in the whole growth of its revolutionary class significance.

Just as it did in the revolutionary underground.

Where the iron will of Bolshevik tactics was forged.

Where the dialectic of Marxist theory was refined.

Where the fatal blows were struck against opportunism, an opponent more terrible than the gendarmerie of the tsarist butchers.

Until the class hurricane broke out in 1870.[59]

We must strike a similarly pitiless blow against the cinema opportunists and marauders who have used the 'opportunity' to unleash their shameless philistinism.

The pressure of the Revolution has not weakened.

Who is responsible for the fact that we cannot see the wood for the trees of trivial squabbling unscrupulously misused by an anaemic leadership, that we cannot see the stumps on which we shall grow the vast branches of *Bolshevik cinema*?

Bismarck said, 'You need three things to win a war: money, money, and more money.'

---

* (Note from the editors of *Sovetskii ekran*.) While giving space to this interesting article by S.M. Eisenstein and G. Alexandrov, we cannot but express our astonishment at the fact that directors whose works to a significant degree define many of the landmarks in the development of revolutionary Soviet cinema have for some reason felt that in Sovkino they are working 'in the "underground"'. Furthermore there are no grounds for tarring the whole of revolutionary cinema with the same brush . . . . However, this article signals a number of internal confusions in production and to clarify these we shall be giving space in our next issues to a series of articles by directors and activists in Soviet cinema.

123

The Iron Chancellor of Soviet cinema has selected the same formula as his motto: Soviet cinema needs three things: money, money and only money. And everything will be all right.

That is not so. It does of course need money but it needs three other things as well. These three things are: school, school and more school.

A school for ideological leadership. A school for highly qualified production. A school for film theory based on Marxist principles. (Without the latter both the first two are pointless.)

Let this year not sound with the fanfares of production.

Let it smash like granite through the dykes of the *idealistic* theory that weighs so heavily on Soviet cinema and with which our cinema has no chance of becoming Bolshevik.

The fact that a particular Mongolian film, a particular peasant film or a particular Parisian film is not too bad (we shall live to see it) has no significance for those kinds of film in general.[60] Here we have in mind the general level, the *results of the planning policy* of our production organisations and not the results of private initiative.

Let this year (when the need arises), because of the magnificent market, drive the theoretical drills more deeply under the vast bulk of reactionary traditionalism with its mass of growth that is stifling everything that is genuinely revolutionary.

The year is different and we shall blow up this Great Wall of China with a firm alliance between the nascent science of cinema and the film school that is being built.

The 'underground' twelfth year must parade beneath the emblem of the maximum possible refinement of the ideology and theory of real Bolshevik cinema culture.

We shall learn. And we shall teach ourselves how to create a theme for Soviet cinema. It's not the gods who burn the pan. We need a little perseverance and gritting of our teeth to chisel out the unyielding granite of science. Sharpen them up. The teeth will come in handy: after all even the Germany of the 'Iron Chancellor' had its 9 January.[61] Eventually the seventh day of Soviet cinema will come too.

The Revolution keeps up its pressure.

Where is the stagnation when there is such symptomatic ferment at all the stages of qualification for film workers!

1) In situations where there is weak artistic and ideological leadership there suddenly emerges an extremely significant phenomenon: the consolidation of the directors' cadres in production organisations.

We are not summoned. We go of our own accord. We ourselves get involved in the problems of leadership in the matters we are fighting for.

Concealing somewhere the evidence of squabbling and fratricide, the directors – the 'rivals' in Sovkino enterprises – form a bloc in their own metaphorical 'collective farm'. A permanent directors' section with a leadership bureau is organised for the production conference. There is, on the one hand, something in the nature of comradely mutual guarantee and support in questions of qualification and the perfection of their own work and, on the other hand, a focus for heightened attention to the problem of the ideological policy of the principle of the enterprise as a whole. We must put an end to excesses and outrages from within as well. All the more so, when the 'bosses' are fast asleep and the 'outsiders' are in no great hurry.

2) In addition young directors (some of whom have a solid professional record) are joining together into a training workshop at the State Cinema School, GTK, so that they can revise, renew and in cultural terms update their practical baggage and reduce it to a reliable theoretical saddle-bag, so that they can raise their ideological and practical qualifications and, lastly, assist in training the young people entering the school who are still quite green but who represent the future source of genuinely Soviet film directors.

3) At long last there must be an abrupt change in the teaching programmes of the Cinema School itself in favour of a single rigid system based on the principle of producing film engineers, specialist masters in the class-based formation of the consciousness of the mass audience (after years of hot-house cultivation of the creative Impressionism of various artistic 'trends').

4) This is feasible because the theoretical premises upon which it will be possible to construct a scientific approach to cinema are gradually becoming clearer. The theoretical fictions are one by one finding their way into the waste-paper basket. The illusion of contradictory principles (e.g. 'played' and 'non-played') is through practical experience finally being reduced to a dialectical interpretation of contradictions 'in a general identity' which is long overdue.

Genuinely tendentious documentarism (i.e. the really practical so-called 'non-played' film) is already a point of contact and a common language with the extreme trends in the 'played' genre (cf. *October* and Esfir Shub's *Lev Tolstoy and the Russia of Nicholas II*).[62]

It is already possible to *work* in a practical way and not to engage in scholastic sophistry.

5) Slowly but surely and in the closest possible collaboration with the Communist Academy and the State Cinema School the Polytechnic Museum's *research laboratory in audience psycho-physiology* is developing, involving and gathering people and experience in this most necessary and fundamental of labours. For the first time a thought-provoking methodology for reflexological inquiry into the phenomenon of cinema as the sum of stimulants and into the audience as the reflex subject is being elaborated where until now we have found only primitive amateurism.

6) *Komsomolskaya pravda*[63] is gathering into a fighting unit all those who are ready to do battle for genuinely revolutionary culture. The editors have formed a permanent group of people responsible for waging a cultural campaign for Soviet cinema in the pages of the militant press.

7) At long last there must be demonstrably increased attention on the

part of Rabkrin [the Workers' and Peasants' Inspectorate] to cinema, *and not just in the economic sphere*. The Socio-Cultural Department of Rabkrin must regard the problem of *film culture* as one of the most urgent tasks it has to deal with.

It is only the eighth point – the contribution of our production organisations to Soviet film culture – that remains, regrettably, unresolved . . . although it should have been the first point to be dealt with.

But, as far as the other points are concerned, as we can see, we are no longer quite so naked or defenceless in terms of our 'cultural campaign' for film culture, and, if in its triumphant 'fifth year' of production Soviet cinema has achieved a successful take-off, then an unavoidable period of theoretical respite is not so terrible.

Let us resurrect more brutally the question of revolutionary implacability on the front of the principles of Soviet film culture.

Then we shall be able to meet the thirteenth October *with a fully armed Cinema October.*

20. The GTK Teaching and Research Workshop (A Conversation with the Leader of the Workshop, S. M. Eisenstein)[64]

The rapid growth and development of our cinema, the vast accumulation of fundamental and formal experience in recent years, necessitate the most serious professional analysis and the first indications of the wholesome formal paths along which our cinema should develop further.

These considerations suggested the idea of organising a Teaching and Research Workshop. Its tasks include:

1) taking stock of our general, and my personal, experience of production, reducing this material to a unified system and underpinning it with a firm dialectical and reflexological base;[65]
2) involving the most active section of our *young production workers* in this work so that collectively we are working on raising our level of qualification;
3) posing and debating various cinema problems and *experimenting* so that we clear the way and mark out the strongholds for the further movement and development of Soviet cinema.

In the course of the past year I have been working on the methods of the film language of 'intellectual' cinema but this by no means signifies that our research work is moving exclusively in this direction.

We reject absolutely the idea that a 'single Soviet style' is inevitable and attainable and we think that different cultural consumers must be served by films that differ in their formal construction. Whereas an urban worker audience with a quite strongly developed orientational aptitude for films of the old type, for instance those with long unbroken sequences, no longer reacts *strongly* enough, a peasant audience that is significantly less advanced quite simply needs the more outmoded forms of composition.

On the other hand, to maintain that, the moment the idea of intellectual cinema emerged, the previous primitively emotional cinema had had its day, would be hopeless snobbery and a far from realistic policy.

Our responsibilities include: achieving an understanding of all genres and stages of the development of cinema so that we are able to provide every consumer with the product best suited to his particular level of cultural development. For this reason our workshop organises three cycles that are interwoven organically with one another:

1) *Human expressiveness*, a predominantly theatrical field.
2) *Montage expressiveness*, a section that encompasses at one extreme

127

E with members of the Kabuki theatre troupe, Moscow 1928

filmed theatre (the played film of the old type) and at the other the notion of cinema figurativeness [*kinoobraznost'*] and the other methods of Left played cinema (*Potemkin, The Mother*). This section includes the study of the gradual creation of expressiveness through montage. Essentially this section examines cinema that is predominantly emotional while formally it represents a mixture of the elements of educational theatre and flashes of the new cinema.

Finally, the third section, devoted to *ideological expressiveness*, is concerned with the problem of the transition of film language from cinema figurativeness to the cinematic *materialisation of ideas*, i.e. with the problems of the direct translation of an ideological thesis into a chain of visual stimulants.

The sphere of this kind of (intellectual) cinema is that of a synthesis of experience and various methods of film language, a synthesis based on a correct *sociological understanding* of the agitational-educational tasks of cinema.

We pay particular attention to examining the problems of sound cinema: it is, of course, my view that the whole future of our cinema and an as yet unimagined range of opportunities for social influence lies with sound cinema.

The Workshop opened on 23 October [1928] with a lecture-demonstration of the technique of the actor in the Japanese Kabuki theatre given by one of the young artistes of the troupe that is now here on tour: Kawarazaki Tsiojuro. Kawarazaki is one of the leaders of a group of young actors who are trying to breathe new life into Japanese theatre and cinema and this explains his intense interest in our theatre and cinema which he has devoted several months to studying. He demonstrated to both the Workshop and the students at GTK the training and acting methods that the Kabuki actors work with.

The extreme precision and measured treatment of every movement that characterise the classical work of Japanese theatre have enormous educational significance for our actors and this is even more true of the film actor than the stage actor.

The Japanese school of acting, which has developed because the Japanese stage is placed closer to the audience than are European actors, precisely calculates the most minute variations in mime and requires from the Japanese actor the most detailed work: as we should say, he works 'in close-up'.

Kawarazaki demonstrated a series of training dances: budding actors, who begin their drama training at the age of five or six, dance them from childhood. These dances include a number of characteristic and unchanging movements that serve in one combination or another to perform different expressive tasks. Then Kawarazaki demonstrated variants of the characteristic movements according to the different roles being portrayed. He showed us a whole series of 'masks' that are characteristic of Japanese theatre and also the quite remarkable technique of Japanese make-up. After performing excerpts from the classical dramas *Tsyusingura, Tarakoya*, etc., he then broke them down into their individual elements, demonstrating the mechanics of Japanese theatrical movement.

Apart from meetings and lectures of this kind, the Workshop is planning a series of meetings from time to time that will keep us abreast of a number of topics that are relevant to our basic subject: reflexology, dialectical materialism, the sociology of art, etc.

21. Conversation with Eisenstein on Sound Cinema[1]   1929

Sergei Mikhailovich Eisenstein is a proponent of absolute sound cinema. If it is a matter of conveying sounds in cinema, rather than colours, reliefs, etc., we can call this kind of cinema an ideal. When and to what extent it can be realised is another question.

Being a proponent of absolute sound cinema, Eisenstein has quite understandably not pondered the problem of combining sound and non-sound sequences in a sound film.

Sound cinema, he says, can and will convey those sounds that musical instruments could not convey. It goes without saying that the entire film, from beginning to end, must be constructed on the basis of sound cinema. This does not mean that in particular places the film will not have a musical accompaniment. But this music will be constructed quite differently from the way that music is now constructed in our cinemas. Perhaps this music will, to some extent, recall the music of the German composer Meisel:[2] it is a well-known fact that new sound equipment is deployed in Meisel's music. In exactly the same way, the sound in sound films will be organised by means of the cinematic recording of noises and untempered sounds. It goes without saying that this is done – or, rather, should be done – neither anarchically nor by recording sounds 'as they really are' but by the strict organisation of the selection of sounds and it is by no means obligatory for these sounds to correspond to the event that is taking place.

Pauses and silences must be organised in the same way. They must also 'sound'. In a sound film it is quite inconceivable that the sound should suddenly break off and give way to silence or to some musical work merely because you need something to stop the gap. On the contrary both silence and music in cinema should be employed to produce a particular effect. Sometimes the pasting-in of a sequence involving a pause or a (silent) intertitle can have the same significance and produce the same effect as, for instance, Picasso pasting a bit of newspaper on to one of his pictures.

Intertitles, Montage, Shots

Eisenstein does not think that intertitles in sound cinema should be completely replaced by 'sound' intertitles. He admits that an intertitle that the audience merely reads makes far less impression on them than a 'talking' title. But, in spite of this, Eisenstein does not admit the possibility that 'talking titles' might completely replace intertitles in sound cinema. He starts from the premiss that the intertitle in cinema plays a quite independent role, serving as one of the elements of a film and, furthermore, as one of its organic elements. To reinforce this position Eisenstein refers to the intertitle in the film *The Coward*, 'Sit Down!' This produces a powerful effect and has an independent significance. (We do not agree with Eisenstein's position but, for reasons of loyalty, we feel obliged to cite a second example that Eisenstein did not mention because of his characteristic modesty: the intertitle in *The Battleship Potemkin*, 'My boy is very ill.' There is no doubt that this title has a more powerful effect than the one in *The Coward*. But both these titles are the exception rather than the rule.)

Admitting the possibility that some titles can be conveyed through sound images, Eisenstein says:

> Everything depends on the goal that the director sets himself in each individual instance. I am quite prepared to admit that in a single film part of the titles might be written, while others might be conveyed by a sound image. It is even possible to have a combination of titles where the written text does not coincide with the spoken . . . .

Eisenstein's stated views on the montage of sound films deserve the most serious attention. As is well known, one of the principal arguments advanced by the opponents of sound cinema against this new art form is that sound films will supposedly not be amenable to montage; in other words, one of the most powerful elements of contemporary cinema will be missing from them.

To a certain extent this position is correct but it is only correct if the sound film is recorded in accordance with the principle of the fixing rather than the organisation of sounds. If, let us suppose, we shoot a battle scene, fixing both sound and noises on film, then it will really be very difficult to submit that sort of scene to montage. We have not yet mentioned talking pictures where montage is almost impossible because in the course of montage we should cut out bits of phrases and words with the scissors.

But Eisenstein's principle consists in the organisation of sounds. He imagines that the recording of a sound film on this principle would take roughly the following form.

The sound part of the film is shot *separately* from the non-sound part. The sounds, noises and music that are necessary are recorded on film in accordance with a pre-determined plan. It is quite possible for this work to be carried out in parallel with the shooting of the non-sound part of the film, possible for it to be done beforehand, and it is also possible – and quite feasible, thanks to new advances – for it to be carried out later, after the non-sound part and the individual sequences in the film have already been shot.

As a result of this work you have the raw material of sound cinema that is amenable to montage, the material that is then joined to the appropriate sequences of the non-sound film to create a single whole.

With this method and on the basis of this principle the montage of a sound film is not merely quite feasible, it also opens up new and extremely wide-ranging possibilities for sound cinema. It goes without saying that

Eisenstein, as the greatest enthusiast for montage in cinema generally, does not for one moment admit the possibility of a diminished role for montage in sound cinema. On the contrary: he is striving to increase this role and, in any event, to broaden the possibilities for montage in sound films.

Similarly, Eisenstein is not in the least confused by the other short-comings that considerably confuse other proponents of sound cinema and provide its opponents with a weapon. We are referring to the fact that, when we are shooting a sound film and we want to convey voice or speech, it is extremely difficult to alternate the shots. The critical material we have to hand relating to the sound films now being shown in America indicates that very frequently the person whose face is shown on screen in close-up does not speak any more loudly than another person seen in medium or long shot. When here in Moscow we showed the Tri-Ergon talking films we became convinced that the volume of the sound in talking films is very difficult to modulate. People speak at the same volume regardless of the fact that some of them are filmed in close-up and others in medium or long shot. This occurs because it is extremely difficult to regulate the volume in sound cinema. In addition the microphones are not always placed in the same spot as the camera (for a whole number of technical reasons that we shall not go into here).

There is no doubt that this 'discrepancy' considerably confuses the audience. But Eisenstein views this problem somewhat differently. In his opinion it is quite possible to envisage a face filmed in close-up with a scarcely audible voice or, the other way round, a person filmed in long shot may speak exceptionally loudly. The problem, says Eisenstein, does not lie in the fact that the type of shot corresponds exactly to the volume of the sound. It all depends on the intention of the author of the film. In order to eliminate a particular effect or to produce an unexpected effect, you can and must emphasise the discrepancy between the sounds and the distance of the filmed object from the camera. But it goes without saying that here too any element of chance must be excluded. In this context too we must use the technical resources at our disposal to organise these discrepancies according to a predetermined plan.

The last point in our conversation with Eisenstein concerned the question of the application sound cinema might have in relation to one or other of the tendencies in our cinema. We put the question bluntly: did Eisenstein suppose that sound cinema could best be used by the cinematic tendency that he heads, i.e. by non-acted cinema?

'It seems to me,' Eisenstein replied, 'that sound cinema can best be used by those film directors who recognise the enormous role of montage in cinema, who regard montage not as a means of simply gluing together separate bits of film but as the factor that establishes the independence of cinema art.'

This reply underlines yet again the importance that Eisenstein attaches to montage in cinema, and not just in cinema but also in the new art form, sound cinema.

22. The Form of the Script³

'A numbered script will bring as much animation to cinema as the numbers on the heels of the drowned men in the morgue.'

That is what I wrote at the height of the arguments about the forms a script outline should take.

There can be no argument about this question. Because a script is, in essence, not a staging of raw material but a stage in the condition of the material.

On the way from the spirited conception of the chosen theme to its visual realisation.

A script is not a drama. Drama is an independent value even beyond its effective theatrical staging.

But a script is merely a shorthand record of an emotional outburst striving for realisation in an accumulation of visual images.

A script is a boot-tree, preserving the shape of the boot when there is no living foot inside it.

A script is a bottle that is necessary only so that the cork can explode and the character of the wine foam into the greedy gullets of the onlookers.

A script is a cipher. A cipher communicated by one character to another. The co-author uses his resources to imprint in a script the rhythm of his own conception.

The director comes along and translates the rhythm of this conception into his own language,

into film language;

he finds the cinematic equivalent of literary expression.

In this lies the heart of the matter.

But not in an arrangement into a chain of pictures, an anecdotal chain of the events in the script.

That is how we have formulated our requirements of the script.

This has dealt a severe blow to the usual form of *Drehbuch*⁴ with numbers. Written in the worst instance by a simple hack, it provides a traditional visual description of what is to be seen.

That is not where the secret lies. The centre of gravity lies in the fact that the script expresses the purpose of the experience that the audience must undergo.

In pursuit of a methodology for this kind of exposition we came to the film novella, the form through which we are trying to make statements on the screen with hundreds of people, herds of cattle, sunsets, waterfalls and boundless fields.

The film novella, as we understand it, is essentially a future audience's anticipated story of the film that has captivated it.

134

This is the presentation of the material in the stages and rhythms of the captivation and excitement with which it is to 'capture' the audience.

We do not recognise any limitations on the visual exposition of the facts. Sometimes the purely literary arrangement of the words in a script means more to us than the meticulous recording of facial expressions by the writer.

'A deathly silence hung in the air.'

What does this expression have in common with the concrete tangibility of a visual phenomenon?

Where is the hook in the air that silence was to be hung on?

But this is a phrase: or, rather, attempts to realise this phrase in screen terms.

This phrase from the memoirs of one of the men who took part in the *Potemkin* mutiny defined the whole conception of the oppressive and deathly pause at the moment when the threatening rifles of the men who were to shoot their brothers were turned on the tarpaulin that covered those who had been condemned to death and that moved as they breathed.

The script sets out the emotional requirements. The director provides its visual resolution.

And the scriptwriter is right to present it in his own language.

Because the more fully his intention is expressed, the more complete will be the semantic designation.

Consequently, the more specific it will be in literary terms.

It will be the material for a truly directorial resolution. It will 'captivate' him too, and provide a stimulus to a creative elevation to that same high level of expression through the methods of his own field, sphere and specialism.

Because it is important to agree on the level of tension or passion that you should employ.

The heart of the matter lies in this passion.

Let the scriptwriter and the director expound this in their different languages.

The scriptwriter puts: 'Deathly silence'.

The director uses: still close-ups; the dark and silent pitching of the battleship's bows; the unfurling of the St Andrew's ensign; perhaps a dolphin's leap; and the low flight of seagulls.

The audience experiences the same emotional spasm in the throat, the same mounting anxiety as that which seized the author of the memoirs at his writing desk and the director of the film at the cutting bench or while shooting in the boiling sun.

That is why we are opposed to the usual form of numbered detailed script (*Drehbuch*) and why we are in favour of the film novella form.

An example of the first attempt at this, dating back to 1926, is the script for *The General Line*[5] published here.

23. 'The Arsenal'[6]

Everyone interprets the stern words of the directive in his own particular way. This man really has something to say. He does not quote but bellows with conviction. The Song of Roland. Sometimes he wears his voice out. Sometimes his windpipe. But almost always he dons the lustrine coat of film (uni)form.[7] So much the worse for those who iron the creases in its trousers!

There are laws for constructing a building.

There are laws for erecting a barricade (the transfer of objects).

Die erste Kolonne marschiert.

And there is civil war.

For there is clarity of purpose.

D[ovzhenko] is not a partisan. He is a member of the Revolutionary Committee.[8] Chinamen. Bandits. A special purpose detachment. And it all lets. . . .

Twisting things. Twisting style. Twisting methods. This is familiar; it is *October*.

But if *October* is a window of an auction room, *The Arsenal* is a barricade.

A fragment of Expressionism. All right. A fragment of *The End of St [Petersburg]*.[9] Welcome. The loathsomeness of glued-on beards. A Byzantine icon. And a cheap postcard. Acceptable. A tram. A barber's sign. An advertisement column. A sprung bed. A mattress. And two lampposts.

Is the dynamic of street fighting really a static construction?

He has laid his hands on cinema quite by chance.

It might be an axe. Or a machine-gun.

It spatters out, incapable of expression.

There are trains that run outside the timetable. Tickets for them are not on sale. They rush past, filmed at an angle. They stop at one station to burn it down. At another they are blown up by the dynamite that has been laid. They rush further on gun-carriages or a coach-and-six. The people are silent. The horses talk. And the shadows of night chase past.

Dovzhenko is like Ivan and the old woman in the first reel. He is quiet for half an hour and then he dashes out and thrashes about like a lunatic.

I'd rather have this than what most of our people do. Perhaps I might use the bad method of a hackneyed comparison. They sit, like Nikolai (in the same reel), for an hour, for a day, for years, looking with a glazed expression in their eyes at some damn gigantic epoch, then they take a breath and on the screen we see the words: 'I've killed a crow.' Pause. 'The weather was fine.' These people do not even kill canaries. Whereas Dovzhenko overturns trams without even suggesting to the passengers that they 'leave the premises' beforehand.

Dovzhenko can shoot you *in the face*. Both through the content that he puts in the firing line and through the form that he is free from. In this he is unique. The rest of us are like a caravanserai of camels bearing the heavy weight of *form*. To live alongside Dovzhenko is to live alongside dynamite. . . .

There are no teachers of Dovzhenko's genre. I do not think that there will be any students of this genre either. Perhaps this is one of the consumer faults in a planned economy.

But in the final analysis we do not after all require of a man who is dying on the barricades that he should be sure to produce a dozen offspring.

Dovzhenko himself is developing by gigantic strides. Not just in terms of the form that he despises: the form that is trampled underfoot like a pavement. (It is important to move but not to 'Keep to the Path'!)

The Diplomatic Bag, Zvenigora,[10] *The Arsenal.*

An immeasurable distance. No less so ideologically: raucous sham Red adventurism.

The old and the new Ukraine. The Ukraine as it is. The undifferentiated Mother Ukraine.

And the savage class chopper in its most diseased and festering form. That phenomenon that is unacceptable to our class: chauvinism. The class chopper in that whole branch of the most harmful glasshouse of Rightism.

It chopped them so that they howled.

Dovzhenko must go his own way.

He can also bare his breast calmly without armour.

It will not be pierced.

Let him bare it!

Let him.

24. Beyond the Shot[11]

It is a weird and wonderful feeling to write a booklet about something that does not in fact exist.

There is, for example, no such thing as cinema without cinematography.

Nevertheless the author of the present book has managed to write a book about the *cinema* of a country that has no *cinematography*,

about the cinema of a country that has an infinite multiplicity of cinematic characteristics but which are scattered all over the place – with the sole exception of its cinema.

This article is devoted to the cinematic features of Japanese culture that lie outside Japanese cinema and it lies outside the book in the same way as these features lie outside Japanese cinema.

Cinema is: so many firms, so much working capital, such and such a 'star', so many dramas.

Cinema is, first and foremost, montage.

Japanese cinema is well provided with firms, actors and plots.

And Japanese cinema is quite unaware of montage.

Nevertheless the principle of montage may be considered to be an element of Japanese representational culture.

The script,

for their script is primarily representational.

The hieroglyph.[12]

The naturalistic representation of an object through the skilled hands of Ts'ang Chieh in 2650 BC became slightly formalised and, with its 539 fellows, constituted the first 'contingent' of hieroglyphs.

The portrait of an object, scratched with a stylus on a strip of bamboo, still resembled the original in every way.

But then, at the end of the third century, the brush was invented,

in the first century after the 'happy event' (AD) there was paper

and in the year 220 indian ink.

A complete transformation. A revolution in draughtsmanship. The hieroglyph, which has in the course of history undergone no fewer than fourteen different styles of script, has crystallised in its present form.

The means of production (the brush and indian ink) determine the form. The fourteen reforms have had their effect.

In short, it is already impossible to recognise in the enthusiastically cavorting hieroglyph *ma* (a horse) the image of the little horse settling pathetically on its hind legs in the calligraphy of Ts'ang Chieh, the horse that is so well known from ancient Chinese sculpture (Fig. 24. 1).

But to hell with the horse and with the 607 remaining symbols of the *hsiang-cheng*, the first *representational* category of hieroglyphs.

It is with the second category of hieroglyphs – the *huei-i*, or 'copulative' – that our real interest begins.

The point is that the copulation – perhaps we had better say the combination – of two hieroglyphs of the simplest series is regarded not as their sum total but as their product, i.e. as a value of another dimension, another degree: each taken separately corresponds to an object but their combination corresponds to a *concept*. The combination of two 'representable' objects achieves the representation of something that cannot be graphically represented.

For example: the representation of water and of an eye signifies 'to weep',

the representation of an ear next to a drawing of a door means 'to listen',

a dog and a mouth mean 'to bark'

a mouth and a baby mean 'to scream'

a mouth and a bird mean 'to sing'

a knife and a heart mean 'sorrow', and so on.

But – this is montage!!

Yes. It is precisely what we do in cinema, juxtaposing representational shots that have, as far as possible, the same meaning, that are neutral in terms of their meaning, in meaningful contexts and series.

It is an essential method and device in any cinematographic exposition. And, in a condensed and purified form, it is the starting-point for 'intellectual cinema',

a cinema that seeks the maximum laconicism in the visual exposition of abstract concepts.

We hail the method of the (long since) dead Ts'ang Chieh as a pioneering step along this path.

I have mentioned laconicism. Laconicism provides us with a stepping-stone to another point. Japan possesses the most laconic forms of poetry, the *haikai*[13] (that appeared at the beginning of the 12th century) and the *tanka*.

(Fig. 24. 1)

139

They are virtually hieroglyphics transposed into phrases. So much so that half their value is judged by their calligraphic quality. The method by which they are resolved is quite analogous.

This method, which in hieroglyphics provides a means for the laconic imprinting of an abstract concept, gives rise, when transposed into semantic exposition, to a similarly laconic printed imagery.

The method, reduced to a stock combination of images, carves out a dry definition of the concept from the collision between them.

The same method, expanded into a wealth of recognised semantic combinations, becomes a profusion of *figurative* effect.

The formula, the concept, is embellished and developed on the basis of the material, it is transformed into an image, which is the form.

In exactly the same way as the primitive thought form – thinking in images – is displaced at a certain stage and replaced by conceptual thought.

But let us pass on to examples:

The *hai-kai* is a concentrated Impressionist sketch:

> Two splendid spots
> on the stove.
> The cat sits on them.
> (GE-DAI)

> Ancient monastery.
> Cold moon.
> Wolf howling.
> (KIKKO)

> Quiet field.
> Butterfly flying.
> Sleeping.
> (GO-SIN)

The *tanka* is a little longer (by two lines).

> Mountain pheasant
> moving quietly, trailing
> his tail behind.
> Oh, shall I pass
> endless night alone.
> (HITOMASO)

We see these as montage phrases, montage lists.

The simplest juxtaposition of two or three details of a material series produces a perfectly finished representation of another order, the psychological.

Whereas the finely honed edges of the intellectual formulation of the concept produced by the juxtaposition of hieroglyphs are here blurred, the concept blossoms forth immeasurably in *emotional* terms.

In Japanese script you do not know whether it is the inscription of a character or the independent product of graphics.

Born from a cross between the figurative mode and the denotative purpose, the hieroglyphic method has continued its tradition not just in literature but also, as we have indicated, in the *tanka* (not *historically* consistent but consistent *in principle* in the minds of those who have created this method).

Precisely the same method operates in the most perfect examples of Japanese figurative art.

Sharaku[14] was the creator of the finest prints of the 18th century and, in particular, of an immortal gallery of actors' portraits. He was the Japanese Daumier. That same Daumier whom Balzac (himself the Bonaparte of literature) in turn called the 'Michelangelo of caricature'.

Despite all this Sharaku is almost unknown in our country.

The characteristic features of his works have been noted by Julius Kurth.* Examining the question of the influence of sculpture on Sharaku, he draws a parallel between the portrait of the actor Nakayama Tomisaburo and an antique mask of the semi-religious No theatre, the mask of Rozo, the old bonze. (See Fig. 24. 2)

Is this not the same as the hieroglyph that juxtaposes the independent 'mouth' and the dissociated 'child' for the semantic expression 'scream'?

Just as Sharaku does by stopping time so we too do in time by provoking a monstrous disproportion between the parts of a normally occurring phenomenon, when we suddenly divide it into 'close-up of hands clasped', 'medium shots of battle' and 'big close-ups of staring eyes' and produce a montage division of the phenomenon into the types of shot! We make an eye twice as large as a fully grown man! From the juxtaposition of these monstrous incongruities we reassemble the disintegrated phenomena into a single whole but from our own perspective, in the light of our own orientation towards the phenomenon.

The disproportionate representation of a phenomenon is organically inherent in us from the very beginning. A. R. Luria[15] has shown me a child's drawing of 'lighting a stove'. Everything is depicted in tolerable proportions and with great care: firewood, stove, chimney. But, in the middle of the room space, there is an enormous rectangle crossed with zigzags. What are they? They turn out to be 'matches'. Bearing in mind the crucial importance of these matches for the process depicted, the child gives them the appropriate scale.

---

* J. Kurth, *Sharaku*, Munich, 1929, pp. 78-80.

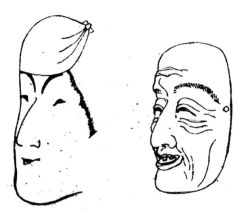

(Fig. 24. 2)

The expression on the mask, also created in Sharaku's day, is the same as that in the portrait of Tomisaburo. The facial expression and the arrangement of masses are very similar to one another even though the mask repesents an old man and the print a young woman (Tomisaburo in the role of a woman). The similarity is striking but nevertheless the two have nothing in common. Here we find a characteristic feature of Sharaku's work: whereas the anatomical proportions of the carved wooden mask are almost correct, the proportions of the face in the print are quite simply impossible. The distance between the eyes is so great as to make a mockery of common sense. The nose, in comparison with the eyes at least, is twice as long as a normal nose could possibly be, the chin is on the whole out of all proportion to the mouth: the relationships between the eyebrows, the mouth, the details in general are quite unthinkable. We can observe the same thing in all Sharaku's large heads. It is just not possible that the great master was unaware that these proportions were wrong. He quite deliberately repudiated naturalism and, *while each detail taken separately is constructed on the principles of concentrated naturalism, their general compositional juxtaposition is subjugated to a purely semantic purpose. He took as the norm for the proportions the quintessence of psychological expressiveness. . . .*

The representation of an object in the actual (absolute) proportions proper to it is, of course, merely a tribute to orthodox formal logic, a subordination to the inviolable order of things.

This returns periodically and unfailingly in periods when absolutism is in the ascendancy, replacing the expressiveness of antiquated disproportion with a regular 'ranking table' of officially designated harmony.

Positivist realism is by no means the correct form of perception. It is simply a function of a particular form of social structure, following on from an autocratic state that has propagated a state uniformity of thought.

It is an ideological uniformity that makes its visual appearance in the ranks of uniforms of the Life Guard regiments. . . .

Thus, we have seen how the principle of the hieroglyph – 'denotation through representation' – split into two.

Following the line of its purpose (the principle of 'denotation') to the principles of the creation of literary imagery.

Following the line of the methods of achieving this purpose (the principle of 'representation') to the striking methods of expressiveness used by Sharaku.

Just as we say that the two diverging arms of a hyperbola meet at infinity (although no one has ever been such a long way away!), so the principle of hieroglyphics, splitting endlessly into two (in accordance with the dynamic of the signs), unexpectedly joins together again from this dual divergence in yet a fourth sphere – theatre.

Estranged from one another for so long, they are once again – the theatre is still in its cradle – present in *parallel* form, in a curious dualism.

The denotation of the action, the representation of the action, is carried out by the so-called Joruri, a silent puppet on the stage.

This antiquated practice, together with a specific style of movement, passes into the early Kabuki theatre as well. It is preserved to this day, as a partial method, in the classical repertoire.

But let us pass on. This is not the point. The hieroglyphic (montage) method has penetrated the very technique of acting in the most curious ways.

However, before we move on to this, since we have already mentioned the representational aspect, let us dwell on the problem of the shot so that we settle the matter once and for all.

The shot.

A tiny rectangle with some fragment of an event organised within it.

Glued together, these shots form montage. (*Of course*, if this is done in the appropriate rhythm!)

That, roughly, is the teaching of the old school of film-making.

> Screw by screw,
> Brick by brick . . . .[16]

Kuleshov, for instance, even writes with a brick: 'If you have an idea-phrase, a particle of the story, a link in the whole dramaturgical chain, then that idea is expressed and built up from shot-signs, just like bricks . . . .'[17]

> Screw by screw,
> Brick by brick . . .

as they used to say.

The shot is an element of montage.

Montage is the assembling of these elements.

This is a most pernicious mode of analysis, in which the understanding of any process as a whole (the link: shot – montage) derives purely from the external indications of the course it takes (one piece glued to another).

143

You might, for instance, come to the notorious conclusion that trams exist merely to block streets. This is an entirely logical conclusion if you confine yourself to the functions that they performed, for example, in February 1917. But the Moscow municipal authorities see things in a different light.

The worst of the matter is that an approach like this does really, like an insurmountable tram, block the possibilities of formal development. An approach like this condemns us not to dialectical development but to [the process of] mere evolutionary 'perfection', in so far as it does not penetrate to the dialectical essence of the phenomenon.

In the final analysis this kind of evolutionising leads either through its own refinement to decadence or, vice versa, to straightforward weakness caused by a blockage in the blood supply. However odd it may seem, there is an eloquent, nay melodious, witness to both these eventualities simultaneously in *The Happy Canary*.[18]

The shot is by no means a montage *element*.

The shot is a montage cell. Beyond the dialectical jump in the *single* series: shot – montage.

What then characterises montage and, consequently, its embryo, the shot? Collision. Conflict between two neighbouring fragments. Conflict. Collision.

Before me lies a crumpled yellowing sheet of paper.

On it there is a mysterious note:

'Series – P' and 'Collision – E'.

This is a material trace of the heated battle on the subject of montage between E (myself) and P (Pudovkin) six months ago.

We have already got into a habit: at regular intervals he comes to see me late at night and, behind closed doors, we wrangle over matters of principle.

So it is in this instance. A graduate of the Kuleshov school, he zealously defends the concepts of montage as a *series* of fragments. In a chain. 'Bricks'. Bricks that *expound* an idea serially.

I opposed him with my view of montage as a *collision*, my view that the collision of two factors gives rise to an idea.

In my view a *series* is merely one possible *particular* case.

Remember that physics is aware of an infinite number of combinations arising from the impact (collision) between spheres. Depending on whether they are elastic, non-elastic or a mixture of the two. Among these combinations is one where the collision is reduced to a uniform movement of both in the same direction.

That corresponds to Pudovkin's view.

Not long ago we had another discussion. Now he holds the view that I held then. In the meantime he has of course had the chance to familiarise himself with the set of lectures that I have given at the GTK since then.

So, montage is conflict.

Conflict lies at the basis of every art. (A unique 'figurative' transformation of the dialectic.)

The shot is then a montage cell. Consequently we must also examine it from the point of view of *conflict.*

Conflict within the shot is:

potential montage that, in its growing intensity, breaks through its four-sided cage and pushes its conflict out into montage impulses between the montage fragments;

just as a zigzag of mimicry flows over, making those *same* breaks, into a zigzag of spatial staging,

just as the slogan, 'Russians know no obstacles', breaks out in the many volumes of peripeteia in the novel *War and Peace.*

If we are to compare montage with anything, then we should compare a phalanx of montage fragments – 'shots' – with the series of explosions of the internal combustion engine, as these fragments multiply into a montage dynamic through 'impulses' like those that drive a car or a tractor.

Conflict within the shot. It can take many forms: it can even be part of . . . the story. Then it becomes the 'Golden Series'. A fragment 120 metres long. Neither the analysis nor the questions of film form apply in this instance.

But these are 'cinematographic':

the conflict of graphic directions (lines)

the conflict of shot levels (between one another)

the conflict of volumes

the conflict of masses (of volumes filled with varying intensities of light)

the conflict of spaces, etc.

Conflicts that are waiting only for a single intensifying impulse to break up into antagonistic pairs of fragments. Close-ups and long shots. Fragments travelling graphically in different directions. Fragments resolved in volumes and fragments resolved in planes. Fragments of darkness and light . . . etc.

Lastly, there are such unexpected conflicts as:

the conflict between an object and its spatial nature and the conflict between an event and its temporal nature.

However strange it may seem, these are things that have long been familiar to us. The first is achieved through optical distortion by the lens and the second through animation or *Zeitlupe* [slow motion].

The reduction of all the properties of cinema to a single formula of conflict and of cinematographic indicators to the dialectical series of one *single indicator* is no empty rhetorical pastime.

We are now searching for a single system of methods of cinematographic expression that will cover all its elements.

The reduction of these to a series of general indicators will solve the problem as a whole.

145

Our experience of the various elements of cinema is quite variable.

Whereas we know a very great deal about montage, we are floundering about, as far as the theory of the shot is concerned, between the Tretyakov Gallery, the Shchukin Museum and geometricisations that set your teeth on edge.[19]

If we regard the shot as a particular molecular instance of montage and shatter the dualism 'shot – montage', then we can apply our experience of montage directly to the problem of the theory of the shot.

The same applies to the theory of lighting. If we think of lighting as the collision between a beam of light and an obstacle, like a stream of water from a fire hose striking an object, or the wind buffeting a figure, this will give us a quite differently conceived use of light from the play of 'haze' or 'spots'.

Thus far only the principle of conflict acts as this kind of denominator:

the principle of optical counterpoint. (We shall deal with this more fully on another occasion.)

We should not forget now that we must resolve a counterpoint of a different order, *the conflict between the acoustic and the optical in sound cinema.*

But let us for the moment return to one of the most interesting optical conflicts:

the conflict between the frame of the shot and the object.

The position of the cinema represents the materialisation of the conflict between the organising logic of the director and the inert logic of the phenomenon in collision, producing the dialectic of the camera angle.

In this field we are still sickeningly impressionistic and unprincipled.

Nevertheless there is a clear principle even in this technique.

A mundane rectangle that cuts across the accident of nature's randomness . . . .

Once again we are in Japan!

Because one of the methods of teaching drawing used in Japanese schools is so cinematographic.

Our method of teaching drawing is to:

take an ordinary sheet of Russian paper with four corners. In the majority of cases you then squeeze on to it, ignoring the edges (which are greasy with sweat!), a bored caryatid, a conceited Corinthian capital or a plaster Dante (not the magician,[20] the other one – Alighieri, the man who writes comedies).

The Japanese do it the other way round.

You have a branch of a cherry tree or a landscape with a sailing boat.

From this whole the pupil cuts out compositional units: a square, a circle, a rectangle. (See Figs. 24. 3 and 24. 4.)

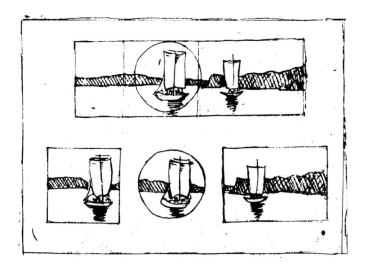

(Fig. 24. 3)

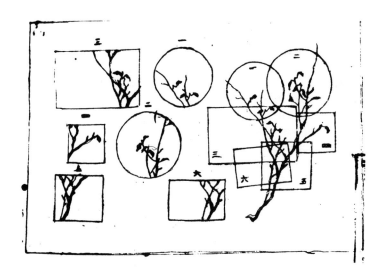

(Fig. 24. 4)

He creates a shot!

These two schools (theirs and ours) precisely characterise the two basic tendencies that are fighting one another in contemporary cinema!

Our school: the dying method of spatial organisation of the phenomenon in front of the lens:

from the 'staging' of a scene to the erection literally of a Tower of Babel in front of the lens.

The other method, used by the Japanese, is that of 'capturing' with the camera, using it to organise. Cutting out a fragment of reality by means of the lens.

Now, however, at a time when the centre of attention in intellectual cinema is at last beginning to move from the raw material of cinema as it is to 'deductions and conclusions', to 'slogans' based on the raw material, the differences are becoming less important to both schools and they can quietly blend into a synthesis.

Eight or so pages back, the question of theatre slipped from our grasp, like a pair of galoshes on a tram, slipped from our grasp.

Let us go back to the question of the methods of montage in Japanese theatre, particularly in acting.

The first and most striking example, of course, is the purely cinematographic method of 'transitionless acting'. Together with extremely refined mime transitions the Japanese actor also makes use of the direct opposite. At a certain moment in his performance he halts. The 'black men' obligingly conceal him from the audience.[21] So, he emerges in new make-up, a new wig: these characterise a new stage (step) in his emotional state.

Thus, for instance, the play *Narukami* is resolved by Sadanji's transition from drunkenness to madness.[22] Through a mechanical cut. And a change in the range (arsenal) of coloured stripes on his face, emphasising those whose duty it is to demonstrate that the intensity is greater than in the first make-up.

This method is organic to film. The forced introduction into film of the European acting tradition of fragments of 'emotional transitions' once more compels cinema to mark time. At the same time, the method of 'cut' acting provides the opportunity to devise entirely new methods. If you replace a single changing face by a whole gamut of faces of varying dispositions – typage – the expression is always more intense than that on the surface of the face of a professional actor, which is too receptive and devoid of any organic resistance.

I have utilised the distinction between the polar stages of facial expression in a pointed juxtaposition in our new film about the countryside.[23] This results in a more pointed 'play of doubt' around the separator. Will the milk thicken or not? Deception? Money? Here the psychological process of the play of motives – faith and doubt – resolves into the two extreme states of joy (certainty) and gloom (disillusionment). In addition, this is heavily underlined by light (which by no means conforms to real life). This leads to a significant heightening of tension.

Another remarkable feature of the Kabuki theatre is the principle of 'decomposed acting'. Shocho, who played the leading female roles when the Kabuki troupe visited Moscow, portrayed the dying girl in *The Mask Maker* through quite disconnected fragments of acting.

Acting with just the right arm. Acting with one leg. Acting merely with the neck and head. The whole process of the death agony was decomposed into solo performances by each 'party' separately: the legs, the arms, the head. Decomposition into shot levels. And each successive fragment became shorter as the unhappy ending – death – approached.

Freed from primitive naturalism and using this method, the actor wins the audience over completely 'with his rhythm', which makes a scene based in its general composition on the most consistent and detailed naturalism (blood, etc.) not only acceptable but extremely attractive.

Since we are no longer distinguishing in principle between montage and what happens within the shot, we can cite here a third method.

The Japanese actor in his work utilises slow tempo to a degree that is unknown in our theatre. Take the famous hara-kiri scene in *The Forty-Seven Samurai*.[24] That degree of slowing down is unknown on our stage. Whereas in our previous example we observed the decomposition of the links between movements, here we see the decomposition of the process of movement, i.e. *Zeitlupe* [slow motion]. I know of only one case of the consistent application of this method, which is technically acceptable in cinema, on a compositionally meaningful level. (It is usually deployed either for visual effect, as in the 'underwater kingdom' in *The Thief of Bagdad*, or for a dream, as in *Zvenigora*.[25] Even more frequently it is used simply for formal trifles and pointless mischief with the camera, as in *The Man with the Movie Camera*.[26]) I have in mind Epstein's *The Fall of the House of Usher*.[27] Judging by press reports, normally acted states [of mind], shot with a speeded-up camera and played back in slow motion on the screen, produced unusual emotional tension. If you bear in mind that the attraction exerted by the actor's performance on the audience is based on the audience's identification with it, you can easily attribute both examples to one and the same causal explanation. The intensity of our perception increases because the process of identification is easier when the movement is decomposed . . . .

Even instruction in handling a rifle can be drummed into the heads of the densest raw recruit if the instructor uses the method of 'decomposition' . . . .

The most interesting link is of course the one between Japanese theatre and sound film which can and must learn from the Japanese what to it is fundamental: the reduction of visual and aural sensations to a single physiological denominator. But I have devoted an entire article to this in *Zhizn' iskusstva* (1928, no. 34)[28] and I shall not return to the subject.

Thus, it has been possible to establish briefly the fact that the most varied branches of Japanese culture are permeated by a purely cinematic element and by its basic nerve – montage.

And it is only cinema that falls into the same trap as the 'left-inclining' Kabuki. Instead of learning how to isolate the principles and techniques of their unique acting from the traditional feudal forms of what they are acting, the progressive theatrical people of Japan rush to borrow the loose formlessness of the acting of our 'intuitivists'. The result is lamentable and saddening. In its cinema Japan also strives to imitate the most appalling examples of the most saleable mediocre American and European commercial trash.

Understand and apply its specific cultural quality to its own cinema – that is what Japan must do!

Japanese comrades, are you really going to leave this to us?

25. Perspectives[29]

In the welter of crises. Imagined and real.

In the chaos of discussions. Serious or pointless (e.g. 'with actors or without?').

Squeezed between the scissors of the need to move film culture forward and demands for instant accessibility.

Trapped by the contradictions between the need to find forms that correspond to the post-capitalist forms of our socialist order.

And the cultural capacity of the class that has created this order.

Strictly observing the basic trend towards mass immediacy and intelligibility to the millions.

We, however, have no right to limit ourselves in our theoretical resolutions to the resolution of this problem and this basic condition.

Parallel with the resolution of the everyday tactical progress of the forms of cinema, we are obliged to work on problems of general principle as a means of developing the prospects for our cinema.

Whereas we now throw all our practical experience into meeting the narrow day-to-day demands of the social consumer, we must in future devote all the more attention to devising the programme for our theoretical Five-Year Plans.

And search out the new functional prospects for a genuinely communist cinema that is clearly distinguished from all past and present cinemas.

The following observations are an attempt to move in that direction.

> It is generally pleasant and useful to understand Marxism. But for Mr Gorky an understanding of Marxism will bring the indispensable benefit of making clear to him how unsuitable is the role of preacher – a man who speaks predominantly in the *language of logic* – for an artist, a man who speaks predominantly in the *language of images*. When Mr Gorky realises this, he will be saved. . . .

That is what Plekhanov once wrote in the Preface to the third edition of *For Twenty Years*.[30]

Fifteen years have passed since then.

Gorky has been successfully 'saved'.

He has, apparently, mastered Marxism.

During this time the role of the preacher has merged with the role of the artist. The *propagandist* has emerged.

But the discord between the language of images and the language of

151

logic continues. There is no way of 'reconciling' them in the language of the dialectic.

In fact the centre of attention on the arts front has now shifted from Plekhanov's antithesis to a different contrast.

Let us deal with this first so that we can then outline the possibilities of a synthetic way out of the first antithesis.

Thus: the contemporary conception of art ranges from one pole to another, that is: from the formula 'art is the cognition [*poznanie*] of life' to the formula 'art is the construction of life'.[31] In my view this polar opposition is profoundly mistaken.

Not on the level of the functional definition of art but in the wrongly based concept that is concealed behind the term 'cognition'.

When we come upon the definition of a concept we ignore at our peril the method of purely linguistic analysis of the actual designation. The words we use are sometimes significantly 'cleverer' than we are.

And our reluctance to examine a definition that has been refined and reduced to a formula and that is the semantic designation of a concept is quite irrational. We should analyse the formula, free it of its extraneous baggage, and its 'popular' associative material that is frequently borrowed and that distorts the essence of the matter.

The dominant associations are of course those that correspond to the class that is dominant in the period of the formulation or maximum application of a particular term or designation.

We have inherited all our 'rational' semantic and terminological baggage from the bourgeoisie.

Along with the dominant bourgeois understanding and reading of these designations and the accompanying associative chains and systems that correspond to bourgeois ideology and orientation.

While every designation, like every phenomenon, has a dual 'reading', what I might call an 'ideological reading'. Static and dynamic. Social and individual.

While the traditionalism of the associative 'context' that corresponds to the previous class-based hegemony constantly confuses us.

And the word-concept, instead of producing a specific semantic 'class differentiation', is written, understood and *used* by us in a traditional manner that in no way corresponds to our class needs.

It was Berkeley who noted the fact of a word's meaning for the analysis of the concept it designated:

> It cannot be denied that words are of excellent use, in that by their means all that stock of knowledge which has been purchased by the joint labours of inquisitive men in all ages and nations, may be drawn into the view and made the possession of one single person.[32]

At the same time he notes what we indicated above: the distortion of the perception of concepts through the one-sided or incorrect application of these designations.

> But at the same time it must be owned that most parts of knowledge have been strangely perplexed and darkened by the abuse of words, and general ways of speech wherein they are delivered.[33]

Berkeley sees the way out of this situation through the eyes of an idealist: not by purging the designations of their social implications on the basis of a class analysis, but by striving towards a 'pure idea'.

> It were therefore to be wished that every one would use his utmost endeavours, to obtain a clear view of the ideas he would consider, separating from them all that dress and incumbrance of words which so much contribute to blind the judgement and divide the atten- tion . . . we need only draw the curtain of words, to behold the fair- est tree of knowledge, whose fruit is excellent, and within the reach of our hand.[34]

Plekhanov approaches the same problem of 'word usage' in quite a different way. He studies the word in its inseparable social-productive context and for the purposes of analysis he restores it from the sphere of the super- structure to the sphere of the basic productive and practical composition and emergence of the word.

Viewed like this, it becomes just as convincing a materialist argu- ment as any of the other research materials that we deploy.

He cites as part of his evidence for basing 'the inevitable necessity of a materialist explanation of history on the most closely studied part of the ideology of primitive society, its art' the linguistic observations of von den Steinen: '. . . Von den Steinen thinks that *drawing (Zeichnen)* developed from *designation of the object (Zeichen), used with a practical aim.*'*[35]

Our traditional acceptance of words, our unwillingness to listen to them attentively and our neglect of this area of research are a cause of con- siderable distress and of oceans of pointless, irrational outbursts by various polemical temperaments!

How many bayonets have, for instance, been broken on the question of 'form and content'!

All because the dynamic, active and effective *act* of 'content' [*soder- zhanie*] as 'containing within oneself' [*sderzhivanie mezhdu soboi*] has been replaced by an amorphous, static and passive understanding of content as *contents* [*soderzhimoe*].

Although nobody would dream of talking about the 'contents' of the

---

* G.V. Plekhanov, *Osnovnye voprosy marksizma* [Fundamental Questions of Marx- ism], Moscow, 1920, p. 33.

play *The Rails Are Humming* or the novel *The Iron Torrent!*[36]

How much inky blood has been spilled because of the persistent desire to understand *form* only as deriving from the Greek *phormos* or wicker basket – with all the 'organisational conclusions' that flow from that!

A wicker basket where those same unhappy 'contents' bob about on the inky floods of the polemic.

Whereas you have only to look in a dictionary, not a Greek one but a Russian dictionary of 'foreign words', and you will see that form in Russian is *obraz* or 'image'. 'Image' [*obraz*] is itself a cross between the concepts of 'cut' [*obrez*] and 'disclosure' [*obnaruzhenie*].* These two terms brilliantly characterise form from both its aspects: from the *individually static (an und für sich)* standpoint as 'cut' [*obrez*], the isolation of a particular phenomenon from its surroundings (e.g. a non-Marxist definition of form, such as Leonid Andreyev's, which confines itself *strictly* to this definition).[37]

'Disclosure' [*obnaruzhenie*] characterises image from a different, socially active standpoint: it 'discloses', i.e. establishes the social link between a particular phenomenon and its surroundings.

Put more colloquially, 'content' [*soderzhanie*] – the act of containing [*sderzhivanie*] – is an *organisational principle*.

The principle of the organisation of thinking is in actual fact the 'content' of a work.

A principle that materialises in the sum total of socio-physiological stimulants and for which form serves as a means of *disclosure*.

Nobody believes that the content of a newspaper consists of a report about the Kellogg Pact,[38] a scandal from the *Gazette de France* or an account of an everyday event like a drunken husband murdering his wife with a hammer on waste ground.

The *content* [*soderzhanie*] of a newspaper is the principle by which the *contents* [*soderzhimoe*] of the paper are organised and processed, with the aim of processing the reader from a class-based standpoint.

Herein lies the production-based inseparability of the sum total of content and form from *ideology*.

Herein lies the gulf that separates the content of a proletarian newspaper from the content of a bourgeois newspaper even though their factual contents are the same.

[Just as it is the practice in newspapers, so it is the practice everywhere else, from the forms of a work of art to the social forms of everyday life.][39]

But where is the error in our use of the term 'cognition'?

Its roots in the Old Norse *kna* (I can)† and the Old Saxon *biknegan*

---

* See: A. Preobrazhenskii, *Etimologicheskii slovar' russkogo yazyka* [Etymological Dictionary of the Russian Language].

† Hence the inseparability in German of *können* ('to be able') and *erkennen* ('to know').

(I take part) have been completely suppressed by a one-sidedly contemplative *understanding* of cognition as an abstractly contemplative function, the 'pure cognition of an idea', i.e. as something profoundly bourgeois.

There is no way in which we can produce within ourselves a revision of our perception of the act of 'cognition' as an act with immediate effects.

Even though reflexology has adequately demonstrated that the process of cognition means an increase in the quantity of conditional stimulants that provoke an active reflex reaction from a particular subject.[40]

Which means that, even in the actual mechanics of the process, there is something active and not passive.

Whereas in *practice*, when we are discussing cognition, we still employ the unnatural formula that separates it from activity and labour, as expressed, for instance, in Ernest Renan's formulation of 'pure cognition'. According to Plekhanov, he demanded: 'in his *Réforme intellectuelle et morale*, a strong government "which would compel the good rustics to do our share of the work while we devoted ourselves to mental speculation".'[41]

Abstract cognition divorced from directly active effectiveness is unacceptable to us.

We have no room for the separation of the cognition process from the productive.

It is no coincidence that in the French text the quotation ends: *'Tandis que nous spéculons . . . .'*

'Spéculons' translates as 'when we devote ourselves to speculation'. It is no coincidence that in our minds this term is linked to a quite different chain of associations.

Abstract science, scientific investigation that has no direct practical result, 'science for science's sake', 'cognition for cognition's sake' – we are prepared to brand these mercilessly like other phenomena that are joined under the generic designation 'speculative' as 'speculation', wherever they occur.

In the conditions of socialist construction there is as little room for speculative philosophy as there is for speculation in basic necessities.

For us, to know is to take part.

In this we base ourselves on the biblical phrase 'And Moses *knew* his wife Sarah . . .'[42] although this in no way implies that he had just become acquainted with her!

Cognition is construction.

The cognition of life is inseparable from the construction of life, from its *re-creation*.

In the age of construction there can be no opposition between these concepts. Even in the form of dissection through research.

The very fact of the existence of our age of socialist construction and of our social order refutes it.

It is the task of the coming age in our art to tear down the Great Wall of China that separates the primary antithesis between the 'language of logic' and the 'language of images'.

We demand from the coming age in art a renunciation of this opposition.

We want to restore the *qualitatively* differentiated and the alienated and individualised into something that is *quantitatively* correlated.

We no longer wish to oppose science to art in the *qualitative* sense.

We want to compare them *quantitatively* and *on this basis merge them into a single new kind of socially active factor*.

Are there any grounds for looking forward to such a path of synthesis?

Synthesis. Because we imagine that this solution is infinitely remote from the narrow formula that insists that 'didactic works must be entertaining and entertaining works must be didactic.'

Are there any grounds? Where is the common ground between the spheres of influence of what are for the time being *mutually antagonistic* areas?

There is no art without conflict. No art as process.

Be it the conflict between the arrow-like flight of Gothic vaults and the inexorable laws of gravity.

The conflict between the tragic hero and the twists of fate.

The conflict between the functional purpose of a building and the conditions dictated by the soil and the building materials.

The victory of the rhythm of verse over the deadening metrics of the poetic canon.

There is struggle on all sides. Formation is born of the clash of opposites. Its scope increases in intensity by constantly involving new spheres of emotional reaction on the part of the perceiver. Until, at its apogee, he is completely involved. Not as a unit, an individual, but as a collective, an audience. Until he himself joins the creative play. And is divided in two.

Collective against collective. Divided into sides. In sport the divided collective fights itself side against side. Sport as the highest form of art completely involves the spectator as creator. As participant. In contemporary terms this means a return through sport to close the circle with the pre-tragic play of the ancients.

In the same 'formal' relationship, of course, as you find in the certain amount of common ground you find between contemporary communism and primitive communism.

Nevertheless.

What about *science*?

Book. Printed word. Eyes. Eyes - brain. That's bad!

Book. Word. *Moving* from corner to corner. That's better! . . . Who has not crammed, running from corner to corner in a four-walled enclosure, book in hand?

Who has not drummed rhythmically with his fist, memorising 'Surplus value is . . . .'

In other words who has not given visual stimulation a helping hand by including some sort of motor rhythm in order to memorise abstract truths?

Even better. Auditorium. Lecturer. Not of course an emasculated educational bureaucrat. But one of those fiery old fanatics (they are becoming rarer and rarer) like the late Professor Sokhotsky, who could talk for hours on integrals and the analysis of infinitely small quantities with the same fire as Camille Desmoulins, Danton, Gambetta or Volodarsky thundered against the enemies of the people and the revolution.[43]

The temperament of the lecturer completely engrosses you. And those around you. The electrified audience in the steely embrace of what has suddenly become rhythmical breathing.

The audience has suddenly become . . . a circus, a hippodrome, a political meeting.

The arena of a single collective passion. A single pulsating interest.

Mathematical abstraction has suddenly become flesh and blood.

You remember the most complex formula – the rhythm of your own breathing. . . .

A dry integral is recalled in the feverish brightness of the eyes. In the mnemonic of *collectively* experienced *perception*.

A further example. The theory of music. Raucous individuals with dusty larynxes try in vain to master the scale of intervals: doh-re, re-mi, mi-fah . . . soh. The piano is taxed to the utmost. In the end both strings and nerves are overstrained. . . . It does not work out. You cannot restore the organic nature of the dissociative process that links voice and hearing. Then suddenly the individual *vibrato* becomes a chorus. And a 'miracle' occurs. In strict measure, interval by interval, the weak little voices are extended and expanded in *collective action*. It sounds out. It sounds out! . . . and it works out! It is achieved.

Suddenly people jump up from their seats. In a strangely measured dance they start to move across the room. What is this? Dionysian ecstasy? No. Jaques-Dalcroze[44] hit on the idea of perfecting the rhythmic memory of his pupils in *solfeggio* by making them mark rhythmic beat *with their whole organism* rather than just their hands. The most delicate nuances of tempo are then mastered with the greatest ease.

But let us move on. Quick march! The collective has been torn in two. Instead of the speaker's chair. Two desks. Opponents. Two 'catapults'.[45] In the fire of the dialectic, in discussion, are forged objective data, the evaluation of a phenomenon, fact.

'Side against side.'

The authoritarian-teleological 'it is so' flies to the devil. Axioms taken on faith collapse. 'In the beginning was the Word . . . .'[46] But *perhaps* it 'was' not? A *theorem* in contradictions requiring proof encompasses *dialectical* conflict.

It encompasses the essence of a phenomenon that can be understood in its contradictions in a dialectically exhaustive manner. Irrefutably.

Extremely intensively. Having mobilised the comprehensive elements of personal *logic* and *temperament* into an inner struggle between opposing points of view.

A complex of conditioned reflexes grown wise with experience. And the direct passion of conditioned reflexes.

In the crucible of the dialectic a new factor in construction has been smelted. A new social reflex has been forged.

What is the difference? What is the gulf between tragedy and essay? Is not the *point of both to provoke internal conflict and in its dialectical resolution to provide the perceiving masses with a new stimulus to activity and a means of creating life [zhiznetvorchestvo]*?

What is the difference between a perfected method of oratory and a perfected method of acquiring knowledge?

The new art must set a limit to the dualism of the spheres of 'emotion' and 'reason'.

It must restore to science its sensuality.

To the intellectual process its fire and passion.

It must plunge the abstract process of thought into the cauldron of practical activity.

Restore the splendour and wealth of gut-felt *forms* to the emasculated speculative *formula*.

Give the clarity of ideological *formulation* to *formal arbitrariness*.

That is the appeal that we are making. Those are the demands we are directing at the coming period of art.

Which art form will be able to meet the challenge?

Purely and solely the medium of cinema.

Purely and solely intellectual cinema. The synthesis of emotional, documentary and absolute film.

Only *intellectual* cinema will be able to put an end to the conflict between the 'language of logic' and the 'language of images'. On the basis of the language of the cinema dialectic.

An *intellectual* cinema of unprecedented form and social functionalism. A cinema of extreme cognition and extreme sensuality that has mastered the entire arsenal of affective optical, acoustical and biomechanical stimulants.

But someone is standing in the way.

Across the path.

Who is it? It is the 'living man'.[47]

He is applying to literature. He is already past the stage door of MKhAT and half-way into the theatre.

He is knocking on the door of the cinema.

Comrade 'living man'! I cannot speak for literature. Nor for theatre.

But cinema is not for you.

To cinema you are a 'right-wing deviation'.

You represent a demand at less than the highest level of technical resources and possibilities and, consequently, of the obligations of cinematic expression. The level of development of the means of production dictates the forms of ideology. You are a prescription that corresponds to the lowest stage of industrial development in the field of art.

As thematic material you are too much like a wooden plough for a highly industrialised art form like cinema in general and intellectual cinema, in its aspirations, in particular.

In addition, cinema is as suited to you and you to cinema as is the second hand of a stop-watch to the gutting of a white fish!

The 'living man' is entirely appropriate within the confines of the cultural limits and the cultural limitations of the resources of theatre . . . .

And not of Left theatre but of MKhAT in particular.

Of MKhAT and the MKhAT-like tendencies, now extravagantly celebrating their 'second childhood' around this demand. And this is entirely logical and consistent.

In fact nothing has become of Left theatre because it could not adapt. It split up and either moved into its next stage of development – cinema – or returned to its previous form of the AKhRR type.

Between them there remains only Meyerhold,[48] not the theatre but the master.

But cinema, which for reasons of *Realpolitik* cannot renounce certain MKhAT influences, must stubbornly pursue its course towards intellectual cinema as the highest form of development of the possibilities of cinema technique.

It is the same in cinema as in agriculture.

So far we have evidence of rather dubious progress so that, for example, in Belorussia the number of wooden ploughs has grown relatively faster than the number of metal ploughs. This, of course, also marks some 'progress' in the agricultural mechanisation of the countryside, but, even at its highest stage, it is inappropriate progress.[49]

Filling the screen with 'living man' would mean precisely the same 'inappropriate progress' towards the industrialisation of our cinema culture.

Cinema can – and consequently must – convey on the screen in tangible sensual form the pure, dialectical essence of our ideological debates. Without recourse to intermediaries like plot, story or living man.

Intellectual cinema can and must cope with themes like 'Right-Wing Deviation', 'Left-Wing Deviation', 'Dialectical Method', 'The Tactic of Bolshevism'.

Not just in characteristic 'vignettes' or scenes but in the exposition of whole *systems and systems of ideas*.

159

Like 'The Tactic of Bolshevism' rather than 'The October Revolution' or '1905', to take just one example.

Just the method and the system themselves, using concrete raw material, of course, but with a quite different orientation and from a different point of view.

Schemes that are more primitive either in their theme – psychological and psychologically reflective – or in their method of exposition – 'through intermediary protagonists' – remain the lot of less highly industrialised media of expression.

Of theatre and cinema of the old acted type.

But the lot of the new cinema, which is alone capable of encompassing dialectical conflict in the formation of understanding, is the task of irrevocably inculcating communist ideology into the millions.

It is the last link in the chain of the media of cultural revolution, stringing everything together and working towards a single monistic system from collective education and complex teaching methods to the newest forms of art; it ceases to be an art and moves on to the next stage in its development.

It is only through this resolution of its problems that cinema will really deserve the designation 'the most important of the arts'.

It is only in this way that it will differ fundamentally from bourgeois cinema.

It is only in this way that it will become part of the approaching age of communism.[50]

26. The Dramaturgy of Film Form[51] (The Dialectical Approach to Film Form)

> According to Marx and Engels the system of the dialectic is
> only the conscious reproduction of the dialectical course
> (essence) of the external events of the world.
>
> (Razumovsky, *The Theory of Historical Materialism*,
> Moscow, 1928)

Thus:

the projection of the dialectical system of objects into the brain

– *into abstract creation* –

– *into thought* –

produces dialectical modes of thought – dialectical materialism –

PHILOSOPHY.

Similarly:

the projection of the same system of objects – in concrete creation – in form –
produces

ART.

The basis of this philosophy is the *dynamic* conception of objects:
being as a constant evolution from the interaction between two contradictory
opposites.

Synthesis that *evolves* from the opposition between thesis and antithesis.

It is equally of basic importance for the correct conception of art and
all art forms.

In the realm of art this dialectical principle of the dynamic is embodied in

CONFLICT

as the essential basic principle of the existence of every work of art and every
form.

FOR ART IS ALWAYS CONFLICT:

1. because of its social mission,
2. because of its nature,
3. because of its methodology.

1. Because of its social mission, since: it is the task of art to reveal the
contradictions of being. To forge the correct intellectual concept, to form the
right view by stirring up contradictions in the observer's mind and through
the dynamic clash of opposing passions.

2. Because of its nature, since: because of its nature it consists in the
conflict between natural being and creative tendentiousness. Between organic
inertia and purposeful initiative.

161

The hypertrophy of purposeful initiative – of the principle of rational logic – leaves art frozen in mathematical technicism. (Landscape becomes topography, a painting of St Sebastian becomes an anatomical chart.)

Hypertrophy of organic naturalness – of organic logic – dissolves art into formlessness.

(Malevich becomes Kaulbach,
Archipenko a waxworks show.[52])

Because:

the limit of organic form
(the passive principle of being) is
NATURE
the limit of rational form
(the active principle of production) is
INDUSTRY

and:

at the intersection of nature
and industry stands
ART.

1. The logic of organic form
versus
2. the logic of rational form produces in collision the
dialectic of the art form.

The interaction between the two produces and determines the dynamic. (Not just in the sense of space-time, but also in the field of pure thought. I similarly regard the evolution of new concepts and attitudes in the conflict between normal conceptions and particular representations as a dynamic – a dynamisation of the inertia of perception – a dynamisation of the 'traditional view' into a new one.)

The basis of distance determines the intensity of the tension: (viz., for instance, in music the concept of intervals. In it there can be cases where the gap is so wide that it can lead to a break, to a disintegration of the homogeneous concept of art. The 'inaudibility' of certain intervals.)

The spatial form of this dynamic is the expression of the phases in its tension – rhythm.[53] This applies to every art form and, all the more so, to every form of its expression. Thus human expression is a conflict between conditioned and unconditioned reflex.

(I do not agree on this point with Klages[54] who
1. considers human expression not dynamically as process but statically as result and
2. attributes everything that moves to the field of the 'soul' and, by contrast, only that which restrains to 'reason', in the idealistic concept of 'reason' and 'soul' which here corresponds indirectly with the ideas of conditioned and unconditioned reflex.)

The same is equally true for every field, in so far as it can be understood as art. Thus, for instance, logical thought, viewed as art, also produces the same dynamic mechanism: 'The intellectual lives of Plato or Dante . . . were largely guided and sustained by their delight in the sheer beauty of the *rhythmic relation* between law and instance, species and individual, or cause and effect.'[55]

This also applies in other fields, e.g. in language, where the strength, vitality and dynamism derive from the irregularity of the particular in relation to the rule governing the system as a whole.

In contrast to this we can see the sterility of expression in artificial, totally regulated languages like Esperanto. It is from this same principle that the whole charm of poetry derives: its rhythm emerges as conflict between the metric measure adopted and the distribution of sounds that ambushes that measure.[56]

The concept of even a formally static phenomenon as a dynamic function dialectically symbolises the wise words of Goethe that

'Architecture is frozen music.'[57]

We shall employ this concept further. And, just as in homogeneous thought (a monistic attitude), both the whole and the minutest detail must be permeated by a *single principle*, so, together with the conflict of *social conditionality* and the conflict of *reality*, that same principle of conflict serves as the foundation stone for the *methodology* of art. As the basic principle of the rhythm that is to be created and of the derivation of the art form.

3. *Because of its methodology*: shot and montage are the basic elements of film.

MONTAGE
Soviet film has stipulated this as the nerve of film.

To determine the essence of montage is to solve the problem of film as such.

The old film-makers, including the theoretically quite outmoded Lev Kuleshov, regarded montage as a means of producing something by describing it, adding individual shots to one another like building blocks.

Movement within these shots and the resulting length of the pieces were thus to be regarded as rhythm.

A fundamentally false notion! It would mean defining an object exclusively in terms of its external course. Regarding the mechanical process of sticking the pieces together as a principle. We cannot characterise this kind of relationship between lengths as rhythm.

It would give rise to a metre that was as opposed to rhythm as such as the mechanical-metric Mensendick system is opposed to the organic-rhythmic Bode school in the case of bodily expression.

According to this definition (which Pudovkin also shares as a theorist) montage is the means of *unrolling* an idea through single shots (the 'epic' principle).[58]

But in my view montage is not an idea composed of successive shots stuck together but an idea that DERIVES *from the collision between two shots that are independent of one another* (the 'dramatic' principle). ('Epic' and 'dramatic' in

163

relation to the methodology of form and not content or plot!!) As in Japanese hieroglyphics in which two independent ideographic characters ('shots') are juxtaposed and *explode* into a concept. THUS:

Eye + Water	=	Crying
Door + Ear	=	Eavesdropping
Child + Mouth	=	Screaming
Mouth + Dog	=	Barking
Mouth + Bird	=	Singing
Knife + Heart	=	Anxiety, etc.*

Sophistry? Not at all! Because we are trying here to derive the whole essence, the stylistic principle and the character of film from its technical (-optical) foundations.

We know that the phenomenon of movement in film resides in the fact that still pictures of a moved body blend into movement when they are shown in quick succession one after the other.

The vulgar description of what happens – as a *blending* – has also led to the vulgar notion of montage mentioned above.

Let us describe the course of the said phenomenon more precisely, just as it really is, and draw our conclusions accordingly.

Is that correct? In pictorial-phraseological terms, yes.

But not in mechanical terms.

For in fact each sequential element is arrayed, not *next* to the one it follows, but on *top* of it. *For:*
the idea (sensation) of movement arises in the process of superimposing on the retained impression of the object's first position the object's newly visible second position.

That is how, on the other hand, the phenomenon of spatial depth as the optical superimposition of two planes in stereoscopy arises. The superimposition of two dimensions of the same mass gives rise to a completely new higher dimension.

In this instance, in the case of stereoscopy, the superimposition of two non-identical two-dimensionalities gives rise to stereoscopic three-dimensionality. In another field: concrete word (denotation) set against concrete word produces abstract concept.

As in Japanese (see above), in which *material* ideogram set against *material* ideogram produces *transcendental result* (concept).

The incongruity in contour between the first picture that has been imprinted on the mind and the subsequently perceived second picture – the conflict between the two – gives birth to the sensation of movement, the idea that movement has taken place.

---

* Abel Rémusat, 'Recherches sur l'origine de la formation de l'écriture chinoise' [Research on the Origin of the Formation of Chinese Script], *Académie des inscriptions et belles-lettres, Paris: Mémoires*, vol. 8(ii), Paris, 1827, pp. 1-33.

The degree of incongruity determines the intensity of impression, determines the tension that, in combination with what follows, will become the real element of authentic rhythm.

Here we have, in the temporal sense, what we see emerging spatially on the graphic or painted surface.

What does the dynamic effect of a picture consist of?

The eye follows the direction of an element. It retains a visual impression which then collides with the impression derived from following the direction of a second element. The conflict between these directions creates the dynamic effect in the apprehension of the whole.

I. It may be purely linear: Fernand Léger, Suprematism.[59]

II. It may be 'anecdotal'. The secret of the fabulous mobility of the figures of Daumier and Lautrec[60] consists in the fact that various parts of the bodies of their figures are depicted in spatial situations (positions) that vary temporally. See, for instance, Lautrec's 'Miss Cissy Loftus':

A logical development of position A for the foot leads to the elabortion of a corresponding position A for the body. But from the knee up the body is already represented in position A+a. The cinematic effect of the still picture is already visible here: from hips to shoulders we already have A+a+a. The figure seems alive and kicking!

III. Primitive Italian Futurism lies somewhere between I and II: the man with six legs in six positions.[61] (Between I and II because II achieves its effects by retaining natural unity and anatomical cohesion, whereas I achieves this through purely elementary elements, while III, although undermining nature, is not yet pushed as far as abstraction.)

IV. It can be of an ideographic kind. Like the pregnant characterisation of a Sharaku[62] (eighteenth-century Japan). The secret of his extremely clever power of expression lies in the anatomical *spatial disproportion* of the parts. (You might term I above *temporal disproportion*.) Julius Kurth expresses himself thus in *Sharaku* (he is describing a portrait of an actor, comparing it to a mask):

> While the carving is worked in fairly correct anatomical proportions, the proportions of the picture are quite simply impossible. The space between the eyes requires a spread that defies all reason. In relation to the eyes the nose is almost twice as long as a normal nose could possibly be. There is absolutely no relation between the chin and the mouth . . . . We can make the same observation about all Sharaku's large heads. It is, of course, unthinkable that the master should not have known that all these proportions were false. He has quite deliberately ignored what is formal and, *while the actual drawing of the individual parts rests on a powerfully concentrated naturalism, their composition is subjugated to purely intellectual points of view.*[63]

The spatial calculation of the corresponding size of one detail in relation to another and the collision between that and the dimension determined for it by the artist produces the characterisation: the resolution of the representation.

Finally, colour. A colour shade conveys a particular rhythm of vibration to our vision. (This is not perceived visually, but purely physiologically, because colours are distinguished from one another by the frequency of their light vibrations.) The nearest shade has a different frequency of vibration.

The counterpoint (conflict) between the two – the retained and the still emerging – frequency produces the dynamic of our perceptions and of the interplay of colour.

From here we have only to make one step from visual vibration to acoustic vibration and we find ourselves in the field of music. We move from the realm of the spatial-pictorial to the realm of the temporal-pictorial.

Here the same law rules. Because for music counterpoint is not just a form of composition but the basic rationale for the possibility of sound perception and differentiation. One might also say that in all the cases cited here the same *principle of comparison* operates: it makes possible for us discovery and observation in every field. With the moving image (film) we have, as it were, the synthesis of these two counterpoints: the spatial counterpoint of the image and the temporal counterpoint of music. Characterised in film through what we might describe as:

VISUAL COUNTERPOINT

This concept, when applied to film, allows us to designate various approaches to the problem, to a kind of film grammar. Similarly with a syntax of film expressions in which the visual counterpoint can determine a completely new system of forms of expression. (Experiments in this direction will be illustrated by extracts from my films.) In all this:
The *basic presupposition* is:
  The shot is not a montage element – the shot is a montage cell (a molecule).
This formulation explodes the dualistic division in the analysis:
    of: title and shot
    and: shot and montage.
Instead it is viewed dialectically as three different *phases in the formation of a homogeneous expressive task*. With homogeneous characteristics that determine the homogeneity of their structural laws.
The relationship between the three: *conflict within a thesis* (an abstract idea):

1. is *formulated* in the dialectic of the *title*,
2. is *formed* spatially in the *conflict within* the shot – and
3. *explodes* with the growing intensity of the *conflict montage between the shots*.

Once again this is quite analogous to human psychological expression. This is a conflict of motives. Conceivable, likewise, in three phases:

166

'Cissy Loftus', Henri de Toulouse–Lautrec 1894

1. Purely verbal utterance. Without intonation: spoken expression.
2. Gesticulative (mimic-intentional) expression. Projection of conflict on to the entire expressive body-system of man. ('Gesture' and 'sound gesture' – intonation.)
3. Projection of conflict into the spatial. With the growing intensity (of motives) the zigzag of mimic expression is catapulted into the surrounding space according to the same distorting formula. A zigzag of expression deriving from the spatial disposition of man in space.

Herein lies the basis for a quite new conception of the problems of film form. We cite as examples of conflict:

1. Graphic conflict (Fig. 26. 1).
2. Conflict between planes (Fig. 26. 2).
3. Conflict between volumes (Fig. 26. 3).
4. Spatial conflict (Fig. 26. 4).
5. Conflict in lighting.
6. Conflict in tempo, etc., etc.

(NB Here they are characterised by their principal feature, by their *dominant*. It is obvious that they occur mainly as complexes, grouped together. That applies to both the shot and to montage.)

For montage transition it is sufficient to imagine any example as being divided into two independent primary pieces

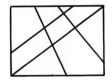 = 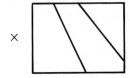 ×

NB The graphic case. It applies also to all other cases. The extent to which the conflict concept extends in the treatment of film form is illustrated by the following further examples:

7. Conflict between matter and shot (achieved by *spatial distortion* using camera angle: Fig. 26. 5).
8. Conflict between matter and its spatiality (achieved by *optical distortion* using the lens).
9. Conflict between an event and its temporality (achieved by slowing down and speeding up [*Multiplikator*]) and lastly:
10. Conflict between the entire *optical* complex and a quite different sphere.

That is how the conflict between optical and acoustic experience produces:
SOUND FILM
which is realisable as
AUDIO-VISUAL COUNTERPOINT.

1. GRAPHIC CONFLICT

2. CONFLICT OF PLANES

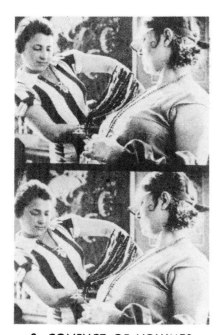

3. CONFLICT OF VOLUMES

4. SPATIAL CONFLICT

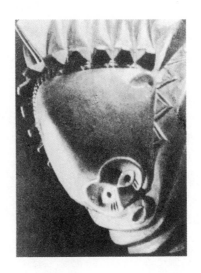

STATIC →← CONFLICT = DYNAMIC CAMERA

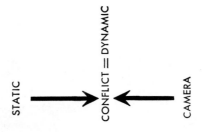

ARTIFICIALLY PRODUCED IMAGES OF MOTION

A. Logical

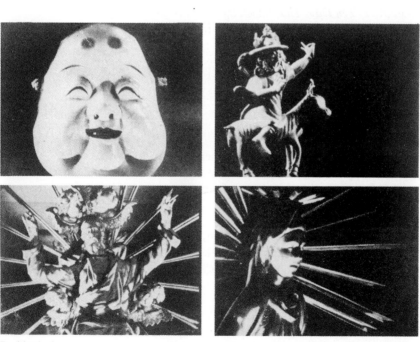

B. Alogical

171

1929

The formulation and observation of the phenomenon of film in the form of conflict provides the first opportunity to devise a homogeneous system of *visual dramaturgy* for every special and particular case of the problem of film.

To create a *dramaturgy of visual film form* that is determined in the same way as the existing *dramaturgy of film material* is determined. . . .[64]

The same standpoint – viewed as an outcome for film composition – produces the following stylistic forms and possibilities and this could constitute a

FILM SYNTAX
A TENTATIVE FILM SYNTAX.

We shall list here:

A series of compositional possibilities that develop dialectically from the thesis that the concept of filmic movement (time lapse) derives from the superimposition of – the counterpoint between – two different stills.

I. *Each moving piece of montage in its own right.* Each photographed piece. The technical determination of the phenomenon of movement. *Not yet composition* (a man running, a gun firing, water splashing).

II. *Artificially produced representation of movement.* The basic optical sign is used for arbitary composition:

A. *Logical*
Example 1. *Ten Days That Shook the World* (*October*).
Montage: repetition of a machine-gun firing by cross-cutting the relevant details of the firing.
Combination a):

Brightly lit machine-gun. Dark one.
Different shot. Double burst:
Graphic burst and light burst.

Combination b):

Machine-gun.
Close up of the machine-gunner (Fig. 26. 6).
Effect almost of double exposure with rattling montage effect.
Length of the pieces – two frames.

Example 2. *Potemkin* (1925).
Representation of a spontaneous action, *Potemkin* (Fig. 26. 7). Woman with pince-nez. Followed immediately – without a transition – by the same woman with shattered pince-nez and bleeding eye. Sensation of a shot hitting the eye.

B. *Alogical*
Example 3. *Potemkin*.
This device used for symbolic pictorial expression. *Potemkin*. The marble lion leaps up, surrounded by the thunder of *Potemkin*'s guns firing in protest

172

against the bloodbath on the Odessa Steps (Fig. 26. 10).

Cut together from three immobile marble lions at Alupka Castle (Crimea). One sleeping. One waking. One rising. The effect was achieved because the length of the middle piece was correctly calculated. Superimposition on the first piece produced the first jump. Time for the second position to sink in. Superimposition of the third position on the second – the second jump. Finally the lion is standing.

Example 4. *Ten Days*.
The firing in Example 1 is symbolically produced from elements that do not belong to the actual firing. To illustrate General Kornilov's attempted monarchist *putsch* it occurred to me that his militarist *tendency* could be shown in the cutting (montage), but creating the montage material itself out of religious details. Because Kornilov had betrayed his tsarist tendency in the form of a curious 'crusade' of Mohammedans (!) (his 'Wild Division' from the Caucasus) and Christians (all the others) against the . . . Bolsheviks. To this end a Baroque Christ with beams streaming (exploding) from its halo was briefly intercut with a self-contained egg-shaped Uzume mask. The temporal conflict between the self-contained egg shape and the graphic star produced the effect of a simultaneous explosion (a bomb, a shot) (Fig. 26. 8).

Example 5. *Ten Days*.
A similar combination of a Chinese sacred statue and a madonna with a halo (Fig. 26. 9). (NB As we see, this already provides the opportunity for tendentious (ideological) expression.)

Another example of more primitive effect from the same place: in the simple cross-cutting between church towers leaning in opposite directions.

So far the examples have shown *primitive-psychological* cases – using *only* the optical superimposition of movement.

III. The case of emotional combinations not merely of the visible elements of the pieces but principally of the chains of psychological association. *Associational montage (1923-4)*. As a means of sharpening (heightening) a situation emotionally.

In Case I we had the following: two pieces A and B following one another are materially identical. According to the position of the material in the shot they are, however, not identical:

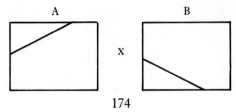

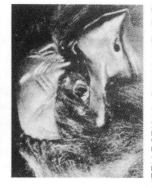

INTELLECTUAL DYNAMIZATION

These two combined produced dynamisation in space – the impression of spatial dynamic:

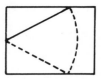

The degree of difference between positions A and B determines the tension of the movement. But let us take a new case:

Shot A and shot B are, in terms of material, *not identical*. The associations of the two shots are identical: associatively identical. By analogy this *dynamisation of the material* produces, not in the spatial but in the *psychological, i.e. the emotional, field*:

EMOTIONAL DYNAMISATION.

Example 1. *The Strike* (1923-4).

The shooting down of the workers is cut in such a way that the massacre is intercut with the slaughter of a cow. (Difference in material. But the slaughter is employed as an appropriate association.) This produces a powerful emotional intensification of the scene.

NB In this case the homogeneity of gesture plays a very great role in generally achieving the effect (the homogeneity of the dynamic gesture: movement within the shot – or of the static gesture: the graphic attitude of the shot). Here is an excerpt from the first version of this scene in the montage list (1923):

1. The head of a bull.
2. The butcher's knife strikes a downward blow.
3. Five hundred workers fall down a hill.
4. Fifty men get up. Hands.
5. A soldier's face. He aims.
6. Shots.
7. The bull standing. It twitches and falls.
8. Close-up. Convulsions of the hind legs. A hoof kicks into the blood.
9. Rifles.
10. Semi-close-up. People get up. Wounded.
11. Imploring hands raised towards the camera.
12. Butcher with blood-stained rope approaches the camera.
13. Hands.
14. The butcher approaches, etc.

This principle was subsequently also used by Pudovkin in *The End of St Petersburg* (1927) when he intercut shots of stock exchange and battlefield. And, in *The Mother* (1926), the ice breaking and the workers' demonstration.

This method may decay pathologically if the essential viewpoint – the emotional dynamisation of the material – gets lost. Then it ossifies into lifeless literary symbolism and stylistic mannerism. We may cite the following as an example:

Example 2: *Ten Days*.
The mellifluous peace overtures of the Mensheviks at the Second Congress of the Soviets (during the storming of the Winter Palace) are intercut with harp-playing hands. A purely literary parallelism that does nothing to enliven the material.

Similarly in Otsep's *The Living Corpse*,[65] with the intercutting (in imitation of *Ten Days*) of church cupolas or lyrical landscapes into the speeches of the prosecution and the defence counsels in the court. The same mistake as that above.

On the other hand, the predominance of purely dynamic effects may have a positive result:

Example 3: *Ten Days*.
The pathos of the adherence of the cycle battalion to the Second Congress of the Soviets is dynamised by the fact that, when their delegates enter, abstractly spinning cycle wheels (association with the battalion) were intercut. These resolved the pathetic content of the event as such into a perceptible dynamic. The same principle – the emergence of a concept, of a sensation from the juxtaposition of two disparate events – led on to:

IV. *The emancipation of closed action from its conditioning by time and space.*
The first attempts at this were made in the *Ten Days* film.

Example 1. (*Ten Days*)
A trench packed with soldiers seems to be crushed by the weight of an enormous cannonball descending on the whole thing. Thesis brought to expression. In material terms the effect is achieved through the apparently chance intercutting between an independently existing trench and a metal object with a similarly military character. In reality they have absolutely no spatial relationship with one another (Fig. 26. 11).

Example 2: *Ten Days*.
Similarly in the scene of Kornilov's *putsch* attempt, which puts an end to Kerensky's Bonapartist plans. In this sequence one of Kornilov's tanks, emerging from the trench, shatters the plaster figure of Napoleon that stands on Kerensky's desk in the palace of Petrograd and has purely symbolic meaning (Fig. 26. 12).

This method of making whole sequences in this way is now mainly being employed by Dovzhenko: *The Arsenal* (1929). Also by Esfir Shub on her Tolstoy film (1928).[66] In addition to this method of dissolving the accepted forms of handling film material I should like to cite another example, which has, however, not been realised in practice.

In 1924-5 I was very concerned with the idea of the filmic representation of real (actual) man. At that time the prevailing trend was that living man could only be shown in film in *long* dramatic scenes. And that cutting (montage) would destroy the idea of real man.

Abram Room established the record in this respect in *The Bay of Death*[67] by using eighty metre-long uncut dramatic scenes. I felt (and feel) that such a concept is utterly unfilmic.

For what really is, in linguistic terms, a precise characterisation of man?

His raven-black hair . . .
The waves in his hair . . .
His flashing, bright blue eyes . . .
His steely muscles . . .

Even when it is not so exaggeratedly phrased, every description, every verbal representation of a man (see above!) becomes an accumulation of waterfalls, lightning conductors, landscapes, birds, etc.

Why then should cinema in its forms follow theatre and painting rather than the methodology of language, which gives rise, through the combination of concrete descriptions and concrete objects, to quite new concepts and ideas? It is much closer to film than, for instance, painting, where form derives from *abstract* elements (line, colour). In film, by contrast, it is precisely the material *concreteness* of the shot as an element that is the most difficult aspect of the process of formation. Why not then lean rather more towards the system of language, where the same mechanism exists in the use of words and word complexes?

Why is it, on the other hand, that montage cannot be avoided even in the orthodox feature film?

The differentiation in montage pieces is determined by the fact that each piece has in itself no reality at all. But each piece is itself in a position to evoke a certain association. The accumulation of associations then achieves the same effect as that provoked in the audience by purely physiological means by a theatrical play that is unfolding in reality.

E.g. Murder on stage has a purely physiological effect. Perceived in a *single* montage sequence it acts like an item of *information*, a title. It only begins to work *emotionally* when it is presented in montage fragments. In montage pieces, each of which provokes a certain association, the sum of which amounts to a composite complex of emotional feeling. In traditional terms:

1. A hand raises a knife.
2. The eyes of the victim open wide.

3. His hands clutch the table.
4. The knife jerks.
5. The eyes close.
6. Blood spurts out.
7. A mouth shrieks.
8. Drops fall on to a shoe . . .

and all that kitsch! In any event each *individual piece* is already almost *abstract* in relation to the *action as a whole*. The more differentiated they are, the more abstract they become, aiming only at provoking a certain association. Now the following thought arises quite logically: could one not achieve the same effect more productively if one did not adhere so slavishly to plot but materialised the notion of *murder* in a free accumulation of associative material? Because the most important thing is to convey the representation of murder, the feeling of murder as such. Plot is only one of the means without which we still do not know how to communicate something to the audience. At any rate an attempt of this sort would produce the most interesting variety of forms. Let someone try it! Since 1923-4, when this thought occurred to me, I have unfortunately not had the time to carry out this experiment. Now I have turned to quite different problems.

But, *revenons à nos moutons*,[68] which will bring us closer to these tasks. Whereas, with 1, 2 and 3 the suspense was calculated to achieve purely physiological effects, from the purely optical to the emotional, we must also mention here the case in which the same conflict tension serves to achieve new concepts, new points of view, in other words, serves purely intellectual ends.

Example 1: *Ten Days*.
Kerensky's rise to (untrammelled) power and dictatorship after July 1917. Comic effect is achieved by *intercutting titles denoting ever higher rank* ('Dictator', 'Generalissimo', 'Minister of the Navy and the Army', etc.) with five or six sequences of the staircase in the Winter Palace with Kerensky ascending the *same* flight each time.

Here the conflict between the kitsch of the ascending staircase and Kerensky treading the same ground produces an intellectual resultant: the satirical degradation of these titles in relation to Kerensky's nonentity.

Here we have a counterpoint between a verbally expressed, conventional idea and a pictorial representation of an individual who is unequal to that idea.

The incongruity between these two produces a purely *intellectual* resolution at the expense of this individual. Intellectual dynamisation.

Example 2: *Ten Days*.
Kornilov's march on Petrograd took place under the slogan 'In the Name of God and the Fatherland'. Here we have an attempt to use the representation

for anti-religious ends. A number of images of the divine were shown in succession. From a magnificent Baroque Christ to an Eskimo idol.

Here a conflict arises between the concept 'God' and its symbolisation. Whereas idea and image are completely synonymous in the first Baroque image, they grow further apart with each subsequent image. We retain the description 'God' and show idols that in no way correspond with our own image of this concept. From this we are to draw anti-religious conclusions as to what the divine as such really is.

Similarly, there is here an attempt to draw a purely intellectual conclusion as a resultant of the conflict between a preconception and its *gradual tendentious discrediting by degrees* through pure illustration.

The gradual succession continues in a process of comparing each new image with its common designation and *unleashes a process that, in terms of its form, is identical to a process of logical deduction.* Everything here is already intellectually conceived, not just in terms of the resolution but also of the method of expressing ideas.

The conventional *descriptive* form of the film becomes a kind of reasoning (as a formal possibility).

Whereas the conventional film directs and develops the *emotions*, here we have a hint of the possibility of likewise developing and directing the entire *thought process.*

These two attempts were received in a very hostile fashion by the majority of the critics. Because they were understood in purely political terms. I willingly concede that it is precisely *this form that is best suited to express ideologically critical theses.* But it is a pity that the critics completely overlooked the filmic opportunities that could be derived from it. In both these attempts we find the first, still embryonic attempts to construct a really quite new form of filmic expression.

A purely intellectual film which, freed from traditional limitations, will achieve direct forms for thoughts, systems and concepts without any transitions or paraphrases. And which can therefore become a

SYNTHESIS OF ART AND SCIENCE.

That will become the really new watchword for our epoch in the field of art. And really justify Lenin's statement that 'of all the arts . . . cinema is the most important.'[69]

One of my next films, which is intended to embody the Marxist world-view, will be devoted to an experiment in this direction.

27. The Fourth Dimension in Cinema[70]

I

Exactly a year ago on 19 August 1928, before I had started work on the montage for *The General Line*, I wrote about the visit of the Japanese theatre in 'An Unexpected Juncture':

> [In the Kabuki] a single monistic sensation of theatrical 'stimulation' takes place. The Japanese regards each theatrical element not as an incommensurable unit of the various categories of affect (on the various sensual organs) but as a single unit of *theatre* . . . .
>
> Addressing himself to the sensual organs, he bases his calculations on the final *sum* of stimulants to the brain, ignoring *which* path that stimulation takes.[71]

This characterisation of the Kabuki theatre was to prove prophetic.

It was this method that lay at the basis of the montage for *The General Line*.

Orthodox montage is montage by *dominants*, i.e. the combination of shots[72] according to their predominant (principal) sign. Montage by tempo. Montage by the principal direction within the frame. Montage by length (duration) of sequences, etc. Montage by foreground.

The dominant signs of two shots side by side result in a particular conflicting relationship that produces a particular expressive effect (I have in mind here a *pure montage* effect).

This situation covers every level of intensity in montage juxtaposition or shock:

from a complete opposition between the dominants, i.e. a sharply contrasting construction,

to a scarcely noticeable 'modulation' from shot to shot. (All cases of conflict are of necessity cases of complete absence of conflict.)

As for the actual dominant, we must in no way regard it as something independent, absolute and invariably stable. There are technical ways of treating a shot so that its dominant can be more or less specifically defined, but never absolutely.

The characteristics of the dominant are variable and profoundly relative.

The revelation of its characteristics depends on the actual combination of shots for whose combination it is itself the condition.

A circle? an equation with two unknown quantities?

A dog, chasing its own tail?

No, simply a precise definition of what is.

In fact, even if we have a *series* of montage shots:

(1) A grey-haired old man,
(2) a grey-haired old woman,
(3) a white horse,
(4) a snow-covered roof,

it is far from clear whether this series works on 'old age' or 'whiteness'.

This series might continue for a very long time before we finally come upon the signpost shot that immediately 'christens' the whole series with a particular 'sign'.

That is why it is better to place this kind of indicator as near as possible to the beginning (in 'orthodox' construction). Sometimes it is even necessary to do this . . . with an intertitle.

These reflections completely exclude a non-dialectic postulation of the question of the unambiguity of the shot in itself.

The shot never becomes a letter but always remains an ambiguous hieroglyph.

It can be read only in context, just like a hieroglyph, acquiring specific *meaning, sense* and even *pronunciation* (sometimes dramatically opposed to one another) only *in combination with* a separate reading or a small sign or reading indicator placed alongside it.

The General Line was edited in a different way from orthodox montage by individual dominants.

The 'aristocracy' of unambiguous dominants was replaced by the method of 'democratic' equal rights for all the stimulants, viewed together as a complex.

The point is that the dominant (with all due obeisance to its relativity) is far from being the only stimulant in the shot, even if it is the most powerful. For example, the 'sex appeal'[73] of the American heroine-beauty is accompanied by various stimulants: texture – like the material of her dress; light – the character of the lighting; race and nation (positive: the 'all-American type' or negative: the 'coloniser-oppressor' for a Negro or Chinese audience); social class, etc.

In a word a whole complex of secondary stimulants always accompanies the *central* stimulant (like the sexual one in our example).

This is precisely what happens in acoustics (in the particular instance of instrumental music).

There, alongside the resonance of the basic dominant tone, there is a whole series of secondary resonances, the so-called overtones and undertones. Their collision with one another and with the basic tone, etc., envelops the basic tone with a whole host of secondary resonances.

Whereas in acoustics these secondary resonances become merely 'interference', in music (which is calculatedly composed) they are one of the most remarkable means of influence for Left composers like Debussy and Scriabin.[74]

It is exactly the same in optics as well. All sorts of aberrations, distortions and other defects that are present and that can be remedied by systems of lenses, can, if calculatedly composed, produce a whole series of compositional effects (changing a 28 lens to a 310).

In combination with a calculation of the secondary resonances of the actual filmed material this produces, by analogy with music, the visual *overtonal* complex of the shot.

This is the method on which the montage of *The General Line* is constructed. This montage is not constructed on the *individual dominant* but takes the sum of *stimuli* of all the stimulants as the dominant.

That distinctive montage *complex within the shot* that arises from the collisions and combinations of the individual stimulants inherent within it,

of stimulants that vary according to their 'external nature' but are bound together in an iron unity through their reflex physiological essence.

Physiological, in so far as the 'psychic' in perception is merely the physiological process of a *higher nervous activity*.

In this way the physiological sum total of the resonance of the shot *as a whole*, as a complex unity of all its component stimulants, is taken to be the general sign of the shot.

This is the particular 'feeling' of the shot that the shot as a whole produces.

And for the montage shot this is the same as the Kabuki method for its individual scenes (see the beginning).

The basic sign of the shot can be taken to be the final sum total of its effect on the cortex of the brain as a whole, irrespective of the ways in which the accumulating stimulants have come together.

The *sum totals* thus achieved can be put together in any conflicting combination, thereby opening up quite new possibilities for montage resolutions.

As we have seen, because of the actual genetics of these methods, they must be accompanied by an extraordinary *physiological* quality.

Just like the music that constructs its works on a special deployment of overtones.

Not the *classicism* of Beethoven, but the *physiological* quality of Debussy or Scriabin.

Very many people have remarked on the extraordinary physiological quality of the effect of *The General Line*.

This is precisely because it is the first film to be edited on the principle of visual overtone.

The actual *method* of montage can be interestingly verified.

If, in the brilliant classical distances of the future, cinema uses both overtonal montage and, simultaneously, montage by dominant sign (tonic), then, as always, the new method will in the first instance always assert itself by highlighting the principle of a problem.

In the first stages of its emergence overtonal montage had to take a line in sharp *contrast* to the dominant.

It is true that in many cases, even in *The General Line*, you will find such 'synthetic' combinations of tonal and overtonal montage.

For example, the 'diving under the icons' in the 'religious procession' or the grasshopper and the mowing-machine are edited *visually* according to their *sound* association with a deliberate revelation and their spatial similarity.

But the methodologically significant constructions are, of course, those that are without a dominant. Or those in which the dominant appears in the shape of a purely physiological formulation of the task (which is the same thing). For instance, the montage of the beginning of the 'religious procession' is carried out according to the degree to which the individual shots are 'saturated with fervour' and the beginning of the *sovkhoz* sequence is graded according to its 'carnivorousness'. The conditions of the extra-cinematic disciplines that place the most unexpected signs of equality between materials are logically, formally and in an everyday context absolutely neutral vis-à-vis one another.

There is also a mass of cases of montage junctures that make a resounding mockery of orthodox scholastic montage by dominants.

The easiest way to demonstrate this is to run the film on a 'cutting table'. It is only then that the complete 'impossibility' of the montage junctures that *The General Line* abounds in is quite clearly revealed. At the same time the extreme simplicity of its metre and its scale is revealed.

Whole long sections of reels comprise shots that are quite equal in length or of absolutely primitive repeated shortness. The entire, complex, rhythmically *sensual* nuancing of the combination of shots is carried out almost exclusively in accordance with the 'psychophysiological' resonance of the shot.

It was on the cutting table that I myself discovered the extremely sharply defined uniqueness of the montage of *The General Line*.

When I had to cut and shorten it.

The 'creative ecstasy' that accompanies the assembly of the shots and the composition of the montage, the 'creative ecstasy' when you hear and feel the shots, that moment had already passed.

Cutting and shortening do not require inspiration, only technique and skill.

There I was, winding the 'religious procession' on the table and I could not fit the combination of shots into one of the orthodox categories (where you can lord it because of your pure experience).

On the table, *immobile*, the sign that dictated their selection was quite unintelligible.

The criteria for their assembly turned out to lie outside the usual formal cinematic criteria.

And here is revealed yet one more curious feature of the similarity between the visual overtone and the musical.

It cannot be sketched in the statics of the shot, just as musical overtones cannot be sketched into the score.

Both emerge as a real constant only in the dynamics of the musical or cinematic *process*.

Overtonal conflicts, which are foreseen but not 'recorded' in the score, emerge only through dialectical formation when the film passes through the projector or an orchestra performs a symphony.

The visual overtone proves to be a real piece, a real element . . . of the fourth dimension.

Of what is spatially unrepresentable in three-dimensional space and only emerges and exists in the fourth dimension (three plus time).

The fourth dimension?!

Einstein? Mysticism?

It is time to stop being frightened of this 'beast', the fourth dimension. Einstein himself assures us:

> The non-mathematician is seized by a mysterious shuddering when he hears of 'four-dimensional' things, by a feeling not unlike that awakened by thoughts of the occult. And yet there is no more common-place statement than that the world in which we live is a four-dimensional space-time continuum.[75]

With such an excellent instrument of cognition as cinema even its primitive form – the sensation of movement – is resolved by the fourth dimension. We shall soon acquire a concrete orientation in this fourth dimension and feel just as much at home as if we were in our bedsocks!

And then the question would arise of a fifth dimension!

Overtonal montage emerges as a new montage category in the series of montage processes that we are already familiar with.

The direct *applied* significance of this method is *immense*.

And that is just as true for the burning question of the moment in cinema – for sound film.

In the article I have already cited at the beginning, referring to the 'unexpected juncture' – the similarity between the Kabuki and sound cinema – I wrote about the contrapuntal method of combining the visual and sound image: 'To master this method you have to develop within yourself a new *sense: the ability to reduce visual and sound perceptions to a new denominator* . . .'.[76]

Whereas *sound* and *visual* perceptions are *not reducible* to a single denominator.

They are constants in different dimensions.

But the visual overtone and the sound overtone are constants in a *single dimension*!

Because, while a shot is a visual *perception* and a tone is a sound perception, *both visual and sound overtones are totally physiological sensations.*

And, consequently, they are of *one and the same kind*, outside the sound of acoustic categories that serve merely as guides, paths to its achievement.

For the musical overtones (a beat) the term 'I hear' is no longer strictly appropriate.

Nor 'I see' for the visual.

For both we introduce a new uniform formula: 'I feel'.*[77]

The theory and methodology of the musical overtone have been elaborated and made known (Debussy, Scriabin).

The General Line establishes the concept of the visual overtone.

The contrapuntal conflict between the visual and the sound *overtones* will give rise to the composition of the Soviet sound film.

II

Is the method of overtonal montage something foreign to cinema, something artificially grafted on to it, or is it simply a quantitative regrouping of a single sign so that it makes a dialectical jump and begins to figure as a new qualitative sign?

In other words, is overtonal montage the next dialectical stage of development of the general montage system of methods and does it stand in staged succession in relation to other kinds of montage?

The four categories of montage with which we are familiar are as follows (there is such a thing as a 'category' of montage, because we characterise montage by the specific quality of the process in various cases, and not by the external 'signs' that attend these processes):

1. *Metric Montage*
The basic criterion is the *absolute length* of the shots. The shots are joined together according to their lengths in a formula-scheme. This is realised in the repetition of these formulas.

Tension is achieved by the effect of mechanical acceleration through repeated shortening of the lengths of the shots while preserving the formula of the relationship between these lengths ('double', 'triple', 'quadruple', etc.).

The primitive form of the method: Kuleshov's montages in three:four time, march-time and waltz-time (3:4, 2:4, 1:4, etc.).

---

* Here it is a question of the same kind of de-individualisation of the *character* of a category of feeling as you find, for instance, in a different 'psychological' phenomenon: when you feel the *pleasure* that derives from extreme *suffering*. Stekel writes of this: 'In cases of affective hypertension pain ceases to be regarded as pain, but is felt as nervous tension . . . . But any powerful nervous tension has a tonic effect, and the heightened tone provokes a feeling of satisfaction and pleasure.'

The degeneration of the method: metric montage using a beat of complex brevity (16:17, 22:57, etc.).

This beat ceases to exert a physiological effect because it contradicts the 'law of prime numbers (relationships)'.

Simple correlations that preserve clarity of perception make for that same maximal effect.

That is why they are always to be found in wholesome classics in every field:

architecture, the colour in a painting, a complex composition by Scriabin – they are always crystal clear in their 'articulation'. The geometricisation of *mises en scène*, the clear schemes of rationalised state enterprises, etc.

Dziga Vertov's *The Eleventh Year* can serve as a similar negative example: the metric module is mathematically so complex that you can only determine its pattern 'with a ruler in your hand', i.e. by measuring rather than perceiving.

This in no way implies that the metre should be 'recognisable' at the moment of perception. Quite the contrary. Even though you are not conscious of it, it is nevertheless an indisputable precondition for the *organisation* of our feeling.

Its clarity joins the 'pulse-beat' of the film and the 'pulse-beat' of the audience 'in unison'. Without this there can be no 'contact' between the two.

Overcomplexity in the metric relationships will instead produce a chaos of perception rather than a distinct emotional tension.

A third instance of metric montage lies between the other two: it is a metric refinement in a complex alternation of shots that have a simple relationship with one another (or vice versa).

Examples: the *lezginka*[78] in *October* and the patriotic demonstration in *The End of St Petersburg*. (The second example can be considered a classic of *purely metric montage*.)

In this kind of montage what lies within each shot is completely *subordinated* to the absolute length of the shot. Hence it adheres to the primitive dominant character of the resolution (the possible 'unambiguity' of the shot).

2. Rhythmic Montage

Here the content within the shot is an *equivalent* element in determining the actual lengths of the shots.

Abstract scholastic determination of the lengths is replaced by a flexibility in the correlation between *actual* lengths.

Here the actual length does not coincide with the mathematical length allotted to it in accordance with the metric formula. Here the practical length of a shot is defined as the derivative of the specific quality of the shot and of the 'theoretical' length allocated to it according to the scheme.

Here it is quite possible to find a case of complete metric *identity* between the shots and the reception of the rhythmic figures exclusively through the combination of shots in accordance with signs within the shot.

187

Formal tension through acceleration is here achieved by shortening the shots, not just in accordance with the basic scheme's formula of repetition, but also in violation of this canon.

Best of all by introducing more intensive material into the same temporal signs.

The 'Odessa Steps' may serve as a classic example. There the 'drumbeat' of the soldiers' feet descending the steps destroys all metrical conventions. It occurs outside the intervals prescribed by the metre and each time it appears in a different shot resolution. The final build-up of tension is produced by *switching* from the rhythm of the soldiers' tread as they descend the steps to another, new form of movement – the next stage in the intensification of the same *action* – the pram rolling down the steps.

Here the pram works in relation to the feet as a direct staged accelerator.

The 'descent' of the feet becomes the 'rolling down' of the pram.

Contrast this with the previously cited example from *The End of St Petersburg*, where the tensions are resolved by cutting the *same* shots down to minimal cellular montage.

Metric montage is quite adequate for that kind of simple march-time resolution.

But it is not adequate for more complex rhythmic tasks.

Its forcible application 'come what may' to these sorts of cases leads to montage failures. That is what happened, for example, in *Storm over Asia*[79] with the religious dances. This montage, edited on the basis of a complex metric scheme that had not been adjusted to the specific weighting of the shots, could not achieve the necessary rhythmic effect.

And in many cases this provokes bewilderment among specialists and inconsistent perception among the lay audience. (This kind of case can be artificially corrected by the musical accompaniment, as happened in this particular example.)

I have called the third type of montage:

3. *Tonal Montage*
This term appears for the first time. It is the next stage after rhythmic montage.

In rhythmic montage by *movement* within the shot we mean actual transposition (either of an object within the scope of the shot or of the eye along the guiding lines of an immobile object).

But here, in this instance, movement is understood in a wider sense. Here the concept of movement embraces *all sorts of vibrations* that derive from the shot.

But to assert that, from the standpoint of perception, it is characterised by the emotional tonality of the shot, i.e. by an apparently 'impressionistic' measurement, is a simple delusion.

The characteristics of the shot can be measured just as precisely here as in the simplest instance of 'ruler' measurement in primitive metric montage.

Only the units of measurement are different here. And the actual amounts to be measured are different.

For example, the degree of light variation in a piece cannot only be gauged by a selenium light-element but can be fully perceived in all its gradations by the naked eye.

If we give a conventional emotional designation of 'more gloomy' to a shot that is to be predominantly resolved by lighting, this can be successfully replaced by a mathematical coefficient for a simple degree of illumination (a case of 'light tonality').

In another instance, where we designate the shot as a 'sharp sound', it is extremely easy to apply this designation to the overwhelming number of acutely angled elements of the shot that prevail over the rounded elements (a case of 'graphic tonality').

A play on combinations of degree of soft-focus[80] or various degrees of sharpness is the most typical example of tonal montage.

As I said above, this case is constructed on the *dominant* emotional resonance of the shot. Some examples: 'Fog in the port of Odessa' (the beginning of the 'Mourning for Vakulinchuk' sequence in *Potemkin*).

Here the montage is built exclusively on the emotional 'resonance' of individual shots, i.e. on the rhythmic vibrations that do not produce spatial transpositions.

In this regard it is interesting that, alongside the basic tonal dominant, a second, accessory *rhythmic* dominant of shots is operating in the same way.

It acts as a link between the tonal construction of this particular scene and the rhythmic tradition, whose furthest development is tonal montage as a whole.

Because rhythmic montage is a special variant of metric montage.

This secondary dominant is realised in the scarcely perceptible ripple on the water, the slight bobbing of vessels at anchor, the slowly swirling mist, the seagulls landing slowly on the water.

Strictly speaking, these too are elements of a *tonal* order. The movements are transpositions of material edited according to their tonal, rather than their spatial-rhythmic, sign. For here the spatially incommensurable transpositions are combined according to their emotional resonances.

But the principal indicator for the assembly of the shots remains entirely in the sphere of the combination of shots according to their basic optical light variations (degrees of 'obscurity' and 'illumination'). And it is in the structure of these variations that the identity with a minor harmony in music is revealed.

In addition, this example gives us a model of a *consonance* in internal combinations of movement as *transposition* and movement as *light variation*.

Here too the intensification of tension follows the *intensification* of the same 'musical' sign of the dominant.

The scene of the 'delayed harvest' (in the fifth reel of *The General Line*) may serve as a particularly graphic example of this build-up.

In both the construction of the film as a whole and this particular case its basic method of staging has been observed.

Namely, conflict between 'content' and its traditional 'form'.

An emotional structure applied to non-emotional material. The stimulant has been separated from its characteristic situation (e.g. the treatment of the erotic in the film) right down to paradoxical tonic constructions. The industrial 'monument' turns out to be a typewriter. There is a wedding . . . but between a bull and a cow. And so on.

Thus the thematic *minor* of the harvest is resolved by the thematic *major* of the storm, the rain. (And even the harvest – a traditionally major theme of fertility under the sun's blazing rays – is used to resolve the minor theme and is in addition soaked by the rain.)

Here the increase in tension proceeds by internal reinforcement of the resonance of that same dominant chord. The growing *pre-storm 'oppressiveness'* of the shot.

As in the previous example, the tonal dominant – movement as light variation – is here accompanied by a second dominant, a rhythmic one, i.e. movement as transposition.

Here it is realised in the growing force of the wind, condensed from air 'streams' into the watery 'torrents' of rain.[81] (A complete analogy with the soldiers' feet passing to the pram.)

In this general structure the role of the rain and wind is quite identical to the link between the rhythmic rocking and the haziness of the lens in the first example. In fact, the *character* of the relationships is the direct opposite. In opposition to the consonance of the first example we have here the reverse.

The heavens gathering into a black stillness are contrasted with the strengthening dynamic force of the wind, that grows and condenses from air 'streams' to watery 'torrents' – the next stage of intensity of the dynamic attack on women's skills and the delayed rye.

Here this collision between two tendencies – the intensification of the static and the intensification of the dynamic – provides us with a clear instance of *dissonance* in tonal montage construction.

From the point of view of emotional perception the 'harvest' sequence is an example of the *tragic* (active) minor key, as distinct from the *lyrical* (passive) minor like the 'port of Odessa' sequence.

It is interesting that both examples are edited according to the first appearance of movement, which follows movement as transposition. That is, according to 'colour':

in *Potemkin*, moving from dark grey to misty white (real-life equivalent: 'dawn'), in the harvest sequence, from light grey to lead black (real-life equivalent: 'the approaching storm'), i.e. according to the frequency of light variations, that are *increasing in frequency* in one instance and *decreasing*, according to the sign, in the other.

We have a complete repetition of the picture of simple metric construction, but perceived in a new and significantly higher category of movement.

The fourth montage category can be justly called:

4. Overtonal Montage

As we can see, overtonal montage, as I characterised it at the beginning of this essay, is the furthest organic development of tonal montage.

As I have already indicated above, it distinguishes itself by taking full account of all the stimulants in the shot.

This characteristic enhances perception from a *melodically emotional colouring to a direct physiological sensation*.

I think that this also marks an advance on the other stages.

These four categories are the *methods of montage*. They become a *montage construction* proper when they enter into conflicting relationships with one another (as in the examples cited).

In this process, replacing one another in accordance with the scheme of their interrelationships, they move towards more refined variants of montage that flow organically from one another.

Thus, the transition from the metric to the rhythmic method arose from the emergence of conflict between the length of the shot and movement within the shot.

The transition to tonal montage resulted from the conflict between the rhythmic and tonal principles of the shot.

Lastly, overtonal montage resulted from the conflict between the tonal principle of the shot (the dominant) and the overtonal.

These considerations provide us in addition with an interesting criterion with which to evaluate montage construction from the standpoint of its 'pictorial quality' [*zhivopisnost'*]. Pictorial quality as opposed to cinematic. Aesthetic pictorialism as opposed to physiological animation.

To pass judgment on the pictorialism of a *shot* in cinema is naive. It is for people with a reasonable knowledge of painting but absolutely no qualifications in cinema. This kind of judgment could include, for example, Kazimir Malevich's[82] statements on cinema. Not even a film novice would now analyse a film shot as if it were an easel painting.

I think that the criterion for evaluating the 'pictorialism' of a montage construction, in the broadest sense of the term, must be this: is the conflict resolved within one of the montage categories, i.e. without a conflict arising between different montage categories?

Cinema begins where the collision between different cinematic measures of movement and vibration begins.

For example, the 'pictorial' conflict between a figure and the horizon (whether static or dynamic is irrelevant), or the alternation of differently lit shots purely according to the conflicts between the light variations, or between the forms of the object and its illumination, etc.

We should also note the characteristics of the effect of individual montage variants on the 'psychophysiological' complex of the perceiver.

The first category is characterised by the primitive motor of effect. It is capable of leading the audience into specific outwardly motor states.

This is how the hay-making sequence in *The General Line*, for example, is edited. The individual shots move – 'unambiguously' – in a single movement from one side of the frame to the other, and I really laughed when I watched the more impressionable section of the audience as they rocked slowly from side to side with the increasing acceleration or when the shots got shorter. The effect was the same as that of a drum and brass playing a simple march.

We call the second category rhythmic, although it could also be called primitive emotional. Here the movement is more subtly calculated, because the emotion is also the result of movement, but of movement that never reaches the primitive external transposition.

The third category – tonal – could be called melodic emotional. Here the movement, which in the second case had already ceased to be transposition, clearly passes over into emotional *vibration* of a still higher order.

The fourth category – a new influx of pure physiologism – repeats with the greatest intensity the first category, once more finding a new stage in the intensity of the direct motor effect.

In music this is explained by the fact that, from the moment when overtones appear in parallel with the underlying resonance, there also appear so-called beats, i.e. kinds of vibrations that once again cease to be perceived as tones but are perceived rather as purely physical 'parallaxes' on the part of the perceiver. This applies to strongly pronounced timbre instruments where the overtonal principle is greatly preponderant.

They sometimes achieve the sensation of physical 'parallax' almost literally: very large Turkish drums, bells, organ.

In some places in *The General Line* I managed to achieve conflicting combinations of the tonal and overtonal lines. Sometimes they also collide with the metric and rhythmic lines. For example, individual junctions in the religious procession: 'diving' beneath the icons, the melting candles and the panting sheep at the moment of ecstasy, etc.

It is interesting that, while making our selection, we quite unconsciously produced evidence of the essential equality between *rhythm* and *tone*, establishing the same kind of staged unity between them as I had previously established between the concepts of *shot* and *montage*.

Hence, tone is a stage of rhythm.

For those who are afraid of such gradational reductions to a common denominator and of the extension of the characteristics of one stage into another for the purposes of research and methodology, I shall recall a quotation concerning the basic elements of the dialectic:

> These, apparently, are the elements of the dialectic. These elements may be presented in a more detailed way thus: . . .
>
> (11) an endless process of deepening the human cognition of objects, phenomena, processes etc. from appearances to essence and from the less profound to the more profound essence.
>
> (12) from coexistence to causality and from one form of connection and interdependence to another, deeper and more general.
>
> (13) repetition, at the highest stage, of certain traits, characteristics etc. of the lowest stage and
>
> (14) return, as it were, to the old. . . . [83]

After this quotation I think that there will be no objection to the next order of montage, established as an even higher category of montage, i.e. intellectual montage.

Intellectual montage is montage not of primitively physiological overtonal resonances but of the resonances of overtones of an intellectual order,

i.e. the conflicting combination of accompanying intellectual effects with one another.

The gradation is here determined by the fact that there is no difference in principle between the motive force of a man rocking to and fro under the influence of primitive metric montage (viz., the hay-making example) and the intellectual process within it, for the intellectual process is the same oscillation – but in the centres of higher nervous activity.

Whereas in the first case under the influence of 'tap-dance montage' (*chechëtochnyi montazh*) the hands and feet quiver, in the second case this quivering, provoked by an intellectual stimulant combined differently, produces an identical reaction in the tissues of the higher nervous system of the thought apparatus.

Whereas, judged as 'phenomena' (appearances), they seem in fact to be different, judged as 'essence' (process), they are, of course, identical.

The application of the experience of work on lower lines to categories of a higher order gives us the opportunity to carry the attack into the very heart of objects and phenomena.

Hence, the fifth category was the case of the intellectual overtone.

The sequence of the gods in *October* may serve as an example of this. In it all the conditions for their juxtaposition are conditioned by the class-intellectual (class, because, whereas the emotional 'principle' is universally human, the intellectual principle is profoundly coloured by class) resonances of the shot of 'god'.

193

1929

These shots were assembled on a descending intellectual scale and lead the notion of god back to a block of wood.

But this, of course, is not yet the intellectual cinema that I have been announcing for some years now.

Intellectual cinema will be the cinema that resolves the conflicting combination of physiological overtones and intellectual overtones,[84] creating an unheard-of form of cinema which inculcates the Revolution into the general history of culture, creating a synthesis of science, art and militant class consciousness.

As we see it, the question of the overtone has enormous significance for the future.

We must examine the problems of its methodology all the more attentively and conduct a thorough investigation of it.

28. The Principles of the New Russian Cinema[1]

I should say at the outset that it is not the purpose of our film to provide an agreeable way of passing the time or a source of entertainment. For us film is always a very serious matter which has an educational and cultural *raison d'être*. Since we started production we have tried to find serious scientific bases for all artistic questions and especially for cinema so that we can uphold this principle. For the past four years or so a sort of university of cinema has been organised in Moscow where young people are trained to be directors, cameramen or actors. This university (which is, I think, quite unique) also includes centres for experimental research where questions of cinema theory and practice are discussed and things can be tried out.

But this is not the only organisation working for cinema. The Universities of Moscow and Leningrad have wholly specialised centres, employing all sorts of methods, for the psychological analysis of the audience.

There are other organisations that maintain contact with the audience in order to study it better, like the Society of Friends of Soviet Cinema[2] which has cells in all the large factories, in the villages, everywhere, and whose purpose is to investigate all aspects of what the factory or Red Army audience thinks of the films. It questions them on the film forms employed, their comprehension of the film, what shocks them, what does correspond to the demands of the public and what does not. These data are collected and analysed and the lessons learnt are then applied.

Let us now move on to the particular ideas that gave birth to our cinema. You are aware that new art forms are always drawn and derived from new social forms. The idea that governs our cinema is the same idea that not long ago governed our Revolution. It is the predominance of the collective element over the individual element.

You are aware of the role that collectivism plays in Russian social life, in our Revolution. I do not have to tell you this but I want to show you how this conception determines all aspects of our cinema: the commercial, the production, the aesthetic and the artistic. Let us first of all examine the commercial aspect.

We have a cinema monopoly: all film production and distribution is the monopoly of the state. This greatly facilitates the achievement of our educational and cultural aims. You are well aware that educational films do not bring in as much money as pornographic films or very successful adventure films. We therefore require of our great historical or adventure films that are shown abroad in large cinemas that they make the money we need to build cinemas in the villages and mobile cinemas that can reach the most distant corners of our vast republic. The role of these mobile cinemas is vital to the development of the culture of the small national republics that are part of the Soviet Union.

The culture of these national minorities could not develop under tsarism and Russian culture was imposed on everybody. Now our policy in this respect is quite different and we are trying to develop all the local cultures.

Some small republics could not by themselves sustain a film company that would work on the themes that interested them. In the Muslim republics, for example, the emancipation of women is still a burning issue, for which film is a necessary propaganda instrument. But this is only possible with state support because the small Muslim republics are too restricted to secure production.

The same applies to films for the peasantry. Films of the kind that you will not be seeing are very important: they are not commercial but their purpose is to explain to the peasants how to use machines.

People often say, as an argument against state control of cinema, that a monopoly of production, by suppressing competition, can harm the quality of a work of art. This is not so.

If you have read our newspapers you will have noticed that in all spheres one thing has replaced commercial competition for our factories and that is the competition of self-respect.

For example, a Moscow factory challenges a Leningrad factory by saying that it will produce more, better and more cheaply. So a competition between the two factories begins. It lasts six months or a year and it is a purely sporting matter.

The same thing happens in cinema: the film studios throw down the same challenges in respect of the quality of their films. That is a valuable stimulus to their work.

The collectivist movement also plays a large role in the production of films. When we first choose a subject our interest is not determined by the shock to our nervous system, by our amusement or our curiosity. When we choose a subject it is always one that interests the masses and means something to everyone.

Like all other branches of industry we have a Five-Year Plan for our production. It is a plan that fixes the principal themes and the principal questions which are to be developed in cinema in the course of those five years. We reserve a space for unforeseen themes furnished by current events but there is a general plan that we adhere to. The issues that we attack through our cinema are always the most topical issues of the day. *The General Line*, for instance, has as its theme the issue of industrialisation and the co-operative organisation of villages. Similarly, the moral and family issues for which the new conditions are forcing us to seek new solutions give rise to new film themes. Once a theme has been found, we place an order with a professional scriptwriter or director who turns it into a script. When the script is finished, we discuss it collectively in the factories or in places with a special interest in the issue that is being dealt with. If it is a peasant film, like *The General Line* that I am unable to show you, we discuss the script with peasants, and every peasant, knowing that it is a film made for his benefit, shows an interest, gives his opinion, says what he thinks of the subject, assists and contributes to it through his familiarity with the background, and the interests involved and thus fulfils the role that we want him to fulfil.

When production starts the masses and collectives also contribute to the shooting. In the great mass films like *The General Line* and *Ten Days That Shook the World*,[3] for example, the great mass scenes are almost entirely played by actors who are workers, voluntary and unpaid extras. In *Ten Days*, when we were shooting the storming of the Winter Palace, two or three thousand workers turned up every day or night with bands all prepared to play the scenes that we wanted them to play. The street shooting was played entirely by volunteers: almost all of them had played a more serious game in 1917 than ten years later in 1927! This gives us the opportunity to recreate the atmosphere and the truth of events. I always say that the masses can only be used like this in our country because there are not many countries where you can lead two or three thousand armed workers on to the streets with impunity!

When the film is finished, and before it is shown in cinemas, we send it to factories and villages, and the classes represented in the film subject it to very severe criticism. Showing a film that you have just finished is quite a difficult job. You have to take it to the factory, listen to what people say about it, change your film when required, add what is necessary to ensure that it faithfully expresses what you intend. On the other hand, however, you have direct contact with the creative masses, with the audience, and with the people you are working for . . . .

Let us now pass on to film formulas. The collectivist movement plays a large part in this as well. The need to make films that have a collective value has helped us to smash the eternal triangle of conventional drama that comprises the husband, the wife and the lover: every American and French film has the same plot. But, if you compare our historical films depicting the development of the masses and their history with American films on historical subjects, you will see the difference straight away. In America there are always two lovers together in the foreground and only the background changes. Today it is the French Revolution, tomorrow the Commune, but the characters are always the same and the historical events are of no interest.

What is there the accessory becomes for us the essential.

We want to get inside life. If we are making a film about life in the navy we go to Odessa or Sebastopol, move in the sailors' milieu, study the atmosphere, the feelings of these people and in this way we manage to recreate the feeling of the milieu that interests us. If it's a peasant film like *The General Line* we go to a village, we spend our time among the peasants and in this way we manage to express local colour and the feeling of the land. The same goes for actors and various interpreters.

We have already said that it is not only professional actors who can perform in cinema: we find that ordinary people can express their feelings better, can be more natural, than professional actors. Occasionally it is a question of time. Whereas an actor playing an old man has one or two days to prepare for as well as rehearse his part, a real old man already has a sixty years' lead on work at his part: he ought therefore to manage better than an actor. But non-professional actors create a lot of difficulties for us. You have to search out in a crowd the faces, expressions and heads that you want and that correspond to the idea that you are forming of the script. You have to find among real people the characteristic expression that is floating in your imagination.

When you have at last found the right person, other difficulties begin. You take this person on and you ask them: would you like to be filmed, sir (or madam)? Almost always, people say yes. But almost at once they add that they will only be photographed *en famille*. It is a photographic tradition: the husband, the wife, the children, the grandmother refuse to be separated and it is difficult to make them understand that you do not need them all. Occasionally it is quite impossible. In *The General Line*, for instance, there is one woman who only agreed to be photographed on condition that she had her mother-in-law beside her because her husband was in another town and she was afraid that people would say bad things about her!!! In this case there is a device you can use: you arrange the shot so that you cut out the person you do not want and leave them outside the frame.

It is more complicated if you want a person who in real life is very honest to play a 'negative' role in the film. It is very easy to play a positive role but very difficult to play a scoundrel because you are always afraid that the character you are representing on the screen will be mistaken for you in everyday life and that your neighbours and acquaintances will take the evil deeds committed on the screen to be real.

In this case you have to resort to tricks again. In *Tens Days* everyone wanted to play the Bolsheviks and no one wanted to play the Mensheviks. In that case we used a very simple process: we gave the actors the text of an inflammatory speech and they spoke it with great fervour. After this we added titles that said the exact opposite and the result was what you have not seen in *Ten Days*!

There are other difficulties as well. While working on *The General Line* we had to go to very primitive regions where there were many medieval traditions and extraordinary difficulties. We had, for instance, to shoot a wedding scene. The first day we had gathered about twenty girls who were to act in this wedding. Everything was going well and we had started shooting, but on the second day not one girl turned up to be filmed. We could not discover why and we made enquiries to find out what could have happened. We were then told that the old women who are always opposed to progress had persuaded the girls that the cameras were able to photograph through their clothes, and that girls who were quite decent when they were being filmed would when projected be as naked as nymphs!!! Naturally nobody wanted us to film them any more and we had to explain to them afterwards that their fears were unfounded. But the interesting thing to note is the premonition of X-rays in this village which imagined that you could photograph through something.

Now the same general idea dominates the new forms of cinema that we are in the process of investigating. The mass film is not regarded as the last stage in the development of Soviet film. It gave us the opportunity to smash the tradition of the triangle and it gave us the opportunity to look for other modes of expression in film. I do not want to belittle the role of people making pure documentaries or abstract films. The great difference between their research and research into mass films is that the abstract film is not concerned to organise or provoke the predominantly social emotions of the audience whereas the mass film is primarily concerned to provoke the audience's emotion. We no longer have the adventure film, the detective film, etc. at our disposal: we have therefore to look to the image itself and to methods of cutting to find the means of provoking the emotions we are seeking.

It is a question that greatly concerns us. After working on this for some time we have managed to accomplish the greatest task of our art: filming abstract ideas through an image, making them in some way concrete. We have done this, not by translating an idea through some kind of anecdote or story, but by finding directly in an image or in a combination of images the means of provoking emotional reactions that are predicted and calculated in advance.

I do not know if I am explaining myself sufficiently clearly but I think the idea is intelligible enough on its own. It is a matter of producing a series of images that is composed in such a way that it provokes an affective movement which in turn triggers a series of ideas. From image to emotion, from emotion to thesis. In proceeding in this way there is obviously a risk of becoming symbolic: but you must not forget that cinema is the only concrete art that is at the same time dynamic and can release the operations of the thought process. The thought process cannot be stimulated in the same way by the other arts, which are static and which can only provoke a thought response without really developing it. I think that this task of intellectual stimulation can be accomplished through cinema. This will also be the historic artistic achievement of our time because we are suffering from a terrible dualism between thought (pure philosophical speculation) and feeling (emotion).

In early times, the times of magic and religion, science was simultaneously an element of emotion and an element of collective knowledge. With the advent of dualism things became separated and we have, on the one hand, speculative philosophy, pure abstraction, and, on the other, the element of pure emotion. We must now go back, not to the primitive stage of the religious state but towards a similar synthesis of the emotional element and the intellectual element.

I think that only cinema is capable of achieving this grand synthesis, of providing the intellectual element with its life-giving sources, both concrete and emotional. That is our task and that is the path that we should follow. It will be the starting-point for the new film that I want to make: it must make our worker and our peasant think dialectically. This film will be called *Marx's 'Capital'*.[4] It will not be a story that unfolds but an essay to make the illiterate and ignorant audience understand and learn the dialectical way of thinking.

I had a lot of marvellous things to tell you about *The General Line* before projecting it but unfortunately I cannot tell you them because they would no longer be concrete.

In conclusion I want to tell you once again that we consider our films to be a collective production, because we are seeking to express the ideas and the interests of the creative masses as well as possible in our works and, if our films do have a power and a mood, it is merely the expression of the power and mood, and of the will, of the creative masses who are putting enormous effort into building socialism in our Union.

Now you have been deprived of your dessert. We cannot show you the film and, if by way of dessert you want to put questions to me, play a little game with me, a sort of ping-pong of questions and answers, I am entirely at your disposition. But do not put any questions that are too complicated: that is all I ask of you.

We now quote the most typical of the questions put to Eisenstein by the audience.

Q.: *Is Inkizhinov[5] a professional actor?*

A.: Yes, he is a professional actor. Pudovkin works with actors: that is one point on which our views differ. He is doing something very interesting: he is looking for something between a professional actor and the people that I use in my films. He takes an actor like Inkizhinov and uses him once as if he were not an actor. He lets him play a role that corresponds to his temperament and his natural calling. He is thus at the same time an actor and a real person: but such coincidences are rare and that is why Pudovkin almost always uses each actor in only one film.

Q.: *What should we think of talking films?*

A.: I think that a 100 per cent talking film is nonsense and I believe that everyone agrees with me.

But sound film is much more interesting and the future belongs to it. Particularly Mickey Mouse films. The interesting thing about these films is that sound is not used as a naturalistic element.

They look for the sound equivalent of a gesture or a plastic scene, i.e. not the sound that accompanies it in reality but the equivalent of this optical fact in the acoustic domain.

In Japanese theatre hara-kiri scenes are illustrated by sounds that correspond to what you see through the emotional and sentimental reaction that they give you. You have the same thing in the Mickey Mouse films where the sound accompaniment is provided by an association or a pure equivalence.

Q.: *What do you think of 'Bed and Sofa'?*[6]

A.: It is a very interesting film from the point of view of its subject. We have a lot of films in this genre that we desperately need because they confront questions of family morality and other questions that currently preoccupy us. It is a sort of didactic theatre where all sorts of questions are debated. I do not want to say that what I have told you here about the intellectual film is obligatory or that this is the only form that should and can exist in our country. In our country, in the USSR, every stage of cultural development must have the film forms that correspond to it and that are intelligible to it. If you are making a film for the villages you cannot have the same system of montage and cutting as you use for films that are destined for the towns because the peasant perceives things at a different speed: peasants cannot see and respond to an image at the same projection speed that a town-dweller is accustomed to.

Q.: *Do you explain things to your actors or do you surprise them like the Cine-Eyes?*

A.: The most interesting part of my work is not the actual shooting but what takes place beforehand because I have to be like a kind of detective and try to capture the expressions and movements that are characteristic of the person who has to play the role, the expressions that are in some way an organic part of him. When I have found these movements I combine them in a way that might produce a quite different expressive effect. Each movement in itself expresses nothing: it is a purely relative question. The Cine-Eyes are doing something different: they fix the movements and the expressions just as they are in daily life. I take natural and intrinsic details, I combine them differently, I try to extract new expressions and effects from them.

Q.: *Do you sincerely believe that the Russian peasant is capable of making useful criticisms of your film?*

A. Of course I must say that the best criticisms come either from critics who understand art, but these are unfortunately very rare, or from primitive peasants, genuinely sincere and direct people. Most people who fall between these categories are of no use to us in films. They are people who have been deprived of their spontaneous *élan* and who know absolutely nothing of what might interest us.

Q.: *What do you think of Surrealism?*

A.: It is very interesting because Surrealism works, I may say, in a way that is dramatically opposed to ours. It is always interesting to understand and evaluate things on diametrically opposed ground: I must admit that on one level we might find common ground and speak the same language. The systems of expression in Surrealism and in our work are basically very close to one another. Both appeal to the subconscious but they use it in inverse fashion.

I have read the Surrealist manifestos: very great spontaneity and direct expression are acknowledged as the best thing in the Surrealist genre. We are doing the same thing but in different directions. The task of *The General Line*, for instance, was to instil pathos into events which in themselves are neither pathetic nor heroic. It is very simple and very easy to instil pathos into something like the encounter between *Potemkin* and the squadron because the subject is inherently pathetic but it is much more difficult to find a means of instilling pathos and provoking a great and powerful emotion if all you have as your subject is a cream separator.

Then you must search for new ways of attacking the subconscious and thereby provoking the elements of pathos and ecstasy that you need for this subject.

I must add to the subject of Surrealism that the extremes meet or, if you take Marx's formulation, opposite objects have the possibility of changing places and combining. That is probably why the personal sympathies between us are quite strong. But from the theoretical point of view we are very different: the Surrealists seek to expose subconscious emotions while I seek to use them and play with them to provoke emotion.

Q.: *Could an independent artist with anarchist tendencies develop freely in Russia?*

A.: I think that the most fertile ground for that is France.

Q.: *French reporters who have been there tell us that laughter is dead in Russia. Is this true?*

A. There are so many things to make fun of that you can be sure that people still laugh at them. When I tell them the tale of my evening here I think that they will laugh a lot!

29. **Rin-Tin-Tin Does His Tricks for Noted Russian Movie Man**[7]

Sergei Eisenstein, Rin-Tin-Tin and several members of the Artkino Guild and a reporter from the *Boston Herald* met for luncheon at the Hotel Vendome. Rin-Tin-Tin did not actually stay for lunch, although at one point he volunteered to make lunch of the reporter.

The little meeting began somewhat ominously in a drawing room. Rin-Tin-Tin, who had trotted over from the Keith Albee Theater to have his picture taken with Mr Eisenstein, was lying around on an oriental rug. Dave Niles of the Artkino Guild and other organizations made a friendly gesture towards the canine star, who remained noticeably indifferent. The dog's owner, Lee Duncan, then issued a sudden warning that Rin-Tin-Tin, when left alone, automatically put himself 'on guard'. Mr Niles desisted.

'If I say the word,' said Mr Duncan, 'you could go right over and pat him or even pull his ear.' Mr Duncan, however, did not say the word, and Rin-Tin-Tin's ear was not pulled.

Rin-Tin-Tin Performs

A little later, after everybody had come in, including Mr Eisenstein, Mrs Ralph Adams Cram, Mrs Felix Frankfurter, Mrs Cornelia Stratton Parker, Courtney Crocker and Henry Wadsworth Longfellow Dana, Rin-Tin-Tin went through his tricks. He yawned, stretched, smiled, scratched an imaginary flea on his right shoulder and another on his left shoulder. Towards the end of his repertoire, all in fun as it turned out, he growled, snarled and showed his teeth at the reporter.

At the time this seemed like the height of unpleasantness but the real unpleasantness was yet to come: Rin-Tin-Tin, just to prove that his heart was gold, kissed the reporter with moist decision upon the end of his nose. Mr Eisenstein, the famous Russian director, en route to Hollywood, seemed unimpressed with the performance.

With that over, the guests reluctantly bade adieu to the Warner Brothers star, and entered the dining room. There they were entertained by Mr Eisenstein who, in the space of an hour or so, answered approximately 100 questions about Russia, Russian movies, the Russian soul and his own business.

Mr Eisenstein, director of *Potemkin, Ten Days That Shook the World, Old and New* and other films, is a young man apparently in his early 30s. His hair is light brown and bushy, receding slightly from his temples. He spoke fluently and well, taking the occasion a little less seriously than his hosts, packers of the Artkino Guild Theater.

Rin-Tin-Tin doing his tricks for noted Russian movie man

He seemed, likewise, less worried than his hosts about the possible effect of Hollywood upon his art.

As his contract allows, he will go home in three months if he finds that his ideas are too much frowned upon in California. He is confident that an 'artistic success' can be a commercial success – even in the movies – if the subject is wisely chosen. He does not know just what he will do here; that is, he says, a Paramount business secret.

He has had no experience with sound pictures, but he does not fear the new technique; his four years with the legitimate stage plus his six years with the movies are enough training, so he thinks, for his direction of the talkies.

'You destroy illusions about Russia,' one woman told him.

'Illusions ought always to be destroyed,' he said. 'The truth is better.'

What director does he think is best in America? The man who directs the Mickey Mouse films, animated cartoons with sound. Eisenstein likes them. Russia itself, he says, is in too serious a mood to produce any humor. If ever she does, it will be satirical. Even in fun the Russians will be serious.

30. The Dynamic Square[8]

It is possible that, at first glance, this article may seem too
detailed or its subject not of sufficiently 'profound' value,
but it is my wish to point out the basic importance of this
problem for every creative art director, director and cameraman. And I appeal to them to take this problem as seriously
as possible. For a shudder takes me when I think that, by
not devoting enough attention to this problem, and permit-
ting the standardisation of a new screen shape without the
thorough weighing of all the pros and cons of the question,
we risk paralysing once more, for years and years to come,
our compositional efforts in new shapes as unfortunately
chosen as those from which the practical realisation of the
Wide Film and Wide Screen now seems to give us the opportunity of freeing ourselves.

S.M.E.

Mr Chairman, Gentlemen of the Academy,

I think this is one of the great historic moments in the development of the
figurative potential of the screen. At a time when the incorrect handling of
sound is on the point of ruining the *figurative* achievements of the screen –
and we all know only too many examples where this has actually occurred! –
the arrival of the wide screen with its opportunities for a new screen shape
throws us once again headlong into questions of purely spatial composition.
And much more – it affords us the possibility of reviewing and reanalysing
the whole aesthetic of figurative composition in cinema which for thirty years
has been rendered inflexible by the inflexibility of the proportions of a screen
frame determined inflexibly once and for all.

Gee, it *is* a great day!

All the more tragic therefore the terrible enslavement of the mind by
traditionalism and routine that manifests itself on this happy occasion.

The card inviting you to this meeting bears the representation of
three differently proportioned horizontal rectangles, 3 × 4, 3 × 5 and 3 × 6,
as suggestions for the proportions of the screen for wide film projection. They
also represent the limits within which the creative imagination of the screen
reformers and the authors of the coming era of a new frame shape revolves.

I do not wish to be either exaggeratedly symbolic or rude and compare the creeping rectangles of these proposed shapes to the creeping men-
tality of the film reduced thereto by the weight upon it of the commercial
pressure of dollars, pounds, francs or marks, according to the locality in
which the cinema happens to be suffering!

But I must point out that, in proposing these proportions for discussion, we only reinforce the fact that for thirty years we have been content to see excluded 50 per cent of compositional possibilities as a result of the *horizontal shape* of the frame.

By 'excluded' I mean all the possibilities of *vertical, upright composition*. And instead of using the opportunity afforded by the advent of wide film to break that loathsome upper part of the frame, which for thirty years – and, in my own case, for six years – has bent and bound us to a passive horizontalism, we are on the verge of emphasising this horizontalism still more.

It is my purpose to defend the cause of this 50 per cent of compositional possibilities which have been exiled from the light of the screen. It is my desire to intone the hymn of the male, the strong, the virile, active, *vertical* composition!

I am not anxious to enter into the dark phallic and sexual ancestry of the vertical shape as a symbol of growth, strength or power. It would be too easy and possibly too offensive for many a sensitive listener!

But I do want to point out that the movement towards a vertical perception launched our hirsute ancestors on their way to a higher level. This vertical tendency can be traced in their biological, cultural, intellectual and industrial efforts and manifestations.

We started as worms creeping on our stomachs. Then we ran horizontally for hundreds of years on our four legs. But we only became something like mankind from the moment when we hoisted ourselves on to our hind legs and assumed the vertical position.

Repeating the same process locally in the verticalisation of our facial angle too.

I cannot, nor need I, enter in detail into an outline of the whole influence of the biological and psychological revolution and shock that followed from that paramount change of attitude. It will be enough to mention man's activities. For many years man was herded into tribes on an endless expanse of fields, bound to the earth in an age-long bondage by the nature of the primitive plough. But he marked in vertical milestones each step in his progress to a higher level of social, cultural or intellectual development. The upright lingam of the mystic Indian beliefs of ancient times, the obelisks of the Egyptian astrologers, Trajan's column incarnating the political power of Imperial Rome, the cross of the new spirit ushered in by Christianity. The high point of medieval mystical knowledge burst upright in the Gothic ogive arch and spire. Just as the era of precise mathematical knowledge shouts its paean in the sky with the Eiffel Tower! And assails the vault of an amazed heaven with armies of skyscrapers and the infinite rows of smoking chimneys or trellisses of oil-pumps of our great industries ranged along the skyline. The endless trails of wandering wagons have heaped themselves upon one another to form the tower of a Times or Chrysler building. And the camp fire, once the homely centre of the travellers' camp, has now paused to vomit its smoke from the unending heights of factory chimneys. . . .

By now, surely, you will have deduced that my suggestion for the optical frame of the supreme and most synthetic of all arts (all of whose possibilities are included in the cinema notwithstanding the fact that it doesn't use them!) is that it must be vertical.

Not at all.

For in the heart of the super-industrialised American, or the busily self-industrialising Russian, there still remains a nostalgia for infinite horizons, fields, plains and deserts. An individual or nation achieves the height of mechanisation yet marries it to our peasant and farmer of yesteryear.

The nostalgia of 'big trails', 'fighting caravans', 'covered wagons' and the endless breadth of 'old man rivers'. . . .

This nostalgia cries out for horizontal space.

And on the other hand industrial culture too sometimes brings tribute to this 'despised form'. It abandons the unfinished Brooklyn Bridge to the left of Manhattan and attempts to surpass it by the Hudson Bridge to the right. It constantly expands the length of the body of poor *Puffing Billy* to that of the Southern Pacific locomotives of today. It lines up endless outspread chains of human bodies (legs, as a matter of fact) in the unnumerable rows of music-hall girls – and, indeed, what limit is there to the other horizontal victories of the age of electricity and steel!

Just as, in contrast to her pantheistic horizontal tendencies, Mother Nature provides us at the edge of Death Valley or the Mojave Desert with the huge 300-foot-high General Sherman and General Grant trees, and the other giant sequoias, created (if we may believe the geography text-books of every country) to serve as tunnels for coaches or motor cars to pass through their pierced feet. Just as, in contrast to the infinite horizontal *contredanse* of the waves, at the edge of the ocean, we encounter the same element shot upright to the sky as geysers. Just as the crocodile stretched out basking in the sun is flanked by an upright standing giraffe accompanied by an ostrich and a flamingo, all three clamouring for a decent screen frame appropriate to their upright shape!

So neither the horizontal nor the vertical proportion of the screen *alone* is ideal for it.

In actual fact, as we saw, in the forms of nature as in the forms of industry, and in the mutual encounters between these forms, we find the struggle, the conflict between both tendencies. And the screen, as a faithful mirror, not only of conflicts emotional and tragic, but equally of conflicts psychological and optically spatial, must be an appropriate battleground for the skirmishes of both these optical-by-view, but profoundly psychological-by-meaning, spatial tendencies on the part of the spectator.

What is it that, by readjustment, can in equal degree be made the figure for both the vertical and horizontal tendencies of a picture?

The battlefield for such a struggle is easily found – *it is the square*, the rectangular space form exemplifying the equal quality of the length of its dominant axes.

The one and only form that is equally fit, by alternately suppressing right and left or up and down, to embrace all the multitude of expressive rectangles in the world. Or used as a whole to engrave itself by the 'cosmic' imperturbability of its *squareness* in the psychology of the audience.

And this specially in a *dynamic* succession of *dimensions* from a tiny square in the centre to the all-embracing full-sized square of the whole screen!

The 'dynamic' square screen, that is to say one providing in its dimensions the opportunity of impressing, in projection, with absolute grandeur every geometrically conceivable form of the picture limit.

(Note here, firstly, that this means that dynamism in the changeable proportion of the projected picture is accomplished by masking a part of the shape of the film square – the frame.

And note, secondly, that this has nothing to do with the suggestion that the proportions 1:2 (3:6) furnish a 'vertical possibility' by so far masking the right and the left that the remaining area has the form of an upright standing strip. The *vertical spirit* can never be attained in this way: first, because the occupied space comparative to the horizontal masked space will never be interpreted as something *axially opposed to it*, but always *as a part* of the latter and, second, because, in *never surpassing the height* that is bound to the horizontal dominant, it will never impress as an opposite space axis – the one of uprightness. That is why my suggestion of squareness puts the question in a quite new perspective, notwithstanding the fact that varityped masking has been used even within the dull proportions of the present standard film size, and even by myself – in the opening shot of the Odessa Steps in *Potemkin*.)

No matter what the theoretical premises, only the square will afford us a real opportunity at last to produce decent shots of so many things that have been banished from the screen until today. Glimpses along winding medieval streets or of huge Gothic cathedrals overwhelming them. Or these replaced by minarets if the town portrayed should happen to be oriental. Decent shots of totem poles. The Paramount building in New York, Primo Carnera,[9] or the profound and abysmal canyons of Wall Street in all their expressiveness – shots available to the cheapest magazine – yet banished for thirty years from the screen.

So much for my form.

And I believe profoundly in the rightness of my statement because of the synthetic approach upon which its conclusions are based. Furthermore, the warm reception for my statement encourages me to believe in the theoretical soundness of my argument.

But the lying form of the screen (so appropriate to its lying spirit!) has a host of refined and sophisticated defenders. There exists even a special and particular literature on these questions and we should leave our case incomplete if we did not critically review the arguments therein contained for the form that it prefers.

209

The memorandum distributed to us before this meeting . . . and brilliantly compiled by Mr Lester Cowan (assistant secretary of the Academy) provides a brief and objective survey of all that has been written regarding the proportions of the screen.[10] Most of these writings share a preference for the horizontal frame.

Let us examine the arguments that have brought different authors from different sides and specialisations to the same, unanimously acclaimed, and wrong suggestion.

The principal arguments are four: two from the dominion of aesthetics, one physiological, and one commercial.

Let us demolish them in the order quoted.

The two aesthetic arguments in favour of the horizontal shape of the screen are based on deductions deriving from traditions in the art forms of painting and stage practice. As such they should be eliminated from the discussion without even being considered, for the greatest errors invariably arise from the attempt to transplant practical results based upon the resemblance of the superficial appearances of one branch of art to those of another. (An entirely different practice is the discovery of similarity in *methods* and *principles* of different arts corresponding to the psychological phenomena that are identical and basic to all art perceptions – but the present superficially exposed *analogies*, as we shall see, are far removed from this!)

Indeed, from the methodological similarity of different arts it is our task to seek out the strictest differentiation in adapting and handling them according to the organic specifics that are typical for each. To impose the adoption of the laws that are organic to one art upon another is profoundly wrong. This practice has something of adultery in it. Like sleeping in another person's wife's bed. . . .

But in this instance the arguments in themselves bring so mistaken a suggestion from their own proper dominion that it is worth while considering them to demonstrate their falsity.

Firstly, Loyd A. Jones discusses the various rectangular proportions employed in artistic composition and gives the results of a statistical study of the proportions of paintings. The results of his research seem to favour a ratio of base to altitude considerably larger than 1, and probably over 1.5.[11]

A statement that is startling in itself. I don't repudiate the enormous statistical luggage that was doubtless at the disposal of Mr Jones in enabling him to make so decisive a statement.

But as I set about summoning up my pictorial recollections gathered through all the museums that I have so lately visited during my rush through Europe and America, and recalling the heaps of graphic works and compositions studied during my work, it seems to me that there are exactly as many upright standing pictures as pictures disposed in horizontal lines.

And everyone will agree with me.

The statistical paradox of Mr Jones derives probably from an undue weight being placed upon the compositional proportions of the nineteenth-century pre-Impressionist period – the worst period of painting – the 'narrative' type of picture. Those second- and third-rate paintings, which were far removed from the progressive high road of painting development, are far more numerous even today than the new schools of painting – even in comparison with Picasso and Léger – as petty-bourgeois oleographs in most concierges' offices in the world!

In this 'narrative' group of painting the 1:1.5 proportion is certainly predominant, but this fact is absolutely unreliable if considered from the point of view of pictorial composition. These proportions in themselves are 'borrowed goods' – entirely unconnected with pictorial space organisation, which is a problem for painting. These proportions are barefacedly borrowed – not to say stolen! – from the stage.

The *stage composition* each of these pictures intentionally or unintentionally reproduces is a process that is in itself quite logical, since the pictures of this school are occupied not with pictorial problems but with 'representing scenes' – a painting purpose even formulated in *stage* terms!

I mention the 19th century as specially abundant in this type of picture, but I do not wish to convey the impression that other periods are entirely lacking in them! Consider, for example, the Hogarth series *Marriage à la Mode* – satirically and scenically in their 'represented' anecdotes a most thrilling series of pictures . . . and nothing more.

It is remarkable that in another case, where the author of the painting was, practically and professionally, also the stage composer (or 'art director' as we would say in Hollywood), this phenomenon has no place. I mean the case of the medieval miniature. The authors of the tiniest filigree brushwork in the world, on the leaves of gilded bibles or *livres d'heures* (do not confuse with *hors d'oeuvre!*), were at the same time the architects of the various settings of the mysteries and miracles. (For instance, Fouquet and an innumerable mass of artists whose names have been lost to posterity.[12]) Here, where, owing to the subject, we ought to have the closest reproduction of the aperture of the stage – we miss it. And find a freedom entirely devoid of such bounds. And why? Because at that time *the stage aperture did not exist.* The stage was then limited far off to right and left by Hell and Heaven, covered with frontally disposed parts of sets (the so-called mansions) with an infinite blue sky shining above them – as in many Passion Plays of today.

Thus we prove that the supposedly 'predominant' and characteristic form of the painting by itself belongs properly to another branch of art.

And from the moment at which painting liberates itself by an Impressionistic movement, turning to purely pictorial problems, it abolishes every form of aperture and establishes, as an example and an ideal, the framelessness of a Japanese impressionistic drawing. And, symbolic as it may be, it is the time for the dawning of photography. Which, extraordinary though it may seem, conserves in its later metempsychosis, the moving picture, certain (*vital* this time) traditions of this period of maturity of one art (painting) and the infantilism of its successor (photography). Notice the relationship between Hokusai's *One Hundred Views of Fuji*[13] and a similar number of camera shots made with an equally pronounced tendency towards shooting two planes of depth – one through another (specially *Fuji Seen Through a Cobweb* and *Fuji Seen Through the Legs*, or Edgar Degas, whose startling series of compositions of women in the bath, *modistes* and *blanchisseuses*, is the best school in which to acquire a training in ideas about spatial composition within the limits of a frame – and about frame composition too which, in these series, restlessly jumps from 1:2 over 1:1 to 2:1).

This is, I think, the right point at which to quote one of Miles's[14] arguments which is much more closely concerned with the pictorial element here discussed than with the physiological where it was intended to be placed. For Miles, 'the whole thing (the inclination towards horizontal perception) is perhaps typified in the opening through which the human eye looks; this is characteristically much wider than it is high!'

Let us suppose for a moment this argument to be true in itself, and we can even provide him with a brilliant example for his statement, one even '*plus royaliste que le roi*'. Still, it won't help him! But, by the way, the example is the typical shape of a typical Japanese landscape woodcut. This is the only type of standardised (not occasional) composition known which is compositionally unlimited at the sides by the bounds of a frame and typified in its vertical limit by a shaded narrow strip from brightest white to, at its topmost, darkest blue, rushing in this limited space through all the shades of this celestial colour.

The last phenomenon is explained as the impression of the shadow falling on the eye from the upper eyelid, caught by the supersensitive observation of the Japanese.

It might be presumed that we have here, in this configuration, the fullest pictorial testimony to the above view of Miles. But once more we must disappoint: inasmuch as the idea of a framed picture derives not from the limits of the field of vision of our eyes but from the fact of the usual 'framedness' of the glimpse of nature we catch through the frame of the window or the door – or stage aperture as shown above – similarly, the composition of the Japanese derives from the absence of door frames, doors being replaced by the sliding wall panels in a typical Japanese house which thus opens on to an infinite horizon.

But even supposing that this shape represents the proportions of the field of vision, we must still consider another remarkable phenomenon of Japanese art: the materialisation on paper of the above-mentioned absence of side boundaries in the form of the horizontal *roll picture*, born only in Japan and China and not found elsewhere. I would call it *unroll picture*, because unwound horizontally from one roll to another it shows interminable episodes of battles, festivals, processions: for example, the pride of the Boston Museum, the many-feet-long *Burning of the Palace of Yedo*. Or the immortal *Killing of the Bear in the Emperor's Garden* in the British Museum. Having created this unique type of horizontal picture out of the supposed horizontal tendency of perception, the Japanese, with their supersensitive artistic feeling, then created, illogical though it may seem to Mr Miles, *the opposite form* – through a purely aesthetic need for counterbalance, for Japan (with China) is also the birthplace of the *vertical roll picture*, the tallest of all vertical compositions (if we disregard the Gothic vertical window compositions). Roll pictures are also found to take the form of curiously shaped coloured woodcuts of upright composition, with the most amazing compositional arrangement of faces, dresses, background elements and stage attributes.

This, I hold, shows pretty clearly that even if the diagnosis of perception as horizontal were correct (which should by no means be regarded as proven), vertical composition is also needed as a harmonic counterbalance to it.

This tendency towards harmony and perceptive equilibrium is quite different from the 'harmonic' and 'aesthetic' argument introduced by another group of defendants of the horizontal screen.

To quote Mr Cowan's summary:

> Howell and Bubray, Lane, Westerberg and Dieterich agree that the most desirable proportions are those approximately 1.618:1, which correspond to those of the so-called 'whirling square' rectangle (also known as the 'golden section'), based on the principles of dynamic symmetry which have predominated in the arts for centuries. For simplicity the ratio 5:3 (which equals 1.667:1, or 8:5 (equalling 1.6:1) are generally advocated instead of 1.618:1 . . . .

'Predominance in the arts for centuries' should in itself be a cause for the most profound suspicion when we are considering applying the idea to an entirely and basically new form of art, such as the youngest art, the art of cinema.

Cinema is the first and only art based entirely on dynamic and speed phenomena,* and yet it is as *everlasting* as a cathedral or a temple; having, with the latter, the characteristics of the static arts – i.e. the possibility of intrinsic existence by itself freed from the creative effort giving it birth (the theatre, the dance, music – the only dynamic arts before the cinema – lacked this possibility, the quality of everlastingness independent of the performing art that accomplished it, and by this means are characteristically distinct from the contrasting group of static arts).

Why should a holy veneration for this mistaken 'golden section' persist if all the basic elements of this newcomer in art – the cinema – are entirely different, its premises being entirely different from those of everything that has gone before?

Consider the two other denominations of the 'golden section', de-

---

* The gramophone record, also a dynamic form made everlasting, has to be considered now as part of the film.

nominations that are symptomatic of the tendency of these proportions: the 'whirling square', the principle of 'dynamic symmetry'.

They are the *cry* of the static hopelessly longing for dynamism. These proportions are probably those most fitted to give the maximum tension to the eye in causing it to follow one direction and then reverse to follow the other.

But – have we not attained, by the projection of our film on to the screen, a 'whirling' square that exists in reality?

And have we not discovered in the principle of the rhythmic cutting of the strip 'dynamic symmetry' that exists in reality?

A tendency that is practically attained and triumphantly materialised by *cinema as a whole*. And therefore does not need to be promoted by the *screen shape*.

And why the hell should we drag behind us in these days of triumph the melancholy souvenir of the unaccomplished desire of the static rectangle striving to become dynamic?

Just as the moving picture is the tombstone of the Futuristic effort towards dynamism in the static painting.

There is no logical basis for preserving this mystical worship of the 'golden section'. We are far enough away from the Greeks who, exaggerating their extraordinary feeling for harmony, used a proportion for their irrigation channels that was based upon some sacred harmonic formula which was not dictated by any practical consideration. (Or was that the case of war trenches? I don't remember exactly but I do remember that some practical channelling process was determined by considerations that were purely abstract, aesthetic and unpractical.)

The imposition by force of these centuries-old proportions on the months-young wide screen would be as illogical as this Greek business was. And, to finish with all this painting tradition, *if* it be desired to establish the relationship of the screen frame to *something else*, why on earth not use for comparison the intermediary between painting and the moving picture – the postcard or amateur photograph?

Well, here we can insist that, at least in this field, justice be done to both tendencies equally by the mere fact that our pocket Kodak snaps with the same facility and accuracy either vertical or horizontal shots of our kid, pa, ma or grandma, whether they are lying in the sunshine on the beach, or posing hand in hand in their wedding, silver-wedding or golden-wedding dresses!

The second aesthetic argument emerges from the domain of the theatre and the musical show, and, as reproduced by Mr Cowan, runs as follows:

> . . . another argument for wide film rests on the possibility inherent in sound pictures which were lacking (were they really lacking??? – S.E.) in the silent pictures of presenting entertainment more of the nature of the spoken drama of the stage. (Rayton.)

Preserving my usual politeness, I shall not say outright that this is the most terrific plague hanging over the talkie. I won't say it, I shall only think it, and shall confine myself to an observation with which everyone must agree, viz., that the aesthetics and laws of composition of the sound film and talkie are far from being established. And to argue at such a moment, from this most doubtful indication of the laws of development of talkies, to consider the present misuse of the talking screen as the basis for a suggestion that will bind us for the next thirty years to come to the proportion of that thirty months' misuse of the screen, is, to say the least, presumptuous.

Instead of approaching the stage, the wide screen, in my view, should drag the cinema still further away from it, opening up for the magic force that is montage an entirely new era of constructive possibilities.

But more of that later – as dessert.

The third distinctly formulated argument for horizontal proportion derives from the domain of physiology. It does not prevent it from being as wrong as those that preceded it. Dieterich and Miles have pointed out that the wider picture shows itself more accessible to the eye by virtue of the physiological properties of the latter. As Miles says:

> The eyes have one pair of muscles for moving them in the horizontal but two pairs for moving them in the vertical. Vertical movements are harder to make over a wide visual angle. As man has lived in his natural environment, he has usually been forced to perceive more objects arranged in the horizontal than in the vertical (!!! – S.E.). This has apparently established a very deep-seated habit which operates throughout his visual perception. . . .

This argument sounds very plausible. But its plausibility largely disappears the moment our research glides from the surface of the face, provided with its horizontally disposed perceptive eyes, towards . . . the neck. Here we could paraphrase exactly the same quotation in the directly opposite sense. From here the mechanism of bending and lifting the head as opposed to its turning movement from right to left provides for exactly the opposite conditions of muscular effort. The lifting and bending of the head (vertical perception) is carried out just as easily as eye movement from left to right (horizontal perception). We see that also in this case, in the purely physiological means of perception, the Wisdom of Nature has provided us with compensatory movements tending to the same all-embracing square harmony. But that is not all.

My example, as well as my counter-example, has established another phenomenon of the perceptive auditor: the phenomenon of *dynamism in perception*. In the horizontal dimensions of the eyes and vertical dimension of the head.

And this alone overthrows another of Dieterich's arguments:

215

On physiological grounds that the total field covered by the vision of both eyes (for fixed head position), and also the field comfortably covered by the vision of both eyes, both approximate a 5 × 8 rectangular form, although the actual boundaries of these fields are somewhat irregular curves . . . .

For fixed head position . . . but the *unfixed* head position has just been established and that argument thereby loses its force.

(By the way, the only really insuperably bound and fixed position of the head in a movie theatre is when it is at rest on one's sweetheart's shoulder. But we cannot pause to consider such facts, even though they concern at the very least 50 per cent of the audience.)

There remains the last argument – the economic.

The horizontally extended form corresponds most closely to the shape left for the eye by the circle overhanging the back of the stalls, and by the series of boxes each overhanging the other. The absolute limit of screen height in these conditions is estimated by Sponable as 23 foot to every 46 foot possible horizontally.

If we are to remain governed by strictly economic considerations – we might well allow that by using vertical compositions we should oblige the public to move to the more expensive front seats clear of overhang.

But another fact comes to our rescue – and this is the unfitness of the present shape and proportions of the cinema theatre of today for *sound purposes*.

Acoustics help optics!

I have not the time to examine references in looking up the ideal proportions for a sound theatre.

I faintly recall from my dim and distant past study of architecture that, in theatre and concert buildings, the vertical cut should, for optimum acoustics, be parabolic.

What I do remember clearly is the shape and the typical proportions of two ideal buildings. One ideal for optical display: let us take the Roxy (New York). And one for auditive display: the Salle Pleyel in Paris – the peak of acoustic perfection hitherto attained in a concert hall.

They are *exactly* opposite in proportions to each other. If the Salle Pleyel were to lie upon its side it would become a Roxy. If the Roxy were to stand upright it would become a Salle Pleyel. Every proportion of the Roxy split horizontally into stalls and circles is the direct opposite of the strictly vertical, receding into depth, corridor-like Salle Pleyel.

The sound film – the intersection of optic and auditive display – will have to synthesise, in the shape of its display hall, both tendencies with equal force.

In days to come the sound theatre will have to be reconstructed. And its new shape – in intersecting the horizontal and vertical tendencies of 'ye olde Roxy' and 'ye olde Pleyel' for these new, coming days in which optic and acoustic perception will be mingled – will be the one most perfectly appropriate to the dynamic square screen and its display of vertical and horizontal affective impulses.*

And now, last but not least, I must energetically challenge one more creeping tendency that has partly triumphed over the talkies and that now stretches out its unclean hands towards the Grandeur Film hastening to force it into still more abject subservience to its base desires. This is the tendency to smother entirely the principles of montage, already weakened by the 100 per cent talkies. We are still waiting for the first powerful example of the perfectly cut and constructed sound film that will establish anew the montage principle as the basic, everlasting and vital principle of cinematographic expression and creation.

I refer to innumerable quotations, quotations accepted in part even by such great masters of the screen as my friend Vidor[15] and the Great Old Man of all of us – D.W. Griffith. For example: '. . . Dance scenes need no longer be "followed" as there is ample room in a normal long shot for all the lateral movement used in most dances . . . .' (The 'moving camera' is a means of producing in the spectator a specific dynamic feeling, and not a means of investigation or following a dancing girl's feet. See the rocking movement of the camera in the reaping scene of *The Old and the New* and the same with the machine-gun in *All Quiet on the Western Front.* – S.E.)

'. . . Close-ups can be made on the wide film. Of course, it is not necessary to get as close as you do with the 35mm camera, but, comparatively speaking, you can make the same size of close-up . . . .' (The impressive value of a close-up lies not at all in its absolute size, but entirely in its size in relation to the optical affective impulse produced by the dimension of the previous and following shots. – S.E.)

'However, with the wide film very few close-ups are needed. After

---

* The actual reconstruction and readjustment of currently existing theatres in order to adapt them to new forms of screen would cost (regardless of the artistic value that would result from any particular kind of adaptation), by estimate of the experts of the Motion Picture Academy, about \$40,000,000. But mechanical genius has found a way out. By the method of first taking the picture on a 65mm Grandeur negative. Reducing it so as to confine it where desired to the limits of a 35mm positive (not covering the whole field provided in the smaller-sized celluloid, owing to its different proportion), and finally throwing it on to the screen by magnifying lenses, enlarging it in dimension and transforming its proportion in accordance with the wall of the cinema theatre. This same procedure could equally well be used for vertical composition which, as shown by drawing, by a very slight alteration of the horizontal line could provide for the equally vertical, and then (when reduced) would likewise not exceed the dimension of the ordinary screen. It remains to bewail the partial and very slight loss of the limits of the vertically composed picture and that wail only applies to the worst circle and stall seats, and even there there would only be a very slight loss.

all, the main reason for close-ups is to get over thought (!!! S.E.) and with the wide film you can get all the detail and expression in a full-sized figure that you would get in a six foot close-up with the 35mm film . . . .' (Although preferring, as far as my personal tastes are concerned in *screen* acting, the almost imperceptible movement of the eyebrow, I none the less acclaim the possibility of a whole body expressing something. But still, we cannot permit the expulsion of the close-up – the fixing of attention by the isolation of a desired fact or detail, an effect that is certainly not achieved by merely providing the body with a disproportionate increase in absolute size. – S.E.)

Close-ups, moving camera shots, the absolute dimensional variation of figures and objects on the screen, and the other elements concerned with montage are far more profoundly bound up with the expressive means of cinema and cinema perception than the task of merely facilitating the view of a face, or the 'getting over of a thought' on it involves.

As we have proclaimed (and as Alexandrov tried to show in humble essay form in that piece of irony, *Romance sentimentale*,[16] so grievously misunderstood in its intentions) – with the coming of sound, montage does not die but develops, amplifying and multiplying its possibilities and its method.

In the same way the advent of the wide screen marks one further stage of enormous progress in the development of montage, which once more will have to undergo a critical review of its laws; laws mightily affected by the change of absolute screen dimension, making quite a number of the montage processes of the olden-day screen impossible or unsuitable, but on the other hand providing us with a gigantic new agent of impression: the rhythmic assemblage of varied screen shapes, the attack upon our field of perception of the affective impulses associated with the geometric and dimensional variation of the successive possible dimensions, proportions and designs.

And, accordingly, if, to many of the qualities of normal screen montage laws we must proclaim, 'le roi est mort!' yet with much greater strength we must cry 'vive le roi!' to welcome the new hitherto unimaginable montage possibilities of Grandeur Film!

31. **Help Yourself!**[1]   1932

Discussions on 'amusement' and 'entertainment' unsettle me considerably. . . .

Having expended no small effort in 'captivating' and 'involving' audiences in a single burst of general absorption, the word 'amusement' sounds somewhat contrary, alien and inimical to me.

When people say that a film should 'entertain', I seem to hear someone saying, 'Help yourself!'

In a manner worthy of Ivan Ivanovich Pererepenko who

if he regales you with snuff, always licks the lid of the snuff-box first, then taps it with his finger and, as he proffers it, says, if he knows you, 'May I be so bold, my dear sir, as to ask you to help yourself?' and, if he does not know you, 'May I be so bold, my dear sir, although I do not have the honour to know your rank, name and patronymic, to ask you to help yourself?'

I am with Dovgochkhun, Ivan Nikiforovich;
for a short 'Help yourself'.
And a film must 'help' and not 'entertain',
grip and not amuse,
give the audience a charge and not squander the energy that it brings into the cinema.

'Entertain' is not such an innocuous term at all: behind it there is a very concrete active process.

And these pointers and discussions have first of all, of course, to bear 'grip' in mind.

While amusement and entertainment must be understood precisely as a mere quantitative (and in no sense qualitative) commutation of the subject matter itself.

When we had gripping films we did not talk about entertainment.

We did not have time to be bored.

But then we lost this 'grip' somewhere.

We lost the knack of making gripping films. And we began to talk about entertaining films.

But we cannot realise the latter without mastering the method of the former.

Many people perceive the slogan of entertainment as countenancing a certain 'Nepmanism',[2] in the worst sense of its perverted understanding of the ideological premisses of our films.

We must master the method again: embody the directive in stirring works.

Nobody will help us in this.

We must do it ourselves.

I want to talk about how we should do this and how we should go about it.

The rehabilitation of the ideological premiss, not as something to be introduced externally 'to please Repertkom'[3] but as the basic animating force that fertilises the most enthralling part of a director's work, the director's 'treatment', is the task of this article.

There is a quite concrete reason for this: the formulation of the teaching for the third, or graduand, class in the GIK faculty of direction, from which, according to the teaching programme, the students must graduate with a creative mastery of directorial work.

The Talmudists of methodology, the learned 'would-be Marxists', may abuse me, but I want to approach this subject and the teaching itself without ceremony, in an everyday 'workmanlike' fashion.

In any case nobody yet has any concrete notion of how to master this problem, whether he hides behind learned quotations or not.

For quite a long time, for years, I myself agonised about the supernatural power, transcending common sense and human reason, that seemed indispensable to an understanding of the *Mysteries of Udolpho*[4] of creative film direction, to a dissection of the music of creative film direction!

A dissection of the music of creative film direction, but not as if it were a corpse – that is what we have to work on with the graduands at GIK.

We approach this problem without ceremony and not from the positions of preconceived scholastic methods.

And it will not be from the corpses of outmoded works that we shall examine the processes of production.

The anatomy theatre and the dissection room are the least appropriate laboratories in which to study theatre.

And the study of cinema must proceed hand in hand with the study of theatre.

Constructing cinema from the 'idea of cinema' and abstract principles is barbarous and absurd. It is only through a critical comparison with earlier forms of spectacle that we shall be able to master critically the specific methodology of cinema.

> Criticism must consist in comparing and contrasting a given fact, not with an idea, but with another fact; for this purpose it is only important that both facts, as far as possible, be carefully investigated, and that they both present, in relation to one another, different moments of development.[5]

We shall study this matter in the living creative process.

This is the first time it has been done in this way.

We shall have simultaneously to create both a working process and a method.

We are not proceeding in Plekhanov's way, from preconceived positions of 'method in general' to the concrete particular case, but we expect, through particular concrete work on particular material, to arrive at the methods of cinematic creation for the director.

To do this, we shall bring out the 'intimate' creative process of the director in all its phases and all the twists in its formation in 'full view' of the audience.

There are many surprises in store for a youth filled with illusions.

In one respect a digression towards 'entertainment' is at our disposal.

Let us cite the greatest of all 'entertainers', Alexandre Dumas *père*, whose son, Dumas *fils*,[6] says of him: 'I have the honour to present my father, a grown-up child to whom I gave birth when I was very small.'

Who has not been delighted by the classic proportions of the compositional labyrinth of *The Count of Monte Cristo*?!

Who has not been bowled over by the deadly logic that weaves and interweaves the characters and events as if these interrelationships had existed in that form from its very inception?

Lastly, who has not imagined the sudden flash of inspiration for that 'fat Negro' Dumas, the ecstasy when he conceived a single, bird's-eye view of the future structure of the novel in all its details and subtleties . . . with the title *The Count of Monte Cristo* emblazoned across the front?

'If only I could do that' is the echo of that vision . . . . And how pleasantly uplifting it is to learn, by sampling the recipe, how such a remarkable composition is really conceived and put together.

How the work on the book involved brutal application and not divine inspiration.

It is really 'black man's work' – not that of the fat Negro sponger, but work worthy of the Negro labourer on the plantations.

Dumas, actually of Negro descent, was born in Haiti, like Toussaint L'Ouverture, the hero of my next film *The Black Consul*.[7]

The nickname of Dumas's grandfather, General Thomas-Alexandre Dumas, was the 'Black Devil'.[8]

And the 'fat Negro' was the name given to Dumas by his detractors and rivals.

A certain Eugène de Mirecourt,[9] whose high-sounding name concealed the humbler Jacquot, wrote of Dumas:

Scratch the hide of Monsieur Dumas and you will find a savage . . . .
He breakfasts on hot potatoes, taken straight from the coals, and devours them . . . without even removing the skins – he is a negro!
But, because he needs 200,000 francs a year to disport himself, he hires anonymous intellectual deserters and translators to do his literary work and pays them wages that would be degrading even for negroes working under the mulatto's lash.

221

'Your father was black!' someone shouts to his face. 'My grandfather was an ape,' he replied, laughing.

To his friend Béranger, who had begun to succumb to rumours about the 'fat Negro's literary piracy', Dumas wrote: 'Dear old friend. The only "negro" I employ is my left hand, which holds the book open while my right hand works twelve hours a day.'[10]

He was exaggerating slightly. He had collaborators but 'in the same way that Napoleon had generals'.[11]

It is difficult to bring yourself to work with such frenzy. But even more difficult to achieve anything without doing so.

Miracles of composition are merely a matter of perseverance and time spent during the 'training period' of one's own autobiography.

Measured by its productivity, this period of romanticism was distinguished by the dizzying speed of its creative tempos: in eight days (between 17 September and 26 September 1829) Victor Hugo wrote 3,000 lines of *Hernani*, which stood classical theatre on its head; he wrote *Marion Delorme* in twenty-three days, *Le Roi s'amuse* in twenty days, *Lucretia Borgia* in eleven days, *Angelo* in nineteen days, *Mary Tudor* in nineteen days and *Ruy Blas* in thirty-four days.

This is echoed quantitatively too.

The literary legacy of Dumas *père* numbers 1,200 volumes.

The same opportunity to create such works is equally accessible to all.

Let us examine *The Count of Monte Cristo* in particular.

This is how Lucas-Dubreton tells the story of its composition:

In the course of a Mediterranean cruise, Dumas had passed near a little island, where he had not been able to land because 'it was *en contumace*'. It was the island of Monte-Cristo. The name struck him at the time. A few years later, in 1843, he arranged with an editor for the publication of a work to be called *Impressions de Voyage dans Paris*, but he needed a romantic plot. Then one day by good luck he read a story of twenty pages, *Le Diamant et La Vengeance*, which was laid in the period of the second Restoration and was included in Peuchet's volume, *La Police Devoilée*. It caught his fancy. Here was the subject of which he had dreamed: Monte-Cristo should discover his enemies hidden in Paris!

Then Maquet had the idea of telling the story of the love-affair of Monte-Cristo and the fair Mercedes and the treachery of Danglars; and the two friends started off on a new track – *Monte-Cristo*, from being travel impressions in the form of a romance, turned into a romance pure and simple. The Abbé Faria, a lunatic born at Goa whom Chateaubriand saw vainly trying to kill a canary by hypnotising it, helped to increase the mystery; and the Château d'If began to appear on the horizon. . . .[12]

That is in fact how works are put together.

To experience this as it takes place and so participate in the process yourself seems to me the most useful and productive thing for the students to do.

The 'methodologists' who preach otherwise and who promote their formulas are simply . . . blackamoors – and not even the blackamoors of Peter the Great.

But the 'chance' element here is much less than it seems and the 'regularity' within the creative process can be detected and revealed. There is method. But the whole evil consists in the fact that not even a fig will grow from preconceived methodological positions. In just the same way, a tempestuous flow of creative potential that is not regulated by method will yield even less.

This kind of analysis of the formation of a work of art will reveal, step by step, the strictest regularity, deriving from basic social and ideological premisses through each curve in the superstructure.

And the gold fever of money-making and self-enrichment that characterised the epoch of Louis-Philippe is no less a determining factor in the gilded legend of the fabulous riches of the former sailor who becomes an all-powerful count than are Dumas's childhood memories of Scheherazade or the treasures of Ali Baba.

And the very fact that a sailor could become a count meant that 'anyone' could.

In the general rush for gold and aristocratic titles, the sailor Dantès, who became the mythically rich Count of Monte-Cristo, served as a splendid 'social ideal' for the bourgeoisie who were feverishly enriching themselves.

It is no coincidence that this character is given the features of an idealised self-portrait.

For Dumas himself, like others, bathed greedily in the murky sea of suspect gold accumulated through the dubious speculations of the reign of the 'bourgeois king'.

'A million? That's exactly what I normally carry around on me for pocket money!'

This remark represented to an identical degree the unattainable ideal both of the 'fat Negro' himself – then the literary master of the newspaper, the *feuilleton* and the drama of the Paris of his day, recklessly spending money – and of the countless greedy hordes of innumerable delinquent *sans-culottes* and adventurers who swamped Paris at that time.

However, one can only sense how precisely these social, economic and ideological premisses determine every slight convolution of form, and how inseparably their processes are linked if one follows the complete creative cycle in 'slow motion' on one's own and bearing full responsibility for it.

The most interesting thing of all would, of course, be to take someone like Goethe or Gogol and force him in front of an audience to write a third part of *Faust* or to rewrite the second volume of *Dead Souls*.

But we do not even have a live Alexandre Dumas at our disposal.

So we are turning the third-year students at GIK into *a collective director and film constructor*.

The instructor is no longer *primus inter pares*, the first among equals.

The collective – and later each member individually – will have to pick its way through all the difficulties and torments of creative work, through the whole process of creativity from the first faint glimmering hint of the theme through to a decision on whether the buttons on the leather coat of the last extra are suitable for filming.

The task of the instructor is merely, by a timely dextrous shove, to push the collective towards the 'right' and 'rewarding' difficulties and towards the right and clear postulation of the questions, the answers to which lead to something constructive and not to fruitless cartwheeling 'around' the work.

That is how people are trained to fly in the circus.

The trapeze is mercilessly held back or the pupil is shown the fist if his 'timing' is wrong.

No great harm if he falls past the safety net on to the front seats in the stand. Next time he won't 'make a mess' of it.

But at each stage in the unfolding creative process the background material of instructions and of experience of our 'legacy' is placed just as carefully, at the right time and in the right place, in the hands of the 'warriors' who are confused or stuck.

But that is not all. If they are not guided by a single comprehensive synthetic giant, then at every turn they will encounter, in addition to their 'legacy', a 'living heir' who constitutes a powerful technician in his own sector.

In the past three years the systematic course of special subjects at GIK (then still GTK) has been replaced by a thin coating of infrequent episodic lectures by all sorts of 'prominent' film workers.

These people rushed into GIK, just as they would jump on a tram, strange and unrelated to one another, and, like passengers rushing as quickly as possible to the exit, they would blurt out something episodic and disjointed in their forty-five minutes' worth and then speed once more out of the sight of their proselytes into the orbit of their private activities.

This 'little episode' must also be rebuilt from the roots!

Within the plan of the general course of specialisms a speaker should be invited at the proper time to deal with a particular concrete case, at a particular stage in the general development of the creative process, and to deal with a particular question in which he really is a 'past master'.

All this is directed towards 'high-calibre' and thoroughly responsible work.

In doing away with these 'little episodes' in teaching, we shall also have done with the wretched 'little episodes' produced by the graduating students.

These short little film 'studies' by the graduands, which are unco-ordinated, wretched but self-satisfied, even shorter on intelligence than they are on footage, must be discarded as wholly unsuitable.

After he has worked on a graduation project on the scale of, say, the Cathedral of Christ the Saviour (now happily dismantled into bricks), an architect will always know how to build something accessible to everyone . . . a public convenience.

But, if your graduation project was one small *pissoir*, it is a risk to undertake anything else!

Yet we have seen this happen year after year with our graduates.

There has to be a complete break.

Nevertheless there will be a little film for our brother. Nevertheless Soyuzkino will not give us much.

Soyuzkino has shelf upon shelf of its own for film.

Nevertheless we can no longer shoot just little episodes.

But in practice a film is broken up into separate episodes.

But these little episodes are held together by the single pivot of a single ideological, compositional and stylistic whole.

The art does not lie in some fanciful shot or unexpected and 'exaggerated' camera angle.

The art lies in the fact that every fragment of a film should be an organic part of an organically conceived whole.

These organically devised and filmed fragments of a single, great, meaningful and general conception must be excerpts from something whole rather than wandering 'orphaned' studies.

It is through these filmed excerpts, through the unfilmed but staged episodes that precede and follow them, through devising the montage plans and lists that will place these parts in the whole, that creative 'irresponsibility' will be really and crucially eradicated among the students.

Their work will be thoroughly monitored and will at the same time be a crucial demonstration of how and to what extent they are capable of re-alising in practice a firmly designated general conception, although at this stage it is not yet their own individual conception but one that has been collectively worked out: this in itself will teach them the harsh lesson of self-discipline,

a self-discipline that will be all the more necessary at the moment when the conception becomes individual and the student's own.

But before this last stage, before this last frontier, which already borders on production outside the school, the students run the 'gauntlet' of a long line of 'past masters', dead and alive.

At a certain stage this will involve a long discussion of the type, image and character of the roles. The ashes of Balzac, Gogol, Dostoyevsky and Ben Jonson will be stirred.

225

The problem of the personification of a particular type of image or character will arise. Here we can count on Kachalov's confessions of how he played the Baron, Batalov will speak, or Max Strauch will tell us about the mechanics of creating the role of Rubinchuk.[13]

We shall wend our way through the forests of plot construction, dismantle the skeletons of the Elizabethans with Aksionov, listen to Dumas *père* and Viktor Shklovsky on plot construction in scripts and on the compositional method in the works of Weltmann.[14]

Then, after discussing dramatic situations with the late Webster, and with Zarkhi and Wolkenstein, we shall turn our attention towards the way in which a situation is 'clothed' in words.[15]

Alexei Maximovich Gorky will probably not refuse to initiate us in the methods he used to write the dialogues in *The Lower Depths* or *Egor Bulychov*. Nikolai Erdman will tell us how he does it.[16]

And Babel will tell us about the specifics of the texture of image and word and about the technique of extreme laconicism of semantic means of expression. Babel, who perhaps knows better in practice than anyone else the great secret of how ' . . . there is no iron that can enter the human heart with the same chilling effect as a full stop properly placed.' About how his remarkable and vastly underestimated play *Sunset* was created so inimitably through this laconicism.[17]

Apart from anything else, this play offers perhaps the best example of fine theatrical dialogue in recent years.

All this will crop up at the appropriate stages in the single progressive creative process of our collective director working on his film.

The division of the different stages into independent analytical digressions is by no means so terrible. The construction of the theme and the plot can sometimes take place quite independently of the elaboration of the words. Are not *The Government Inspector* and *Dead Souls* brilliant examples of treatments of subjects 'set' by someone else?![18]

The question of musical accompaniment for the sound medium . . . . The question of the physical milieu . . . . The analysis of a sizeable number of models from our 'legacy' and other items, each viewed from the angle of a specialised narrow specific quality: how it, and it alone, can be particularly useful?!

James Joyce and Emile Zola.

Honoré Daumier and Edgar Degas.

Toulouse-Lautrec or Stendhal.

And the problem of the correct ideological formulation of a question about the approach to the theme and the social comprehension of the work will be analysed thoroughly and at length by specialists in Marxism-Leninism. In this way we can count on securing the mobilised experience and skilled support of the leaders among those who have to fight their way through to making films.

But the most serious and interesting part of this work – the central part of creative direction – is training people in 'treatment' and working through with them the process of how it proceeds and is achieved.

We work essentially on such unexperimental trivia with such an oversimplified perception of our tasks that we simply do not have the opportunity to observe works which display genuine, living, creative interrelationships between their social treatment and conception and which give evidence of form.

Our works are on such an oversimplified level that they recall the well-known caricature of the automatic sausage factory: pigs go into one side of a box with a handle and sausages come out on the other side.

Between the schematic skeleton of 'sloganising' and the empty skin of outer 'form' there are no layers of actual, living flesh and muscle, nothing organic, no interactions or links.

Then people are surprised that the skin hangs formlessly and the mechanistically perceived 'social significance' of the subject matter stares through it in its oversimplified way.

The muscle and flesh are not enough.

That is why Gorky's *Egor Bulychov and the Others* was greeted with such unanimous enthusiasm. Even though the play did not yet constitute an answer to a single basic question: the people depicted in it were not yet our people; they were not contemporaries.

And we are still waiting for Alexei Maximovich.[19]

On the other hand, here is flesh. Here is muscle.

And this flesh was made today, when all around us on stage and screen we no longer see the 'men in cases' but simply the cases without the men.[20]

Instead they are tightly packed with cheap quotations.

Our works are like the spikes on the barbed wire of harsh truth, covered with muslin, and we are astonished that blood does not flow through this wire and that the muslin does not beat with a poisoned pulse.

It is one step from the sublime to the ridiculous.

But there are a couple of hundred steps from a sublime premiss of an idea, formulated into a slogan, to a living work of art.

If we take those steps alone we shall achieve the ridiculous result of compromising rubbish.

We must begin to learn to make three-dimensional vivid works, leaving behind the two-dimensional flat clichés of the 'direct line' from the slogan to the story, without going through a transformer.

We had to trace in our own work the way in which a seriously determinant ideological outlook does in fact have the effect of defining a work, although that was in somewhat unusual social conditions.

It happened in Hollywood.

'Among People'[21] at Paramount.

It concerned the script treatment of a high-quality work.

Although not devoid of all ideological flaws, Theodore Dreiser's *An*

American Tragedy,[22] whatever else it is, is a first-class work, even if it is not a class-based work from our point of view, a work that has every chance of being counted as a classic of its time and place.

But, from the moment that we produced our first draft script it became obvious that two irreconcilable viewpoints – the 'front office's' and ours – were bound to clash over this material.

'Is Clyde Griffiths guilty or not guilty in your treatment?' was the question put by the 'boss' of Paramount's California studies, Ben (B.P.) Schulberg.[23]

'Not guilty,' was our reply.

'Then your script is a monstrous challenge to American society! . . .'

We explained that we thought the crime committed by Griffiths was the summary result of the social relationships whose influence he had been subjected to at every stage of the development of his life and character that unfolded in the course of the film.

'For us this is, essentially, the whole interest of the work. . . .'

'We'd rather have a simple and powerful whodunit about a murder . . . and about the love between a boy and a girl,' someone told us with a sigh.

The possibility of two such fundamentally opposite treatments of the central character should not surprise you.

Dreiser's novel is as broad and boundless as the Hudson River, as immense as life itself and it permits of any opinion of itself. Like any 'neutral fact' of nature itself, his novel is 99 per cent a statement of facts and one per cent attitude towards them. This epic of cosmic truth and objectivity had to be 'screwed together' into a tragedy, which was unthinkable without the direction and the emphasis provided by a particular world-view.

The bosses were disturbed by the question of guilt and innocence from a quite different standpoint: guilty meant unsympathetic. The leading hero would suddenly be unsympathetic. What would the verdict of the box-office be?

And if he was not guilty. . . .

It was because of the problems surrounding this 'damned question' that *An American Tragedy* had lain dormant in Paramount's file for more than five years.

It was even undertaken by Griffiths (this time not Clyde but the patriarch of cinema, David Wark[24]) and by Lubitsch,[25] and many others besides.

With their customary prudence the bosses shirked a decision in our case too.

They suggested that we complete the script 'as you feel it'[26] and then they would see. . . .

From what I have said it is quite clear that in our case, as distinct from the others, the substance of the difference of opinion did not revolve around the resolution of a particular situation but lay much deeper and more centrally in the problem of the basic social treatment as a whole.

It is interesting now to trace how in this way an adopted position starts to determine the moulding of the separate parts and how it, and it alone, through its own requirements, impregnates the problems of situational resolution, psychological profundity, the 'purely formal' aspect of the construction of the work as a whole, how it directs one towards quite new, 'purely formal' methods which, when generalised, may even be assembled into new theoretical realisations of the leading disciplines of cinema as such.

It would be difficult to set out the whole plot of the novel: you cannot produce in five lines what it took Dreiser two bulky volumes to do. We shall only touch upon the central point of the external plot aspect of the tragedy – the murder itself, although the tragedy lies, of course, not in the murder but in the tragic path pursued by Clyde who is driven by the social system to murder. In our script this was the principal focus of attention.

The case revolves around the fact that Clyde Griffiths, having seduced a young girl in the workshop where he was foreman, was unable to help her procure an abortion, which is strictly forbidden in the USA even now.

He sees himself being forced to marry her. But this would completely destroy all his visions of a career, because it would upset his marriage to a wealthy heiress who is hopelessly in love with him.

The situation is itself profoundly characteristic of America, where among the middle ranks of industry there is not yet the caste-based exclusiveness that would make this kind of *mésalliance* impossible. There the patriarchal 'democracy' of the fathers still prevails, with their memories of how they themselves walked the streets *sans-culotte* in search of prosperity. With the next generation we come closer to the financial 'aristocracy of Fifth Avenue': in this respect the difference in attitude of Clyde's uncle and cousin towards him is characteristic.

One way and another Clyde faces a dilemma: either he must relinquish for ever his career and social success or . . . he must dispose of the girl.

Clyde's adventures in his clashes with American reality up to this moment have succeeded in 'moulding' him psychologically so that after a prolonged inner struggle (not with moral principles, it is true, but with his own enervated lack of character), he decides on the latter.

He carefully conceives and prepares the murder: a capsized boat – apparently an accident.

He plans every detail with the excessive care of the inexperienced criminal which subsequently entangles the novice inevitably in an inescapable net of incontrovertible evidence.

He takes the girl out in a boat.

In the boat the conflict between pity and aversion for the girl, between his characterless indecision and his greedy desire to escape to glittering material comforts, reaches its apogee.

Half-consciously, half-unconsciously, in a wild inner panic, the boat is capsized.

The girl drowns.

Clyde abandons her, saves himself as he had previously planned and falls unexpectedly into the very net he had woven for his own salvation.

The affair of the boat is executed in the way that all such incidents take place:

it is neither fully spelt out nor fully realised – it is an undifferentiated tangle.

Dreiser handles the affair so 'impartially', leaving the further form and development of events logically not to the plot but . . . to the processes of law.

It was imperative for us to sharpen the *actual* and *formal* innocence of Clyde within the specific act of committing the crime.

It was only then that we could make sufficiently clear our 'monstrous challenge' to a society whose very mechanism drives a rather characterless lad to such a predicament and then, invoking morality and justice, puts him in the electric chair.

The sanctity of the *formal* principle in the codes of honour, morality, justice and religion in America is the principal and fundamental thing.

It is the focus for the endless game of advocacy in the courts, and among the lawyers and parliamentarians. The essence of what the formal argument is about is something quite different. The essence comes to him who is formally most flexible.

Hence Clyde's conviction, which he, in essence, deserves for the role that he, in essence, played in the affair (which is nobody's concern), given his *formal* innocence, would be seen in the American context as something 'monstrous' – a judicial murder.

Such is the shallow but obvious and unshakeable psychology of the American that accompanies him everywhere.

And it was not from books that I came to know this side of the American character. . . .

It was therefore imperative to develop the boat scene into one of indisputably clear *formal* innocence, without in any way whitewashing Clyde himself or removing his guilt.

We chose this treatment: Clyde wants to commit murder, but he *cannot*. At the moment when decisive action is required, he falters. Simply because he is weak-willed.

However, before his inner 'defeat', he manages to provoke in Roberta (the girl) such a feeling of alarm that, when, already inwardly defeated and ready to 'take everything back', he leans towards her, she recoils from him in terror. The boat is off balance. When he, trying to support her, accidentally hits her in the face with his camera, she finally loses her head and, in her terror, she stumbles and falls and the boat capsizes.

For greater emphasis we show her rising to the surface again. We even show Clyde trying to swim to her. But the machinery of crime has been set in motion and it follows its course through to the end, even against Clyde's will: with a weak cry, Roberta shies away from him in fear and, as she cannot swim, she drowns.

Clyde, who is a good swimmer, reaches the shore and, coming to his senses, continues to act in accordance with the fateful plan of action he has prepared for the crime, and from which he has only deviated slightly.

There is no doubt that in this form the situation is made psychologically and tragically more profound.

The tragedy is heightened to an almost Grecian 'blind Moera, fate'[27] that, once summoned into action, will not relax her grip on the person who has 'provoked' her.

Reaching a tragically heightened 'causality' that, once it claims its rights, drives the inexorable course of its process, once it has been brought to life, to its logical conclusion.

In this crushing of an individual human being by a 'blind' cosmic 'principle', by the inertia of the process of laws over which he has no control, we find one of the basic premises of classical tragedy, the representation of the passive dependence of man at that time on natural forces. This is analogous to what Engels, in relation to another period, wrote about Calvin: 'His predestination doctrine was the religious expression of the fact that in the commercial world of competition success or failure does not depend upon a man's activity or cleverness, but upon circumstances uncontrollable by him.'[28]

An ascent to the atavism of original cosmic principles, seen through an accidental situation of our day, always 'intensifies' a dramatic scene to the heights of tragedy.

But our treatment was not limited to this. It was pregnant with a significant sharpening of the whole series of stages and of the further course of action. . . .

In Dreiser's book Clyde's rich uncle provides him with the 'apparatus' of defence 'to preserve the honour of the family'.

The defence has in essence no doubts about the crime.

Nevertheless they invent a 'change of heart' experienced by Clyde under the influence of his love and pity for Roberta.

That is not bad, considering that it was made up 'on the spot'.

But it becomes more evil when there *really* was a change of heart. When that change took place for very different reasons. When really there was no crime. When the lawyers are convinced that there was a crime. And it is with this outright lie, that is so near the truth and at the same time so far from it, that they try in this false fashion to whitewash the accused and save him.

It becomes still more dramatically evil when, moving along a different adjacent moment, the 'ideology' of your treatment upsets the proportions of Dreiser's dispassionate narrative which in another place would be epic.

The whole second volume is almost completely filled with the trial of

Clyde for Roberta's murder and his prosecution to conviction and the electric chair.

In just a few lines it is demonstrated that the true aim of Clyde's trial and conviction has, however, no relation to him whatsoever. There is only one aim: to create the necessary popularity among the farming population (Roberta was a farmer's daughter) for the prosecuting attorney Mason to ensure his election as judge.

The defence lawyers take on a case they know to be hopeless ('at best ten years in the penitentiary') on that same level of political struggle. They belong to the opposite political camp (but by no means to a different class) and their basic aim is to harm by any means the candidate they despise.

For one side, as for the other, Clyde is merely a means.

A plaything in the hands of 'blind' Moera – fate, 'causality' *à la grecque* – Clyde also becomes a plaything in the hands of the far-from-blind machine of bourgeois justice, a machine that is no more than an instrument for the political adventurism of very knowing political careerists.

Thus the fate of a particular case, Clyde Griffiths, is tragically expanded and generalised into a real general 'American tragedy', a typical story of a young American at the beginning of the 20th century.

The whole tangled web of the trial was almost entirely omitted from the construction of the script and it was replaced by the pre-election hullabaloo that showed through the contrived symbolism of the courtroom, which serves as a private drill-ground for pre-election scuffles rather than as an end in itself.

But the basic treatment of the murder determines the tragic deepening and the powerful ideological force of yet another part of the film and another figure.

The mother.

Clyde's mother is the head of a religious mission. Blind fanaticism. She has such a powerful belief in her absurd religious dogma that her figure assumes a certain monumentalism that inspires respect and deference, and a certain aura of martyrdom.

This happens even despite the fact that she is, in essence, the first concrete embodiment of the guilt of American society in relation to Clyde: her teaching and her principles, her orientation towards God and celestial matters rather than towards training her son for work were the first prerequisites for the unfolding tragedy.

In Dreiser's book she fights to the last for her son's innocence. She herself works as a trial reporter for a provincial paper in order to be present at his trial. She, like the mothers and sisters of the black Scottsboro boys,[29] travels around America speaking to collect enough money for an appeal when everyone else has abandoned Clyde.

The mother acquires the definite sacrificial grandeur of a heroine. In Dreiser's book this grandeur radiates sympathy for her moral and religious doctrines.

In our treatment Clyde, in his death cell, confesses to his mother that, although he did not kill Roberta, he had intended to.

His mother believes in the ultra-Christian concept that 'the word is the same as the deed'[30] and that a sinful thought is the same as a sinful deed. She is stunned.

With an unexpected grimace that is the reverse of the grandeur of Gorky's mother she too betrays her son.

She goes to the governor with a petition for clemency. She is flustered by the point-blank question: 'Do you yourself believe in your son's innocence?' At this critical moment for her son, the mother remains silent.

The Christian sophism of the unity of the ideal (a deed in thought) and the material (a deed *de facto*), an amusing parody of the principles of the dialectic, leads to the final tragic denouement.

The petition is ignored and the dogma and dogmatism of its bearer are equally discredited. This moment cannot be washed away by her tears when she takes her final farewell of her son whom she has delivered with her own hands as a sacrifice into the jaws of the 'Christian Baal'. The more poignant the sadness in these last scenes becomes, the more bitterly they lash out at this shaman's ideology.

Here the curious formalism of American dogmatism finds a polar opposite, as it were, in the contrasting principle of Messianism, which turns out in fact to be the same soulless dogmatism of formal principle in religion. And this is unavoidable in so far as both feed equally on the same social and class premises.

In our view our treatment succeeded in tearing off not perhaps 'all' and certainly not 'each and every one' of the 'masks' from this monumental figure, but some of them at least.

In so doing we managed to correct what Sergei Dinamov[31] quite rightly remarked about Clyde's mother in his foreword to the Russian translation of *An American Tragedy*:

> The characters in *An American Tragedy* are taken from the bourgeois and petty bourgeois milieu. Dreiser, describing them precisely and with apparent indifference, almost avoids showing his own attitude towards them. This permits us to think that in the majority of these characters Dreiser himself does not disclose his approval. There is something different about two characters: Clyde's mother and the Rev. McMillan. . . . Dreiser has betrayed his usual realistic manner in his portrayal of this fanatical woman, he has idealised her, given her character hints of winning and genuine sympathy. . . . A narrow-minded and ignorant woman grows into a courageous, purposeful heroine who remains unbowed under the blows that life rains down on her. The pastor McMillan is just as sympathetically drawn: he is Clyde's last consoler in those terrible hours when he is preparing convulsively for the fatal flow of current. The sin is punished by

death, redeemed by humility, absolved by God: these Christian moral maxims of McMillan crown the novel and Dreiser does not expose the falsehood of these positions. . . . Dreiser's artistic method in relation to Clyde's mother and McMillan is a retreat from realism. Dreiser's objectivity is the objectivity of a progressive petty bourgeois writer who has his limitations. . . .

We 'reconstructed' the mother as far as we could.

We 'chucked' pastor McMillan out of the script altogether.

And Dreiser was the first to welcome everything that our treatment brought to his work.

It is no coincidence that we are all now witnesses to his steady migration from the petty-bourgeois camp towards ours.

In our treatment the tragedy within the framework of this novel is actually 'consummated' far earlier.

The cell. The shadow of the electric chair. The brightly polished spittoon (which I saw myself at Sing-Sing) at his feet. All this is no more than an end to one particular embodiment of the tragedy that continues to be enacted relentlessly every hour and every minute and which rages throughout the United States far beyond the confines of the cover of the novel.

But the choice of such a 'dry' and 'hackneyed' formula of social treatment leads to more than just a sharpening of situations and a more profound revelation of characters and roles.

It has a profound effect too on purely formal methods. It was particularly due to this, and deriving from it, that the concept of 'inner monologue' in cinema was formulated, an idea that I have been carrying around for six years before the advent of sound made its practical realisation possible.

As we have already seen, we needed such an exceptionally differentiated refinement of exposition of what was happening inside Clyde before the actual moment of the 'boat incident' that merely to show its external manifestations would not have solved the problem.

The whole arsenal of knitted brows, rolling eyes, 'held' breaths, contorted figures, stony faces or close-ups of the convulsive play of hands was not enough to reveal all the subtleties of the inner struggle in all its nuances. . . .

The camera penetrated 'inside' Clyde, it began to fix aurally and visually the feverish *train of thought*, alternating with the external action – the boat, the girl sitting opposite him, his own actions.

The form of the 'inner monologue' was born.

These montage sketches were marvellous.

Even literature is almost powerless in this respect. It is limited either to the primitive rhetoric of Dreiser's account of Clyde's inner babblings or to the even worse falsehood of the pseudo-classical tirades of O'Neill's heroes, who conduct secondary monologues in 'asides' revealing 'what they are thinking' while they tell the audience what they are saying (*Strange Interlude*).[32]

Theatre is even more lame in this respect than orthodox literary prose.

Only cinema is capable of depicting the whole train of thought in a disturbed mind.

If literature can do it, it will only be a literature that goes beyond the · bounds of its orthodox limitations.

This problem is exceptionally brilliantly resolved within the cruel framework of literature's limitations in the immortal 'inner monologues' of the insurance agent, Leopold Bloom, in James Joyce's remarkable *Ulysses*.*

It is no coincidence that, when Joyce and I met in Paris, he was so intensely interested in my plans for 'inner film monologues' with far broader possibilities than those in literature.

Despite his almost total blindness, he wanted to see those parts of *Potemkin* and *October* that follow similar lines in the film sector of expressive culture.[33]

The 'inner monologue' as a literary method of abolishing the distinction between subject and object in the exposition of the hero's experiences in crystallised form is first observed in literature and dated by researchers to 1887 in the work of Edouard Dujardin, *Les Lauriers sont coupés*.[34]

As a theme, as a world-view, as a 'feeling', an object of description but not a method of it, one can of course find it even earlier. 'Sliding' from the subjective to the objective and back is especially characteristic of the writing of the Romantics: E. T. A. Hoffmann, Novalis, Gérard de Nerval (on the latter see René Bizet's *La Double Vie de Gérard de Nerval*).[35]

But as a method of literary style, rather than plot structure, as a specific method of exposition, a specific method of construction, we find it first in Dujardin. It reaches its absolute literary perfection in Joyce and Larbaud[36] thirty-one years later.

None the less, it can of course find its full expression only in cinema.

For only the sound film is capable of reconstructing all the phases and all the specifics of a train of thought.

What wonderful sketches those montage lists were!

Like thought itself they sometimes proceeded through visual images, with sound, synchronised or non-synchronised . . .

sometimes like sounds, formless or formed as representational sound images . . .

now suddenly in the coinage of intellectually formed words, as 'intellectual' and dispassionate as words that are spoken, with a blank screen, a rushing imageless visuality . . .

now in passionate disjointed speech, nothing but nouns or nothing but verbs; then through interjections, with the zigzags of aimless figures, hurrying along in synchronisation with them.

---

* I referred to Joyce's significance for cinema in *Na literaturnom postu* shortly before I left for Europe and America. [See above, pp. 95-99.]

Now visual images racing past in complete silence,
now joined by a polyphony of sounds,
now by a polyphony of images.

Then both together.

Then interpolated into the external course of action, then interpolating elements of the external action into themselves.

As if on their faces were represented the inner play, the conflict of doubts, of explosions of passion, of voice, of reason, in 'slow motion' or 'speeded up', marking the different rhythms of the one and the other and jointly contrasting with the almost complete absence of external action: the fever of inner debates as opposed to the stony mask of the face.

How fascinating to listen to your own train of thought, especially in its affect when you catch yourself wondering: what do I see? how? what do I hear?!

How do you talk 'within yourself' as distinct from 'outside yourself'? What is the syntax of inner language, as distinct from external? What quiverings of inner words accompany the corresponding visual image? What contradicts what? How does reciprocity work?

You listen and study in order to understand the structural laws and assemble them into the construction of an extremely tense inner monologue of the struggle of tragic experience.

How fascinating!

And what momentum for creative invention and observation!

And how obvious it is that the raw material of sound film is not *dialogue*.

The true material of sound film is, of course, monologue.

And how unexpectedly, in its practical embodiment of the unforeseen particular concrete instance of expressiveness, it reminds us of the 'last word' on montage form in general that I foresaw theoretically long ago,

of the fact that montage form as structure is a reconstruction of the laws of the thought process.

Here the particular treatment, fertilised by a new rather than an existing formal method, goes beyond its limits and generalises the theory of montage form as a whole into a new realm of theory and principle. (However, this by no means implies that the *thought process as a montage form* always necessarily has to have a train of thought as its *subject*!)

[However, Mr Schulberg ('B.P.') and Washington 'D.C.' (District of Columbia) combined to prevent the 'red dogs' (our official soubriquet in Fascist circles) from realising all *this* on the screen, launching their 'monstrous challenge' to American society and effecting this 180° advance in sound film culture. . . .

We parted like ships at sea . . . .][37] My notes are drowning in unopened suitcases, buried like Pompeii in my one-room suite under a pile of books: there is not even room to unpack them. My notes are drowning while they wait to be realised.

. . . But von Sternberg made the film and he directly and literally did 'just the reverse', excising everything that our script was based on and restoring everything that we had discarded.

The idea of 'inner monologue' never even occurred to Sternberg. . . .

Sternberg confined himself to a 'straightforward' detective story.

The grey-haired lion Dreiser himself fought for our 'distortion' of this work and took Paramount, who had made an outwardly correct version of his story, to court.

Two years later the screen saw O'Neill's *Strange Interlude* and double and treble expositions of talking heads surrounding the silent face of the hero aggravated the clumsy unwieldiness of his cuneiform dramaturgy. It was a bloody mockery of what might be achieved through montage using the correctly resolved principle of inner monologue!

Work of a similar type. The resolution of the film through the treatment. Evaluation through the treatment. But the most important thing is to effect a constructively artistic and formally fruitful role for this 'boring', 'obligatory', 'imposed' ideology and ideological restraint.

To effect this through the living organism of the work rather than through a schema is the fundamental task facing our collective director, the direction collective of the third-year course at GIK.

And, although we shall use every method to find a shock theme from among the multi-faceted thematic ocean that surrounds us in order to find the actual theme for this work, I nevertheless believe that our first experiment on this road will be the resolution of a film on a subject that has long been waiting for its resolution: the theme of 'youth of the 20th century' – 'youth in the USSR'.

Paramount publicity picture for Sternberg's film, sent by E to Ivor Montagu and inscribed 'An American Tragedy as directed by great Von Joe'

32. In the Interests of Form[38]

'Our cinema is on course towards ideological saturation.'

That is the theme that the newspaper *Kino* has placed on the agenda, very appropriately, for the anniversary of October.

Théophile Gautier[39] spent his spare time engrossed in dictionaries.

He thought it was the most useful form of reading.

At least he mercilessly rebuffed from literary consultation the young authors who blushed with a glow of denial when he asked them if they did the same.

I also have a bad habit with dictionaries.

A kind of ailment. A weakness.

A preconceived notion that the first salvation of a word or term from the confusion that surrounds it is above all a simple dictionary of definitions.

Not so much encyclopaedic as etymological.

It does not always solve the problem but it always leads to profitable reflections.

'Ideological saturation'.

'Ideology'.

'Idea'.

In the olden days probably nobody looked in a Greek dictionary.

But in the meantime.

Somewhere between Ibycus, a poet who was more popular for his cranes than for his verse, and the Phrygian Mount Ida A. F. Pospishil has found a refuge for *idea*.[40]

Idea.

On p.476 we read: '. . . ἰδέα Ionic. (1) appearance, exterior; (2) image, type, method, feature, quality . . .; especially: method of exposition, form and type of speech; (3) idea, prototype, ideal.'[41]

These three points are the three mammoths of cinema.

And these are the three mammoths that I shall talk about.

Once more let us recall their genetic inseparability . . . *idea* (third meaning), *method of exposition* (second meaning) and *exterior, appearance* (first meaning).

'That's new?' – 'As new as the name Popov', Sasha Chyorny[42] wrote about these kinds of 'discoveries'.

But, if it is not new, it belongs to those truths that we ought to repeat to ourselves every day both before breakfast and before lunch. And, if you do not have dinner, before you go to sleep.

Mainly in one's waking hours.

And you must start to put this into practice.

This is the principal group that it is most appropriate to consider for the fifteenth anniversary of October.

238

And now is just the right time when our cinema could easily be driven into opportunism through a false understanding of the principle of entertainment, on the one hand, and the bad tradition of the thinly disguised *agitka*,[43] on the other.

Hardly anyone inclines towards thematic opportunism.

What is more, the steel ranks of consultants[44] will not let it through into the film.

So it will be predominantly a matter of opportunism of form.

In my view cinema's basic ailment today is one that affects the second and third points of the tripartite totality of the materialised ideology.

Soviet cinema has been so intimidated by the Ku-Klux-Klan of 'Formalism' that it has almost eradicated creativity and creative searches in the field of form.

If Formalism as a scientific literary tendency invites attack and censure, it has first and foremost a complete and formulated platform.

But in cinema 'Formalism' was rather created 'by analogy' – and not so much by the film workers themselves as by the critics who were looking for a label to attach themselves to.

If any film-maker began to contemplate or work on the problem of the means of expression to embody an idea, the shadow of suspicions and accusations of Formalism would fall on him straight away.

'Formalists' were signed up like recruits.

Without a chance to sober up and come to.

Just as the young Lomonosov[45] was once apparently signed up as a recruit for the Russian king.

Just as when Russia was converted to Christianity, hordes of people, anyone who dared to mention form, were christened Formalists.

Unfortunately those hordes did not in actual fact exist: there were two or three people honestly contemplating the problems of form. Unfortunately, as subsequent developments have shown, there were not more of them . . . .

Christening these people Formalists was as over-hasty as calling people who study the symptoms of syphilis . . . 'syphilitics'.

At a certain stage this extreme form of persecution is quite permissible.

A few people overdid it, perhaps, but that could be tolerated.

Engels wrote about neglect of form, form that people forget, in a letter to Mehring dated 14 July 1893:

> Otherwise there is only one other point lacking, which, however, Marx and I always failed to stress enough in our writings and in regard to which we are all equally guilty. We all, that is to say, laid and were bound to lay the main emphasis at first on the derivation of political, juridical and other ideological notions, and of the actions arising through the medium of these notions, from basic economic facts.

But in so doing we neglected the formal side – the way in which these notions come about. . . . It is the old story: form is always neglected at first for content . . . but I would like all the same to draw your attention to this point for the future.[46]

Our cinema has also to some extent neglected problems of form. Especially in recent years.

And forgotten, it is now beginning to ache like a neglected tooth.

We are full of content, but in the field of form we are lame in all four legs.

Our failings today lie not in the ideology of films but in form.

In form that cannot be ideology.

The plot anecdote is still satisfactory in defiance even of our traditions.

In fact: sometimes it is both vociferous and sharp-eyed, despite the fact that it is swaddled by the seven nannies of consultation. . . .

However, it is not in the devices of Formalism, real or imaginary, that we need to look for ways of recovering film form for the present day.

And not just in a correct representation of the contents.

A good idea in itself.

Excellent content.

Or an agitational *lubok*.[47]

Or something emerges, based on a false understanding of the years of entertainment, that . . . simply takes fright.

Protruding sadly from most of the thin grey soup of our mediocre screen production we see the Gogolian nose[48] with the sorrowful sigh.

'It's a depressing world, gentlemen!'[49]

And this is at a time of enormous revolutionary upsurge and enthusiasm.

Form has to catch up.

Our government inspectors,[50] the consultants, are terrible.[51]

Sickeningly meticulous.

But none of these government inspectors can help us in this.

The only person who can help us here is the 'last' inspector, 'supernatural' in Gogol, who stands behind all the others.

In Nikolai Vasilevich's [Gogol's] work he is a very mystical figure.

People have tried to identify him with everyone from God Himself to the most sacred person of Our Lord and Emperor Nikolai Pavlovich.

Ours will be simpler, even though he is 'inside' us.

This is not a matter of an 'inner Party card'[52] that is independent of any attachment to a district committee.

An inner Party card, independent of Party membership, should be in the inside pocket of all those who approach our fifteenth October as filmmakers.

That is the very real, personal, inner 'government inspector' whom

we must look straight in the face and be true to to the very end.

Unfortunately it seems to turn out all too often to be a real Khlestakov. . . .[53]

Ideological Khlestakovism concealed behind fine phrases.

Its inevitable accompaniment in form . . . 'Labardan'.[54]

This Labardan of form and brain produces Khlestakovism in the field of ideology.

It is a well-known fact that words are produced to conceal ideas as either Talleyrand or Metternich said.[55]

The screen was silent for too long to learn to lie.

You can lie your way round our consultants about theme and plot.

You can prattle on or start lying through your teeth.

But there comes a point when you do not lie.

The director can spend hours prattling on at the actors with abstract ideas of how this or that should be done.

But there comes a moment when you cannot get away with prattle.

'Come out and do it. Show me yourself.'

And that does not just happen with the actor.

In the ideology of 'explication' it is always possible to lie.

And never actually *do* anything.

Form is *always ideology*.

And form always turns out to be *real ideology*.

That is, ideology that *really* applies and not what passes for ideology in the idle prattle of the talkers.

Where the talent is wasted.

They prattle on about enthusiasm, pathos or the heroic with ease:

you can pick someone else's words from a newspaper and speak them yourself, thinking about Marusya[56] so that your voice sounds more passionate. Because of the content of your speech you were carried away by your passion.

But when you start to shoot and edit: there is no Masha.

If the scissors cut without enthusiasm then the film will run without enthusiasm.

If you filmed without hatred, none of the atrocities on the screen will kindle hatred.

Our screen is pitiless in 'tearing each and every mask' off those who make films.

Sometimes, when Maruska does walk into the actual film, it then becomes a work that is not about enthusiasm at all but about Katya and Masha, Dunya, Parasha or Foma and Yerema.

But the screen, whether silent or sound, yells about this at the top of its voice.

The form of the film produces a film-maker with a small head.

The men who dodged the call-up into the tsarist army liked to pretend to be deaf. But the old stagers, the army officer and the call-up doctor,

found them out: in a simple manoeuvre they just happened to drop a coin behind the conscript.

He turned round involuntarily.

And the 'deaf' man was unmasked.

So it is with form: if you do not give a rouble of full ideological value, then the kopek you do give will tinkle and show up as false.

An enormous amount of methodological work is now going on to master and teach the secrets of creativity. Of cinematic images and cinematic form.

But in the first instance it is not form that we must teach as a matter of urgency. And it is not form that we must investigate and contemplate.

It is absolutely crystal clear that our first task among creative film-workers is to teach ideology.

Ideological training, rather than the ideological 'stocks' that some extremists had in mind.

And I shall talk about this training in the interests of form.

As an old, experienced, inveterate . . . 'Formalist'.

In the sixteenth year of the Revolution a film-worker should no longer be 'at the service' of the Revolution – he must 'belong' to it.

Otherwise there will be no cinema.

Form is above all ideology.

But ideology is no longer 'for hire'.

There is no closed distribution of ideology in nature.

But without an ideology that is thoroughly understood by the creative film-worker what more can you expect from him than commonplace vulgarity? Not the grandeur of the events surrounding him and the 'official' viewpoint of what should fire enthusiasm for the construction of socialism.

Dostoyevsky wrote to N. N. Strakhov[57] from Florence on 26 February 1869 about finding the new revolutionary realism that we are looking for and about its methods: '. . . commonplace events and an official view of them are, in my view, not yet realism but its opposite. . . .'

It is only when they are thoroughly immersed in Marxist-Leninist ideology that creative film-workers will be able to engage completely responsibly in the actual realisation of the theory and practice of Leninism through cinema.

That is the programme for the enormous psychological work that our leading Party cadres must do on those people both within the ranks of the Party and outside it who have been called on to record and reproduce the greatest epoch in human history in unsurpassable images and forms.

This is the only guarantee of the ideological saturation of our cinema.

This is the only *possibility* for its ideological saturation.

It is in the full acknowledgment of ideology as the fundamental principle of the perfection of form that the basis for the further victorious advance of Soviet cinema as the mightiest of the arts lies.

As the mightiest cultural weapon in the hands of the proletariat.

33. **Through the Revolution to Art:**   1933
Through Art to the Revolution[1]

The October Revolution is fifteen years old.

My artistic activity is twelve years old.

My family traditions, my upbringing and my education had prepared me for a completely different field.

I was trained as an engineer. But a subconscious and undeveloped inclination towards work in the sphere of art prompted me even within the framework of engineering towards architecture, a field that was closer to art, rather than towards the mechanical and technological side.

However, it needed the whirlwind of Revolution sweeping past to emancipate me from my inertia, from my once projected path, and make me surrender to the inclination which, left to its own devices, would not have dared to reveal itself.

This is my first debt to the Revolution.

It needed the overthrow of all the foundations of the country, a complete transformation in its views and principles, and two years of technical engineering work on the Red Fronts of the North and West for the bashful student to cast off the fetters placed on him from the cradle by a solicitous parent's hand and abandon an almost completed education and a secure future to throw himself into the unknown prospects of a life of artistic activity.

Leaving the front I found myself not in Petrograd to complete my course but in Moscow to start a new life.

Although the first distant rumblings of the approaching *revolutionary* art were already seething and trembling around me, I, having fallen greedily on art *in the general sense*, was completely captivated by art in the general sense.

In our first steps our link with the Revolution was a purely superficial one.

To make up for this I, armed with my technical engineering methods, greedily tried to penetrate ever deeper into the origins of creativity and art, where I instinctively foresaw the same sphere of precise knowledge that my short experience in the field of engineering had inculcated in me.

My one-man struggle, against the windmills of mysticism that the solicitous hands of obliging sycophants had placed at the approaches to the mastery of artistic methods to confuse anyone in their right mind who wanted to master the secrets of artistic production, passed through Pavlov, Freud, a season with Meyerhold, a confused but feverish plugging of the gaps in my knowledge of this new field, an excessive amount of reading and my first steps in independent set design and production work at the Proletkult Theatre.

My campaign proved to be less like Don Quixote's than it seemed at first. The sails of the windmill broke off and that single dialectic that lies at the basis of every phenomenon and every process gradually began to make itself felt in that mysterious field.

By this time I had already long been a materialist by nature.

At this stage an unexpected correspondence suddenly appeared between what I had encountered in the analytical work I had been doing on the thing that fascinated me and what was happening around me.

My art students, to my considerable astonishment, suddenly drew my attention to the fact that in teaching them their artistic alphabet I was using exactly the same method as the political education instructor on social questions who was sitting next to me.

That superficial shock was enough to ensure that it was the dialectics of materialism rather than aesthetics that gleamed on my work table.

The fighting year 1922. A decade ago.

The experience of my personal research and creative work in my particular branch of human activity merged with the philosophical experience of the social basis of each and every socio-human manifestation through my study of the founders of Marxism.

But the matter does not end there. Through the study of its brilliant teachers the Revolution became entrenched in my work in another way.

My link with the Revolution became one of vital interest and utter conviction.

In my creative work this was signified by the transition from the extreme rationalism and almost abstract theatrical Eccentrism of *Wise Man* (a reworking in circus form of A.N. Ostrovsky's comedy *Enough Simplicity for Every Wise Man*) through the agitational and propagandist poster-plays *Can You Hear me, Moscow?* and *Gas Masks*[2] to the revolutionary screen epics *The Strike* and *The Battleship Potemkin*.

The desire for ever closer contact with the Revolution determined the trend to an ever deeper immersion in the dialectical principles of militant materialism in the field of art.

Together with the weight of their response to direct social requirements, my next films will include attempts at experimental practical 'mediation' [*oposredstvovanie*] of the secrets of creativity and of the opportunities for cinematic expressiveness to master the most effective methods of revolutionary art and to equip pedagogically the generation of young Bolsheviks who are coming to take the place of the cinematic masters of the Revolution's first Five-Year Plans.

The centre of gravity of my latest works (*October, The Old and the New*) lies in the field of experimentation and research.

As far as my personal creativity is concerned, my systematic scientific and pedagogical practice are inseparably intertwined (at the State Institute of Cinematography, GIK).

My theoretical works on the basic principles of film art are being written.

My *Weltanschauung* appears to have taken shape. I have accepted the Revolution. My activity is devoted entirely to furthering its interests.

The question remains of how far I am consciously and inflexibly determined.

At this point my journey abroad intervenes.

Abroad is the severest test that biography can set a Soviet man whose development is automatically and indissolubly linked with the development of October. It is the test of free choice.

Abroad is the severest test for a 'master of culture' to examine consciously 'whom he is for and whom he is against'.

Abroad is the severest test for a creative worker as to whether he is on the whole capable of creation outside the Revolution and whether he can go on existing outside it.

This test appeared for us when we were confronted by the golden hills of Hollywood and we passed it, not with a heroic pose of arrogant rejection of the earth's charms and blessings, but with our creative and constructive instincts modestly and organically rejecting the opportunity to create in a different social atmosphere and in the interests of a different class.

This inability to create on the other side of the demarcation line between the classes reflects the strength and power of the revolutionary pressure of the proletarian revolution as a whirlwind sweeping away all those who oppose it and as a still more powerful whirlwind engulfing those who have chosen to march in step with it.

That is how everyone in the galaxy of active Soviet artists acts, feels and thinks.

Many of us have come through the Revolution to art.

All of us summon you through art to the Revolution!

34. Pantagruel Will Be Born[3]

'What's on the sign must be in the shop': that is what people sometimes say about a shop.

Sometimes they say it about people they meet.

We have to say it about Comrade Weissman's article.

What is the title/sign?

'Gargantua is growing'.

The article/shop provides an explanation.

Gargantua is apparently our sound cinema.

Figuratively speaking? Yes.

Figuratively accurate? No.

Gargantua, as his biographer Rabelais reports, was born from the left ear of Gargamelle. The ear – and, what is more, the left one.

Our sound film has been born . . . in precisely the opposite way – not from the ear but *from the eye of silent cinema* (if not from the 'Cine-Eye').[4]

More accurately, from a mote in the eye of silent cinema, from the worst vestiges of theatre within it.

Does the name on the sign correspond to the goods inside the shop of the article?

Undoubtedly, if you accept the mistaken associations that accompany the excerpts from my article 'Help Yourself!'.[5]

We are not responsible for the selection of these excerpts, their montage or the series of individual associations that Comrade Weissman makes with them . . . .

The fact that 'in literature and in the theory of theatre Idealists of all shades have reflected the thought process by means of inner monologue' and that 'the Idealist method readily operates through the method of inner monologue' can in no way itself serve as an argument against inner monologue and the Idealist philosophy that necessarily accompanies it.

If we follow these lines of argument we should have to walk everywhere on foot on the grounds that many Idealists have travelled, and do travel, by tram.

And the phrase 'the dialectic of nature' would have to be eliminated altogether because the Idealists also frequently use the term 'dialectic'.

There is the Idealist dialectic and there is the material dialectic.

Why should there not be a similar dual and directly opposite notion inherent in the idea of inner monologue? A reverse side to the philosophical 'reverse side' . . . that Comrade Weissman supplies 'inner monologue' with?

I do not deny that I made a mess of my statement of this problem in my article (and it was not the principal problem in the article, but rather an illustration of it).

But Comrade Weissman, resenting my confusion, somewhat prema-

246

turely and pointlessly blows his hurt and spongy Sologubisms[6] in my direction.

Since I am afraid of making yet another mess of a problem that, in my view, is of prime importance with regard to our approaches to the real forms of sound film dramaturgy, I shall permit myself to provide a detailed analysis and statement of this problem in the wider space of the printed pages of *Proletarskoe kino*,[7] where it will appear in due course and without any special prompting from Comrade Weissman.

Because of a shortage of time and space I cannot dwell here even on the obvious distortions that are clearly based simply on careless reading.

The 'mystery of the individual monologue' rests *entirely* on the conscience of Comrade Weissman.

So does inner monologue as a means of sowing the doctrine of removing the boundaries between the subjective and the objective.

There is a parallel with the Proustian method of 'fixing the alteration of reality without in any way intervening in it'[8] when Comrade Weissman himself refers to my work 'Beyond the Shot',[9] which revolves around the problem of the deconstruction [*raz"yatie*] of reality and its new montage accumulation from our class standpoint, etc., etc.

On the other hand, I cannot fail to notice that what Comrade Weissman so loftily calls 'only a half-way stage that we stopped at very briefly' *does in fact involve an extremely serious reconstruction of precisely that 'architectonic of cinema action'* that Comrade Weissman writes about as if it were something that had apparently long been defined, immanent and well known to him.

It is a curious architectonic that includes, for example, the unexpected assertion 'that dialogue in sound film must live in truncated form, quite unlike dialogue in theatre'. Statements about 'laconicism' and 'maximal tension' are 'commonplaces' that have long been familiar even beyond the bounds of cinema.

We do not wish to see the elements of sound film truncated by eunuch-signs taken from other art forms.

We wish to find an approach to the elements of external continuity that renews from within the specific qualities and the new aspects of the possibilities of sound film.

Comrade Weissman's assertion that in sound film 'we must not forget that the language of cinema is the language of movement' is no more than an 'aphorism', and not a very original one at that.

We must not merely not forget this 'language of movement': we must unfortunately devise it in its entirety.

Almost from scratch.

The dramaturgy of sound film, whether it derives from theatre or silent film, has the chance, simultaneously with the transition to this new form, to make a quantum 'leap' as great as the leap in human means of social intercourse from the stage of diffuse consciousness and inarticulate sound to the stage of articulate meaningful speech and conscious thought.

None of the traditions of Aristotle's severed heads will help us here.[10]

The signs are refashioned but not 'resewn' with the transition from one stage of development to another.

Patched-up clothes are no good when it is a matter of the transition to a new quality.

It was Plekhanov who used to talk about how, in the final analysis, all phenomena can be reduced to 'movement'.

To talk simply of movement is to say everything and at the same time to say nothing.

The language of cinema is the language of movement (plus the word in sound film).

But the language of theatre is also the language of movement (plus the word if it is not mime).

Movement and movement.

But the 'movement' is different in each case.

And it defines the specific character of the two fields.

In a single general basic social determinant that defines their superstructure.

Based on a definite field of human phenomena ('movement') that is characteristic of its own field, the art form adopts the appropriate law of structure that is specific to it.

Thus, it seems to us that theatre is in the first instance *a reconstruction of the actions and deeds of man as a social being.*

It is this fact that has determined and does determine the specific character of the concept of theatrical dramaturgy, of the articulation, the structure and construction that develop and change as part and parcel of the cause of social development, while none the less preserving their characteristic features as forms of spectacle.

Cinema seems to us *by its specific character to reproduce phenomena according to all the indications of the method that derives from the reflection of reality in the movement of the psychic process.* (There is not one specific feature of cinematic phenomenon or method that does not correspond to the specific form of the process of human psychic activity.)

It is in the realisation of this and in its constructive application that, in our view, *the key to the approach to a specific dramaturgy of sound film lies.*

In terms of both its quality and its stage of development it will stand in the same relationship to theatrical dramaturgy as does the thought process to mere walking.

It is along this path that we shall find both the specific expressive methods of sound film and the rules of construction for its component elements.

Among their endless variety there will doubtless be a place for the much-vaunted *element of dialogue*, one that does not resemble theatrical dialogue at all. *For it will be constructed on the basis of the real specific character of its field and will, in reality, not resemble theatre.*

However paradoxical it may seem, this will be a structure of dialogue re-

constructed on the basis of the specific character of the means of expression of sound film as the structure of 'inner monologue'.

That is part of what we understand by 'montage form as the reconstruction of the thought process'.

Have I made a mess of it again?

Possibly.

Even so it will still be a long way from Comrade Weissman's pitiful castrato-truncated dialogue.

For Comrade Weissman's information:

the experiment of 'inner monologue' as a particular form of plot resolution is a 'half-way stage' but only in the sense that Gargantua the father is a half-way stage between Grangousier the grandfather and Pantagruel the grandson (you can judge for yourself how appropriate the analogy is).

I shall wait for a bit with my whistle.

I shall whistle when I have spent some time in practical work on this problem (the next stage beyond 'inner monologue').

But to make up for it: I shall get there in the end.

35. To Your Posts!¹¹

A registry office. And what is more – a local one. A local registry office.

And what is more – a consultation about divorce.

The local registry office is an inexhaustible source of curiosities and comic situations.

'Your surname?'

'Oh, I'm sorry, I can't say!'

'Why?'

'Well, you'd laugh at me.'

'??!'

'But I've got such a funny surname.'

'??!!'

(The registrar's mind begins to reverberate with indistinct contours that hint at 'funny' surnames in the style of Barkov¹² or Rabelais: you can see from the announcements on the back pages of *Izvestiya* that they are the kind of names that people change.)

'Nevertheless . . . .'

'Oh, I can't. Everybody laughs when I tell them my surname.'

(The hints are obviously becoming stronger and the questioner's voice is becoming correspondingly more avuncular.)

'Well, there are only a few surnames like that. We sometimes have to listen to the most unexpected things.'

But the client has no desire whatsoever to give his name.

'No, no, no . . . . You'll laugh.'

He is met with an excursion into the class origins of the creation of contemptuous and insulting names that are inseparable from the general system of capitalist repression and humiliation.

And in the end, after every imaginable and unimaginable guarantee not to laugh, it turns out that his surname is:

'Schoolboy' [*Shkol'nik*].

Possibly somebody might laugh at that.

Probably they would.

But the questioner feels rather angry disappointment at the lost outpourings of his solicitous humanity – and all for the sake of a schoolboy!

But the schoolboy is delighted. There has been none of the usual laughter. His trust has been won over.

And very quickly the questioner is engulfed in a stormy torrent, the fantastic details of the insane story of an average happy marriage that suddenly, after twelve days (!), breaks down in divorce with a claim about the material, moral and physical loss suffered by the impetuous schoolboy.

This time it really is like Rabelais. . . .

But what can we say about the torrent of divorce cases that come up endlessly: after a week, three days, two, and even one straight after the registration ceremony.

There are girls who will not agree to make love outside marriage.

So people marry them. Then the following morning they get divorced.

It is an infamy that is wrapped up in the two certificates of two perfectly legal civil acts.

These cases are dealt with without direct reference to the courts.

But there might be evidence of a more criminal nature . . . and the nastiest evidence is cited by 'intellectual partners' who divorce after five or six years of marriage.

'This woman is the scourge of my life. . . .'

'You were a nobody when I took you up. . . .'

'If it weren't for me, you'd never have got through university. . . .'

The usual bickering.

But it reaches its height when we come to the matter of 'Article 10', on what the law calls the division of property, which in practice means the moment of the inevitable division into two equal parts of eleven silver spoons, the five teacups that survive from what was once a complete service of crockery, and three enamel saucepans of various sizes. . . .

It is here, in the face of 'Article 10', that the last remnants of the masks of goodwill, good manners and good breeding slip away.

The instincts of petty jealousy and petty possessiveness have full rein.

From beneath the nervously rolled cuffs of the usually so well-poised but now disturbed and deranged 'intellectual' there emerge the bared jowls of the same kulak and property-conscious psychology that we see in Efimov's caricatures.[13]

> As Marxists you should know that the consciousness of people lags in its development behind their actual situation. Collective farmers are, in terms of their situation, no longer individual peasants but part of a collective, but their consciousness is still that of the old order of private ownership.*

These words of Comrade Stalin are not only applicable to individual collective farms.

These words are applicable wherever you smell not the scent of socialist ownership but the acrid stench . . . of private ownership.

And especially where the forms of equitable distribution have not yet been finally and clearly sketched in by law and practice.

---

* J.V. Stalin, 'Itogi pervoi pyatiletki' [The Results of the First Five-Year Plan], *Izvestiya*, 10 January 1933.

Recently this kind of acridly stinking wave has regularly swamped the squabbles between creative groups of various specialisms in their fights over the division of the spoils from the 'author's' cake.

The directors have interfered with the rights of the scriptwriters.

There is bickering over the cameramen's pretensions to direction.

Everyone is very highly strung – with ironically twisted lips.

Sudden attacks and counterattacks in the press.

Repressed anger.

Making the handles of the cameras quiver as they are cranked.

The scriptwriters' pens[14] skip across the paper as they divert their attention to writing 'letters to the editor' rather than to the images of socialist realism.

The directors roll up their sleeves, searching for the place where they can strike the 'enemy' like a snake.

Below the belt without fail.

The atmosphere becomes more oppressive and, just as in *Dead Souls* when any poor devil approaches the town of N, stories circulate. Rumours circulate, gossip circulates. And possibly facts.

Personal notes and private correspondence that are far from being publishable in terms of their quality are dragged from grandmothers' stockings on to the pages of the press.

Compromising shots that have been excised are circulated.

And everywhere you find a prosecutor. A prosecutor. A prosecutor.

A director with a freshly made 'world name', appearing before a Soviet court, demands that it take into account the damage that will be done to his 'world reputation' if the co-authorship suit that has been brought against him is proven. . . .

And everywhere you find a prosecutor. A prosecutor.

Rumours descend from the hilltops that in the country that is building socialism it is none the less possible to 'buy out' a cameraman from another creative collective, for instance, in return for a few small crumbs from the co-authorship payments. . . .

Perhaps the prosecutor is not yet omnipresent enough. . . .

The prosecutor. The prosecutor. The prosecutor.

Whereas somewhere, as they say, Bonaparte appeared in Gogol but in fact it was really Chichikov,[15] in our cinema now dyed-in-the-wool Chichikovism is parading as the real Bonaparte as far as the apportionment of author's payments is concerned. . . .

And it is a matter precisely of dead souls.

Dead souls crawling into living ones.

Or living souls taken as corpses!

We by no means wish this self-seeking scramble between the living and the dead under the Darwinian slogan of consuming and devouring each other to be opposed with the slogan, 'love thy neighbour as thyself'.

We should like to oppose this rage of passions with a cool exposition of the apportionment of the stages of authorship in the making of a film. In my view, a confusion between two of them, with an inadequate demarcation between them, lies at the bottom of the majority of our disagreements.

Let us try and gain some understanding of the matter.

A certain specialism enters cinema under two names.

Like a two-headed eagle.[16]

Or St Cyril and St Methodius.[17]

One is described as a director [*rezhissër*].

The other is called a producer [*postanovshchik*].

By misusing the twaddle of our discussions we have quite ceased to respect both the designation and the word.

And ceased seeing both the essence and meaning that lie beneath many words and designations.

That is why this specialism emerges in this way.

One man likes to describe himself as a producer.

Another prefers to be called a director.

The only criterion, apparently, is the alliterative correspondence with the resonance of your own surname.

If your surname sounds such that you cannot construct any alliterative correspondence with it at all, then you write the two together:

producer-director or director-producer.

None the less. . . .

None the less there are two great differences.

And the underestimation of these two great differences is one of the basic causes of our squabbles, one of the basic causes of the legitimate protest against the appropriation by the 'director' of author's rights and, on the other hand, the insufficient respect for the legitimacy of the moral right of the 'producer' to a share in the author's loot.

The producer is the 'author of the production'.

The director is the 'executor of the production'.

It is the fault of the directors themselves that the low quality of the 'authorship of the production' forces them themselves to overlook the most important link between making a film and the location of the basic 'authorship' in film work.

It is the link that lies between the written script, on the one hand, and the rehearsed cry of the actor, the crew at 'strike up' and the snipping of the editor's scissors, on the other.

At the same time this very link is precisely the only one that is able to justify the reverent esteem that prevails over the director's rank in the iconography of cinema ('Director – that's a proud name'?!).

It is precisely this link – the focus for the director's creativity over the picture – that is most often generally absent as a creative stage.

Its palliative substitute for a one-and-a-half-month honeymoon period is the pair: 'preparatory period' and 'shot-by-shot analysis' [*raskadrovka*].

253

A genuine script is, if possible, not a half-finished product but it is undoubtedly a semi-virgin: it is not a virgin – a subject – but it is also not a married woman, a mother of a family – a film.

The completeness of a script is an ideological-emotional whole embodied in plot action of a certain visibility and mobility in general terms.

It requires a visual and motive screen equivalent that is specifically cinematic.

The lines of a script are subject to replacement by the duration on screen of images of people first of all perceived speculatively and then encountered in the flesh, of abstract intimations of a landscape engraved with the contours of actual species of trees, etc.

This is the creative stage in the crystallisation of a film, like the crystallisation of love in Stendhal, when the rhythm of the pulsating, ideologically saturated emotion of a script begins its transformation into the forms of articulation of a screen story through screen methods.

Between a script and the accounting methods of a 'director's' shot-by-shot analysis there is this stage of the creation by the 'producer' of a screen equivalent for a script, a stage that precedes the 'shooting'.

But it is much more complicated than this.

It is not merely a matter of creating an equivalent.

The crux lies in the treatment.

In that 'revelation' of the intention of the author (if that he be) that is particular to him and that his methods permit or in the introduction of a profound social significance into the work of a scriptwriter who is incapable of raising himself above the accumulated charm of organised peripeteia.

Sometimes co-authorship outgrows authorship. . . .

But, on the other hand, this is far from being a case of simple 'alteration' or a deliberate artificial shuffling or juggling so that the director can 'make himself felt'. There have been cases like that.

We are not talking about the real treatment stage.

In everyday practical terms it cannot be distinguished from the doctor's straightforward function: it is not a matter of the depth of the treatment and the creative mastery of material of someone else's authorship but merely of an excursion occasioned by someone else's inventiveness.

Lastly, it sometimes involves both scriptwriter and director in a case of genuine and collective collaboration and co-authorship.

This last case least frequently leads to conflicts.

This is the basic link in a production: the 'authorship of the production'.

Direction is something quite separate.

Let us begin with the fact that it is possible to be the director of a production that is not one's own.

For some reason this happens frequently and quite naturally in theatre.

Especially in the Moscow Gorky Art Theatre and its subsidiaries.[18]

In a Sakhnovsky production the direction is like that.[19]
In a Simonov production the direction is like that.[20]

But Meyerhold writes literally the 'author of the production' and, if Nikolai Vasilevich Gogol were to receive royalties, he would rightly have to cede half of them to Vsevolod Emilevich.[21]

It is appropriate here to express regret that our cinema lacks the American equivalent of this, because America is richly acquainted with this phenomenon even in cinema.

A production by (the now deceased) Thomas Ince.[22] But several directors are shooting, each directing separate parts of the production.

A production by (the still healthy) Cecil. B. DeMille.[23] But someone else is sweating over the direction.

This produces marvellous results both in terms of the artistic well-being of the production and in terms of shooting experience.

A director like this works or, expressed in accounting terms, this part of the director's work is carried out not 'for royalties' but for basic pay at a special rate.

This in no way negates or reduces the highly creative and inventive qualities required of the producer himself or another director to carry out this work.

At this stage of the work the director is completely equal in creative terms to the cameraman, the actor, the lighting engineer and everyone who collectively 'realises' the film.

The difference in pay is attributable to the greater sphere of responsibility, for instance, of a director in comparison, say, to an assistant cameraman, while, in creative terms, the working responsibility falls to each of them in equal measure.

The creative working respect and the working creative equality in the work being created involve all the members of the collective identically and in equal measure.

It is no mere coincidence that we live in a country where 'every cook should know how to run the government'[24] and where a driver in charge of a bus and a People's Commissar in charge of a People's Commissariat – a whole sector of the government – are equal shock-workers in the construction of socialism.

Nor, in our sector of general labour, is there any room for grudges.

Film is and will remain an equal collective work of all those who participate in it.

The degree of figuratively creative demand made of each person and of each specialism is regulated, we repeat, by the scale of their payments.

In terms of their creative investment all those who realise the film are equal.

This, I think, also resolves the problem of the cameraman's co-authorship. A full and equal co-author is one who has participated either in writing the script or on an equal basis in the 'authorship of the production'.

Any member of the collective can be a co-author of the production but this will be over and above his basic creative work on the picture overall.

A cameraman who has not played a part in the 'co-authorship of the production' has just as little right to a share in the royalties as a director who has really been 'only a director' and not a 'producer'.

Similarly, only a scriptwriter who has actually played a part in the production of a script has the right to be called the 'author of the script'.

We must separate St Cyril from St Methodius. Muir from Merrilees.[25] The producer from the director.

Not as individuals but in recognition of their activities as creative stages in a single process.

A failure to distinguish between them will lead to a large number of misunderstandings and false claims and counterclaims.

But a recognition of them should have a fruitful result in raising this most important and hitherto unnoticed creative link to the proper and principled heights of the artistic responsibility for the treatment of the script.

This will immediately be reflected in the quality of production.

By collating the literary script and the director's script it will be easy to establish immediately whether we are dealing with a slavish shot-by-shot analysis or with a new creative advance in the work which has taken place after the scriptwriter's authorship through the creative consciousness of the producer.

That is how it strikes me both in theoretical and judicial terms.

Practice is, of course, more diverse.

From amicable agreements to . . . criminal abuses.

You also, of course, come across forms that are based on straightforward exploitation.

The more amicable understandings there are that are based on complete collectivism, the better.

Prosecution is concerned with crimes.

But unfounded grudges and claims on the part of someone, albeit a genius, who is 'only a director' against a scriptwriter, or against him on the part of a cameraman who was not involved in the 'co-authorship of the production' but who merely shot the film, albeit with utterly brilliant mastery, must be shown their place.

Because, in addition to the 'author's' royalties, there are also the 'bonuses' for quality.

We must approach this matter like grown-ups.

We must stop being schoolboys.

We shall not exchange the practice of the most collective of arts for the divorce chairs of the registry office.

We must have a clear awareness of our creative posts.

And we must fill them with the utmost responsibility.

We must put an end to 'kulak-like' scuffles and squabbles. And respond in a harmonious and creative manner to the summons 'to our creative posts'.

It is this that will help us to bring our cinema rapidly to the heights required by that summons and by the practical measures taken in the film industry by the Party and the Government.

36. Georges Méliès's Mistake[26]

One particular stallion made a mistake. Or perhaps it was a donkey. Somehow or other a hinny emerged. And then a mule.

The mule and the hinny arrived and grew from strength to strength.
Because they met the economic needs of the social and property structure.

There were probably many others who made mistakes.

But they did not grow from strength to strength because they did not
meet a particular prerequisite.

In San Francisco there was Burbank, in Tambov Michurin.[27]

They produced unheard-of fruits.

These fruits became common because they met the needs of the food
structures of our organism.

One particular illusionist and conjuror made a mistake: he was
Georges Méliès. It happened in 1894 when the dawn of cinema was breaking.

Méliès made a mistake: he filmed his subject twice on the same strip
of negative.

To err is human and Méliès probably made other mistakes in his
work. But for some reason this mistake was consolidated and became part
of the treasury of cinema's means of expression.

It is reasonable to suppose that there were, and are, some grounds for
this.

These grounds are to be found in the structure of our process of
perception in general.

Really.

The principle of superimposition is the basic premiss through which
we perceive space fully.

The eyes of a fish stare motionless to the side in diametrically opposite directions. Since its two fields of vision never cross, a fish is deprived
of the opportunity of perceiving space stereoscopically. It would have to pick
its way painfully through the scale of the evolution of species so that, when it
reached the half-way stage of the ape on its way towards mankind, its eyes
would move from the side of its head to join in the middle of its snout and
form a face.

It is only when the field of vision reaches this state that even primates
start to shield one another, as S. Zuckerman writes (*The Social Life of Mon-
keys and Apes*, New York, 1932), for they are the only mammals capable of
stereoscopic vision, i.e. of a complete perception of the three dimensions in
space (see also H.M. Jolinson in *Journal of Animal Behaviour*, Boston, 1914,
who notes the absence of this capability in chickens and dogs).

Hence in apes and men – through the process of the superimposition
of two flat images one on top of the other – we observe for the first time the
complete three-dimensional assimilation of reality.

258

It is interesting that, when we resort to the graphic method of fixing a three-dimensional phenomenon, to graphic representation that inevitably gives way to the fullness of speculative representation, human practice is forced to slip back into the deconstruction of a three-dimensional body into two flat images.

A judgment of three-dimensional value is broken down into two right-angled projections.

Into façade and plane, to put it more colloquially.

But that is not all.

We know that consciousness is the reflection of the objective progress of social reality. This is counting from the moment when social reality on the boundaries of primitive society begins to take on concrete forms.

But what is there left for the primitive consciousness that is being formed to reflect?

In essence, it scarcely exists.

Its function in relation to consciousness remains to a certain extent for the animal organism to perform.

Really.

If we observe carefully the comparative anatomical and physiological development of the organism, we see that the development of the most primitive forms of thought reproduces them and the processes of their development in precisely the same way as the consciousness of an advanced human being reproduces in mirror image the structure and processes of development of the social organisms to which he belongs.

The transition from two separate flat images to the stage of the same images intersecting and producing a relief is fully reflected in the development of animal perception at the initial stage of the approach to the future realisation of reality.

In precisely this transition from the independent accumulation of 'impressions' to the representation of a phenomenon by means of the super-imposition of comprehensive impressions of the particular phenomenon.

Even in the tradition of the linguistic depiction of these designations we have preserved a trace, a stage of two-dimensional sense, in the three-dimensional realisation of a phenomenon.

'Two-dimensional' terms are an impression, *Eindruck, impression,* as opposed to three-dimensional terms like representation, *Vorstellung, représentation.*

If this position is correct as a starting-point for assimilating phenomena, then at a higher stage, at the stage of forming judgments, we once again encounter the same structure.

Primitive superimposition figures once more in this new capacity but it is now in the form of juxtaposition.

Juxtapositions that lie at the basis of those constructions and judgments that we make in relation to real phenomena, before we subject them to social re-creation through revolutionary pressure.

As we can see, the method of superimposing one image upon another is like a copy of all the progressive stages in a single historical process towards the assimilation and realisation of reality.

It is interesting to note that even the actual history of the development of trick photography – from Méliès's chance discovery to the natural developments in the further mastery of the techniques of trick photography – follows the same paths, beginning with the mechanical superimposition of two images and ending with the synthetic organics of the trick shot (the 'transparency'[28] method).

Let us add to this the fact that the basic cinematic phenomenon – the motor perception of a screen image – is based on the same superimposition of two successive immobile phases of motion in the consciousness of the perceiver.*

We have seen that the multiple superimposition of images is like a copy of the thought process at the various stages of its development. It is likewise incumbent on this method, from the standpoint of means of expression, to realise everything from the primitive optical 'trick' to a means of revealing more profoundly and consciously what it is representing.

By this we understand the applicability of the technical methods expounded in this book as means of expression.

Of the reality that we are calling on the actual film camera to penetrate – so that we move from the routine monitoring of an illusory, composed reality to an authentic unity of images joined in juxtaposition in order to reveal their sense.

All the varieties of the immeasurable number of forms taken by trick photography must be grouped together from these opposite poles and interact.

---

* Link's experiments have demonstrated clearly that the process of perceiving cinematic motion is above all a psychological process.

37. An Attack by Class Allies[29]

The *rentier* Lenglumé, emerging from his bed recess, cannot remember where he has spent the night.

Suddenly the bed recess begins to snore.

Someone else emerges.

A stranger. Someone he does not know. An outsider. A cook by trade.

The red-nosed Mistingue emerges.

Neither can remember what they were doing or where they were the night before or how they ended up together in Lenglumé's recess.

In their pockets they discover: a woman's cap, a blond plait of hair, a woman's shoe and lots and lots of coal dust and lumps of coal.

The newspaper says that a woman has been murdered in the Rue de Lourcine. By two unknown men. . . . In a coal cellar. . . .

One of the murderers' distinguishing features is a yellow umbrella with a monkey's head.

Lenglumé turns pale: he was on his way home with an identical umbrella.

This is the plot of Labiche's one-act vaudeville *The Affair of the Rue de Lourcine*.[30]

The revellers Lenglumé and Mistingue, who had been up to no good the night before at Madame Moreau's, had got so drunk that they had been locked up in the coal cellar but they were quite convinced that they were criminals . . . . They begin a panic concealment of the traces of their imagined crime. A never-ending kaleidoscope of ridiculous situations unfolds. They try to destroy the umbrella. To gas imaginary witnesses. To kill one another, and so on.

I have cited Labiche not just because, when we are talking about a bitingly taut story-line, we cannot help recalling Labiche or Scribe[31] but, principally, because of the denouement of this vaudeville.

It transpires that the newspaper report does actually correspond to reality but the newspaper itself does not: it dates from 1837 whereas the action of the play unfolds in the 1860s.

Justin the servant has mistakenly slipped this old newspaper under Madame Lenglumé's vase of flowers instead of a new one and, when he realises what has happened, he is unable to correct his mistake:

'Never mind, Madame only reads the report about dogs run over by carriages.'

The vaudeville that a couple of my friends, Bartenev and Kalatozov, have written about me should also have ended with the same reference to the dates of the material that they handled in such a panic-stricken way as if it were a special edition dealing with a sensational murder or a directive for immediate action.

261

For the authors of this vaudeville, using not just our films but also our 'theoretical pronouncements', remain resolutely on the threshold of 1929, that is, nearly five years ago. And there have been quite a few of the latter (the 'pronouncements'), if not of the former, since then . . . .

However, by distorting these pronouncements in an offensive manner and turning them into a 'ruptured montage' of their own juxtapositions, they simply ignore everything that has been written since.

This leaves them in the same position of confusion as that other pair, Mistingue and Lenglumé, in relation to the 1837 newspaper.

Our esteemed authors have obviously never read my article 'Help Yourself!'.[32] Otherwise how can you explain the fact that, when they were discussing my views on dramaturgy, they did not . . . help themselves to it?

I agree that, given the general state of preparedness of these authors in the problems of dramaturgy, which is obvious from their very curious statements on the 'drift' [*samotëk*] of dramaturgical construction (of which more below), my arguments about 'inner monologue' were perhaps rather too difficult for them, but everything else, everything concerning the dramaturgy and the dramaturgical saturation of the script for *An American Tragedy*[33] is clear and intelligible enough. It does not require or assume any special preparation either in matters of dramaturgy in general or on the level of the clarification of my attitude to these problems.

However, there is no doubt that our authors have not read this article, for I cannot possibly believe that this is a simple careless suppression of material that does not fit the straitjacket of their notion of me, into which their preconceptions are driving me.

If this is simply an archaeological exercise in the 'history of cinema' then let us call it that!

One way and another our authors could stay put in those distant times.

I might, of course, apply to them the calendar-based vaudeville finale of *The Affair of the Rue de Lourcine*, which their article fully deserves, and conceal from our friends the calendar with the date 1929.

But I shall not do this for two reasons.

First, it might cast a shadow over the theoretical value of the cinematic past in those years where we are dealing with a quite normal historical stage in the general course of development of cinema.

I should be very glad to repent of anything the authors suggested but, after running once again through the archive material they are using, I am once again convinced that the 'murderousness' of past misdemeanours that are attributed to me on that evidence is precisely akin to Lenglumé's participation in the murder in the Rue de Lourcine.

Second, I consider it necessary to discuss this article for prophylactic purposes as something harmful and as an indicator of the model new adversity that our cinema is being subjected to.

I have therefore permitted myself to christen with the term 'an attack by class allies' the type of pronouncement that the article by our esteemed authors represents.

'An attack by class allies' – that is, by people who are profoundly well-intentioned but who stray away from the historical stages and the progressive links in the processes of development. Sometimes they simply even stray away from the facts, and all this in the name of their preconceived notions and their facile labels.

Third and last, because we have a tradition of juggling with a whole series of significations, not by any means in our original authentic reading and understanding of them, but by ascribing to them intentions that they were far from proclaiming originally.

Let us take this step by step.

First, let us cite the characteristics of bourgeois art:

> . . . The ideological disintegration of bourgeois art is accompanied by the disintegration of the organicism of individual works of art. . . . Bourgeois works of art increasingly dissolve into separate parts that are outwardly, but not organically, connected to one another (in cinema this means episodicism in films) or, by excluding content, they are transformed in the final analysis into a construction without a subject. . . . In bourgeois art the tendency towards outward contrast between individual phenomena, towards the construction of a work as the sum of the individual parts and individual details is growing stronger. . . .

And so on.

Then in order to make an equation between this art and 'what we were doing between 1924 and 1929 and why' they make the following assertions about our work. I have numbered them:

> It is no accident that at this time the Formalist theory of montage was firmly established as the basis of cinema, as opposed to theatre (ONE!), a theory that Eisenstein formulated as: 'Cinema is, first and foremost, montage' (TWO!).
>
> In considering montage as the principal distinction between cinema and the other arts (THREE!), Eisenstein understood it, not as an ideologically creative process of development of a particular work of art (FOUR!), but as a process of mechanical juxtaposition, collision between individual frames and sequences (FIVE!).

Let us begin with number three. The authors draw a similar conclusion from my article 'Beyond the Shot' (February 1929).[34]

But that article began like this:

> This article is devoted to the cinematic features of Japanese culture that lie outside Japanese cinema. . . .

Cinema is: so many firms, so much working capital, such and such a 'star', so many dramas.

Cinema is, first and foremost, montage. . . .

Nevertheless the principle of montage may be considered to be an element of Japanese representational culture. . . . [p.138]

There follow a couple of dozen lines analysing the script, poetry, figurativeness, drawing, the art of theatre, the art of acting and sound formation of the Japanese.

There follows a conclusion: 'Thus, it has been possible to establish briefly the fact that the most varied branches of Japanese culture are permeated by a purely cinematic element and by its basic nerve – montage' [pp.149-50].

It is well known that, in historical terms, art first becomes acquainted with the principle of montage to its full extent at the cinema stage. But, as we can see, this article was written specifically as a kind of illustration, on the basis of the particular instance of Japanese culture, of the thesis that the principle of montage is common to all the arts, on an equal footing with other features, and does not represent a caste-based privilege of cinema.

This in no way diminishes the fact that montage is at its most specific and significant as a method of influence in the field of cinema.

May we ask: *are statements two and three malicious or naive?*

Statements four and five: the authors have misquoted. In fact, what would their 'statements' look like if they were 'reinforced' by this extract from the same article: after an analysis of the artistic methods of Sharaku we read:

. . . Just as Sharaku does by stopping time so we too do in time by provoking a monstrous disproportion between the parts of a normally [i.e. 'neutrally' – S.E.] occurring phenomenon, when we suddenly divide it into 'close-up of hands clasped', 'medium shots of battle' and 'big close-ups of staring eyes' and produce a montage division of the phenomenon into the types of shot! We make an eye twice as large as a fully grown man! From the juxtaposition of these monstrous incongruities we reassemble the disintegrated phenomenon into a single whole *but from our own perspective, in the light of our own orientation towards the phenomenon.* [p.141]

(My emphasis – so that this time our authors will not miss the main point!)

If our author friends think this over, they might realise that the only thing that is 'mechanistic' in this assemblage is the process connected with the acetone. The rest requires the most serious 'ideological and creative' skills and action.

Furthermore, they must bear in mind that the example cited does not even concern an instance of particular ideological responsibility, but is just 'any old suggestion' – that is, the first idea that came into my head.

It transpires that, even in this instance where no single attitude towards the phenomenon has been determined in advance, we must not make use of the montage phrase in our construction . . . .

May we ask: should we call statements four and five 'malicious' or 'naive'?

But perhaps our authors wish to hide behind statements that date from the even more distant past. For instance, a statement of the offensive term 'attraction', which this spring celebrates the tenth anniversary of its disturbing presence in the world.

I quote *Lef* (1923, no.3) about it:

Theatre's basic material derives from the audience: the moulding of the audience in a desired direction (or mood) is the task of every utilitarian theatre. . . . The instrument of this process consists of all the parts that constitute the apparatus of theatre . . . because, despite their differences, they all lead to one thing – which their presence legitimates – to their common quality of *attraction*. [p.34]

I went on to offer a characterisation of an attraction:

An attraction (in our diagnosis of theatre) is any aggressive moment in theatre, i.e. any element of it that subjects the audience to emotional or psychological influence, verified by experience and mathematically calculated to produce specific emotional shocks in the spectator . . . . These shocks provide the only opportunity of perceiving the ideological aspect of what is being shown, the final ideological conclusion. (The path to knowledge encapsulated in the phrase, 'through the living play of the passions', is specific to theatre.) [ibid]

Thus, in order to begin to subject the audience to the 'attractional effect of an object', you must:

(a) have a clear idea of the ideological conclusion towards which you are directing the audience;
(b) examine closely the ideological aspect of the work as it unfolds;
(c) know or find out which 'emotional shocks' to the audience and which combinations provide the best way of revealing that ideological aspect (in some cases it might be a newsreel, in others a situation comedy, and in still others a drama of large-scale characters, etc.);
(d) know or find out which emotional and psychological effects and which combinations of them will put the audience in the appropriate emotional state (in some cases this may be a collective mass experience, in others the actions and sufferings of the hero, and in yet others the lyricism of a musical score, etc.);

(e) know or find out which elements (attractions) in the proposed show are capable of achieving which psychological or emotional results among the audience.

This is after all somewhat different from the idiotic 'games with the children's bricks' of means of influence that have been attributed to me!

So I ask: is the nod towards the attraction in the context of these authors malicious or naive?

Perhaps our authors are so immersed in summer gardens and music-halls that they cannot contemplate the notion of an attraction outside the circus or variety show? In that case, I ask them to read the 'demarcation' between the attraction and the stunt in the same article, and not to let their benevolent attention linger on the *particular example* of the circus montage of attractions as deployed in one *particular* production of *Wise Man* (1923) but to remember especially among all the examples of attractions that the notion of an attraction stretches as far as 'Romeo's soliloquy' and includes even *The Cricket on the Hearth*.[35]

Perhaps our authors imagine that this recognition of the elements of a show, which has opened up the possibility of a particular method of constructing works that goes beyond the traditional story-line, in some way excludes plot or drama as a matter of principle?

The article provides an answer to this too: by providing us with the possibility of other methods of composing a show, the montage of attractions at the same time admits:

> to the weave of this montage whole 'illusory sequences', and a plot integral to the subject, not something self-contained or all-determining but something consciously and specifically determined for a particular purpose, and an attraction chosen purely for its powerful effect. [p.35]

In other words: the aim of maximising the ideological class effect remains all-determining.

The presence or absence of a story-line is regarded as historically relative, like the other fluctuations and variations in means of influence, depending on the relevant stages in the battle, life and requirements of the class.

Whereas, eight or ten years ago, compositions that were not based on story-lines in the traditional sense of the word predominated, this in no way excludes the possibility that nowadays the story-line may serve as the means to achieve maximum effect.

As we can see, the notion of attraction by no means contradicts this: on the contrary, it provides for it and gives us not a bad method of understanding the art of its composition.

That disposes of statements two, three, four and five.

I shall preface the first proposition with a discussion of the principal quotation in italics upon which the characterisation of my views as 'reactionarily Formalistic' is based.

Bartenev and Kalatozov quote from my article 'Beyond the Shot': 'I opposed him [i.e. Pudovkin – ed.] with my view of montage as a *collision*, my view that the collision of two factors gives rise to an idea' [p.144].

It required the combined efforts of both our authors to write the following commentary on this passage:

> It is curious that the 'collision between two factors' is employed, not to express the artist's idea, his intentions, but so that it, i.e. the idea, should emerge. But, once the idea has emerged in montage and does not find expression in it, the need for a script, as a general plan, a sketch for the future film, consequently no longer arises.

We, for instance, always thought that the script was not a 'sketch' or plan for a 'future' work but the backbone of what was being, and the spine of what had been, filmed.

But this is not the main point: do our comrades really not understand that in the discussion from which they have quoted a fragment we are talking precisely about the expression of an idea by means of cinema and about the methods of expressing it in the particular field of montage?

Do they really think that the work of the director consists in crumbling fragments hysterically, 'mechanistically' sticking them together and waiting expectantly for an idea to 'emerge'?

Do they really think that, if I wanted a gunpowder blast, I should take at random, let us say, some soft caviare and join it by means of a lighter to a box of fruit drops?

I should obviously use certain chemicals. Not just any. But very specific ones. And not in random proportions. But very specific ones. I should mix them in the appropriate proportions and, using a lighter, I should get the explosion I required.

In precisely the same way I shall set myself the aim of conjuring up the ideas that I want to emerge in the consciousness of the audience for a film. I shall select from the wide variety available a series of episodes, situations and images. Not just any and not in random proportions. Only those that, in the unity of their totality, will evoke the required idea among the audience. I shall mix them in the appropriate proportions and, letting the film run, I shall achieve the required and predetermined ideological effect.

That is how it is with drama as a whole.

And it is just the same in its minutest link, the montage phrase.

Not just any two fragments and not in random proportions.

But precisely and solely those which, when combined, will evoke the image, concept or idea that I shall determine in advance and that I wish to evoke.

Perhaps our authors thought that I had in this context ignored the 'inner content' of the shot?

Not at all. The shot, just like montage, is rigidly determined by the preconceived eventual emotional semantic effect.

Is it really not clear to these authors that a collision between marmalade and ground shin-bone will not produce an explosion?

While they sob their hearts out for dramaturgy our authors cannot see the wood for the trees: they ignore the main point in the passages that they cite:

in my conception of montage there is a tendency to extend the dramatic principles of the whole to the smallest expressive link: the montage pair of fragments and the internal construction of the shot.

The relevant pages of my article 'Beyond the Shot' are also devoted to a demarcation between the epic and dramatic conception of the realisation of purpose by means of montage as one cinematic method:

> If we are to compare montage with anything, then we should compare a phalanx of montage fragments – 'shots' – with the series of explosions of the internal combustion engine, as these fragments multiply into a montage dynamic through 'impulses' like those that drive a car or a tractor. [p.145]

Similarly the drama itself is driven through peripeteia by collisions, impulses and explosions and, the more refined its action is in terms of story-line, the more precise this movement is.

The search for dramaturgical principles in a particular instance (the dramaturgy of the *montage phrase* in *October*), following its resolution *as a whole* (the dramaturgy of the plot in *Potemkin*) *on the way towards their unification in later stages of work*, is a quite normal process of consecutive realisation and exploration of the field of cinema which, to this day, is still far from being fully understood.

It is here that I see my response to the first of the five statements on my 'montage Formalism' 'as a counterweight to dramaturgy'.

Let the story-line at the stage it was then at be partially relaxed. Partially because our researches have gone deeper than the story-line and because they have demonstrated the possibilities of other non-story [*vnefabul'nyi*] constructions of our work.

However, I think that to run down this period unreasonably and undeservedly would be a historical underestimate.

The dull traditional 'story for story's sake' of the American cinema as a stage in the development of cinema in general is what we had at the moment we split its skull with the principles of other possible structures.

This was our first denial.

A first denial that was necessary so that, once we had overcome it, we could by that same token return to works with a story-line, but on a quite different level, of a different quality and with a different degree of ideological and experimental wealth:

not to the *American* 'story for story's sake' but to our own story as a means of disclosing the social processes that we have made meaningful and our attitude towards them.

The period of both our first denial and our second were equally determined by the reflection of the stages of development of our social reality in the theatrical and formally creative achievements of Soviet film-makers during these stages.

All the more so since a number of the basic principles of film theory, as I have shown above, in no way lose their validity at these various stages but their mutual exclusion concerns only the private spheres of practical application at a particular stage of development.

Our authors are probably not acquainted with this sort of notion of the history of the development of Soviet cinema.

They prefer to swim along like Ilovaisky,[36] studying personal biographies for their own sake, quite ignorant of the strange situation in which at various stages, none the less, the same 'ruptured psyche' can produce at one stage the 'purged plot' (e.g. *The Strike*) and at another the monolith of 'dramaturgical saturation' (*Potemkin*).

On the contrary our authors resolve this problem extremely easily: the 'purgative' attitude towards plot is explained away as 'petty-bourgeois anarchism'.

And they have an even simpler explanation in the case of *Potemkin*: I quote their remarks:

> The point is that Eisenstein came upon the script in haphazard fashion. His script has been written by history insofar as he, with proper consistency and great artistic veracity, basically reflected in his film the emotionally saturated events of the mutiny on board the battleship *Potemkin*. . . .

Copying these lines, the typewriter blushes with shame for our authors in spite of the fact that at that moment they were enjoying a higher philosophical education.

The Soviet public is working intensively on script problems, attracting writers to work in cinema and convening a conference.[37]

But at a moment like this two of our friends can find nothing more intelligent to do than proclaim as the tool of script-writing, the 'bludgeon'.

Really.

Take a good piece of history.

A hundred thousand roubles. Eighteen thousand metres of film.

And the drama? . . . 'It'll take care of itself. . . .'

'Hey, we're lost!' we add. We are lost because of a 'theory' presented at a moment of heightened argument about problems relating to the script as it now stands.

Why approach writers, why search out literary figures, why study dramatists when it transpires that history itself will scribble out the script in its spare time?

If this assertion is absurd in 'general' terms, it is no less absurd in a 'particular' case, i.e. when applied to a particular film. This is above all relevant to the justice of the assertions about 'proper consistency' and 'veracity' in reflecting events.

Meanwhile. . . .

The film's first dramatic success – the scene on the quarter-deck and the beginning of the mutiny – is a complete historical 'distortion', starting with the fact that nothing like the scene with the tarpaulin that is depicted on film happened, ever did happen, or ever could happen. During the filming the studio consultants had their heads in their hands over the 'absurdity' of our device, warning that the public would laugh at this kind of improbability. . . .

Let us go on: if our esteemed authors had ever chanced to find themselves under a hail of bullets in a crowded street, they would probably have noticed how that street emptied in a flash.

At the same time the Odessa Steps sequence runs for *six minutes* and it would do our friends no harm to analyse its *dramaturgical structure* in order to discover the complex devices that were deployed to stretch a momentary event out over half a reel without ever disclosing its patent lack of authenticity.

It would be interesting to find out which annals of 1905 foretold the imaginary episode with the baby's pram. . . .

You could draw up a much longer list.

And the ending? We are all familiar with the end of the historical *Potemkin*. . . . And many people remember how the *Potemkin* actually sailed through the squadron. . . .

At the same time the *break in the drama of 'Potemkin' is precisely here* . . . – *the socially reinterpreted ending* . . . – *the reworking of the historical finale*. . . .

'Today we're happy and tomorrow we'll be happy,' Suvorov used to say. 'Dear God, just give us the wit.'

That is how we gradually move up to the underlying assertion by our friends: '. . . as a result of these latter tendencies in Eisenstein's work there have clearly emerged a fragmentation of the thought process, an understanding of reality as the sum of external phenomena and not of the organic whole. . . .'

And so on, and so on. I have already examined clearly enough the extent to which the unsubstantiated nature of this assertion is based on my dramaturgical and montage conceptions as a whole. There remains one more example, also printed in bold type, and concerning the 'interrupted play' around the cream separator in *The Old and the New*. This example concerns the play of 'doubts' and 'certainties', stretched to opposite poles to heighten the tension surrounding the separator – that is, after the drama and the montage – and it involves my notion of acting as the third sphere of the film sphere.

First, we must not forget that the isolated examination of a phenomenon taken out of its natural context is fallacious and methodologically unsound.

With that said, the 'polarised play of doubts' around the separator is surrounded:

(a) by scenes of purely realistic acting (a meeting, ploughing, an attempt to distribute money to the artels, the damage to the tractor, etc.);
(b) by scenes constructed in identical fashion with the experience of an individual character (the priest, the scene with Martha) and a single experience through the scale of various characters (the ecstasy of the religious procession, the anger after the 'deception' with the rain) both being acted through a 'scale of transitions'. The possibility of the latter device was described by me as one more organic possibility among others in cinema;
(c) lastly, one image permeates the whole film – Martha Lapkina. If she has not been regenerated quickly enough for the script requirements that preceded the decree of 23 April [1932],[38] that is only because, at the time the film was being made (1926), the changes accepted in the scripts of that period had not yet attained the speed that enabled them to be accomplished fully in the course of six reels of film. . . .

Comrades! Let us be 'historical'. . . .

This list alone tells us that the 'organics' are by no means *confined* to 'interrupted play'.

But it does nothing to negate the assertion that this kind of play has a complete right to exist and to be considered just as organic as other kinds. You should not forget that we are talking about the application of this method to a scene of 'high tension'. As a particular method, intensive polarisation into *contrasts* is always the most powerfully effective.

The *conflict* in this particular instance is achieved, however, by a *contrasting* construction.

But it certainly does not follow from this that conflict is always achieved through contrast.

Or that each contrasting construction is at the same time an embodiment of conflict or, in particular, that conflict and contrast are not 'two entirely different things'!

But this last point is evidently not clear to our 'friends' and it is to this fact that I am most probably partly indebted for another of their judgments on me. That is, precisely, that '. . . Eisenstein does not progress beyond a mechanistic understanding of conflict'.

In fact, if you substitute contrast for conflict in my understanding you will get not something mechanistic but something possibly even worse.

But in that case the question arises as to whose current account and whose conscience the mechanistic and 'ruptured' nature of thought relates?

My current account? Or the conscience of my commentators?

That is why I said 'partly' above, because the question of ascribing ruptured thought to me derives most probably directly from the fund of personal prejudices of my 'commentators'.

271

Branding something as a vice, each of us is particularly eager to try and see in or ascribe to someone else the vice that we ourselves are suffering from.

Then we turn angrily on the spectre we have ourselves created.

It is a peculiar way of distancing ourselves exterritorially from our own mistakes.

Can we not detect the same state of affairs in this particular instance?

While the actual character of the article bears witness to the presence in the authors' thinking of characteristics that are at least as sad as 'rupture', we find by happy coincidence concrete and even 'tangible' evidence that precisely this vice is present in large measure in the authors.

Photographed, developed and fixed on film. . . .

The model of the interpretation of the film *The Old and the New* through 'ruptured thinking'.

This can be interpreted in two ways:

either the object of the interpretation – that is, the film itself – was the product of ruptured thinking, or the thinking derived from its perceived consciousness was itself ruptured.

I repeat that, by happy coincidence, we have to hand an objective psychogram of the perception of *The Old and the New*.

It even has a title: *Salt for Svanetia*.[39]

The collation of the interpretation and the object of the interpretation, I submit, finally resolves the question of which of the two sides in this dispute is in fortunate possession of ruptured thinking!

In truth it is only the second of my commentators, only Kalatozov, who rightfully bears the responsibility for it.

It transpires, then, that in fact it is there, to *Salt for Svanetia*, that everything the authors write about 'ruptured' thinking should be readdressed.

For *Salt for Svanetia* is essentially similar to the inebriated commentaries on *The Old and the New* on the part of the man looking at Svanetia. Here, tangibly imprinted on film, is what Kalatozov sees as the method of *The Old and the New*. . . .

In some places he not only sees but sees double (e.g. the pregnant women!).

Why not suppose that he sees my cinematic concepts in the same way? Tortured and distorted?

I have, to my complete surprise, turned everything that was offensive against the authors themselves. Thoroughly, if not very delicately. But I shall stop here and not start to draw further hasty conclusions and fall into their trap of regarding this as an indicator of 'petty-bourgeois anarchism' or as a 'reactionary Formalist position'.

After all, in their case, apart from their theoretical illiteracy, there is evidence of straightforward montage illiteracy in practice. . . .

In addition our authors, even though they might not have expected it, have in their own article insured themselves against that sort of conclusion.

In fact, if we join together the beginning and end of our friends' article, like a poisonous snake, into a circle, we shall see that its sharp-tongued beginning clings brutally to its own tail.

The beginning states: 'The ideological disintegration of bourgeois art is accompanied by the disintegration of the organisation of individual works of art.'

While at the end we read: 'American films are always dramaturgically saturated and the majority possess a very organic development.'

And: 'It is thus characteristic that in this cinema the tendencies towards the disintegration of the organicism of the work do not emerge so distinctly.'

That is: the assertion that their development is *very organic* is not enough for this fact to be considered . . . 'characteristic'.

Characteristic of what?????!

Or does American cinema not follow the general law postulated at the beginning?

Or is American cinema not bourgeois?

Or is bourgeois cinema not disintegrating?

Or is the disintegration of bourgeois art not accompanied by an organic disintegration in individual works of art?

These are the enormous questions inadvertently raised by the contradictions in our esteemed authors.

The questions are enormous but the answer is extremely simple: you ought not to draw conclusions and make generalisations too hastily about cinema culture as a whole from the fact that nowadays we need story, story-line and coherent plot, as distinct from those days when we managed without them.

It is particularly inadvisable to regard as the focus for the localisation of the 'organic disintegration' only the traditionally accepted forms of dramaturgy and, in addition, theatrical traditions as applied to cinema.

However, the presence or absence of story and story-line have not yet exhausted and do not determine the completeness of the unity of dramaturgical purpose, even less the completeness of the manifestation of cinema culture as a whole.

This sort of miscalculation of the whole complex of the means of influence of cinema and the forced reduction, through an equals sign, of the completeness of a work to the presence or absence in it of a traditional story-line, are very typical examples of the mechanistic oversimplification of a complex problem and specimens of the crudest vulgarisation.

Crudest in so far as they lead in one and the same article to an inescapable contradiction.

The path of oversimplification is generally a dangerous one but in this field it is especially dangerous.

Even such an apparently extremely 'decadent' method of literary construction as the method of 'scattered diary entries', that was so character-

273

istic of the decadent psychology of Ernst Theodor Amadeus Hoffmann in *Kater Murr*, suddenly turns up as a method used by a monolithic intellect like Balzac (in the particular instance of *The Muse of the Department*).

At this particular stage we need plot.

Just as at a different stage we managed without it.

We shall also examine critically the experience of the West in devising our plots [*syuzhetoslozhenie*].

But the new forms of plot-based cinema that we need will only emerge on the crest of a comprehensive process of denial: that is, taking considerable account of what was achieved in the period 1924-9 in cinema to get the better of Americanism.

Slinging mud at the *preceding stage of development* instead of assimilating its achievements into the following period is an utterly pointless and dubious form of embroidery.

It is not a genuinely critical assimilation of our cultural achievements!

Our authors are mistaken: by the assimilation of culture they apparently mean the straightforward 'minor skill' of borrowing and transferring external forms and methods rather than the creative assimilation of their founding principles.

That is the kernel of the matter!

(And you don't find kernels merely in nuts. . . .)

Now writers are being summoned to theatre. A sensible, fruitful, rational measure.

We have twice had to work on a director's treatment of fully fledged literary works: Dreiser's *American Tragedy* and Blaise Cendrars's *Sutter's Gold*.[40]

I can only say from experience that we have perhaps never found a more satisfactory source to fertilise our directorial and dramaturgical intentions.

American capital chose to sit on these works at the script stage. This is the only evidence for the degree of their dramaturgical 'saturation' with what American 'ideologues' are so afraid of.

Now writers are joining our circle.

Their reserves of creative experience are vast.

But we shall not overestimate these reserves.

Writers are not Varangians.

And a good writer is not necessarily a guarantee of a good film.

Assimilating a good writer into a fully fledged cinematic work;

and assimilating the full creative value of a writer in a cinematic work – these are the two enormous tasks for the present day in the field of cinema theory and practice.

We must study writers.

And writers must study cinema.

And we should not bewilder people who are fresh to cinema with articles like the one I have just discussed.

Otherwise literature will once again rush away from cinema and directors without scripts or scriptwriters will once again start to write their own scripts: that is, they will once again be no better off than they were when 'saving drowning men was a matter for the drowning men themselves'.

38. Cinema and the Classics[41]

As well as working with contemporary authors it is very important for film-makers to pay attention to the literary classics. However, work on the classics must not be organised along the lines of superficial borrowing but as a matter of studying all the elements that constitute their specificity. We must interpret their signs and observe how a particular element should develop into a new one, passing through different stages in time and class. This applies equally to the technique of depicting characters and to the means and methods of embodying them. It applies to an even greater degree to what first and foremost we must learn from them, namely: the composition of the plot. It seems to me that in all the energetic efforts to assimilate the classics not enough attention has been devoted to this element, the correction of their characteristics for historical and class reasons.

Neither the method nor the character of the depiction of the old man Grandet,[42] nor the specific quality of the dramatic embodiment of Shylock, can be directly translated into the depiction of a kulak. Similarly, the scene of Fortinbras's arrival, if directly borrowed, would do little to help elaborate a scene depicting the arrival of the head of the political sections. In exactly the same way the specific quality of the pathetic structure of Mark Antony's speech over Caesar's dead body requires a more complicated qualitative re-interpretation if it is to suit, let us say, a scene depicting the murder of a *selkor*.[43] Without the same kind of alteration *Lysistrata* would scarcely produce the dramatic elaboration of the scenes of women's rebellions that regularly break out in our scripts.

Only a more acute recognition of the qualitative differences will permit us to utilise productively the permissible common denominator in the treatment.

39. For Elevated Ideological Content,   1934
for Film Culture!¹

I am developing my activity in three spheres: 1) the creative, 2) the academic, and 3) theory and research.

On these three I report as follows.

Contrary to the gossip in the communiqué that in terms of creativity I have become overgrown with grass like a burial mound, my creative work does of course come first (or, rather, my creative works – all three of them).

The subject of my work is *Moscow*.²

Despite a number of flattering proposals, like a full-length feature film on *Stenka Razin and the Princess*,³ I am none the less sticking firmly to the subject of *Moscow*.

My work on this theme has so far not been greeted by my immediate superiors with any great enthusiasm, encouragement, interest or – most important of all – understanding.

In the meantime this has by no means discouraged the very intense thinking that I have done on a theme that has captivated me very profoundly.

A whole number of scenes have recently taken quite clear shape.

The thematic orientation is made explicit in the clear approach to the fundamental problems of the present day.

The gigantic construction of the metro is already being promoted as one of the central items of material in order to realise the main thematic link, the new Moscow. The standpoint through which it becomes the principal link in the film is already clear.

You can already hear in concrete terms a number of scenes and you can see others.

You cannot speak in such concrete terms of the production prospects. Unfortunately they do not just depend on me. I had wanted the cameras to start rolling last autumn.

I am waiting impatiently for the arrival of Fadeyev⁴ who has expressed a desire to take part in work on the script. In addition to him we shall probably attract a number of other comrades because the work is important and complex.

I am very enthusiastic about *Moscow*. Above all about the subject. And not just about the subject, but also about the fact that it gives me the opportunity to join in the liquidation of the absolutely scandalous hiatus on the film culture front, which is possibly even more flagrant than that on the organisational and economic front.⁵

I am burning with a desire to launch an attack not just using high-quality ideological content but also involving a cultural campaign for film culture.

In the academic 'sector' of my work we are trying to develop the fight for this in all directions.[6]

As far as my own personal obligations to the Seventeenth Party Congress are concerned, I have finally completed redrafting my detailed academic programme, 'The Theory and Practice of the Subject of Direction'.

Once the comments of my faculty colleagues at the Institute have been incorporated, we shall have a unique historical document.

In the first institution in history for higher education in cinema we shall for the first time have a unified basic programme of education and training for a complex and ideologically responsible specialism like the director's craft.

In collaboration with the dean's office and the teaching staff of the Institute we are now embarking, on the basis of this programme, on devising a plan and programmes to cover every individual discipline in the whole faculty of direction. It is enormously complex and unprecedented work because in institutions of higher education in the arts in general and in GIK in particular things have in the past been put together in an extremely superficial way without any co-ordination of the teaching or logical planning in its execution.

The results of our pedagogical work in the first term have been extremely satisfactory as far as the assessed work submitted by the students is concerned. The method of teaching direction that we have devised, reworked and perfected from year to year, is beginning to produce perceptible results. It is gratifying to see that creative technique and competence in realising projects cannot only be taught but can also be learned.

This forces me to devote myself with even greater enthusiasm and passion to the education and training of Bolshevik cadres among the rising generation of Soviet film-makers. In the main group I am working with there is only one non-Party member out of thirty people.

The Party purge has done a great deal to improve and normalise our work and the Institute is approaching the Party Congress in fine fettle.

As for the third sphere, I am busy for days and nights on the trot writing the first part of my book *Direction*:[7] the theory and practice, summarising my experience as professor at GIK (especially in the last two years) and . . . my fourteen years as director (ten of them in cinema). The book will be bulky: it is based on the 1,500 typescript pages of my course at GIK – and it should reach GIKhL, the publishers, by the spring of this year.

The second and third parts still lie ahead.

But I hope that I shall come to them through the usual cycle of creative productivity.

In the immediate future I shall begin collaborating with the leading young cameramen of Potylikha[8] on a working seminar to improve their qualifications. I have a similar commitment to LenARRK for a cycle of guest lectures on questions of theory, not summarising but attacking, dealing with the film problems that preoccupy us now. I am starting in February.

In between all these things I am managing to read the cuttings from

American and English papers and the letters sent to me in connection with the recent premières in America and England of our Mexican film that has been ruined and distorted by someone else's editing.[9]

I rejoice at the praise I have received for those parts through which the features of the original conception are perceptible and I gnash my teeth with hatred for those film people who, through stupidity and lack of culture, have not allowed us to complete our fourteen months of intensive work which, by all objective criteria, represents an enormous stage in the creative activity of our collective.

40. On Fascism, German Cinema and Real Life. Open Letter to the German Minister of Propaganda, Dr Goebbels[10]

Herr Doktor!

It will scarcely distress you and probably hardly surprise you to learn that I am not a subscriber to the German press that is under your control.

Usually I do not even read it.

So you may be surprised that I have, albeit somewhat belatedly, been informed of your latest speech to the film-makers of Berlin in the Kroll Opera House on 10 February.[11]

On this occasion you made, for the second time, a complimentary reference to my film, *The Battleship Potemkin*.

What is more, you once again – just as you did a year ago – deigned to hold it up as a model of the quality that National Socialist films should emulate.

You are acting very wisely when you send your film-makers to learn from your enemies.

But, in so doing, you make one tiny 'methodological' error.

Allow me to point it out to you.

And do not blame me if what I say is not to your liking.

We are not desperate to teach you – you are thrusting yourself on us.

To err is human.

And your suggestion that Fascism can give birth to a great German cinema is profoundly mistaken.

Even with the most benevolent assistance of the Aryan Holy Ghost that you are now posing as.

Somewhere Engels quotes the English proverb, 'The proof of the pudding is in the eating.'[12]

A considerable period of sadness has already passed but your much-vaunted National Socialism has not produced a single work of art that is in the least bit digestible.

So you will probably have to make quite a few speeches like the two you have already made.

It is a tiresome and thankless task to inspire the German cinema which had considerable achievements in the past but has now fallen into the clutches of Fascism.

I am profoundly convinced and I firmly hope that the German proletariat will not be slow to help you free yourself from this exhausting and, above all, quite fruitless labour.

But, just in case you do have to make another speech about cinema, we must not allow a man who occupies a high position like yours to make the same kind of methodological errors.

To thunderous applause you produced the magnificent outline of a creative programme for German cinema:

> . . . *Real life must once again become the content of film.**

We must take hold of life fearlessly and courageously and not be afraid of difficulties or failures. The greater the failures, the fiercer must be our renewed assault on the problems. Where should we be today if we had lost our courage at every failure? (Loud applause.) Now that trashy entertainment has been eliminated from our public life, you film-workers must return to the theme of the immortal German people and tackle it. Tackle people, whom no one knows better than we do . . . . Every people is what people make of it. (Bravo!) We have sufficiently demonstrated what can be made of the German people. (Tempestuous applause.)

The public is not estranged from art.

And I am convinced that, if we were to show in one of our cinemas a film that really captured our epoch and really was a National Socialist 'Battleship', then the seats would be sold out for a long time.†

When you refer to the *Battleship* I have no doubt that you have in mind not just *Potemkin* but the whole victorious line of our cinema in recent years.

For the rest – it is a really brilliant programme.

We all know that only real life, the truth of life and the truthful depiction of life serve, and can serve, as the basis for true art.

What a masterpiece a truthful film about Germany today could be!

However, you need some good advice to realise your brilliant programme.

You certainly need advice. And not just one bit of advice. Lots and lots of it.

Let us say it straight: you need *the whole Soviet system*!

Because in our days great art, the truthful depiction of life, the truth of life, even life itself, are possible only in a land of Soviets, whatever its previous name.

But truth and National Socialism are incompatible.

He who stands for truth can have no truck with National Socialism.

He who stands for truth stands against you!

How dare you speak of life anywhere when you are bringing death

---

* Emphasis in the original.

† Emphasis in the original. Source: 'Grosse Rede des Reichspropagandaministers vor den Filmschaffenden' [Major Speech by Reich Propaganda Minister to Film-makers], *Deutsche Allgemeine Zeitung*, 11 February 1934.

and exile with the axe and the machine-gun to all that is living and best in your country?

Slaughtering the best sons of the German proletariat and scattering across the surface of the globe the pride of true German science and world culture.

How dare you call on your cinema to depict life truthfully and not make it its first duty to cry out to the whole world about the thousands who are languishing and being tortured in the subterranean catacombs of your prisons, the torture chambers of your dungeons?

How can you have the cheek to talk about truth at all after that Tower of Babel of muddle, impudence and lies that you constructed at Leipzig?[13] And at a moment when you are erecting a new scaffold of lies and treachery in the preparations for the trial against Thälmann?[14]

You go on in your speech like a good shepherd: '. . . I have only to be convinced that there is an honest artistic intention behind a film and I shall defend it by every means. . . .'

You are lying, Herr Goebbels.

You know very well that an honest and artistic film can only be one that fully exposes the hell that National Socialism has plunged Germany into.

You would hardly encourage films like that!

A true German cinema can only be one that summons the revolutionary masses into battle with you.

That really does require courage and daring.

Because, despite the mellifluous tones of your speeches, you are keeping your art and culture in the same iron shackles as the thousands of inmates in your hundreds of concentration camps.

Works of art are not produced in this way, as you imagine them to be. We know, for instance, and have to some extent already demonstrated, that a work of art that deserves the name does, did and always will do so when the compressed, and clearly formulated and determined striving of a class is expressed through an artist.

A genuine work of art is the formally organised striving of a class to consolidate its struggle, its achievements, its social profile in the lasting images of art.

The higher the work of art, the more fully the artist has succeeded in comprehending, feeling and communicating this creative burst of the masses themselves.

That is not how you view class and the masses.

According to you: '. . . Every people is what people make of it. . . .' And there are idiots who shout 'Bravo' at these words.

Just you wait. The proletariat will find its own corrective to your conception, if we can call it that, Herr Demiurge of Divine Power.

Then you will learn who is the real subject of history.

Then you will learn who makes whom and what will be done with you . . . and made out of you.

They say that war gives birth to heroes.

They say that mountains give birth to mice.

But no Goebbels, with pretensions to giving birth to a new Germany like Athena from his own head, is capable of giving birth to a 'great National Socialist cinema'.

However hard you try, you cannot create a 'National Socialist realism'. In this mongrel of lies there would be as much genuine truth and realism as there is socialism in National Socialism.

This quantity has been precisely estimated by Comrade Stalin in his report to the Seventeenth Party Congress.

Not an atom!

> . . . I refer not to Fascism in general but here primarily to Fascism of the German kind, which is wrongly designated National Socialism for, despite the most rigorous investigation, it is impossible to discern in it even an atom of socialism.[15]

It is only the genuine socialist system of the Soviet Union that is capable of giving birth to the grandiose realistic art of the future and the present.

You can only dream about it.

You find it difficult even to guess. You do it wrongly and back to front. You are using the wrong cards. And no tricks will help you.

Paint in the Prussian blue of your lyrical scheming. But know that only genuine socialism and a programme of socialist attack guarantees a creative programme for all forms of art.

The wireless messages from the heroes of the icebreaker *Chelyuskin*[16] bring us the news that, trapped and imprisoned by the ice, they derive new reserves of strength and a surge of creative energy from the report of the Seventeenth Congress on the work of the Central Committee of the Party.

Imprisoned in your fetters for long months, your victims and our beloved heroes Dimitrov, Tanev and Popov were deprived of any contact with the outside world. There was one happy moment when this isolation was broken for a few days. A newspaper got through to them. Its pages carried the same report. That moment, those columns of print, were compensation for all those months of suffering. The day after his return I heard from Tanev's own lips what they meant to your prisoners. They provided a surge of new energy and new feeling for the pitiless struggle.

In those columns there was everything that a 'soldier of the revolution' (the expression is that of Soviet citizen Dimitrov[17]) needed to know a year ago and for many years to come.

In those columns there is everything on which to base the creative programme of a 'soldier of the art of revolution' using all kinds of ideological weapons – literature, art and cinema – in his final battles for a classless society.

It is the best example of socialist realism in action.

283

It is the best model of socialist realism for all sectors of artistic creation.

It is not the empty sonority of your speeches.

After promising your high-level protection for 'honest artistic creativity' in film, you benevolently add: 'But I do not require a film to begin and end with a National Socialist procession. Leave the National Socialist processions to us – we know how to do them better than you do . . . .'

Well said! Well said!

Get back to your drums, Herr Drummer-in-Chief!

Don't play the tune of National Socialist realism in cinema on your magic flute.

Don't imitate your idol, Frederick the Great, and on the flute too.

Stick to the instrument you're used to – the axe.

And don't waste time.

You don't have long to wield the executioner's axe.

Make the most of it.

Burn your books.

Burn your Reichstags.

But don't imagine that a bureaucratic art fed on all this filth will be able to 'set the hearts of men on fire with its voice'.

41. 'Eh!' On the Purity of Film Language[18]

My surname begins with an E. None the less, it is quite immaterial who first says 'Eh!' to the question.[19] The question of the purity of film language.

But one way and another we must all comment on Gorky's statement on language and literature with our reflections on film language.

Film language as a defining concept rather than a critic's turn of phrase is to a certain extent connected with my works and commentaries on them.

For this reason I shall take on the role of sniping at myself.

I do not intend to talk about the talking film. Or rather about the talking part of talking film. It speaks for itself. It even shouts. And its quality, even before we assess it from a cinematic point of view, has so many infelicities of a purely literary sort that its pretensions to cinematic quality can wait a while.

It is not about this language that I want to speak. (It would be absurd for me to do so given my fairly well-known literary style!) I want to talk about the uncultured cinematic language of films as they appear on our screens today.

In the field of film language our cinema has done a great deal for film culture. Much more than fashion has done.

It is true that in the West many of the means of expression that are specifically ours have taken no deeper root than fashion. Little snippets of film, spliced together with the aid of that stuff that smells of pears,[20] appear on the film menu under the name 'russischer Schnitt' or 'Russian cutting' in the same way as the term 'salade russe' is retained on restaurant menus for various vegetables prepared and seasoned in a particular way.

Fashion.

Fashions pass – culture remains. Sometimes the culture behind the fashion remains unnoticed. Sometimes the cultural achievement is thrown out with the outmoded fashion.

As in the West.

Negro sculpture, Polynesian masks or the Soviet way of editing films – for the West these are, first and foremost, exotica.

And just exotica.

No mention can of course be made of the extraction of general cultural values, of the assimilation of principles, of the use of these achievements to move culture forward in principle.

What would it all be for?! Tomorrow the fashion magnates – the Patous, Worths, Mme Lanvins in various fields – will launch a new style. From somewhere in the Congo they will bring ivory tusks that have been carved by colonial slaves in some new way. Somewhere on the plains of Mongolia some yellowed bronze plates made by the slaves of some long past epoch are being dug up.

All is well. It is all to the good. It all helps profits.

The growth of culture? Who cares?

It would seem that this attitude towards culture and cultural achievements has long since come to an end with the October Revolution.

You cannot even force your way into the museums on your day off: the worker and his wife and children are queuing for the Tretyakov Gallery.

You cannot even squeeze into the reading room: there are so many people.

Readings and lectures are all overcrowded. Everywhere you find interest, attention, thrift. A proprietary interest in pre-Revolutionary achievements.

But in cinema there is a purely bourgeois absence of good management. And not only in the estimates. There is thoughtlessness. And not only in the schedules.

There is a complete disregard for, and neglect of, everything that has been done in the field of film culture in the Soviet period, by Soviet hands, on Soviet material and in accordance with Soviet principles.

Splendid: 'We have mastered the classics'.[21] (Whether or not it is splendid is another question – and a very debatable one at that!) Let us enter that on the credit side.

But this in no way invalidates the question. Why must we make these films with the complete disregard for all cinema's expressive means and possibilities that they demonstrate when flashed up on the screen?!

We have mastered theatre actors (better than the classics). Splendid! But the question again arises: 'Should we hold on to auntie's tail?'[22] Even if this auntie is as fine an actress as Tarasova![23]

Or would cinema culture harm her acting rather than promoting it?

Meanwhile the shots are 'rubbish'. The combination of the shots is a 'mess'. And the montage obviously 'jumps about'.

As a result, looking at the screen, you experience a sweet sensation, as if your eye had been gripped by sugar-tongs and ever so gently turned first to the right, then to the left and finally turned full circle and then put back into a confused orbit. They say: 'That's how your eyes are', 'That doesn't matter to the audience', 'The audience doesn't notice', 'The audience won't shout'. Quite right. The reader doesn't shout either. But what is needed is not a shout but a terrifying shout. Gorky's authoritative shout to make literature notice the elements of its own undoing. The reader will not die of the 'mess'. 'Rubbish' will not kill him. And neglect of literary language will not push him into the grave.

None the less it was deemed necessary to take the reader's literary hearing into protection. How does the reader's vision deteriorate when he becomes a film viewer?

How much worse is his ear in conjunction with his eye when he is present at some audio-visual catastrophe that has pretensions to audio-visual counterpoint?

Characteristically, films have begun to be called 'sound' films. Should this mean that what you see does not deserve attention?

But that is how it is.

In this context people say viciously: 'Well, the old devil, he's whining about montage.'

Yes, montage.

For many people montage and the left deviation in Formalism are synonyms.

But in the meantime. . . .

Montage is not that at all.

For those who know, montage is the most powerful compositional means of realising plot.

For those who know nothing about composition, montage is the syntax for the correct construction of each particular fragment of a film.

Lastly, montage is simply the elementary rules of cinema orthography for those who mistakenly put together the fragments of a film the way one would mix potions according to a fixed recipe, pickle cucumbers, marinate plums or soak apples in cranberry juice.

[And the button, the sash, the suspenders, if they also become an end in themselves, can lead to absurdity.][24]

Not just montage. . . .

But I should like to see the freedom of expressive activities of man's hands relieved of these supporting aggregates in the lower part of his toilet.

In films you do encounter individual good shots but in these circumstances the independent pictorial qualities of the shot and its value stand in mutual contradiction. As they are not linked by montage thought and composition, they become mere playthings and an end in themselves. The better the shots, the closer the film comes to being a disjointed collection of beautiful phrases, a shop window of unrelated objects or an album of postage stamps with views.

We do not by any means stand for the 'hegemony' of montage. The time has passed when, for pedagogical and educational purposes, it was necessary to perform a tactical and polemical manoeuvre to ensure the broad mastery of montage as one of cinema's means of expression. But we are duty-bound to confront the problem of literacy in film language.[25] We must demand that the quality of montage, film syntax and film speech not only matches the quality of earlier works but exceeds and surpasses them. That is what the battle for the high quality of film culture requires of us.

It is easier for literature. When you criticise it, you can stand it alongside the classics. Its heritage and achievements have largely been examined down to the tiniest microscopic detail. The analysis of the compositional and image structure of Gogol's prose carried out by the late Andrei Bely stands as a living reproach to any literary flippancy.[26]

None the less, Gogol has also been used in cinema. The last, as it were, flash of purity of montage form in sound cinema was, before it descended into complete formlessness, like a transposition of a Gogol text into visual material.

You could, I think, successfully accompany the magnificent visual poetry of the Dnieper in the first reel of Dovzhenko's *Ivan* by declaiming Gogol's 'Wonderful Dnieper'.[27]

The rhythms of moving shots. Sailing along the shore. Motionless expanses of water cutting in. The magic of Gogol's imagery and his turns of speech are captured in their alternation and changing. All this 'neither stirs nor thunders'. All this 'you see and do not know whether its immense expanse is moving or not and it seems as though it is made of glass', etc. Here literature and cinema provide a model of the purest fusion and affinity. And these fragments also recall Rabelais. His poetic anticipation of the 'imaging' of the theory of relativity in his description of the island '*des chemins cheminants*':

> Seleucus had been of the opinion that the earth really revolved around the poles, rather than the heavens, although the contrary seems to us to be the truth – just as, when we are on the River Loire, the trees along the bank seem to be moving, whereas it is not the trees at all, but ourselves upon the boat, who are in motion.

We have dwelt on this example because it seems like a swansong for the purity of film language on our contemporary screen. Even for *Ivan*. Its later reels nowhere rise to the perfection of this fragment.

People will say: but 'The Wonderful Dnieper' is a poem.

That is not the point at all. On this basis we should have to assume that the structure of the prose of, for instance, Zola would unfailingly display signs of 'naturalistic chaos'.

Yet in one study I happened to see his pages broken up into the strophes of an epic poem. These pages of *Germinal* were recited with almost as much severity as Homeric hexameters.

They covered the episodes leading up to the sinister scene when, during the disturbances before the arrival of the gendarmes, the mob destroys the shop of the usurer and rapist Maigrat. When the infuriated women, under the leadership of La Brute and Mouquette, 'emasculate' the corpse of the despised shopkeeper who, in escaping, had stepped from the roof and broken his skull on the kerbstone. When the bloodied 'trophy' is hoisted on a pole and carried in procession.

> 'What is it they have at the end of that stick?' asked Cécile, who had grown bold enough to look out.
> Lucie and Jeanne decided that it must be a rabbit-skin.
> 'No, no,' murmured Madame Hennebeau, 'they must have been

pillaging a pork butcher's, it seems a remnant of a pig.'

At this moment she shuddered and was silent. Madame Grégoire had nudged her with her knee. They both remained stupefied.[28]

This scene, like the previous scene in which the crowd of women tries to flog Cécile publicly, is itself, of course, related to the stylised quoted transplant episodes that obviously struck Zola in the annals of the French Revolution.

The women's attempt to abduct Cécile echoes the well-known episode of the execution of Théroigne de Méricourt.[29]

The second scene forces us to recall involuntarily a perhaps less well-known and popular episode from Mercier's materials. When the people's hatred for the Princesse de Lamballe, Marie-Antoinette's closest intimate, burst and the popular anger made short work of her at the gates of La Force prison, one of the participants 'cut out her virginal parts and made himself a moustache'.[30] The later commentary on this affair by the journal *Intermédiaire* in 1894 is interesting:

> We are told all about the unfortunate princess's fate. But collectors have no respect for anything! About twenty years ago in one of the châteaux in the neighbourhood of Liège in Belgium I saw the reverentially preserved, completely withered organs of the Princesse de Lamballe, spread out on a satin cushion.

The title of the novel, *Germinal*, deliberately chosen from the names given to the months in that earlier period, suggests a previously stylised adaptation of the episodes.[31] Whereas this reference for purposes of temperament and pathos to an earlier pathos-filled epoch played a considerable part in defining the rhythmic clarity of the form of its literary language, its spread to the treatment of minor episodes is not very felicitous.

Our film *October* suffered in a similar way in the sequence dealing with the events of July 1917. At all costs we wanted the historical incident of the worker Bolshevik who was beaten and murdered by the brutalised bourgeoisie to be imbued with the 'tone' of the Paris Commune. The result was the scene with the ladies hitting the worker with their parasols: the scene is quite different in spirit from the general mood of the period before October.

This passing observation may not be unhelpful. We have to make frequent use of our literary heritage and the culture of the image and language of earlier periods. In stylistic terms it often determines our works quite considerably. And it does us no harm to note our failures as well as our positive models.

Returning once more to the question of the purity of film form, I frequently come across the objection that the craft of film language and film expressiveness is still very young and has no models for a classic tradition. They say that I attack, without contrasting the positive models, getting away with literary analogies. Many even express a doubt as to whether there is anything similar in this 'half art', as many people still think of cinema.

Forgive me. That is how things are.

At the same time our film language, although it has no recognised classics, has acquired great severity of form and expression. At a certain stage our cinema displayed the same strict responsibility for each shot admitted into a montage sequence as poetry did for each line of verse or music for the regular movement of a fugue.

We may cite quite a number of instances from the practice of our silent cinema. As I do not have the time now specially to select other models, I shall permit myself to cite here a sample analysis from one of my own works. It is taken from the materials for my book *Direction* (Part II: *Mise en cadre*),[32] which I am finishing, and it concerns *Potemkin*. In order to demonstrate the compositional interdependence of the plastic aspect of the changing shots I have deliberately chosen an example at random rather than from a climactic scene: fourteen consecutive fragments from the scene that precedes the shooting on the Odessa Steps. The scene where the 'good people of Odessa' (as the *Potemkin* sailors addressed their appeal to the population of Odessa) send skiffs with provisions alongside the mutinous battleship.

The sending of greetings is constructed on a distinct intersection between two subjects:

1. The skiffs speed towards the battleship.
2. The people of Odessa wave.

In the end the two subjects merge.

The composition is basically on two planes: depth and foreground. The subjects dominate alternately, advancing to the foreground and pushing one another into the background.

The composition is constructed: (1) on the plastic interaction between both planes (within the shot), (2) on the change in line and form on each plane from shot to shot (by montage). In the second case the compositional play is formed from the interaction of the plastic impression of the previous shot in collision or interaction with the succeeding one. (Here the analysis is by purely spatial and linear sign. The rhythmic temporal relationship will be examined elsewhere.)

The movement of the composition (see the attached table) takes the following course.

I. The skiffs in motion. A smooth movement parallel to a horizontal cross-section of the shot. The whole field of vision is occupied by the first subject. There is a play of small vertical sails.

II. The intensifying movement of the skiffs of the first subject. (The entrance of the second subject facilitates this.) The second subject comes to the fore with a strict rhythm of motionless vertical columns. The vertical lines sketch the plastic disposition of future figures (IV, V, etc.). The interplay of horizontal waves and vertical lines. The skiff subject is pushed into the background. The plastic subject of the arch appears in the bottom half of the shot.

III. The plastic subject of the arch expands into the whole shot. The play revolves around the change in the frame's articulation from vertical lines to the structure of the arch. The vertical subject is maintained in the movement of small-scale people moving away from the camera. The skiff subject is finally pushed into the background.

IV. The plastic subject of the arch finally occupies the foreground. The arch structure moves into the opposite resolution: the contours of a group forming a circle are sketched in(the parasol completes the composition). The same transition to an opposite also occurs within the vertical construction: the backs of the small-scale people moving into the background are replaced by large-scale static figures filmed from the front. The subject of the movement of the skiffs is maintained by reflection in the expression of the eyes and in their movement along the horizontals.

V. In the foreground a common compositional variation: an even number of people is replaced by an uneven number. Two becomes three. This 'golden rule' in changing the *mise en scène* is supported by a tradition that dates back to the Italian *commedia dell'arte*[33] (the direction of the glances also intersects). The arch motif is once more straightened out, this time into an opposite curve. Repeating and supporting it, there is a new parallel arch motif in the *background*: a balustrade. The skiff subject in motion. The eye passes over the whole breadth of the shot along the horizontal.

VI. Sections I–V provide the transposition from the skiff subject to that of the onlookers, developed in five montage sections. The interval V–VI produces a sudden transition back from the onlookers to the skiffs. The composition, which strictly follows the content, suddenly turns all the signs back in the opposite direction. The line of the balustrade is brought suddenly to the foreground, and repeated in the line of the boat's gunwale. It is echoed by the line where the boat comes into contact with the surface of the water. The basic compositional articulation is the same but the treatment is the opposite. V is static. VI is sketched out through the dynamic of the boat in motion. The division into 'three' along the vertical is maintained in both shots. The central element is texturally similar (the woman's blouse and the canvas of the sail). The elements at the sides are sharply contrasted: the dark shapes of the men beside the woman and the white spaces beside the sail. The articulations along the vertical are also contrasted: three figures cut off by the bottom of the frame become a vertical sail cut off by the top of the frame. In the *background* a new subject appears: the battleship seen from the side, cut off at the top (a preparation for Section VII).

VII. Another sudden change of subject. The background subject, the battleship, moves forward into the foreground (the thematic jump from V to VI serves as a kind of *Vorschlag*[34] to the jump from VI to VII). The angle is turned through 180°: the shot from the battleship towards the sea is the reverse of VI. This time the side of the battleship is in the *foreground* and is cut off by the *bottom* of the frame. In the background is the sail subject, working in verticals. The vertical of the sailors. The static gun-barrel continues the line of movement of the boat in the preceding section. The side of the ship appears to be an arch becoming a straight line.

VIII. This repeats IV with greater intensity. The horizontal play of the eyes spreads into a vertical of waving hands. The vertical subject moves from the background into the foreground, repeating the thematic transfer of attention to the onlookers.

IX. Two faces closer up. Generally speaking, an unfortunate combination with the preceding section. A shot with three faces should have been inserted between them. A repetition of Section V, for instance, but also with greater intensity.

This would have produced a 2:3:2 structure. Moreover the repetition of the familiar group IV–V ending with a new IX would have heightened the perception of the last shot. The situation is saved by a slight enlargement of the close-up.

X. Two faces become one. The arm is raised very energetically up and out of the frame. A correct alternation of faces (if we adopt the correction between VIII and IX): 2:3:2:1. The second pair of shots with the correct enlargement of scale vis-à-vis the first pair (a proper repetition with qualitative variation). The line of odd numbers varies both in quantity and quality (the dimension of the faces is different as is their number, while observing the general characteristics of odd numbers).

XI. Another sudden change of subject. A jump that repeats V–VI but with greater intensity. The vertical *thrust* of the previous shot is repeated in the vertical *sail*. But the vertical of this sail scuds past horizontally. A repetition of the subject of VI with greater intensity. And a repetition of the composition of II with the difference that the subject of the horizontal of the skiffs' motion and the vertical of the motionless columns is here fused into a single horizontal transposition of the *vertical* sail. The composition repeats the thematic line of the unity and identity between the skiffs and the people on the shore (before we move on to the final theme of merger: the shore and the battleship via the skiffs).

XII. The sail in XI dissolves into a multitude of vertical sails, scudding along horizontally (a repetition of Section I with heightened intensity). The small sails move in the opposite direction to the large sail.

XIII. Having dissolved into small sails, the large sail is once more reassembled, this time not into a sail but into the flag flying over the *Potemkin*. There is a new quality in this shot because it is both static and mobile, the mast being vertical and motionless while the flag flutters in the breeze. In formal terms Section XII repeats XI. But the change from sail to banner translates the principle of plastic unification into an ideological and thematic unification. This is no longer just a vertical that in plastic terms joins the separate elements of composition: *this is a revolutionary banner uniting the battleship, the skiffs and the shore.*

XIV. From here there is a natural return from the flag to the battle-ship. XIV repeats VII. Also with heightened intensity.

This section introduces a new compositional group of *interrelation-ships between the skiffs and the battleship* as distinct from the first group of *skiffs and the shore*. The first group reflected the subject: 'the skiffs are bringing greetings and gifts from the shore to the battleship'. The second group will express the *fraternisation between the skiffs and the battleship*.

The mast with the revolutionary flag serves as a compositional water-shed and at the same time as the ideological uniting face for both compositional groups.

Section VII, repeated by the first shot in the second group in Section XIV, appears as a sort of *Vorschlag* for the second group and as an element linking the two groups together, like a 'patrol' sent out by the latter group to the former. In the second group the same role will be performed by the shots of the waving figures, cut into the scenes of fraternisation between the skiffs and the battleship.

You must not think that both the shooting and montage for these sequences were done according to tables calculated a priori. Of course not. But the assembly and the interrelationship of these fragments on the cutting table were clearly dictated by the compositional requirements of film form. These requirements dictated the selection of these fragments from all those available. They established the regularity of the alternation between shots. Actually these fragments, if viewed merely from the standpoint of plot and story, could be arranged in any combination. But the compositional move-ment through them would scarcely prove in that case to be as regular in con-struction.

We should not complain of the complexity of this analysis. In com-parison with analysis of literary and musical form my analysis is still quite obvious and easy.

Setting aside for the moment problems of rhythmic examination, I have in my analysis also examined the alternations of sound and word com-binations.

An analysis of the actual objects of shooting and their treatment through camera angle and lighting, deriving from the requirements of style and of the character of the content, would correspond to an analysis of the ex-pressive quality of the actual phrases, words and their phonetic indication in a literary work.

We are convinced that the requirements that film composition sets itself are just as great as the requirements of the corresponding sections of literature and music.

The audience is, of course, least of all able to verify with a pair of compasses the regularity of the contruction of successive shots in montage. But its perception of regular montage composition involves the same elements as those that distinguish stylistically a page of cultured prose from a page of Count Amori, Verbitskaya or Breshko-Breshkovsky.[35]

Now Soviet cinema is historically correct in joining battle for plot. There are still many obstacles along the path, many risks of a false understanding of the principles of plot. The most terrible of these is the underestimation of the opportunities that a temporary emancipation from the old traditions of plot has given us:

the opportunity to re-examine in principle and once more the bases and problems of film plot

and advance in a progressive cinematic movement not 'back' to plot but 'forward to plot'.

There is no clear artistic orientation at the moment along these paths although individual positive phenomena are already being sketched in.

But, one way or another, we must meet the moment when we master the clearly recognised principles of Soviet plot cinema fully armed with an irreproachable purity and culture in our film language and speech.

We value our great masters of literature from Pushkin and Gogol to Mayakovsky and Gorky not just as masters of plot. We value in them the culture of masters of speech and word.

The time has come to pose the acute question of the culture of film language.

It is important that all film-makers should express their views on the matter.

Above all in the language of montage and the shots of their own films.

The sequence from *Potemkin* to which E refers above (pp. 290-3).

42. At Last!³⁶

There are various forms of fighting.

Tournaments. Duels. Boxing. Tournaments with the visor raised. Hand-to-hand fighting with the visor down. Boxing unmasked. And boxing masked.

French seigneurs and English gentlemen practised another method: they dispatched a lackey with a cudgel to slaughter their objectionable opponent. Pamphleteers suffered particularly from this method.

Finally, there is one more method. When they beat people 'blind'. That is how they slaughter suspects.

Covering the head with a robe and – a knee in the back. These beatings, as they say, do not leave any traces.

In literary fighting, where it is called polemics, all these varieties exist, albeit in a new quality.

Polemics through open articles. Polemics where the author's identity is concealed behind a pseudonym.

The equivalent of the stick would be the editorial 'tail' consisting of a three- or four-line commentary by the editor to undermine an author's viewpoint that they do not like.

But there is also the last variety:

'blind'.

When part of your viewpoint is covered with a robe, i.e. the fact that the article is not published in full is kept quiet.

Usually someone who is beaten up 'blind' remains silent.

I have been involved in various kinds of fighting. The other day I got involved in this last kind of fight. But I do not want to remain silent. For right is on my side. And the actual question concerns not me but Soviet cinema.

What was the nature of the 'seditious' remarks that the editor's pencil deleted from my article for *Sovetskoe kino* to mark the fifteenth anniversary of Soviet cinema?³⁷

I wrote roughly as follows:

The development and history of Soviet cinema move in clear five-year periods.

The fourth is the most remarkable so far.

Three of them have passed and the fourth is upon us.

The fourth will be the most remarkable not just because each new page in our reality is even more remarkable than the one that preceded it.

It is also remarkable in another respect.

Whereas the first five years of our cinema was above all a period of economic and organisational formation and of the first emerging shoots of our own cinema, the second and third five years were already periods that were sharply outlined in stylistic terms. Periods that gave a clearly defined shape to the Soviet cinema of two changing stages.

As successive stages of development they are sharply contrasted with one another.

The least contrast lies in the fact that the third five years was a sound period and the second a silent, although it thundered round the globe.

It is a matter of their stylistic distinction.

A distinction that sometimes verges on mutual exclusion.

And in any event a matter of the strongest contradiction in principle.

Take any film from one five-year period and compare it with any film from the other and the comparisons will speak for themselves:

The Mother and *The Deserter*, *The Arsenal* and *The Golden Mountains*, *Potemkin* and *Counterplan*.[38]

The stylistic difference between each of these three pairs bears the equally distinct imprint of their location in one five-year period or another.

That brings us back to why the impending fourth five-year period in our cinema will be so remarkable.

It will be remarkable because it will be a synthesis which will include in 'distilled' form the greatest achievements of the mutually exclusive styles of the two preceding periods. . . .

This part of my article turned out to be objectionable to the editors. This principled preamble was amputated. They left just my 'evening of reminiscences'.

What could their motive have been? Only one thing: editorial disagreement with the relative evaluation that I give to the different stages of our cinema.

Where could the essence of the disagreement lie? In the fact that, in the editor's view, the features that I expect from the fourth five-year period of our cinema are ones that they have a strong desire to see, and that they want to force me to see in the films produced in the five-year period 1929-34.

The editors did not express their opposition to my point of view: they just removed it from circulation.

For this reason I am free to attribute whatever motives I please to them. They have not said anything about them. But I think that these were their motives.

We can probably add to this the usual hackneyed accusation of 'pessimism', of an 'underestimation of creative potential' and of 'lack of faith in the strength of Soviet cinema'.

This was precisely how N. Zarkhi was 'dissected' for his speech to the Writers' Congress in one issue after another of *Kino*.[39]

Only people with a very weak grounding in the dialectic of development and in questions of how the elements of one stage may be present in another, were capable of reading the nonsensical slogan 'Back to *Potemkin*, to *The Arsenal* and *The Mother!*' into Zarkhi's appeal not to waste the achievements of the second five-year period on the threshold of our entry into the fourth.

Meanwhile the qualities introduced by the second and third five-year periods are extremely varied.

Collating them, we should recall Belinsky's words:

> What a contrast there was between the period of *Pushkin* and that of *Karamzin*, just as the present period contrasts with *Pushkin's* . . . .
> The period of Pushkin was distinguished by a certain frantic mania for poetry: the present period has from its very inception shown a decisive preference for prose.

Belinsky entirely approved of the Pushkin period.

But here there is an important difference. Conditioned by differing historical and social premisses, the two five-year periods in our cinema that I have mentioned were, however, distinguished from one another by the very same thing.

It must be understood that in this context we are talking about the contrast between poetry and prose in the literary rather than the everyday conception of these terms!

In fact the distinctive differentiation lay in the predominance of poetry in the first period. And of prose in the second period. In the order of things. In the specifics of the selection of the means of influence. In their figurative and compositional structure.

The stage of poetry and the stage of prose.

But it would be a huge POLITICAL error vis-à-vis the *prosaic* five-year period to attribute to it the same characteristics that Belinsky attributes to the post-Pushkin period: 'But, alas! It was not a step forward, not a renewal but an impoverishment, an exhaustion of creative activity. . . .' There are many who are enamoured of the first five-year period who are ready to deny any achievement in the second and take the quotation even further: '. . . activity and life came to an end: the thunder of weapons fell silent and the exhausted warriors sheathed their swords, rested on their laurels, each claiming victory for himself, and nobody won in the true meaning of the word.'[40]

We must decisively reject such attitudes. They would be shortsighted, mistaken and pessimistic.

But we must be just as brutal in opposing those who try to claim that the second five-year period is beyond reproach and who wish to gloss over the elements of one-sidedness that are just as characteristic of it as, in another sense, they are of the preceding period.

Whereas the first stage, sometimes at the expense of thematic depth, knew how to captivate audiences with revolutionary subject matter, using all the methods and achievements of the film poetics and the mastery of film language that it had created and was creating, the second period made a sudden break with all the elements of film expressiveness that had characterised the first period.

This was partly facilitated by its as yet incomplete mastery of sound technique. But it was basically a matter of the principles that characterised that particular stage.

In return, this period of prose promoted demands for problematic depth, for a psychological portrayal of man, for a story that was tied together by a plot.

There is no point in my saying it 'promoted demands' because there were few occasions when this period achieved the heights of its own demands.

Perhaps the most successful film in this respect was *Counterplan*, which was a particularly clear polar opposite to the preceding period.

You would have to be conceited or blind not to see the one-sided limitations of both periods on a par with their valuable contributions towards our general cultural development.

And you would have to be blind or short-sighted not to foretell and foresee that the next stage must be a stage of synthesis, absorbing all the best things introduced or proclaimed by the previous stages.

Yesterday we could foretell and foresee this. Yesterday we could not publish our foresights and assumptions.

Today we see this. Today we can talk about it. Today the fine film *Chapayev*[41] can say the same thing from the screen on our behalf.

What is *Chapayev's* remarkable achievement based on?

On the fact that, without forfeiting any of the achievements or contributions to film culture of the first stage, it has organically absorbed, without any surrenders or compromises, everything that the second stage promoted as a programme.

Taking all the experience of poetic style and pathos that characterised the first stage and all the thematic depth revealed in the living image of man that stood at the centre of attention of the second five-year period, the Vasilievs have been able to produce unforgettable images of people and an unforgettable picture of the period.

The composition of this film is remarkable. It is not a return to the old plot forms that were filmed in the first stage of our cinema. It is not 'back to plot'. But 'forward to a new kind of plot'.

Preserving the epic form that was popular in the early days of our cinema, the film-makers have been able, within that framework, to sketch in the kind of brilliant gallery of heroic individuals that could previously really only have been achieved in films that were tied together by a plot with a traditional story-line. Shakespeare? Shakespeare's successors? Certainly, even if they are not the descendants of Lear, Macbeth or Othello. In the poetics of its

299

composition *Chapayev* does not come near to them. Nevertheless within the boundaries of its style it can count Shakespeare, the Shakespeare of no less remarkable dramaturgy – the Shakespeare of the historical chronicles.

The appearance of *Chapayev* does, I think, mark the end of the discord between the epochs.

In chronological terms, *Chapayev* opens the fourth five-year period in our cinema.

In terms of principle as well.

The appearance of *Chapayev* signifies the start of the fourth five-year period in Soviet cinema, the start of a five-year period of great synthesis, when all the achievements of the whole preceding era of Soviet cinema in their uncompromisingly high quality become at the same time the property of the many millions of the masses, infecting them with the new energy of heroism, struggle and creativity.

The victory of *Chapayev* is the first victory on this road.

None of us has ever doubted the great strength of our cinema.

But we did not want to proclaim as great victories films that, in our view, did not quite deserve it. We kept quiet about a lot of films.

But this was not pessimism.

It was the high standard we set our cinema as a criterion.

But now, during Soviet cinema's great celebration, we can, with a complete and well-founded feeling of enormous joy, exclaim over this new and uncompromising proof of our cinema's strength:

'At last!'

Notes

Throughout these notes Eisenstein is referred to as E. The following are the principal editions of E's writings hitherto available in English: some of them are referred to in the notes. They are listed in chronological order.

J. Leyda (ed. and trans.), *The Film Sense*, New York, Harcourt Brace Jovanovich, 1942, and London, Faber & Faber, 1943.

J. Leyda (ed. and trans.), *Film Form, Essays in Film Theory*, New York, Harcourt Brace Jovanovich, 1949, and London, Dennis Dobson, 1951.

J. Leyda (ed.), *Film Essays and a Lecture*, London, Dobson, 1968, and New York, Praeger, 1970.

S. Eisenstein, *Notes of a Film Director*, New York, Dover, 1970.

L. Moussinac, *Sergei Eisenstein. An Investigation into His Films and Philosophy*, New York, Crown, 1970.

J. Leyda & Z. Voynow, *Eisenstein at Work*, New York, Pantheon, 1982, and London, Methuen, 1985.

H. Marshall (trans.), *Immoral Memories. An Autobiography by Sergei M. Eisenstein*, Boston, Houghton Mifflin, and London, Peter Owen, 1985.

A. Y. Upchurch (trans.), *Sergei M. Eisenstein: On the Composition of the Short Fiction Scenario*, Calcutta, Seagull Books, 1984.

J. Leyda (ed.), *Eisenstein 2: A Premature Celebration of Eisenstein's Centenary*, Calcutta, Seagull Books, 1985.

J. Leyda (ed.), *Eisenstein on Disney*, Calcutta, Seagull Books, 1986.

H. Marshall (ed. and trans.), *Non-Indifferent Nature*, Cambridge University Press, 1987.

Introduction

1. Leonid Andreyev, 'First Letter on Theatre', translated in: R. Taylor and I. Christie (eds.), *The Film Factory, Russian and Soviet Cinema in Documents, 1986-1939*, London and Cambridge, Mass., 1988, pp. 27-31.
2. E would have shuddered at the comparison with Stanislavsky but it is appropriate at least in terms of the revolutionary impact of both their theories in their own time: in this sense the fact that E reacted vehemently against much of what Stanislavsky stood for is strictly irrelevant. Jacques Aumont has rightly pointed out the limitations of the comparison with Brecht (J. Aumont, *Montage Eisenstein*, London and Bloomington, Indiana, 1987, p. 72). The proper comparison is with Meyerhold, not just because of their common historical context and the similarities in their artistic experience, but also because E himself regarded Meyerhold as his 'master' or spiritual father (Aumont, pp. 14 & 203, n. 26; I. Barna, *Eisenstein*, London, 1973, p. 56; M. Seton, *Eisenstein*, London, 1952, pp. 46 & 48). It is a clear sign of E's respect for his 'master' that he personally preserved Meyerhold's papers for posterity after the latter's arrest and official disgrace in June 1939. E saw himself very much in the mould of Leonardo da Vinci, as Seton makes abundantly clear.
3. Aumont argued the case for Eisenstein's coherence in *Montage Eisenstein*, as does Peter Wollen in his chapter on 'Eisenstein's Aesthetics' in *Signs and Meaning in the Cinema* (London, 1969, pp. 19-73).

4. Barna, pp. 37-8.
5. The 'Eccentric' in the title derives from *ekstsentrik*, one of the Russian words for 'clown'. Like E, the members of FEKS (Sergei Yutkevich, Leonid Trauberg, Grigori Kozintsev) progressed from theatre to cinema.
6. Taylor and Christie, p. 58.
7. Ibid., p. 62.
8. Ibid., p. 58.
9. Ibid., p. 59.
10. The concept of the *naturshchik* or 'model actor' derived from the theory and practice of the Kuleshov Workshop and had certain similarities with Meyerhold's theory of 'biomechanics'.
11. E's critique has something in common with Shklovsky's remark that 'Mussolini talking interests me. But a straightforward plump and bald-headed man who talks can go and talk off screen. The whole sense of a newsreel is in the date, time and place. A newsreel without this is like a card catalogue in the gutter' (V. B. Shklovskii, 'Kuda shagaet Dziga Vertov?' [Where Is Dziga Vertov Striding?], *Sovetskii ekran*, 10 August 1926, p. 4): Taylor and Christie, p. 152.
12. E is here playing with the concept of 'photogeny' or 'the photogenic' elaborated in France by Louis Delluc in his *Photogénie* (Paris, 1920), and by Jean Epstein in *Bonjour cinéma* (Paris, 1921).
13. The exchange of letters between E and Valerian Pletnyov has been translated in J. Leyda (ed.), *Eisenstein 2: A Premature Celebration of Eisenstein's Centenary* (Calcutta, 1985), pp. 1-7.
14. For details of *Potemkin's* reception in the West, see: H. Marshall (ed.), *The Battleship Potemkin* (New York, 1979), pp. 117-235, and: G. Kühn, K. Tümmler and W. Wimmer (eds.), *Film und revolutionäre Arbeiterbewegung in Deutschland 1918-1932* (Berlin, GDR, 1975), vol. 1, pp. 323-69.
15. In the English-speaking world this statement is usually attributed to E's 1928 article 'An Unexpected Juncture', which Jay Leyda translated as 'The Unexpected' in *Film Form*, pp. 18-27, but it was in fact first used here. E was not averse to recycling his examples and arguments, or indeed in some instances even his articles.
16. 'K predstoyashchemu kinosoveshchaniyu' [Address to the Imminent Cinema Conference], *Zhizn' iskusstva*, 27 September 1927, p. 1. For detailed analyses of the events of 1928 and their significance see: R. Taylor, *The Politics of the Soviet Cinema, 1917-1929* (Cambridge, England, 1979, Ch. 6, and: D. Youngblood, *Soviet Cinema in the Silent Era, 1918-1935* (Ann Arbor, Michigan, 1985), Ch. 7.
17. Shklovsky's 'Art as Technique' is translated in: L.T. Lemon and J.J. Reis (trans.), *Russian Formalist Criticism, Four Essays* (Lincoln, Nebraska, 1965), pp. 3-24.
18. Seton, p. 168, and H. M. Geduld and R. Gottesman (eds.), *The Making and Unmaking of 'Que Viva Mexico!'* (London and Bloomington, 1970), pp. 309-11.
19. Seton, pp. 247-8.
20. It is perhaps worth remembering that the Vasilievs, who directed *Chapayev*, had been E's pupils at GIK.
21. E elaborated this periodisation in 'The Middle of the Three' [Srednyaya iz trëkh], *Sovetskoe kino*, 1934, no. 11/12 (November/December), pp. 54-83. I had originally intended to include a translation in this volume but for reasons of space it had to be omitted. Leyda has included it as 'Through Theatre to Cinema' in *Film Form*, pp. 3-17.

1922

1. Source: S. Yutkevich and S. Eizenshtein, 'Vos'moe iskusstvo. Ob ekspression-izme, Amerike i, konechno, o Chapline', *Ekho*, 7 November 1922. Sergei I. Yutkevich (1904-85), Soviet film director, was at that time a student at both GVYRM, under Meyerhold (see below, no. 6), and Vkhutemas.
2. Claude Blanchard (1896-1945), French journalist and writer on film.
3. *The Phantom Carriage (Körkarlen)*, directed by Viktor Sjöström (Sweden, 1920), and also known in English as *Thy Soul Shall Bear Witness*.
4. Not identified. The French names cited by Yutkevich and Eisenstein in this article have been transliterated by them into Russian with a considerable degree of in-accuracy. Yutkevich recalled (in an interview with the Editor in Moscow in March 1983) that he and Eisenstein had been considerably influenced by a special film issue of the French avant-garde journal *Crapouillot*, but I have been unable to trace the particular issue concerned.
5. Aleksandr Ya. Tairov (1885-1950) founded the Moscow Kamerny (i.e. Chamber) Theatre in 1914: it stood for an Expressionist style of production and acting as opposed to the naturalism of Stanislavsky's Moscow Art Theatre.
6. Vsevolod E. Meyerhold (1874-1940), Russian and Soviet theatre director and actor, who joined the Moscow Art Theatre at its inception in 1898 and later ran an experimental studio there. His ideas on acting and the training of actors, which later developed into the system of biomechanics, led him to work elsewhere and to set up his own studio in 1913. After the Revolution he was in charge of GVYRM (see above, n. 1); he also ran his own theatre in Moscow until his denunciation and arrest in 1938.
7. Louis Delluc (1890-1924), French film director, film theorist and acknowledged 'father' of French film criticism. His book *Photogénie*, Paris, 1920, also influenced Eikhenbaum and Tynyanov in their *Poetika kino* [Poetics of Cinema], Moscow, 1927, published in English as Volume 9 of *Russian Poetics in Translation*, Oxford, 1982. Delluc's work has not been translated into English. The films referred to here are *La femme de nulle part (The Woman from Nowhere)* (France, 1922) and *Fièvre (Fever)* (France, 1921).
8. The reference is to the Petrograd group formed in the autumn of 1922 under the title FEKS (*Fabrika ekstsentricheskogo aktëra*), the Factory of the Eccentric Actor, led by Grigori M. Kozintsev (1905-73), Leonid Z. Trauberg (b. 1901) and Yut-kevich. Their proclaimed models included circus and music-hall techniques and American cinema.
9. Probably Dr Emile Galtier Boissière, author of popular pamphlets on such varied topics as alcoholism, cycling and venereal disease.
10. The naturalistic acting methods deployed by the Meiningen Players, the court theatre troupe founded by Duke George II and his morganatic wife, influenced Stanislavsky when they visited Russia in 1890. They also influenced the style of early film acting, notably in the films of Yakov A. Protazanov (1881-1945).
11. A polemical reference to the Russian woman painter V.D. Polenova (1844-1927), known primarily for her realistic landscapes, but who also painted religious and biblical subjects.
12. *Father Sergius (Otets Sergii)*, directed by Yakov Protazanov for the privately owned Ermoliev company and starring Ivan Mosjoukine (RSFSR, 1918). The film was based on the story by Lev Tolstoy.
13. *Don Juan et Faust* (France, 1923). ·
14. *Le Lis de la vie*, a film ballet starring René Clair (see 1926, n. 37) (France, 1920).
15. *Das Kabinett des Dr Caligari* (Germany, 1919), one of the most important ex-amples of German Expressionist cinema. The names of the artists are incorrect:

the sets were designed by three members of the *Sturm* group, namely: Hermann Warm, Walter Röhrig and Walter Reimann. Rodstadt and Arpke have not been identified.

16. Léon Moussinac (1890-1964), leading French critic and film historian, instigator of the film society movement in France and one of the earliest and foremost proponents of Soviet cinema in the West. His book, *Le cinéma soviétique*, was published in Paris in 1928.

17. 'Rio Jim' was the nickname of William S. Hart (1870-1946) and derived from the role he played in *The Passing of Two-Gun Hicks* (USA, 1913). Sessue Hayakawa (1889-1973) was a Japanese actor who appeared in many non-Japanese films from Cecil B. De Mille's *The Cheat* (USA, 1915) to *The Bridge on the River Kwai* (Great Britain, 1957). Roscoe ('Fatty') Arbuckle (1887-1933) was one of the leading stars of early Hollywood slapstick comedies.

18. Alexandre Millerant (1859-1943), President of the French Republic from 1920 to 1924.

19. Ilya Ehrenburg (1891-1969) wrote a paean to cinema in *A vsë-taki vertitsya* [And Yet It Turns], Berlin, 1922.

20. A 'heliotrope auntie' is Eisenstein's mocking way of characterising the taste of the petty bourgeoisie that was emerging under the New Economic Policy, NEP. As a pejorative term it is somewhat akin to the contemporary term 'blue-rinse brigade'. According to Naum Kleiman, E elsewhere summarised popular taste of the 20s as 'velour sofas and pink lampshades'.

1923

1. Source: S. M. Eizenshtein, 'Montazh attraktsionov', *Lef*, 1923, no. 3 (June/July), pp. 70-1, 74-5.

2. *Enough Simplicity for Every Wise Man*, the comedy by Alexander N. Ostrovsky (1823-86), was reworked by Sergei M. Tretyakov (1892-1939) for Proletkult in 1923.

3. Proletkult, the Proletarian Culture organisation, aimed to produce a specifically proletarian culture for post-Revolutionary Soviet audiences. The organisation's ideas were seen by Lenin and others as a challenge to the authority of the Party. E clearly also regarded the Proletkult's ideas as extreme: he left the organisation after a dispute over the authorship of the script for *The Strike* in the winter of 1924/5.

4. *The Dawns of Proletkult (Zori Proletkul'ta)* was a stage performance based on the works of various proletarian poets. It was staged as a response to Meyerhold's 1920 version of Emile Verhaeren's *The Dawns*.

5. *Lena* was a play by Valerian F. Pletnyov (1886-1942), based on the events in the Lena goldfield in Siberia in 1912 and staged at the Moscow Proletkult Theatre in October 1921. When E and Proletkult parted company he and Pletnyov indulged in a vitriolic public exchange of letters.

6. Boris I. Arvatov (1896-1940), art critic, was a member of Proletkult and later also of LEF.

7. *The Mexican (Meksikanets)*, a stage version of the story by Jack London, was E's first theatrical production (with Smyshlyayev) in January–March 1921. E also designed the sets and costumes.

8. Valentin S. Smyshlyayev (1891-1936), originally an actor and director with the Moscow Art Theatre, worked in the 1920s as a director with Proletkult. The work referred to later in this paragraph is properly entitled *Tekhnika obrabotki stseni-*

cheskogo zrelishcha [The Technique of Treatment for the Stage Show] and was published by Proletkult in booklet form in 1922.

9. Pletnyov's *On the Abyss* (*Nad obryvom*) was produced by Proletkult in 1922.

10. Alexander A. Ostuzhev (1874-1953) was a classical actor.

11. Charles Dickens's *The Cricket on the Hearth* was produced at the Moscow Art Theatre in 1915.

12. During E's production of *Can You Hear Me, Moscow?* (*Slyshish', Moskva?*) squibs were let off under the seats in the auditorium. The play was written by E's collaborator Sergei M. Tretyakov.

13. Georg Grosz (1893-1959), the leading German satirical draughtsman of this century, known especially for his bitter satires on the bourgeoisie of Weimar Germany.

14. Alexander M. Rodchenko (1891-1956), Constructivist artist and photographer and one of the founders of photo-montage.

15. The Russian word *montazhër* is now principally used to mean 'editor' but at that time could also indicate 'producer' or 'director'.

16. The Russian *ekstsentrik* means initially 'clown' but was adopted by the Petrograd-based Factory of the Eccentric Actor (FEKS). See 1922, n. 8.

17. A Georgian chant used by Christians, the pun being in the sound 'Allah'.

18. The New Economic Policy, introduced by Lenin at the end of the Civil War in spring 1921, marked a limited return to private enterprise and was designed to restore the Soviet economy to 1913 levels. The 'Nepman' and 'Nepwoman', the nouveaux riches who emerged in the following years, were a constant object of satire. See 1922, n. 20.

19. E's first film was made for this part of the production.

20. Alexander N. Vertinsky (1889-1957) was a popular singer and film actor who emigrated in 1919 but returned in 1943.

21. *Lezginka:* a Caucasian dance.

1924

1. Source: 'Montazh kinoattraktsionov', a typescript, dated October 1924, held in the Eisenstein archive, TsGALI, Moscow, as yet unpublished in Russian in its complete form and reproduced by kind permission of the USSR Union of Film-Makers. It has recently been discovered that a distorted version of this article was in fact published by Alexander Belenson under his own name in his *Kino segodnya, Ocherki sovetskogo kinoiskusstva (Kuleshov – Vertov – Eizenshtein)* [Cinema Today, Essays on Soviet Cinema (Kuleshov – Vertov – Eisenstein)], Moscow, 1925. In this and subsequent documents E is somewhat inconsistent in his use of the Russian equivalents of 'effect' and 'affect'. The Editor was initially tempted to improve on the original by making the English translation more systematic but ultimately felt it fairer to both E and the reader to reproduce E's usage. Both *vozdeistvie* and *effekt* are therefore translated as 'effect', *deistvennost'* as 'effectiveness' and *vozdeistvuyushchii* as 'effective', while *affekt* and *affektivnyi* are rendered as 'affect' and 'affective' respectively. The reader should however constantly bear in mind the possibility of the alternative meaning. Similarly, *sopostavlenie* has been translated as either 'comparison' or 'juxtaposition' but retains both meanings in Russian.

2. The Cine-Eyes (*Kinoki*, singular: *Kinoglaz*) were the documentary film-makers grouped around Dziga Vertov (pseudonym of Denis A. Kaufman, 1896-1954). The group published two major, and numerous minor, attacks on fiction film and on the concept of 'art' as a manifestation of bourgeois culture to be torn down 'like the

Tower of Babel': 'We. A Version of a Manifesto' ['My. Variant manifesta'] in the Constructivist journal *Kino-Fot*, no. 1, 25-31 August 1922, pp. 11-12, and 'The Cine-Eyes. A Revolution' ['Kinoki. Perevorot'] on pp. 135-43 of the same issue of *Lef* as E's 'The Montage of Attractions'. Both Cine-Eye documents are translated in: A. Michelson (ed.), *Kino-Eye, The Writings of Dziga Vertov*, Berkeley, Calif., 1984; London, 1985, pp. 5-9, 11-21; and R. Taylor and I. Christie (eds.), *The Film Factory: Russian and Soviet Cinema in Documents*, London and Cambridge, Mass., 1987, pp. 69-72 and 89-94.

3. See 'The Montage of Attractions', pp. 33-38 above.
4. *Cine-Pravda (Kinopravda)* meaning 'Cinema Truth' and pointing the analogy with the name of the Party newspaper *Pravda*, was the name of the newsreel produced by the Cine-Eye group in twenty-three issues between June 1922 and 1925.
5. See 1923, n. 12.
6. *Alogizm*: a neologism coined by E to denote an action or event that had no logical explanation in its particular context.
7. *The Extraordinary Adventures of Mr West in the Land of the Bolsheviks (Neobychainye priklyucheniya Mistera Vesta v strane bol'shevikov)* (USSR, 1924) was directed by Lev Kuleshov (1899-1970) and satirised Western notions of the Bolsheviks. It was Kuleshov who first developed the notion of montage as the essence of cinema specificity.
8. *Intolerance* (USA, 1916) was made by D.W. Griffith (1875-1948).
9. *The Palace and the Fortress (Dvorets i krepost')* (USSR, 1923) was directed by Alexander V. Ivanovsky (1881-1968).
10. *Andrei Kozhukhov* (Russia, 1917) was directed by Yakov Protazanov after the February Revolution and starred Ivan Mosjoukine as the revolutionary Populist hero. It was still in distribution in 1924. *Stepan Khalturin* (USSR, 1925) was made by Ivanovsky.
11. See 'The Montage of Attractions', pp. 33-38 above.
12. The reference is to the play *Nathan der Weise* by the German dramatist Gottfried Ephraim Lessing (1729-81).
13. *Naturshchik:* a 'model' or 'mannequin', the word used by E, Kuleshov and others to denote an actor who functioned as a mere tool of the director and expressed his emotions through specific physical actions.
14. See 1923, n. 3.
15. See 1923, n. 12.
16. E's reference is to Guillaume-Benjamin-Arnand Duchenne, called Duchenne de Boulogne (1806-75). The first French edition of the work cited was: *Physiologie des mouvements démontrée à l'aide de l'expérimentation électrique et de l'observation clinique* [Physiology of Movements Demonstrated with the Aid of Electrical Experimentation and Clinical Observation], Paris, 1867. I can find no trace of an 1885 edition. The work was translated into English as *Physiology of Motion*, ed. and trans. E.B. Kaplan, Philadelphia, 1949.
17. Literally: 'Isolated muscular action does not exist in nature'.
18. The original text has 'two' but this is clearly erroneous.
19. H. Nothnagel, *Topische Diagnostik der Gehirnkrankheiten* [The External Diagnosis of Brain Diseases], Berlin, 1879.
20. In German in the original: the English translation is 'thalamus', where the optical nerve ends originate.
21. *Gas Masks (Protivogazy)* by Tretyakov was produced by E at the Proletkult theatre in 1923. Cf. 1923, n. 12.
22. See 1922, n. 17.
23. See n. 1 above.
24. Russian: *prozodezhda*, a term frequently used by the Constructivists.

1925

1. Source: 'K voprosu o materialisticheskom podkhode k forme', *Kinozhurnal ARK*, 1925, no. 4/5 (April/May), pp. 5-8.
2. The implication here is that the past has prepared the present like a factory process.
3. *The Strike* was originally intended as one of the episodes in this larger cycle.
4. *Massovost'* meaning 'mass quality' or 'mass character', by analogy with *klassovost'* meaning 'class quality' or 'class character' and *partiinost'* or 'Partyness'.
5. E is referring here to earlier debates about whether cinema could be considered an autonomous art form in its own right or whether it was more properly regarded as an adjunct of another art form, such as theatre, literature or painting.
6. The reference is to *Novyi zritel'*, 1925, no. 5. For Pletnyov, see 1923, n. 5.
7. Mikhail Koltsov (1898-1942), the journalist who was later to become editor of *Ogonëk* and *Krokodil*, reviewed *The Strike* ('Stachka', *Pravda*, 14 March 1925, p. 8), describing it as 'the first revolutionary work that our screen has produced', but in the film journals it was criticised, among other things, for a 'discrepancy between ideology and form'.
8. See 1924, n. 2.
9. See 1924, n. 4.
10. *Cine-Eye (Kinoglaz)*, a six-reel 'exploration of "life caught unawares"', directed by Vertov, was released on 13 October 1924.
11. Khrisanf N. Khersonsky (1897-1968), the critic and scriptwriter, wrote a hostile review of *The Strike* and participated with E, Pletnyov, Abram Room and others in a discussion of the film at the headquarters of ARK in Moscow on 19 March 1925.
12. AKhRR, formed in 1922, consisted of artists who adhered to the traditions of nineteenth-century social realism exemplified by the Wanderers (*Peredvizhniki*), a group whose leading members were Ilya Repin and Vasili Vereshchagin.
13. See 1924, n. 6.
14. *Cine-Pravda* no. 19, released in May 1924, was variously subtitled 'A Trip with a Movie Camera from Moscow to the Arctic Ocean' and 'On the Train Summer and Winter'.
15. Source: 'Metod postanovki rabochei fil'my', *Kino*, 11 August 1925.
16. See 1924, n. 1.
17. See above, n. 4.
18. See 1923, n. 12.
19. See 1922, n. 15.
20. Mary Pickford (1893-1979) and her then husband Douglas Fairbanks (1883-1939) were just as popular in the Soviet Union as in the West. When they visited Moscow in 1926 they made a brief appearance in a film entitled *The Kiss of Mary Pickford (Potselui Meri Pikford)*. Their favourable comments on E's *The Battleship Potemkin* were used to advertise the film to Soviet audiences.
21. Unfortunately E did not always get his bibliographical references right: this is presumably a reference to V. Lindsay, *The Art of the Moving Picture*, New York, 1915. I am particularly grateful to the staff of that remarkable institution, the Motion Picture, Broadcasting and Recorded Sound Division of the Library of Congress, for their assistance in tracing this work. However, although Lindsay devotes one chapter of his book to censorship, he nowhere produces the list that E mentions.

1926

1. Source: 'Konstantsa. (Kuda ukhodit *Bronenosets Potëmkin*), dated 1926 and first published in: N.I. Kleiman and K.B. Levina (eds), *Bronenosets Potëmkin*, Moscow, 1968, pp. 290-2.
2. *The Thief of Bagdad* (USA, 1924), starred Douglas Fairbanks.
3. *The Station Master* (*Kollezhskii registrator*) (USSR, 1926) was directed by Yuri Zhelyabuzhsky and based on a story by Pushkin.
4. *Subbotnik*: an unpaid extra day of labour for the state introduced to help rebuild the Soviet economy.
5. Muir and Merrilees was an exclusive foreign-owned department store in Moscow before the Revolution, somewhat similar in style to Harrods in London. The site is now occupied by the state-owned store TsUM.
6. E had studied the later works of Vladimir M. Bekhterev (1857-1927), in particular, *Ob obshchikh osnovakh refleksologii kak nauchnoi distsipliny* [The General Principles of Reflexology as a Scientific Discipline], 1917, and *Kollektivnaya refleksologiya* [Collective Reflexology], 1921.
7. Harold Lloyd (1893-1971), American film comedian, whose best-known films at that time were *Grandma's Boy* (USA, 1922) and *The Freshman* (USA, 1925).
8. Tretyakov's play *I Want a Child* (*Khochu rebënka*) was accepted by Meyerhold for a production with sets by El Lissitzky but never produced for censorship reasons.
9. Source: 'Kak ni stranno – o Khokhlovoi', *Kino*, 30 March 1926, reprinted in: *A. Khokhlova*, Moscow, 1926, pp. 5-9. Alexandra S. Khokhlova (1897-1985), actress wife of the director and film theorist Lev Kuleshov, played the part of the Countess in his *The Extraordinary Adventures of Mr West in the Land of the Bolsheviks* (*Neobychainye priklyucheniya Mistera Vesta v strane bol'shevikov*) (USSR, 1924) and the role of Edith in his *By the Law* (*Po zakonu*) (USSR, 1926). Khokhlova's acting style exemplified Kuleshov's theories about the actor as *naturshchik* or 'model'.
10. International Women's Day is celebrated in the USSR on 8 March each year.
11. Lon Chaney (1883-1930), American actor known as the 'man of a thousand faces', played the title roles in *The Hunchback of Notre Dame* (USA, 1923) and *The Phantom of the Opera* (USA, 1925). Erich von Stroheim (1885-1957), Vienna-born American director and actor known at the time of E's article primarily for his films *Foolish Wives* (USA, 1922), *Greed* (USA, 1923-5) and *The Merry Widow* (USA, 1925). Richard Barthelmess (1895-1963), American actor, appeared in Griffith's *Broken Blossoms* (USA, 1919) and *Way Down East* (USA, 1920) and in Henry King's *Tol'able David* (USA, 1921).
12. Rudolph Valentino (1895-1926), legendary Italian-born star of Hollywood silent films such as *The Four Horsemen of the Apocalypse* and *The Sheik* (USA, 1921), *Blood and Sand* (USA, 1922), *Monsieur Beaucaire* (USA, 1924) and *The Son of the Sheik* (USA, 1926). Ramon Novarro (1899-1968), Mexican-born Hollywood actor, starred in *The Prisoner of Zenda* (USA, 1922) and *Ben-Hur* (USA, 1926).
13. Priscilla Dean (b. 1896) starred in Tod Browning's *The Virgin of Stamboul* (USA, 1920).
14. The reference here is to the type exemplified by the screen roles played by Gloria Swanson (1899-1983), Barbara La Marr (1896-1926) and Leatrice Joy (1899-1985).
15. i.e. Mack Sennett's 'Bathing Beauties'.
16. Carol Dempster (b. 1902) appeared in a number of D.W. Griffith's films: *A Romance of Happy Valley, The Girl Who Stayed at Home, True Heart Susie* and *Scarlet Days* (USA, 1919), *The Love Flower* (USA, 1920), *Dream Street* (USA, 1921), *One Exciting Night* (USA, 1922), *The White Rose* (USA, 1923), *America* and *Isn't Life Wonderful?* (USA, 1924), *Sally of the Sawdust* (USA, 1925), *That Royle Girl* and *The Sorrows of Satan* (USA, 1926).

17. *The Bear's Wedding* (*Medvezh'ya svad'ba*), directed by Konstantin Eggert from a script by Anatoli Lunacharsky (then People's Commissar for Enlightenment) based on the short story *Lokis* by Prosper Mérimée and starring Lunacharsky's wife Nataliya Rozenel, was a greater box-office success in Moscow in the winter of 1926 than E's *Potemkin*. It is a horror story set in the forests of Lithuania with the stock elements of werewolves and hereditary insanity.

18. Ekaterina V. Geltser (1876-1962), Russian classical ballerina who appeared in factories, etc. after the Revolution.

19. *Sarafan*: a long Russian peasant dress.

20. GUM is the Russian abbreviation for State Universal Store, the large department store on Red Square in Moscow opposite the Kremlin. These film titles were presumably intended to depict Khokhlova the 'Eccentric' in everyday situations.

21. Nikolai P. Okhlopkov (1900-67), Soviet actor and director, worked in Meyerhold's theatre in the 20s and began with bit parts in cinema: *Old Knysh's Gang* (*Banda bat'ki Knysha*) (USSR, 1924), *The Bay of Death* (*Bukhta smerti*) and *The Traitor* (*Predatel'*) (USSR, 1926).

22. Source: 'Sergej Eisenstein über Sergej Eisenstein, den *Potemkin*-Regisseur', *Berliner Tageblatt*, 7 June 1926. The interview was conducted at the beginning of that month during E's second visit to Berlin. Translated by Leyda and included as 'A Personal Statement' in *Film Essays*, pp. 13-17.

23. See 1923, nn. 3 and 4.

24. For Meyerhold, see 1922, n. 6. Vladimir V. Mayakovsky (1893-1930), the Futurist poet and dramatist, had written a number of articles on theatre and film since 1913 and was the author of several film scripts.

25. Konstantin S. Stanislavsky (1863-1938) was co-founder in 1898 of the Moscow Art Theatre and the leading exponent of both the theory and practice of psychological realism and naturalism on stage. For Tairov, see 1922, n. 5.

26. This error was made by the *Frankfurter Zeitung* and later repeated by the American press.

27. See 1923, n. 2.

28. See 1923, n. 12.

29. See 1924, n. 21.

30. The 'happy ending' (Russian: *kheppi end*) became a shorthand way of criticising the faults of Hollywood in general.

31. Antaeos was a figure in Greek mythology who derived his strength from his contact with the earth.

32. *Faust* (Germany, 1926) was directed by F.W. Murnau and starred Emil Jannings. E and Tisse became acquainted with both men during the shooting of the film in the spring of 1926. *Metropolis* (Germany, 1926) was directed by Fritz Lang: again E and Tisse visited the studio during the shooting.

33. This paragraph did not appear in the published version.

34. Source: 'O pozitsii Bela Balasha', *Kino*, 20 July 1926, and: 'Bela zabyvaet nozhnitsy', *Kino*, 10 August 1926. This article is a polemical response to the Russian publication of an article by Béla Balázs (1884-1949), the Hungarian film theorist, author and scriptwriter: 'O budushchem fil'my' (On the Future of Film) in *Kino*, 6 July 1926. An English translation is available as Document no. 54 in R. Taylor and I. Christie (eds), *The Film Factory: Russian and Soviet Cinema in Documents*, London and Cambridge, Mass., 1988. The article, an extract from a lecture delivered by Balázs to the German Cameramen's Club, appeared in German as 'Filmtradition und Filmzukunft' (The Tradition of Film and the Future of Film) in *Filmtechnik*, 12 June 1926, pp. 234a-5b.

35. This is E's paraphrase of Balázs's statement: 'As long as the cameraman comes last, cinema will be the last art. The sentence ought to be turned on its head'.

36. Ilya G. Ehrenburg (see 1922, n. 19) lived in Paris from 1908 to 1917 and again from 1921 to 1923.

37. Francis Picabia (1897-1949), one of the founders of Dada, wrote the script for *Entr'acte* (France, 1924), directed by René Clair (the pseudonym of René Chomette, 1898-1981). The painter Fernand Léger (1881-1955) made the experimental short film *Le ballet mécanique* in 1924. Henri Chomette (1896-1941), brother of René, made a number of abstract films including *Jeux des reflets et de la vitesse* (France, 1923) and *Cinq minutes de cinéma pur* (France, 1925).

38. Novokhopyorsk is a district on the Khopyor River south-east of Voronezh.

39. Three mythical firebirds from Russian folklore.

40. *Filmtechnik* was not in fact the official organ of the club, but represented its interests. The co-editor was Guido Seeber, whose book *Der Trickfilm*, Berlin, 1927, was translated into Russian as *Tekhnika kinotryuka*, Moscow, 1929. *Variété* (Germany, 1925), set in a circus, was directed by E.A. Dupont and starred Emil Jannings.

41. Prometheus-Film was founded in December 1925 by three prominent members of the German Communist Party (KPD), including Willi Münzenberg, to market Soviet films in Germany and engage in German-Soviet co-productions.

42. Eduard K. Tisse (1897-1961) was the cameraman for all E's films from *The Strike* to *Ivan the Terrible*. They visited Germany together in 1926.

43. UFA was the largest film production company in Germany in the 1920s.

44. Günther Rittau (1893-1971) was joint cameraman on *The Nibelungs* (Germany, 1924) and *Metropolis* (Germany, 1926), both directed by Fritz Lang. See above, n. 32.

45. UFA was taken over in 1927 by Alfred Hugenberg, the press baron and leader of the nationalist DNVP and strong supporter of Hitler. After the Nazis came to power in 1933 UFA formed the backbone of Goebbels's propaganda effort in film.

46. The somewhat obscure implication of this statement is that the German censors should not have tried to ban the film as their ban was both unnecessary and counterproductive.

47. Another neologism by E, this time derived from the English word 'star'. In the 20s E worked largely without professional actors. Balázs, by contrast, insisted on the importance of great actors: See 'Nur Stars' [Only Stars], *Filmtechnik*, 1926/7, p. 126.

48. The 'iron five' (*zheleznaya pyatërka*) were E's assistants: Grigori Alexandrov, Maxim Strauch, M. Gomorov, A. Levshin and A. Antonov, who wore striped shirts during the filming in Odessa. See: H. Marshall (ed.), *The Battleship Potemkin*, New York, 1978, pp. 63-7.

49. See 1924, n. 1.

50. Quotation from Isaak Babel's 'The Death of Dolgushov', one of his *Red Cavalry* stories: I. Babel, *Collected Stories*, Harmondsworth, 1961, p. 76. See 1928, n. 5.

51. E analyses this sequence in '"Eh!" On the Purity of Film Language'. See below, pp. 000-000.

52. This phrase was used at that time by LEF and others to denote straightforward montage that clarified rather than obscured.

53. Valerian V. Osinsky (1887-1938), journalist, diplomat, Party functionary and one of the leading organisers of the October Revolution.

54. *The Ten Commandments* (USA, 1923) was directed by Cecil B. DeMille.

55. Source: 'Dva cherepa Aleksandra Makedonskogo', *Novyi zritel'*, 31 August 1926, p. 10.

56. A member of an evangelical sect that emerged among the peasantry in southern Russia in the 1860s.

57. *Our Hospitality* (USA, 1923), starring Buster Keaton, involved a paddle-steamer called 'Our Hospitality'.

58. *The Magnanimous Cuckold* (*Velikodushnyi rogonosets*), a play by Fernand Crommelynck (1888-1970), was first produced by Meyerhold in April 1922.
59. See 1923, n. 2.
60. Meyerhold's 1923 version of Marcel Martinet's *La Nuit* was entitled *Earth Rampant* (*Zemlya dybom*).
61. See 1924, n. 21.
62. Evgeni L. Nikolai (1880-1951), Soviet physicist who worked on the dynamics of solids.
63. Nikolai R. Erdman's (1902-70) *The Warrant* (*Mandat*) was produced by Meyerhold in 1925.
64. The dances in Meyerhold's 1924 production of *Give Us Europe!* (*Daësh' Evropu!*) by Ehrenburg and Kellermann were choreographed by Kasyan Ya. Goleizovsky (1892-1970).
65. The actors in Meyerhold's 1924 production of Ostrovsky's *The Forest* (*Les*) wore coloured wigs.
66. Tretyakov's *Roar, China!* (*Rychi, Kitai!*) was produced at the Meyerhold Theatre in 1926. *The Storm* (*Shtorm*) by Vladimir N. Bill-Belotserkovsky (1885-1970) was produced at the Moscow Trade Union Theatre in 1925. *The Meringue* (*Vozdushnyi pirog*) by Boris S. Romashov (1895-1958) was the most successful play in the 1925 Moscow theatre season.
67. Source: 'Germanskaya kinematografiya. Iz putevykh vpechatlenii', *Vestnik rabotnikov iskusstv*, 1926, no. 10 (October), pp. 8-9.
68. Films by Fritz Lang. See above, nn. 44 and 32.
69. *The Chronicles of the Grey House* (*Zur Chronik von Grieshuus*) (Germany, 1925) was based on the story by Theodor Storm.
70. *The Last Laugh* (*Der letzte Mann*) (Germany, 1924) was directed by F.W. Murnau (1888-1931).
71. *The Fire* (*Das Feuer*) (Germany, 1924) starred Asta Nielsen.
72. See above, n. 32.
73. *Waltz Dream* (*Ein Walzertraum*) (Germany, 1925) was directed by Ludwig Berger.
74. Russian: *agitka*: a short punchy film with a clear and simple political message usually related to a single issue, a genre first developed during the Soviet Civil War for use on the fleet of agit-trains. See: R. Taylor, 'A Medium for the Masses: Agitation in the Soviet Civil War', *Soviet Studies*, 22 (1970/1), no. 4 (April 1971), pp.561-74; and R. Taylor, 'The Birth of the Soviet Cinema', in: A. Gleeson, R. Stites and P. Kenez (eds), *Bolshevik Culture: Experiment and Order in the Russian Revolution*, Bloomington, Ind., 1985, pp. 192-202.
75. Thea von Harbou (1888-1954), then wife of Fritz Lang, was the scriptwriter for his German films including *Metropolis*.
76. Kuleshov: see 1924, n. 7. *The Death Ray* (*Luch smerti*) (USSR, 1925), from a script by Pudovkin, was Kuleshov's fourth film.
77. The story of *Potemkin*'s path through the German censorship is told in: G. Kühn, K. Tümmler and W. Wimmer (eds), *Film und revolutionäre Arbeiterbewegung in Deutschland, 1918-1932* [Film and the Revolutionary Workers' Movement in Germany, 1918-1932], Berlin, GDR, 1975, pp. 323-69.

1927

1. Source: 'Daësh' Gosplan', *Kino-Front*, 1927, no. 13/14 (December), pp. 6-8. The title has echoes of the Meyerhold production of *Give Us Europe!* (see 1926, n. 64).
2. Gosplan is the central state planning organisation for the USSR.
3. Thomas H. Ince (1882-1924), American film producer and director, insisted on detailed and tightly structured shooting scripts for all his films, thus enabling different directors to shoot different sequences at the same time.
4. Boris V. Barnet (1902-65) made *Moscow in October* (*Moskva v Oktyabre*) (USSR, 1927) for the tenth anniversary of the October Revolution. E's *October* and *The End of St Petersburg*, directed by Vsevolod I. Pudovkin (1893-1953), were made for the same purpose.
5. *Chërnyi kabinet*: the postal censorship office in tsarist Russia.
6. The working-class district of Moscow that played an important part in the events of 1905.
7. Nina F. Agadzhanova-Shutko (1889-1974) wrote the scripts for, among others, *The Battleship Potemkin* and Pudovkin's *The Deserter*.
8. E returned to this theme in 1938-9.
9. Sovkino made several unsuccessful attempts to film the Civil War novel *The Iron Torrent* by Alexander S. Serafimovich (1863-1949).

1928

1. Source: 'Nasha anketa sredi deyatelei kino', *Na literaturnom postu*, 1928, no. 1 (January), pp. 71-3.
2. Emile Zola (1840-1902), French novelist and dramatist, exponent of ruthless naturalism. The titles cited by Eisenstein in this article are of novels in the Rougon-Macquart cycle.
3. *The Storm of the Heavens* (*Shturm neba*) was a working title for *The New Babylon* (*Novyi Vavilon*), directed by Grigori Kozintsev and Leonid Trauberg (USSR, 1929).
4. See 1927, n. 9.
5. E had been planning a film version of the collection of Civil War short stories entitled *The Red Cavalry* by Isaak Babel (1894-1939). See 1926, n. 50.
6. Sofia Z. Fedorchenko (1888-1959), Russian writer best known for her collection of Civil War essays entitled *A People at War* [Narod na voine].
7. Probably a reference to the article 'Béla Forgets the Scissors' (see above, pp. 77-81). Although that appeared in *Kino*, the piece by Balázs to which it was a response, 'The Future of Film' [O budushchem fil'my] was published in *Kino-gazeta* on 6 July 1926.
8. Vyacheslav Ya. Shishkov (1873-1945), Russian novelist. The reference is to characters in his novel *Vataga*.
9. Ivan S. Kondurushkin's *Chastnyi kapital pered sovetskim sudom* was published in Moscow in 1927.
10. Davydov's *Maklochane*, Leningrad, 1926, and Burov's *Derevnya na perelome*, Moscow, 1926, were two of the sources that provided Eisenstein with material and inspiration for *The General Line*.
11. Fyodor V. Gladkov's (1883-1958) *Cement* [Tsement] was published in Moscow in 1925.
12. *A Woman of Paris* (USA, 1923) starred Charlie Chaplin and was much discussed by Soviet film-makers in the 1920s.

13. The reference is to German Expressionist films like *The Cabinet of Dr Caligari*. See 1922, n. 15.
14. Eisenstein worked with Babel (see above, n. 5) in the summer of 1925 on a screen adaptation of the latter's collection of short stories *Benya Krik*, which was to be filmed at the same time as the project that became known as *The Battleship Potemkin*. *Benya Krik* never came to fruition.
15. The slogan originated during the French Revolution.
16. Vladimir I. Blyum, Soviet film critic in the 1920s.
17. Mezhrabpom was a joint-stock company producing popular commercially orientated films for audiences both at home and, through its links with Prometheus-Film in Berlin, abroad: one example is *The Bear's Wedding*, see 1926, n. 17. The Lenin quotation comes from his 'Directive on Cinema' of 17 January 1922, translated in Taylor and Christie, *The Film Factory*, pp. 56.
18. Source: 'Chego my zhdëm ot partsoveshchaniya po voprosam kino', *Sovetskii ekran*, 3 January 1928, p. 6. The first Party Conference on Cinema was originally scheduled for January 1928 but was postponed and eventually held from 15 to 21 March 1928.
19. Source: 'Nash *Oktyabr'*. Po tu storonu igrovoi i neigrovoi', *Kino*, 13 and 20 March 1928. The original manuscript is dated 8 March 1928.
20. *Broken Blossoms* (USA, 1919) was directed by D.W. Griffith and starred Lillian Gish.
21. *Zaum* is usually translated as 'trans-sense', denoting the idea of a suprarational force.
22. *Kamernost'*: 'chamber' quality, as opposed to the monumentally epic.
23. Both directed by Pudovkin in 1926 and 1927 respectively.
24. *A Sixth Part of the World* (*Shestaya chast' mira*) (USSR, 1926) was a feature-length documentary directed by Dziga Vertov.
25. *The Eleventh Year* (*Odinnadtsatyi*) (USSR, 1928) was also directed by Vertov.
26. *The Diplomatic Bag* (*Sumka dipkur'era*) (USSR, 1927) and *Zvenigora* (USSR, 1928) were both directed by the Ukrainian film-maker Alexander P. Dovzhenko (1894-1956).
27. A quotation from Griboyedov's play *Woe from Wit* (*Gore ot uma*).
28. See 1926, n. 40.
29. Runich and Khudoleyev were two actors in pre-Revolutionary Russian films.
30. Lavr G. Kornilov (1870-1918) was one of the leading generals on the White side in the Civil War.
31. Alexei V. Efimov (b. 1896), Soviet historian.
32. Source: 'Za "rabochii boevik"', *Revolyutsiya i kul'tura*, 1928, no. 3/4 (March/April), pp. 52-6.
33. The Russian word *golovomoika* can also mean a 'dressing down'.
34. *Red Partisans* (*Krasnye partizany*) (USSR, 1924) was produced by Sevzapkino, Leningrad and directed by Vyacheslav K. Viskovsky (1881-1933).
35. *The Red Web* (*Krasnyi gaz*) (USSR, 1924) was produced by Goskino, Siberia and directed by I. Kalabukhov.
36. *Bulat-Batyr* (USSR, 1927) was directed by Yuri V. Tarich (1885-1967).
37. *The Poet and the Tsar* (*Poet i tsar'*) (USSR, 1927) was directed by Vladimir R. Gardin (1877-1965) and based on Pushkin's last years. *House of Ice* (*Ledyanoi dom*) (USSR, 1928) and *The Lame Gentleman* (*Khromoi barin*) (USSR, 1928) were both directed by Konstantin Eggert for Mezhrabpom. *The Lame Gentleman* was not released until February 1929.
38. *Monsieur Beaucaire* (USA, 1924) starred Rudolph Valentino.
39. *The Little Red Devils* (*Krasnye d'yavolyata*) (USSR, 1923) was directed in Georgia by Ivan N. Perestiani (1870-1959).

40. *The Three Millions Trial (Protsess o trëkh millionakh)* (USSR, 1926) was a satire on the West directed by Protazanov (see 1922, n. 10).
41. *Potholes (Ukhaby)* (USSR, 1927) was directed by Abram M. Room (1894-1976) and scripted by him and Viktor B. Shklovsky (1893-1985). *Lace (Kruzheva)* (USSR, 1928) was directed by Sergei Yutkevich: see 1922, n. 1.
42. This manifesto was first published in an authorised German translation as: 'Achtung! Goldgrube! Gedanken über die Zukunft des Hörfilms' in *Die Lichtbildbühne* on 28 July 1928. The Russian original was first published as 'Zayavka' in *Zhizn' iskusstva*, 5 August 1928, pp. 6-9, from which this has been translated, and *Sovetskii ekran* on 7 August 1928. An English translation appeared under the title 'The Sound Film. A Statement from USSR' in *Close Up*, October 1928, pp. 10-13. Jay Leyda included his own version as 'A Statement' in *Film Form*, pp. 257-9. Grigori V. Alexandrov (1903-83) was E's chief assistant from *The Strike* to *¡Que Viva México!* and later became the leading exponent of the Soviet musical comedy genre. For Pudovkin, see 1927, n. 4.
43. Source: 'Nezhdannyi styk', *Zhizn' iskusstva*, 19 August 1928, pp. 6-9. Translated by Jay Leyda as 'The Unexpected' in *Film Form*, pp. 18-27.
44. The Japanese Kabuki theatre, the popular offshoot of No, visited the USSR in 1928 with the director, actor and dramatist Itakawa Sadanji (1880-1940).
45. The reference is to Meyerhold's notion of an anti-illusionist 'theatre of convention' [*uslovnyi teatr*] as opposed to Stanislavsky's 'theatre of experience' [*teatr perezhivanii*].
46. *Lyubov Yarovaya* [Spring Love], a play by K.A. Trenyov (1876-1945), produced in 1926. *A Life for the Tsar (Zhizn' za tsarya)* was an opera written in 1836 by Mikhail I. Glinka (1804-57) and known since the Revolution as *Ivan Susanin*.
47. *The Collapse (Razlom)*, a play written in 1927 by Boris A. Lavrenyov (1891-1959) and set in the Civil War. *Armoured Train 14-69 (Bronepoezd 14-69)*, also set in the Civil War, was written in 1922 by Vsevolod V. Ivanov (1895-1963).
48. At that time the Bolshoi Theatre symbolised for E everything that was stuffy and outmoded. In 1940 he was to produce Wagner's *Die Walküre* there.
49. One of the most popular plays in the Kabuki repertoire, written in 1748 by Takedo Idsumo, and performed during the 1928 visit to Moscow. The play was also the origin of the Mizoguchi film *The Loyal 47 Ronin* (Japan, 1941-2).
50. See above, n. 45.
51. Quoted from 'The Montage of Attractions': see above, pp. 33-38.
52. An ironic reference to Meyerhold's experiments.
53. Ivan A. Baudouin de Courtenay (1845-1929) was a prominent comparative philologist, a precursor of structural linguistics, who was influential on the Russian Formalist school.
54. See above, pp. 000-000.
55. Monty Banks (pseudonym of Mario Bianchi) (1897-1950) was an Italian-born comic dancer who appeared in numerous British and American films and was once married to Gracie Fields.
56. *The Kid* (USA, 1920) and *The Gold Rush* (USA, 1925).
57. The title of this piece is a reference to Dziga Vertov's documentary film *The Eleventh Year*: see above, n. 25. Source: S.M. Eizenshtein and G.V. Aleksandrov, 'Dvenadtsatyi', *Sovetskii ekran*, 6 November 1928, pp. 4-5. For Alexandrov, see above, n. 42.
58. V.I. Lenin, *Sobranie sochinenii* [Collected Works], vol. XIII, p. 40.
59. i.e. in the Paris Commune.
60. The references are to Pudovkin's *Storm over Asia (Potomok Chingis-khana* – the literal translation being 'The heir to Genghis-Khan', but the film was given a catchier title, as were other Soviet films of the period, when released in Germany) (USSR, 1929), Dovzhenko's *Zvenigora* (see above, n. 26) and the FEKS film *The New*

Babylon (see above, n. 3), set in Paris.
61. The day in 1905 that has become known as 'Bloody Sunday', when a crowd of peaceful demonstrators led by Father Gapon was shot down on its way to petition the Tsar.
62. *Lev Tolstoy and the Russia of Nicholas II* (*Rossiya Nikolaya II i Lev Tolstoi*) (USSR, 1928) was a compilation film directed by Esfir Shub (1894-1949).
63. Literally 'Komsomol Truth', the organ of the Komsomol or Communist Youth League.
64. Source: 'Instruktorsko-issledovatel'skaya masterskaya pri GTK. Beseda s rukovoditelem masterskoi S.M. Eizenshtein', *Sovetskii ekran*, 27 November 1928, p. 4.
65. See 1926, n. 6.

1929

1. Source: Chapter 11, 'Razgovor s Eizenshteinom o zvuchashchem kino', in: V.A. Sol'skii (ed.), *Zvuchashchee kino* [Sound Cinema], Moscow, 1929, pp. 80-6. The exact date of the interview is not known but is assumed to have been late 1928 or early 1929. The following chapter consisted of a similar interview with one of E's co-authors of the 'Statement on Sound' (pp. 113-114 above), Vsevolod Pudovkin.
2. Edmund Meisel (1874-1930), Austrian-born violinist in the Berlin Philharmonic Orchestra, composer for the Deutsches Theater under Max Reinhardt and for Prometheus-Film. Wrote the music for several films, including *Potemkin* and *October* in their German release versions.
3. Source: 'O forme stsenariya', *Byulleten' kinokontory torgpredstva SSSR v Germanii* (Berlin, 1929), no. 1/2 (January/February), pp. 29-32. A partial translation of this piece appeared as 'A Russian View of Scenarios' in the *New York Times*, 30 March 1930. The first sentence is a quotation from 'Literature and Cinema: Reply to a Questionnaire', p. 98 above.
4. The German term for a shooting script.
5. *The General Line* (*General'naya liniya*) was the working and original release title for E's film about the advantages of collectivisation, which he began in 1926. He broke off work on the film to make *October* for the tenth anniversary of the October Revolution and by the time *The General Line* was eventually completed Party policy had changed. The film was therefore generally released as *The Old and the New* (*Staroe i novoe*) on the twelfth anniversary of the Revolution, 7 November 1929.
6. Source: L. Kozlov, 'Eizenshtein i Dovzhenko', *Voprosy kinoiskusstva*, no. 9 (Moscow, 1966), pp. 308-12. The complete text, with corrections, was supplied by Naum Kleiman. The original is dated 7/8 February 1929. *The Arsenal* (*Arsenal*), directed by Dovzhenko (see 1928, n. 26), was released in Kiev on 25 February 1929 and in Moscow on 26 March.
7. The Russian word *forma* can mean both 'form' and 'uniform'.
8. The significance of the distinction made by E here is that Dovzhenko is not just a soldier of the Revolution but a man deeply committed to its ideals.
9. *The End of St Petersburg* (*Konets Sankt-Peterburga*) was made by Pudovkin in 1927 for the tenth anniversary of the October Revolution.
10. These were Dovzhenko's two previous films: see 1928, n. 26. It was at the screening of *Zvenigora* for Glavrepertkom on 23 December 1927 that E first met Dovzhenko.
11. Source: 'Za kadrom', written as a postscript to: N. Kaufman, *Yaponskoe kino* [Japanese Cinema], Moscow, 1929, pp. 72-92. Translated by Leyda as 'The Cinematographic Principle and the Ideogram' in *Film Form*, pp. 28-44.

12. Throughout this piece E uses the Russian *ieroglif* (hieroglyph) rather than *ideogramma* (ideogram).
13. Also known as *haiku*. Historically the *haiku* was the first line of a *tanka*, literally a 'short song'.
14. Toshushai Sharaku, Japanese No actor and painter, produced 140 pictures of Kabuki actors between May 1794 and February 1795. Little is known of him apart from this, except that he died in 1801.
15. Alexander R. Luria (1902-77) was a noted Russian psychologist and pioneer of modern neuropsychology, whose best-known works include *The Nature of Human Conflicts* and *The Mind of a Mnemonist*.
16. The words of a popular Russian song in the 1920s.
17. Lev Kuleshov's theory of montage is expounded at length in his book *Iskusstvo kino* [The Art of Cinema], Moscow, 1929. This extract is from p. 100.
18. *The Happy Canary* (*Vesëlaya kanareika*) (USSR, 1929) was directed by Kuleshov.
19. The Tretyakov Gallery is Moscow's principal museum of Russian art. The collection assembled by Sergei Shchukin before 1917 became the First Museum of Modern Western Painting after the Revolution. In 1923 it was merged with the Second Museum of Modern Western Painting, based on the collection of the Morozov brothers, housed in the Morozov mansion and called the Shchukin State Museum of Modern Western Art. In 1948 the Museum was closed and the collections shared between the Hermitage in Leningrad and the Pushkin Gallery in Moscow.
20. A magician was then performing at the Moscow Hermitage music-hall under the name Dante.
21. The 'black men' in Kabuki theatre serve as prompters and stage-hands and derive their name, and their invisibility, from their black clothes.
22. *Narukami*, one of the most popular plays in the Kabuki repertoire, was written by Suuti Hantsuro. For Sadanji, see 1928, n. 44.
23. i.e. *The General Line*.
24. See 1928, n. 49.
25. *The Thief of Bagdad* (USA, 1924), starred Douglas Fairbanks. *Zvenigora* (USSR, 1928) was directed by Dovzhenko.
26. *The Man with the Movie Camera* (*Chelovek s kinoapparatom*) (USSR, 1929) was directed by Dziga Vertov.
27. *The Fall of the House of Usher* (*La Chute de la maison Usher*) (France, 1928) was made by the Polish-born French director and theorist, Jean Epstein (1897-1953). Henri Langlois described the film as 'the cinematic equivalent of a Debussy creation'.
28. The reference is to 'An Unexpected Juncture': see above, pp. 115-122.
29. Source: 'Perspektivy', *Iskusstvo*, 1929, no. 1/2, pp. 116-22, dated 2 March 1929. Translated by Jay Leyda as 'Perspectives' in *Film Essays*, pp. 35-47. A slightly different version appeared as 'Der Film der Zukunft' in *Vossische Zeitung*, 15 September 1929. See below, n. 50.
30. Published in Moscow in 1914.
31. This was the slogan of LEF.
32. G. Berkeley, 'Introduction' to *A Treatise Concerning the Principles of Human Knowledge*, 1710, reprinted in: A.A. Luce and T.E. Jessop (eds), *The Works of George Berkeley, Bishop of Cloyne*, London, 1949, vol. 2, p. 38.
33. Loc cit.
34. Ibid., p. 40.
35. Translated as 'Fundamental Problems of Marxism' in: *Selected Philosophical Works*, vol. 3, Moscow, 1976, p. 152. The reference is to the German ethnographer, Karl Steinen (1855-1929), whose work *Unter den Naturvölkern Zentral-*

Brasiliens [Among the Primitive Peoples of Central Brasil], Berlin, 1894, had been translated into Russian.

36. *The Rails Are Humming (Rel'sy gudyat)* was a play written in 1927 by Vladimir M. Kirshon (1902-38), a leading member of RAPP, whose pamphlet, *Na kinopostu* [On Cinema Watch], Moscow, 1928, published to coincide with the First Party Conference on Cinema in March 1928, was highly critical of Soviet cinema. For *The Iron Torrent* see 1927, n. 9.

37. Leonid N. Andreyev (1871-1919), Russian writer who moved after the 1905 Revolution from Gorky's critical realist 'Znanie' circle to Idealism and then, after 1917, to anti-Bolshevik activity in Finnish exile. He was one of the first Russian intellectuals to recognise the significance of cinema. See Taylor and Christie, pp. 27-31 and 37-8.

38. The Kellogg Pact, signed in Paris in August 1928, formally condemned war as an instrument of national policy. Initially signed by nine countries, sixty-five eventually adhered to it, including Germany, the USA and the USSR, although the Soviet government later came to interpret the Pact as an attempt by the capitalist powers to encircle the USSR.

39. This paragraph did not appear in the original published version.

40. 'Reflexology' centred on the view that all psychological phenomena had objective physical causes. It was associated above all with the ideas of V.M. Bekhterev: see 1926, n. 6.

41. G.V. Plekhanov, 'Art and Social Life', in: *Selected Philosophical Works*, vol. 5, Moscow, 1981, p. 654. The work Plekhanov is quoting by the French historian and philosopher Ernest Renan (1823-92) is *La Réforme intellectuelle et morale de la France* [The Intellectual and Moral Reformation of France], Paris, 1871.

42. This appears to be a misquotation of Genesis 4: 17: 'And Cain knew his wife; and she conceived, and bare Enoch . . . .' Sarah was, after all, *Abraham's* wife. I am indebted to Mrs Phyllis Hancock for tracing this quotation.

43. Yulian V. Sokhotsky (1842-1929), Professor of Mathematics at the University of St Petersburg and author of a textbook on higher algebra. Camille Desmoulins (1760-94), French revolutionary and journalist. Georges Jacques Danton (1759-94), French revolutionary known for his powerful oratory. Léon Gambetta (1838-82), radical French lawyer, politician and orator, who declared the Third French Republic in 1870 and was then forced to flee the siege of Paris in a balloon, became one of the leading republican politicians. Moisei M. Volodarsky (pseudonym of Moisei M. Goldstein, 1891-1918), leading Bolshevik of Ukrainian Jewish origin, propaganda commissar on the Rumanian front, was murdered by Right Socialist Revolutionaries in 1918.

44. Emile Jaques-Dalcroze (1865-1950), Swiss musician and composer who founded the system of eurhythmics.

45. There is a play on words in this paragraph: the Russian *pul't* means 'desk', while *katapul't* means a 'catapult'.

46. 'In the beginning was the Word and the Word was with God and the Word was God' St John 1: 1.

47. A polemical reference to the debate launched by RAPP in 1927 on the rounded portrayal of the new Soviet 'living man'.

48. See 1922, n. 6.

49. From the report on agriculture to the Fifteenth Party Congress in December 1927 delivered by Vyacheslav M. Molotov (pseudonym of V.M. Skryabin, 1890-1986). This section has been omitted from Leyda's translation.

50. E provided a different ending for the version of this piece printed in *Vossische Zeitung* on 15 December 1929. The full text of this alternative ending is given in: H.-J. Schlegel (ed.), *Sergej M. Eisenstein: Schriften 3*, Munich, 1975, pp. 350-1.

51. This piece, written by E in German, exists in two typescripts, one dated 'Moscow,

29 April 1929' and the other dated 'Zurich, 29 November 1929'. It has not been published in the USSR. Leyda translated and included it as 'A Dialectic Approach to Film Form' (a change of title approved by E) in *Film Form*, pp. 45-63. It was also published in *Close Up*, September 1929. This translation has been done from Schlegel, vol. 3, pp. 200-25, with some alterations established by François Albera, to whom I am extremely grateful.

52. Kazimir S. Malevich (1887-1935), Russian painter and founder of Suprematism. In an unpublished diary entry for 1929 E described Malevich's Suprematism as 'a mixture of mysticism and mystification'. Wilhelm von Kaulbach (1805-74), German painter and graphic artist, known for his neo-classical monumental paintings; court painter to King Ludwig I of Bavaria from 1837. Alexander Archipenko (also Arkhipenko) (1887-1964), Ukrainian-born American sculptor, associated with Cubism and the revival of polychromy.

53. The following line was deleted by E from the original typescript at this point: 'The temporal form of this tension (the phases of tension) is rhythm.'

54. Ludwig Klages (1872-1956), German philosopher and founder of biocentric metaphysics, developed a methodology for a 'science of expression'. His major work, *Der Geist als Widersacher der Seele* [The Spirit as Antagonist to the Soul] was published in three volumes between 1929 and 1932. See above, p. 000.

55. G. Wallas, *The Great Society, A Psychological Analysis*, London, 1914, p. 101.

56. Here E is drawing on the ideas of the Formalist school of literary criticism and, above all, on: Yu. Tynyanov, *Problema stikhotvornogo yazyka* [The Problem of Poetic Language], Leningrad, 1924.

57. J.W. von Goethe, *Conversations of Goethe with Eckermann*, London, 1930, p. 303. The conversation took place on 23 March 1829: 'I have found a paper of mine among other things,' said Goethe today, 'in which I call architecture "petrified music".' A similar metaphor is employed by Schelling in his *Philosophie der Kunst* [The Philosophy of Art], where he refers to architecture as 'frozen music'.

58. Deleted from the original typescript: 'just as we lay (unwrap) bricks'.

59. For Léger, see 1926, n. 37. For Suprematism, see above, n. 52.

60. Honoré Daumier (1808-79), French caricaturist and lithographer, known for his bitter social and political satire. Henri de Toulouse-Lautrec (1864-1901), French painter and graphic artist. 'Cissy Loftus', dating from 1894, depicts an eighteen-year-old Glasgow singer, Marie-Cecilia McCarthy, who played male parts on stage: see J. Adhémar, *Toulouse-Lautrec: His Complete Lithographs and Drypoints*, London, 1965, pl. 105.

61. This painting is by the Italian Giacomo Balla (1871-1958) who was closely associated with Italian Futurism.

62. See above, n. 14.

63. See above, pp. 000-000.

64. A page of the original typescript appears to be missing at this point.

65. *The Living Corpse (Zhivoi trup)* (USSR, 1929) was a Soviet-German co-production, based on the eponymous drama by Lev Tolstoy and directed by Fyodor A. Otsep (1895-1945).

66. i.e. *Lev Tolstoy and the Russia of Nicholas II*.

67. *The Bay of Death (Bukhta smerti)* (USSR, 1926) was directed by Abram M. Room (1894-1976).

68. In French in the original: literally, 'let us return to our sheep' and metaphorically, 'let us go back to what we were talking about'. An old French catchphrase, used by Rabelais, from whom E probably took it.

69. A remark attributed to Lenin by Lunacharsky and recalled in: G.M. Boltyanskii, *Lenin o kino* [Lenin on Cinema], Moscow, 1925, pp. 16-17.

70. Only Part I of this essay, written in Moscow in August and September 1929, was published in Russian in E's lifetime as 'Kino chetyrëkh izmerenii' [Four-Dimen-

sional Cinema'] in *Kino*, 27 August 1929. This appeared in English as 'The Fourth Dimension in the Kino' in *Close Up*, March 1930. Part II, written in London in November and December 1929, appeared for the first time in English as 'The Fourth Dimension in the Kino: II' in *Close Up*, April 1930. Jay Leyda re-translated both as 'The Filmic Fourth Dimension' and 'Methods of Montage' respectively in *Film Form*, pp. 64-71 and 72-83. The complete piece was published in Russian for the first time only in 1964 in *Izbrannye proizvedeniya* [Selected Works], vol. 2, pp. 45-59, as 'Chetvërtoe izmerenie v kino', which is the title given to the present translation, 'The Fourth Dimension in Cinema'.

71. See above, p. 117.
72. The Russian word here is *kuski*, plural of *kusok*, which may also be translated as a 'fragment', 'piece' or 'strip'. See Translator's Note, p. 25.
73. In English in the original.
74. E is using 'Left' here to denote 'avant-garde' composers generally. Claude Debussy (1862-1918) was a French composer, Alexander N. Scriabin (also Skryabin) (1871-1915) was a Russian pianist and composer.
75. A. Einstein, *Relativity: The Special and the General Theory*, London, 1920, p. 65 (the opening sentence of Ch. XVII, 'Minkowski's Four-Dimensional Space'). This quotation does not appear in the published Russian text.
76. See above, p. 119.
77. W. Stekel was a German psychologist and psychoanalyst of the Freudian school. E's quotation is presumably from *Nervöse Angstzustände und ihre Behandlung* [Nervous Anxiety States and Their Treatment], 3rd edn, Berlin/Vienna, 1921.
78. *Lezginka*: a Caucasian dance.
79. See 1928, n. 60.
80. In English in the original.
81. A play on words between the Russian *tok*, meaning a 'stream' and *potok*, meaning a 'torrent'.
82. See above, n. 52.
83. The quotation is from Lenin's 'Conspectus of Hegel's *Science of Logic*' and appears to be a paraphrase of the section reproduced in *Collected Works*, vol. 38, Moscow, 1961, p. 132.
84. E is making a cross-reference here to 'Perspectives': see above, pp. 151-160.

Photograph sent from Mexico to Ivor Montagu and inscribed 'Speaks for itself and makes people jealous!'

1930

1. Source: 'Les Principes du nouveau cinéma russe', *Revue du cinéma*, 1930, no. 9 (April), pp. 16-27. This is the text of the lecture given by E at the Sorbonne in Paris on 17 February 1930. The lecture was intended as an accompaniment to a showing of *The General Line* but, four hours before the performance, the film was banned by the police. Similar lectures were delivered by E during his visits to Great Britain and the United States.

2. The Society of Friends of Soviet Cinema (*Obshchestvo druzei sovetskogo kino* or *ODSK*) was founded in 1926 in an attempt to involve film audiences in the development of Soviet cinema. Its first head was Felix Dzerzhinsky, who was also head of the secret police.

3. *Ten Days That Shook the World* was the original release title of *October* in Germany and derived from the eye-witness account of the Revolution written by John Reed.

4. This project never came to fruition.

5. Valeri Inkizhinov played the leading role in Pudovkin's *Storm over Asia*. See 1928, n. 60.

6. *Bed and Sofa* was the release title in the West of *Third Meshchanskaya Street* (*Tret'ya Meshchanskaya*) (USSR, 1927), directed by Abram Room.

7. E signed a contract with Paramount, which was announced on 1 May 1930, and left almost immediately for the United States, where he was received with the usual razzmatazz. This newspaper report of his visit to New York is all too typical and contrasts with the more serious treatment E received from German newspapers. The British press ignored his visit to London and Cambridge and the only French newspaper to report his presence in Paris was the Communist Party daily *L'Humanité*. Source: Mason Ham, 'Rin-Tin-Tin Does His Tricks for Noted Russian Movie Man', *Boston Herald*, 27 May 1930.

8. This is the text of a lecture delivered by E on 17 September 1930 to a meeting organised by the Technicians Branch of the Academy of Motion Picture Arts and Sciences in Hollywood. The English-language text as delivered in Hollywood and as printed in *Close Up*, vol. 8, no. 1 (March 1931), pp. 3-16, and no. 2 (June 1931), pp. 91-4, warts and all, conveys the flavour of the original. Leyda has produced a more polished version in *Film Essays*, pp. 48-65. I have also tried to clarify the original.

9. Primo Carnera (1906-67), Italian world heavyweight boxing champion 1933-4, was the heaviest of all world champions and was also famous for his great height. He appeared in *On the Waterfront* (USA, 1954) as a dockside hoodlum.

10. This memorandum was compiled by Cowan specifically for the discussion on 17 September 1930 and a copy is held in the library of the Academy of Motion Picture Arts and Sciences, Hollywood.

11. Loyd A. Jones, 'Rectangle Proportions in Pictorial Composition', *Journal of the Society of Motion Picture Engineers*, January 1930. This whole issue was devoted to a discussion of the problem of screen size and ratio.

12. Jean Fouquet (c. 1415-c. 1480), French painter of portraits and miniatures.

13. Kazusika Hokusai (1760-1849), Japanese painter and engraver, was particularly noted for his views of Mount Fuji.

14. Miles and, later, Howell and Bubray, Lane, Westerberg, Dieterich, Rayton and Sponable were participants in the discussions.

15. King Vidor (1894-1982), American film director, was known at that time for *The Big Parade* (USA, 1925) and *The Crowd* (USA, 1928).

16. *Romance sentimentale* (France, 1930) was a short film directed by Grigori Alexandrov in consultation with E.

1932

1. Source: 'Odolzhaites'!', *Proletarskoe kino*, 1932, no. 17/18 (October), pp. 19-29. The title refers to a recurrent phrase in Gogol's short story *How Ivan Ivanovich Quarrelled with Ivan Nikiforovich*. Published as 'Detective Work in the GIK', 'Cinematography *with* Tears' and 'An American Tragedy' in *Close Up*, December 1932, March 1933 and June 1933. Leyda has translated this piece as 'A Course in Treatment' in *Film Form*, pp. 84-107.

2. 'Nepman' was the pejorative term used for the members of the petty bourgeoisie that emerged under the New Economic Policy in the 1920s.

3. Repertkom was the committee responsible for cinema and theatre censorship.

4. *The Mysteries of Udolpho*, a novel by the English writer Ann Radcliffe (1764-1823).

5. Quotation from Lenin's 'What "The Friends of the People" Are' (1894), reprinted in: *Collected Works*, vol. 1, pp. 129-332.

6. Alexandre Dumas *père* (1802-70), French writer, author of historical novels like *The Count of Monte Cristo*. Alexandre Dumas *fils* (1824-95), his son, dramatist and author of *La Dame aux camélias*.

7. Pierre-Dominique Toussaint L'Ouverture (1743-1803), one of the leaders of the black revolt against French rule in Haiti, became Governor-General of the island in 1798. He was summoned to France by Napoleon, incarcerated and died in prison. In 1932 E signed a contract with Soyuzkino for a film based on the novel *The Black Consul* (*Chërnyi konsul*) by Anatoly K. Vinogradov (1888-1946) but it was never started.

8. Thomas-Alexandre Dumas (d. 1803) was in fact Dumas's father. He was the son of a black mother and served as a general under Napoleon.

9. Eugène de Mirecourt (pseudonym of Charles Jean-Baptiste Jacquot) (1812-80) penned an attack on Dumas *père* under the title *Fabrique de romans: Maison A.C. Dumas et cie.* [The Novel Factory: The House of A.C. Dumas & Co.], Paris, 1845, for which Dumas took him to court.

10. Pierre Béranger (1780-1857), French revolutionary poet and song-writer. There is a play on words here: *nègre* is the French for 'ghost-writer'.

11. The term used by Dumas *père* himself.

12. J. Lucas-Dubreton, *The Fourth Musketeer: The Life of Alexander Dumas*, New York, 1928, p. 145.

13. Vasili I. Kachalov (1875-1948), actor at the Moscow Art Theatre and creator of the role of the Baron in Gorky's *The Lower Depths*. Nikolai P. Batalov (1899-1937), actor at the Moscow Art Theatre who played leading roles in Pudovkin's *The Mother* and Ekk's *The Road to Life* (*Putëvka v zhizn'*) (USSR, 1931). Maxim M. Strauch (also Shtraukh) (1900-74), a childhood friend of E, played the role of the old Jewish porter in Natan Zarkhi's *The Street of Joy* (*Ulitsa radosti*) on the stage of the Moscow Theatre of the Revolution in 1932.

14. Ivan A. Aksionov (1884-1935) was a Soviet poet and specialist in Elizabethan drama, Viktor B. Shklovsky (1893-1985) was a Formalist writer, critic and literary theorist who wrote a number of screenplays and Alexander F. Weltmann (Vel'tman) (1800-70) was a Russian novelist.

15. John Webster (c. 1580-1624) was an English dramatist who is best known for his *The White Devil* and *The Duchess of Malfi*. Natan A. Zarkhi (1900-35) was one of the leading Soviet scriptwriters of the time, working with Pudovkin on *The Mother* and *The End of St Petersburg*. Vladimir M. Wolkenstein (Vol'kenshtein) (1883-1963) was a Soviet author, scriptwriter and theorist, whose book *Dramaturgiya* [Dramaturgy] was published in 1923.

16. See 1926, n. 63.

17. Babel's play *The Sunset* (*Zakat*) was written in 1928 and performed at the Moscow Art Theatre.

18. The subjects of *The Government Inspector* and *Dead Souls* were supposed to have been suggested to Gogol by Pushkin.
19. i.e. Gorky, whose real name was Alexei Maximovich Peshkov.
20. The reference is to Chekhov's short story about the straitjacketing effect of provincial life, *The Man in the Case* (*Chelovek v futlyare*).
21. 'Among People' is a literal translation of the title of the second part of the so-called 'Gorky Trilogy', '*V lyudyakh*': it is often translated as 'Into the World'. E is referring to his negotiations with Paramount during his American sojourn.
22. *An American Tragedy* was the novel by Theodore Dreiser (1871-1945) which E and Ivor Montagu reworked for Paramount. Their script was rejected, the project was handed over to Josef von Sternberg (1894-1969) and the film released in 1931.
23. Ben P. Schulberg (1892-1957) was general manager of Paramount's West Coast production during the negotiations with E.
24. The Russian transliteration of Griffith is 'Griffits', hence the possibility of the play on surnames.
25. Ernst Lubitsch (1892-1947), German-born American director best known for his sophisticated comedies which exemplified 'the Lubitsch touch'.
26. In English in the original.
27. Moera was the Greek goddess of fate.
28. F. Engels, *Socialism, Utopian and Scientific*, trans. E. Aveling, London, 1892, pp. xx-xxi.
29. On 31 March 1932 nine black youths were arrested in Scottsboro, Alabama, and charged with raping two white girls. They were tried, convicted and sentenced to death the following month. After a storm of protest from northern liberals the sentences were commuted to long terms of imprisonment and, after a series of appeals, most of the defendants were eventually released.
30. The reference is presumably to Christ's Sermon on the Mount, Matthew 5: 27, 28: 'Ye have heard that it was said by them of old time, Thou shalt not commit adultery: But I say unto you, That whosoever looketh on a woman to lust after her hath committed adultery with her already in his heart.'
31. Sergei S. Dinamov (1901-39), Soviet specialist in American literature, translated *An American Tragedy* into Russian.
32. *Strange Interlude* was written in 1927 by the American playwright Eugene O'Neill (1888-1953).
33. E is probably here referring to sequences in both films that are visually allusive rather than dictated by the requirements of plot development: in *October*, for instance, the sequence where Kerensky is 'compared' to a peacock or the one where, as he climbs the staircase in the Winter Palace, we see an array of gods, and in *Potemkin* the scene where the stone lion 'roars'.
34. Edouard Dujardin (1861-1949), French writer. *Les Lauriers sont coupés* has been translated into English as *We'll to the Woods No More*, Cambridge, Mass., 1938.
35. Ernst Theodor Amadeus Hoffmann (1776-1822) was one of the leading German Romantic writers. Novalis was the pseudonym of the German Romantic poet Friedrich von Hardenberg (1772-1801). Gérard de Nerval was the pseudonym of the French Romantic writer Gérard Labrunie (1808-55). René Bizet's book was published in Paris in 1928.
36. Valéry Larbaud (1881-1957), French writer.
37. The section in square brackets was deleted by E from the original manuscript before publication.
38. Source: 'V interesakh formy', *Kino*, 12 November 1932.
39. Théophile Gautier (1811-72), French writer and critic.
40. Ibycus was a late sixth-century BC lyric poet. According to legend, he was attacked and killed by robbers. As he lay dying, a flock of cranes flew overhead and Ibycus swore that they would avenge him. The story was the subject of a poem by Schiller.

Mount Ida was, according to classical mythology, part of the range of mountains in southern Phrygia where Paris was exposed to the elements, brought up by shepherds, and fell in love with Oenone. Hence the line in Tennyson's poem *Oenone*, 'Mother Ida, many-fountained Ida'.

41. The reference is to: A.F. Pospishil' (ed.), *Grechesko-russkii slovar'* (Greek-Russian Dictionary), 3rd edn, Kiev, 1901, p. 476.
42. A reference to the pseudonym Alexander M. Chyorny (i.e. 'Black') of the Russian satirist, humorist and poet Alexander M. Glikberg (1880-1933).
43. See 1926, n. 34.
44. These consultants were largely Party appointees placed in studios to keep a watchful eye on film production.
45. Mikhail V. Lomonosov (1711-65), Russian scientist and poet, one of the founders of physical chemistry.
46. K. Marx and F. Engels, *Correspondence 1846-1895*, London, 1936, pp. 510-12.
47. *Lubok*: a Russian peasant woodcut.
48. The reference is to Gogol's short story, *The Nose* (*Nos*).
49. The closing words of Gogol's short story *How Ivan Ivanovich Quarrelled with Ivan Nikiforovich*. See above, n. 1.
50. The reference is to Gogol's play *The Government Inspector*.
51. *Groznyi*: the word used to describe Ivan the Terrible [Ivan Groznyi].
52. E means here that film-makers, regardless of their particular political affiliation, should have an inner commitment to the ideals of the Party.
53. Khlestakov is the main character in *The Government Inspector*.
54. *Labardan* is a nonsense word used repeatedly by Khlestakov.
55. The reference is to a remark by the French statesman, Talleyrand (1754-1838), 'Words were given to man to conceal his own thoughts', which was an ironic paraphrase of the words of Doctor Pancras in Molière's play *Le Mariage forcé*: 'Words were given to man to express his own thoughts.'
56. Marusya, Masha and Maruska are all diminutives of the name Marya.
57. Nikolai N. Strakhov (1828-96), Russian philosopher, publicist and literary critic, friend and first biographer of Dostoyevsky.

1933

1. Source: 'Cherez revolyutsiyu k iskusstvu – cherez iskusstvo k revolyutsii', *Sovetskoe kino*, 1933, no. 1/2 (January/February), pp. 34-6. Listed by Leyda in *Film Essays* as 'October and Art'.
2. All three plays were produced by E at Proletkult in 1923.
3. E's article was published alongside 'Gargantua Is Growing' ['Gargantyua rastët'], the article by the the critic Evgeni Weissman (also Veisman) to which it was a response. Gargantua and Pantagruel were characters in the satirical romance *The History of Gargantua and Pantagruel* by François Rabelais (c. 1494-1553). Gargantua was distinguished by his enormous size and voracious appetite, while Pantagruel, his son and the last of the giants, was noted for his strength. Weissman and E are using these names to characterise Soviet film theory: Weissman's article is essentially a critique of E's notion of 'inner monologue' that was developed in 'Beyond the Shot' (see above, pp. 138-150) and 'Help Yourself!' (see above, pp. 219-237). Source: 'Roditsya Pantagryuel'', *Kino*, 4 February 1933.
4. For E's views on Vertov's Cine-Eye, see 1924, n. 2.
5. See above, pp. 219-237.
6. A polemical response to Weissman's identification of E's concept of 'inner monologue' with the views of the writer Fyodor Sologub (1863-1927).

7. The article did in fact appear in *Kino* as 'To Your Posts!': see the following document, pp. 250-257.
8. The principle upon which *Remembrance of Things Past* (*A la recherche du temps perdu*) by the French writer Marcel Proust (1871-1922) was constructed.
9. See above, pp. 138-150.
10. E is here arguing against the simplistic application to cinema of the principles of classical drama as laid down in Aristotle's *Poetics*. The analogy is with the biblical story of Salome serving up the severed head of John the Baptist.
11. Source: 'Po mestam!', *Kino*, 10 March 1933. Leyda lists it as 'In Place!' in *Film Essays*.
12. Ivan S. Barkov (c. 1732-68), Russian poet and translator.
13. Ilya E. Efimov (1889-1938), Chuvash writer, author of a number of satirical works including the poem 'Kolchak' (1919).
14. There is a play on words here in the original Russian as *ruchka* is used to mean both a 'handle' and a 'pen'.
15. Chichikov is the name of the principal character in Gogol's *Dead Souls*.
16. The two-headed eagle was the imperial symbol of tsarist Russia.
17. The two brothers St Cyril and St Methodius were ninth-century Greek missionaries in Central Europe. St Cyril is credited with the development of the Cyrillic alphabet which bears his name.
18. Stanislavsky's Moscow Art Theatre, which had always been closely associated with Gorky's work, was additionally named after him in 1932 to mark the fortieth anniversary of his literary activity.
19. Vasili G. Sakhnovsky (1886-1945), Soviet theatre director, pupil of Komissarzhevsky, who worked at the Moscow Art Theatre from 1926.
20. Ruben N. Simonov (1899-1968), Soviet theatre director and actor, was director of the Vakhtangov Theatre from 1924, and from 1928 to 1937 ran his own theatre studio.
21. For details of Meyerhold's career, see 1922, n. 6.
22. See 1927, n. 3.
23. Cecil B. DeMille (1881-1959), American director and producer, particularly known for his mammoth biblical spectaculars like *The Ten Commandments* (USA, 1923), *The King of Kings* (USA, 1927) and *The Sign of the Cross* (USA, 1932), although E may well have been acquainted with his earlier vamp films and sex comedies as well.
24. A paraphrase of Lenin's views as expressed in *State and Revolution*.
25. See 1926, n. 5.
26. This article was written as the preface to Vladimir Nilsen's *Tekhnika kombinirovannoi kinos"ëmki* [The Technique of Trick Photography], Moscow, 1933. Georges Méliès (1861-1938), French film pioneer, accidentally discovered the principle of superimposition one day when his camera jammed: he is nowadays remembered primarily for the elements of fantasy and inventiveness that characterised his films. Source: 'Oshibka Georga Mel'e', *Sovetskoe kino*, 1933, no. 3/4 (March/April), pp. 63-4.
27. Luther Burbank (1849-1926) was an American plant breeder whose method of hybridisation produced more than 800 new varieties. Ivan V. Michurin (1855-1935) was a Russian geneticist whose ideas on the inheritance of acquired characteristics were adopted by the Soviet government in the 1930s as the official orthodoxy.
28. In English in the original.
29. Source: 'Vylazka klassovykh druzei', *Kino*, 22 and 28 June 1933. Written as a reply to a critique of his position by the directors Sergei I. Bartenev (1900-66) and Mikhail K. Kalatozov (1903-73) under the title 'Obraz i dramaturgiya v tvorchestve Eizenshteina' ['Character and Dramaturgy in Eisenstein's Work'], *Kino*,

16 June 1933. Listed by Leyda in *Film Essays* as 'Sortie by Class Friends'.

30. *The Affair of the Rue de Lourcine* (*L'Affaire de la rue de Lourcine*) was written in 1857 by the French dramatist Eugène Labiche (1815-88).

31. Eugène Scribe (1791-1861), French dramatist.

32. See above, pp. 219-237.

33. See 1932, n. 22.

34. See above, pp. 138-150. Page references given in the text in square brackets are to the present edition.

35. See 1923, nn. 2 and 11.

36. Dmitri I. Ilovaisky (1832-1920) was a Russian historian who reduced history to a series of biographies of tsars and generals.

37. This conference was held in Moscow on 27 June 1933 under the auspices of GUKF in an attempt to promote more fruitful collaboration between film-makers and writers. Apart from E, those present included Pudovkin, Shub, Dovzhenko, Room and the writers Alexander A. Fadeyev (1901-56) and Pyotr A. Pavlenko (1899-1951) who was to collaborate with E on the script for *Alexander Nevsky*.

38. The decree of 23 April 1932 abolished the proletarian-orientated cultural organisations such as RAPP and ARRK as a prelude to the introduction of the doctrine of socialist realism.

39. *Salt for Svanetia* (*Sol' Svanetii*) (USSR, 1930) was directed by Mikhail Kalatozov, one of the critics to whom E is responding in this piece.

40. For Dreiser, see 1932, n. 22. E also worked on a treatment of *Sutter's Gold* when in America. A film version of the book was, ironically, produced in Nazi Germany by Luis Trenker (b. 1893) in *Der Kaiser von Kalifornien* (*The Emperor of California*) (Germany, 1936).

41. A reply to a questionnaire on the occasion of the conference to discuss the thematic plan for 1934. Source: 'Kino i klassiki', *Literaturnaya gazeta*, 23 December 1933.

42. The reference is to Balzac's novel *Eugénie Grandet*.

43. Russian abbreviation for *sel'skii korrespondent* or 'peasant correspondent'.

1934

1. A progress report on E's work on the occasion of the Seventeenth Party Congress, held at the end of January 1934. Source: 'Za vysokuyu ideinost', za kinokul'turu!', *Kino*, 22 January 1934. Listed by Leyda in *Film Essays* as 'For High Ideals, for Film Culture!'.

2. *Moscow* (*Moskva*) was envisaged as a history of the city seen through the four elements: water (the origins of the city), earth (Ivan the Terrible and Peter the Great), fire (the peasant rebellions, the fire of 1812, the class struggle and the Revolution) and air (the construction of the new Moscow). The film was never made.

3. There is no other record of this proposal.

4. See 1933, n. 37.

5. A reference to the continuing interruptions in production because of recurrent shortages of suitable scripts, the so-called 'screenplay crises'.

6. E's work at GIK is covered in Volume 3.

7. E's book on *Direction* [*Rezhissura*] was never completed. Much of the draft material for it is included in Volume 2.

8. The village on the Lenin Hills, then just outside Moscow, where the new studios were built at the end of the 20s and the beginning of the 30s. The complex now houses the studios of Mosfilm.

9. An inflated version of one episode from the Mexican film ¡*Que Viva México*! was released in October 1933 in New York under the title *Thunder over Mexico*.

10. E's riposte to Joseph Goebbels (1897-1945), German Minister for Popular Enlightenment and Propaganda during the Third Reich, was written on 9 March 1934. Source: 'O fashizme, germanskom kinoiskusstve i podlinnoi zhizni. Otkrytoe pis'mo germanskomu ministru propagandy Doktoru Gëbbel'su', *Literaturnaya gazeta*, 22 March 1934. Translated as 'Open Letter to Dr Goebbels,' *Film Art*, Winter 1934, pp. 7-11.

11. The two Goebbels speeches that E refers to in the course of this article were made on 28 March 1933 and 9 February 1934. The second would have been reported in the German press on the following day, hence E's confusion over the date. See: D. Welch, *Propaganda and the German Cinema, 1933-1945*, Oxford, 1983, pp. 16, 97.

12. In English in the original.

13. A reference to the show trial in Leipzig in the autumn of 1933 of the Bulgarian communists Georgi Dimitrov (also Dimitroff), Tanev and Popov, and the Dutchman Martinus van der Lubbe for alleged complicity in the burning of the Reichstag on 28 February 1933. Dimitrov was later found not guilty and released, and he then settled in the USSR.

14. Ernst Thälmann (1886-1944), chairman of the German Communist Party (KPD) from 1924, was arrested and imprisoned in various concentration camps in 1933, and died in Buchenwald.

15. Stalin's speech was reprinted in *Pravda*, 28 January 1934.

16. In the winter of 1933-4 the Soviet steamship *Chelyuskin* sank in the Arctic after colliding with an iceberg. The Soviet press gave wide coverage to the heroism of the rescue operations. E penned an article, 'Nesravnimoe' ['The Incomparable'], on the subject for *Literaturnaya gazeta*, 18 June 1934.

17. The Bulgarians were given Soviet citizenship after their arrival in the USSR.

18. Source: '"E!" O chistote kinoyazyka', *Sovetskoe kino*, 1934, no. 5 (May), pp. 25-31. Translated by Jay Leyda as 'Film Language' in *Film Form*, pp. 108-21. The article is a response to Gorky's observations 'O yazyke' [On Language], published in *Pravda*, 18 March 1934.

19. A reference to the behaviour of the characters Bobchinsky and Dobchinsky in Gogol's play *The Government Inspector*.

20. A jocular reference to acetone, which smells of pears and was used to splice film together in the earlier stages of editing at that time.

21. The administrative and political head of Soviet cinema from 1930 until his dismissal and arrest in January 1938 and summary execution six months later, Boris Z. Shumyatsky (1886-1938), enjoined Soviet film-makers to 'master the classics' partly in order to overcome the shortage of acceptable scripts on contemporary themes.

22. The tail here referred to being that of theatre. 'Tailism' derives from the political debates in the late 1890s between Lenin and the so-called 'Economists' about the proper future path for Russian Social Democracy.

23. Anna K. Tarasova (1898-1973), Moscow Art Theatre actress who was to play leading roles in *The Storm* (*Groza*) (USSR, 1934) and *Peter the First* (*Pëtr Pervyi*) (USSR, 1937-9), both directed by Vladimir M. Petrov (1896-1966).

24. Omitted from the published version.

25. The Russian word here is *kinopis'mo* which literally means 'cinema letter'.

26. Andrei Bely (pseudonym of Boris N. Bugayev) (1880-1934), Russian writer and, in the pre-Revolutionary period, one of the leading figures in Russian Symbolism. In 1933 E chaired a lecture given by Bely at the Polytechnic Museum in Moscow. Bely's book *Masterstvo Gogolya* [Gogol's Mastery] was published in 1934.

27. *Ivan* (USSR, 1932) was directed by Dovzhenko (see 1928, n. 26). Chapter 10 of Gogol's *The Terrible Vengeance* describes the River Dnieper.

28. E. Zola, *Germinal*, Harmondsworth, 1954, p. 353.

29. Théroigne de Méricourt (1762-1817) was one of the participants in the French Revolution. On 31 May 1793, after she had delivered a speech defending the Girondists, she was attacked by a group of Jacobin women and birched: she then went mad.

30. Marie-Thérèse-Louise de Lamballe (1755-92) was imprisoned with Marie-Antoinette, murdered and disembowelled. The quotation is from S. Mercier, *Paris pendant la Révolution* . . . , Paris, 1862, vol. 1, p. 88.

31. Germinal was the name given to the seventh month of the French Revolutionary calendar covering the period from 21 March to 19 April.

32. By analogy with *mise en scène*.

33. The *commedia dell'arte* was a form of popular Italian comedy that reached its height in the 16th and 17th centuries. It was performed by specially trained troupes of actors who improvised on standard synopses involving a group of formalised and familiar characters (such as Harlequin, Columbine, Pierrot and Pulcinella) and a series of stock situations.

34. The German *Vorschlag* denotes a musical 'forestroke', an auxiliary note that anticipates and merges in performance with the principal note.

35. Popular Russian writers at the turn of the century.

36. Source: 'Nakonets!', *Literaturnaya gazeta*, 18 November 1934.

37. 'The Middle of the Three' ('Srednyaya iz trëkh'), translated by Leyda as 'Through Theater to Cinema' in *Film Form*, pp. 3-17.

38. *The Mother (Mat')* (USSR, 1926) and *The Deserter (Dezertir)* (USSR, 1933) were both directed by Pudovkin. *The Arsenal (Arsenal)* (USSR, 1929) was directed by Dovzhenko. *The Golden Mountains (Zlatye gory)* (USSR, 1931) was directed by Sergei Yutkevich and was one of the first Soviet sound feature films. *Counterplan (Vstrechnyi)* (USSR, 1932) was directed by Friedrich Ermler.

39. See 1932, n. 15. Zarkhi defended the importance of scriptwriting at the First Congress of the Union of Soviet Writers in August 1934.

40. Vissarion G. Belinsky (1811-48), Russian literary critic and publicist; see *Sobranie sochinenii v 3-kh tomakh* [Collected Works in 3 Volumes], vol. 1, Moscow, 1948, pp. 75-6.

41. *Chapayev* (USSR, 1934) was directed by Georgi N. Vasiliev (1899-1946) and Sergei D. Vasiliev (1900-59). They were known as the 'Vasiliev Brothers' but were not in fact related to one another. They had both studied under E.

Index

This Index covers the Introduction and the Documents but not the endnotes. I have eschewed separate entries for 'cinema', 'film' and 'Eisenstein' and concentrated instead on specific aspects of all three. As in the notes, Eisenstein is referred to as E. Translations of journal and newspaper titles are given in parentheses and film titles are followed by the name of the director.

actor, in cinema, 198, 286; model actor (*naturshchik*), 4, 7, 48-58, 71-3, 87; *see also* Japan, Kabuki theatre
Agadzhanova-Shutko, Nina F., 92
agitation, 33-4, 45, 48-9, 99, 111, 129, 239
AKhRR, *see* Association of Artists of Revolutionary Russia
Aksionov, Ivan A., 226
Alexandrov, Grigori M., 9, 11, 20, 113-14, 123-6, 218
All Quiet on the Western Front (Milestone), 217
alogism, 42, 63
American Tragedy, An (E film project), 21, 227-37, 262, 274
'Americanism', 31, 42, 44, 72, 75, 81, 108-9, 274
Andrei Kozhukhov (Protazanov), 45
Andreyev, Leonid, N., 1, 154
animation, 145
Arbuckle, Roscoe 'Fatty', 31, 55
Aristotle, 248
Armoured Train 14-69 Ivanov play), 115
ARRK, *see* LenARRK
Arsenal, The (Dovzhenko), 136-7, 178, 297, 298
association, *see* attraction
Association of Artists of Revolutionary Russia (AKhRR), 62, 102, 159
attraction, 3, 12, 23, 33-58, 65, 66, 70, 74, 117, 265-6; definition of, 34, 40-1; sexual, 65-6; *see also* stimulant
audience reaction, and class, 65, 127, 154

Babel, Isaak E., 80, 95, 98, 226
Balázs, Béla, 7-8, 77-81
Balzac, Honoré de, 141, 225, 274, 276
Banks, Monty, 121
Barnet, Boris V., 90
Bartenev, Sergei I., 261-75
Barthelmess, Richard, 71
Batalov, Nikolai P., 226

Battleship Potemkin, The, 4, 6-7, 18, 19, 22, 67-71, 74-6, 78-9, 86, 88, 90, 91, 92-3, 101, 102, 104, 105, 109, 118, 129, 132, 135, 172, 174, 202, 203, 235, 244, 268, 269-70, 280, 281, 290-3, 297, 298; firing-squad episode, 118; skiffs, 68, 190, 290-3; stone lions, 68, 172, 174; Odessa steps sequence, 68-9, 172, 174, 188, 270, 290; final sequence, 68
Bay of Death, The (Room), 178
Bear's Wedding, The (Eggert and Gardin), 72
Bed and Sofa (Room), 201
Beethoven, Ludwig van, 183
Belinsky, Vissarion G., 298
Bely, Andrei, 287
Berkeley, George, 152-3
Bismarck, Otto von, 123
Black Consul, The (E film project), 221
Blanchard, Claude, 29-30
Blyum, Vladimir I., 99
Bode, Rudolph, 51, 163
Bolshoi Theatre, 115
Brecht, Bertolt, 1
Broken Blossoms (Griffith), 101
Bulat Batyr (Tarich), 108
Burbank, Luther, 258

Cabinet of Dr Caligari, The (Wiene), 31, 66
cameraman, role in cinema, 77-9, 81, 255-6
Can You Hear Me, Moscow? (E stage production), 41n., 50, 64, 74, 244
Capital (E film project), 10, 18, 105, 200
career, 1-2, 74-6, 243-5; in Berlin, 6; at La Sarraz, 20; at Sorbonne, 20; in USA, 20-1, 203-5; in Hollywood, 21, 205, 206-18, 227-37, 244, 274; in Mexico, 21; return to USSR, 21
Cendrars, Blaise, 274
censorship, *see* Repertkom
Chaney, Lon, 71

Chapayev (Vasilievs), 23, 96, 299-300
Chaplin, Charles S., 2, 3, 29-32, 34, 42
Chekhov, Anton P., 68
Chomette, Henri, 77
Chronicles of the Grey House, The (Gerlach), 85
Cine-Eye (Vertov film), 62, 63-4
Cine-Eyes (group), *see* Vertov, Dziga
Cine-Pravda (Vertov), 41, 42, 62, 63; *Lenin Cine-Pravda*, 64
circus, 35-6, 39, 60
'classness' (*klassovost'*), 64, 110, 112
Collapse, The (Lavrenyov play), 115
collective, as aspect of cinema, 8, 16, 21-3, 78-9, 127, 196-7, 224
collision, *see* conflict
colour, 17, 113, 131, 166
commerce, versus ideology, 110, 195-6
common denominator, for sound and image, 115-22, 138-50, 185-6
Commune, Charles de la, 30
conflict, as essence of art, 14-19, 23, 144-6, 158, 161-80, 191-2, 267-8, 271; *see* counterpoint
Counterplan (Ermler), 297, 299
counterpoint, 12, 17, 19, 114, 146, 166, 185, 287
countryside, and cinema, 196, 201
Cricket on the Hearth, The (Dickens), 34, 266
critics, role in cinema, 99, 110, 115, 220

Danton, Georges, 157
Darwin, Charles, 53n., 80
Daumier, Honoré, 141, 165, 226
D.E. Trust, The, see Give Us Europe!
Dean, Priscilla, 71-2
Death Ray, The (Kuleshov), 87
Debussy, Claude, 183, 186
Degas, Edgar, 212, 226
Delluc, Louis, 30, 31
DeMille, Cecil B., 255
Dempster, Carole, 72
Deserter, The (Pudovkin), 297
dialectic, Marxist, 4, 10, 14, 16, 19, 23, 60, 123, 127, 130, 151-2, 158, 161-80, 193
Dickens, Charles, *see Cricket on the Hearth, The*
Dimitrov, Georgi, 283
Dinamov, Sergei S., 233-4
Diplomatic Bag, The (Dovzhenko), 102, 137
Direction (E book project), 278, 290
director, role in cinema, 16, 46, 63, 78, 81, 87, 134-5, 250-7, 267

Dnevnik Glumova, see Glumov's Diary
documentary film, *see* non-played film
dominant, *see* music, and cinema
Dostoyevsky, Fyodor M., 225, 242
Dovzhenko, Alexander P., 136-7, 178, 288
Dreiser, Theodore, 227-37, 274
Dumas, Alexandre, 21-4, 226

Earth Rampant (Meyerhold stage production), 83
Eccentrism, 2, 30, 31, 33, 36, 61, 72, 244; *see also* FEKS
Ehrenburg, Ilya G., 32, 77
Einstein, Albert, 185
Eleventh Year, The (Vertov), 102, 104, 187
emotion, and reason, 12, 16, 18, 127, 129, 155-6, 158, 161-80, 199-200; emotional dynamisation, 17, 63, 176-7
End of St Petersburg, The (Pudovkin), 90, 95, 102, 112, 136, 177, 187, 188
Engels, Friedrich, 161, 239-40, 280
Enough Simplicity for Every Wise Man (E stage production), 33-8, 74, 82-3, 244, 266
entertainment, 195, 219
Epstein, Jean, 149
Erdman, Nikolai R., 226
Expressionism, 65-6, 136
Extraordinary Adventures of Mr West in the Land of the Bolsheviks, The (Kuleshov), 42

fabula, see plot
Factory of the Eccentric Actor, *see* FEKS
Fadeyev, Alexander A., 277
Fairbanks, Douglas, 31
Fall of the House of Usher, The (Epstein), 149
Fascism, 280-4
Father Sergius (Protazanov), 31
Faust (Murnau), 76, 85, 88
FEKS, 2, 95; *see also* Eccentrism
Fever (Delluc), 30
film school (GTK and GIK), 9, 11, 21, 125, 127-30, 140, 195, 220, 224-5, 237, 244, 278
Five-Year Plan, 21, 151, 196
Forest, The (Meyerhold stage production), 83
form, 59-64, 66, 153-4, 161-80, 190, 238-42; and content, 5, 15, 16
Formalism, 6, 19, 59, 82, 110, 239, 240, 263, 266, 268, 272, 287
Forty-Seven Samurai, The (Kabuki play),

116, 149
Fouquet, Jean, 211
Freund, Karl, 77, 78
Fuller, Zoe, 31
Futurism, Italian, 165

Gambetta, Léon, 157
Gas Masks (E stage production), 55, 74, 83, 244
Gautier, Théophile, 238
Geltser, Ekaterina, 72
General Line, The 8, 9, 18-21, 76, 93, 95, 105, 135, 181-94, 196-8, 200, 202, 203, 217, 244, 270-2
German cinema, 6, 22, 76, 85-8, 109, 113, 280-4
GIK, *see* film school
Give Us Europe! (Meyerhold stage production), 83
Gladkov, Fyodor V., 97
Glavrepertkom, *see* Repertkom
Glumov's Diary (E short film), 38
Goebbels, Joseph, 280-4
Goethe, Johann W. von, 163, 223
Gogol, Nikolai V., 223, 225, 226, 240-1, 252, 255, 287-8, 294
Gold Rush, The (Chaplin), 121
Golden Mountains, The (Yutkevich), 297
Gorky, Maxim, 151, 226, 227, 285, 286, 294
Goskino, 92
Gosplan, 89
Griffith, David Wark, 31, 42, 44, 72, 217, 228; *The Birth of a Nation*, 81; *Intolerance*, 31, 42
Grosz, George, 34
GTK, *see* film school

Happy Canary, The (Kuleshov), 144
Harbou, Thea von, 86
Hart, William S., *see* Rio Jim
Hayakawa, Sessue, 31
Hoffmann, E. T. A., 235, 274
Hogarth, William, 211
Hokusai, Kazusika, 212
House of Ice (Eggert), 108
Hugo, Victor, 222

I Want a Child (Tretyakov play), 70
Idealism, 124, 153, 246-9
ideology, as motive power for art, 5, 10, 15-17, 20-23, 34, 59-60, 63, 66, 75, 124-5, 129, 152, 154, 161-80, 195, 238-42, 265-7
illusion, 29-30, 35, 74, 113

Impressionism, 46, 62, 125, 140
Ince, Thomas, 89-90, 94, 255
Inkizhinov, Valeri, 200
'inner monologue', 21-2, 236, 246-9
'intellectual cinema', 9, 13, 16-21, 103-4, 127, 129, 139, 148, 151-60, 161-80, 193, 199-201, 261-75
Iron Torrent, The (Serafimovich novel), 93, 95, 154
Ivan (Dovzhenko), 288
Izvestiya ('The News': government newspaper), 250

Jannings, Emil, 85, 88
Japan; drawing, 146, 211-13, 263-4; Kabuki theatre, 11-12, 14-15, 18, 115-22, 129, 143, 148-50, 181-94, 200-1; masks, use of, 129; painting, 141-2, 143, 165; poetry, 120-1, 139-41; script (ideograms), 13, 120-1, 138-50, 164, 182
Jaque-Dalcroze, Emile, 157
Jonson, Ben, 225
Joyce, James, 21, 96, 226, 235; *Portrait of the Artist as a Young Man*, 96; *Ulysses*, 96, 235

Kachalov, Vasili I., 226
Kalatozov, Mikhail K., 261-75
Kaulbach, Wilhelm von, 162
Keaton, Buster, 82
Khersonsky, Khrisanf N., 62
Khokhlova, Alexandra S., 7, 71-3
Kid, The (Chaplin), 121
Kino ('Cinema'), 298
Klages, Ludwig, 52, 162
Kleist, Heinrich von, 122
Komsomolskaya pravda ('Komsomol Truth'), 125
Körkarlen, see *Phantom Carriage, The*
Kozintsev, Grigori M., 2-3
Kuleshov, Lev V., 57, 71, 72, 87, 143-4, 163, 186; serial montage, 14, 17, 18, 143-4, 163
Kurth, Julius, 112, 141, 165

Labiche, Eugène, 261
Lace (Yutkevich), 110-12
laconicism, 139-40
Lame Gentleman, The (Eggert), 108
Lang, Fritz, 87
language, and cinema, 80, 163, 178
Last Laugh, The (Murnau), 85
LEF, 6, 74, 117
Léger, Fernand, 32, 77, 165, 211

LenARRK, 278
Lenin, Vladimir I., 19, 23, 99, 180
Lev Tolstoy and the Russia of Nicholas II
  (Shub), 125, 178
L'Herbier, Marcel, 31
Life for the Tsar, A (Glinka opera), 115
lighting, 146
Lily of Life (Clair), 31
literature and cinema, 60, 95-9, 134,
  158-9, 235, 275, 276, 286, 287, 289-90,
  293
Little Red Devils, The (Perestiani), 109
Living Corpse, The (Otsep), 177
Lloyd, Harry, 68
Lomonosov, Mikhail V., 239
Lubitsch, Ernst, 228
Lunacharsky, Anatoli V., 22, 74
Luria, Alexander R., 141
Lyubov Yarovaya (Trenyov play), 15

Magnanimous Cuckold, The (Meyerhold
  stage production), 82
Malevich, Kazimir S., 162, 191
Man with the Movie Camera, The (Ver-
  tov), 149
Marx, Karl, 105, 161, 202
'massness' (*massovost'*), 59, 61
'material', 10, 12, 13, 17, 40, 46, 61, 66,
  70, 72, 80-1, 83, 90-3, 103-4, 105, 107,
  110-11, 132, 134-7, 148, 160, 172, 178
Mayakovsky, Vladimir V., 74, 294
Meisel, Edmund, 131
Méliès, Georges, 22, 258-60
Meringue, The (Romashov play), 84
Metropolis (Lang), 76, 77, 85-8
Mexican, The (E stage production), 33
Meyerhold, Vsevolod E., 1, 30, 74, 115,
  122, 159, 255
Mezhrabpom/Mezhrabpom-Rus, 99, 100
Michurin, Ivan V., 258
Mickey Mouse, 200-1, 205
Monsieur Beaucaire (Olcott), 109
montage, 3-24, 25-6, 46-7, 63-4, 80, 83,
  113-14, 122, 129, 132-3, 138-50,
  161-80, 181-94, 261-75, 285-94; in *The
  Strike*, 59-60, 69, 75; in *The Battleship
  Potemkin*, 290-3; in *The General Line,
  The*, 181-94; in *Cine-Pravda*, 63; metric, 19,
  186-7, 189, 192; overtonal, 19, 20,
  183-6, 191, 192, 194; rhythmic, 19,
  187-8, 192; serial, *see* Kuleshov, Lev;
  tonal, 19, 188-91, 192; *see also* shot
montage of attractions, 3-5, 6, 7, 15, 20,
  39-58, 65-6, 70, 75, 82, in theatre, 33-8
Moscow (E film project), 277

Moscow Art Theatre (MKhAT), 74, 76,
  117, 158-9, 254-5
Mother, The (Pudovkin), 102, 129, 177,
  297, 298
Moussinac, Léon, 31
music, and cinema, 98, 131, 132, 181-94,
  291, 293; dominant in cinema, 17, 18,
  19, 23, 168, 181-94; *see also* sound
music-hall, 35-7
Mysteries of Udolpho (novel), 220

*Na vsyakogo mudretsa dovol'no prostoty,
  see Enough Simplicity for Every Wise Man*
Nad obryvom, see On the Abyss
New Babylon (Kozintsev and Trauberg),
  95, 124
New Economic Policy (NEP), 67-8, 219
Nibelungs, The (Lang), 85, 87, 97
1905 (projected film series), 91-3; *see also
  Strike, The*
non-played film, 10, 11, 13, 62, 101-6,
  125, 128-9, 133
Novarro, Ramon, 71

October, 8, 9, 11, 13, 18, 21, 89, 90,
  91, 93-4, 95, 96, 101-6, 125, 136, 172,
  177, 187, 197, 198, 203, 235, 244, 268,
  289; script, 94; cycle battalions, 177;
  images of gods, 17-18, 174, 179-80, 193;
  Kornilov, 174, 177, 179-80; Kerensky,
  177, 179
ODSK, *see* Society of Friends of Soviet
  Cinema
Okhlopkov, Nikolai P., 73
*Old and the New, The, see General Line,
  The*
On the Abyss (Pletnyov play), 33
*One Sixth of the World, see A Sixth Part
  of the World*
O'Neill, Eugene, 234, 237
Osoaviakhim, 115
Ostrovsky, Alexander N., 33-8, 244
Ostuzhev, Alexander A., 3, 34, 117
Otsep, Fyodor A., 177

painting, and cinema, 17, 60, 80, 97, 178
Palace and the Fortress, The (Ivanovsky),
  43, 45
Paramount, 227-37
Party; Conference on Cinema, March
  1928, 9, 100, 108, 123; 17th Congress,
  January – February 1934, 278, 283
Phantom Carriage, The (Sjöström), 30
photogeny, 30, 56-7, *see also* Delluc,
  Louis

332

Picabia, Francis, 77
Picasso, Pablo, 32, 211
Pickford, Mary, 31, 66, 71
plan, *see* Five-Year Plan
Plekhanov, Georgi V., 151, 153, 155, 221, 248
Pletnyov, Valerian F., 33, 60; *see also* Proletkult
plot, 22-3, 40-1, 47, 59, 61, 75, 105, 114, 266, 268, 276, 293-4; *fabula* and *syuzhet*, 25, 59-60
Poet and the Tsar, The (Gardin), 108
poetry, and prose in cinema, 23
Potholes (Room), 110-11, 112
Pravda ('The Truth': Party newspaper), 61, 71
Proletarskoe kino ('Proletarian Cinema'), 247
Proletkult, 6, 33-8, 40, 48, 51, 59, 74, 75, 76, 111, 244
propaganda, 15, 151
Protivogazy, see Gas Masks
psychologism, 7, 70
Pudovkin, Vsevolod I., 11, 17, 18, 95, 112, 113-14, 144, 163, 177, 200, 267
Pushkin, Alexander S., 294, 298

Que Viva México!, 21, 279

Rabelais, François, 246-9, 250, 288
Rabkrin, 126
Rails are Humming, The (Kirshon play), 154
raw material, *see* material
Red Cavalry (E film project), 95
Red Partisans (Viskovsky), 108
reflexology, 125, 127, 130, 155
Renan, Ernest, 155
Repertkom, 220
rhythm, 162-3, 165, 166
Rin-Tin-Tin, 20, 203-5
Rio Jim, 31, 32
Rittau, Günther, 78
Roar, China! (Meyerhold stage production), 84
Rodchenko, Alexander M., 34
Romance sentimentale (Alexandrov), 218
Room, Abram M., 178
rupture, 271-2

Sally of the Sawdust (Griffith), 72
Salt for Svanetia (Kalatozov), 272
Schopenhauer, Arthur, 56
Schulberg, Ben P., 228, 236
screen ratio, 206-18

Scriabin, Alexander N., 183, 186, 187
script, 4, 12-13, 22, 40, 44-5, 46, 98, 107, 134-5, 250-7, 269, 275
scriptwriter, 13, 46, 81, 134-5, 250-7, 269, 274-5, 276
Serafimovich, Alexander S., 95
sex, use of, 65-6, 71-2, 182
Shakespeare, William, 34, 266, 276, 299-300
Sharaku, Toshushai, 141-2, 143, 165, 264
Shishkov, Vyacheslav Ya., 97
Shklovsky, Viktor B., 14, 226
shot, relationship to montage sequence, 17, 18, 79-81, 138-50, 161-80, 181-94, 268, 287, 290
Shub, Esfir I., 125, 178
Shumyatsky, Boris Z., 21
Sixth Part of the World, A (Vertov), 102, 104
slow motion, 145, 149, 168
Slyshish', Moskva?, see Can You Hear Me, Moscow?
Smyshlyayev, Valentin S., 33
social command, 98
Society of Friends of Soviet Cinema (ODSK), 195
Sologub, Fyodor, 247
sound, 10-11, 12, 19, 20, 22, 29-30, 113-14, 115-22, 129, 131-3, 161-80, 185, 236, 248, 285, 287, 299; 'Statement on Sound', 11, 12, 19, 22, 113-14, 119; as substitute for intertitle, 131-2
Sovetskii ekran ('Soviet Screen'), 123
Sovetskoe kino ('Soviet Cinema'), 296
Sovkino, 9, 93, 107, 124
Soyuzkino, 21, 225
Stalin, Joseph V., 251, 283
Stanislavsky, Konstantin S., 1, 74, 76, 122
Staroe i novoe, see General Line, The
Station Master, The (Zhelyabuzhsky and Moskvin), 68
Steinen, Karl von den, 153
Stendhal, 226
Stenka Razin and the Princess (film project suggested to E), 277
Stephan Khalturin (Ivanovsky), 45
stereoscopic cinema, 113
Sternberg, Josef von, 237
stimulant, 12, 19, 65-6, 68, 83, 117-18, 122, 125, 154, 155; *see also* attraction
Storm, The (Bill-Belotserkovsky play), 84
Storm Over Asia (Pudovkin), 124, 188

Strauch, Maxim M., 37, 226
Strike, The, 4, 5, 6, 7, 9, 19, 43, 47, 59-64,
  65, 68-9, 75, 79, 83, 86, 90-2, 95, 96, 105,
  176-7, 244, 269; role of script, 59-60;
  absence of plot, 59, 61, 75; Cine-Eye
  qualities, 68; hosing sequence, 68-9;
  slaughter sequence, 43-4, 65, 176-7
Stroheim, Erich von, 71
stunt, *see* trick
Suprematism, 165
Surrealism, 201-2
Sutter's Gold (E film project), 274
synthesis, 4-5, 10, 13, 16, 17, 18, 20, 23-4,
  60, 129, 151-60, 161-80
syuzhet, see plot

Tairov, Alexander Ya., 30, 74
Talleyrand, Charles, M. de, 241
Tarasova, Anna K., 286
Ten Commandments, The (DeMille), 81
Ten Days That Shook the World, see October
Thälmann, Ernst, 282
theatre, and cinema, 1-2, 8, 11, 17, 22, 39,
  40, 42, 53, 60, 62, 63-4, 74-5, 76, 80,
  82-4, 97, 111-12, 113-14, 115-22, 127-8,
  129, 149, 158-9, 160, 178, 235, 286;
  Chinese theatre, 116; Kabuki, *see* Japan
The Thief of Bagdad (Walsh), 67, 149
*Third Meshchanskaya (Street), see Bed and
  Sofa*
The Three Millions Trial (Protazanov), 110
Tisse, Eduard K., 20, 67, 78, 85
Toulouse-Lautrec, Henri de, 165, 226
Towards the Dictatorship (projected film
  series), 59, 61
Trauberg, Leonid Z., 2
Tretyakov, Sergei M., 51n., 70
trick, in theatre, 34-5; in cinema, 55, 60,
  83, 260
typage, 198, 200-1

UFA, 78, 86

Valentino, Rudolph, 71
Variété (Dupont), 77n., 104
Veidt, Conrad, 71
Veisman, Evgeni, *see* Weissman
Vertov, Dziga, 4, 5, 6, 7, 11, 39, 41, 46,
  62, 63-4, 98, 102, 149, 187, 201
Vidor, King, 217
Virgin of Stamboul, The (Browning), 71-2
Volodarsky, Moisei M., 157
Voltaire, 69

Waltz Dream (Berger), 86

Wanderers, The, 62
War and Peace (novel), 145
Warrant, The (Meyerhold stage pro-
  duction), 83
Webster, John, 226
Weissman, Evgeni, 246-9
Weltmann, Alexander F., 226
*Wise Man, see Enough Simplicity for Every
  Wise Man*
Wolkenstein, Vladimir M., 226
Woman from Nowhere, The (Delluc), 30, 31
Woman of Paris, A, (Chaplin), 97, 99
women, role in cinema, 71-3
Workers' and Peasants' Inspectorate, *see*
  Rabkrin

Year 1905, The, see 1905
Yutkevich, Sergei I., 2, 29-32

Zarkhi, Natan, 226, 298
zaum, 102, 105
Zemlya dybom, see Earth Rampant
Zola, Emile, 95, 226, 288-9
Zvenigora (Dovzhenko), 102, 124, 137, 149